Catalyzing Development through ICT Adoption

Harleen Kaur • Ewa Lechman • Adam Marszk
Editors

Catalyzing Development through ICT Adoption

The Developing World Experience

 Springer

Editors
Harleen Kaur
Department of Computer Science and
  Engineering
School of Engineering Sciences
  and Technology
Hamdard University
New Delhi, India

Ewa Lechman
Faculty of Management and Economics
Gdańsk University of Technology
Gdańsk, Poland

Adam Marszk
Faculty of Management and Economics
Gdańsk University of Technology
Gdańsk, Poland

ISBN 978-3-319-85936-1   ISBN 978-3-319-56523-1   (eBook)
DOI 10.1007/978-3-319-56523-1

Printed on acid-free paper

This Springer imprint is published by Springer Nature
The registered company is Springer International Publishing AG
The registered company address is: Gewerbestrasse 11, 6330 Cham, Switzerland

Foreword

This is the second year since the adoption of the 17 Sustainable Development Goals (SDGs) by world leaders in September 2015 at a historic United Nations Summit. Over the next 15 years, countries will mobilize total efforts to end all forms of poverty, fight inequalities, and tackle climate change. Information and communication technologies (ICTs) have the potential to accelerate socio-economic development of all countries in support of the 2030 development agenda for sustainable development.

Today, seven billion people (95% of the global population) live in an area that is covered by a mobile-cellular network. Mobile-broadband networks (3G or above) reach 84% of the global population. Over two-thirds of the population lives within an area covered by a mobile-broadband network. Information and communication technology services are increasingly becoming more affordable. For instance, mobile-broadband services have become more affordable than fixed-broadband services. By end of 2015, average mobile-broadband prices corresponded to 5.5% of gross national income per capita worldwide. Although in the developing world, more than half of all people are not yet using the Internet and there exists large differences in terms of broadband speeds and quality, the situation in terms of ICT adoption is improving.

The progress being made has significant impact in the developing world in education, health, agriculture, commerce, and almost every facet of human life. Even in the world's 48 least developed countries, there is a new wave of hope and adoption of the latest ICT services and applications that include the use of Big Data to mitigate epidemics and road network planning. Financial inclusion is also on top of the agenda and is playing a key role for the development of these countries as it extends services at affordable cost to sections and low-income segments of society.

I have no doubt that the stage is already set for catalyzing development through ICT adoption. Policy makers and telecommunication regulators are encouraged to, however, create an enabling environment in order to encourage the private sector to invest into the ICT sector and get more and more people to have easy access to ICT and to develop the necessary skills that will enable them to fully use these new tools.

Capacity building remains a key success factor as new technologies are constantly introduced into the market such as Big Data, Internet of Things, and Artificial Intelligence. These technologies have immense potential to accelerate economic growth that in turn could result in most countries achieving the targets of the 2030 sustainable agenda covering economic, social development, and environmental protection.

Cosmas Zavazava
Projects and Knowledge Management
International Telecommunication Union (UN) (ITU)
Geneva, Switzerland

Preface

The Context

Recently, the world has witnessed unprecedented advancements in terms of speed and geographical coverage and diffusion of information and communication technologies (ICTs). Broad empirical evidence shows that even the most economically backward countries are adopting ICTs to eradicate their technological deprivation.

ICTs are universally acknowledged as a powerful tool for development and are often promoted as pivotal to bringing about social and economic growth. The revolutionary feature of modern ICTs – mainly the Internet and mobile telephony – facilitates low cost and speedy interaction among network participants. The full potential of new technologies can be easily unleashed when they are deployed as an economic development accelerator in least developed countries. ICTs bring to developing markets new business models, innovations, capital-labor substitution, and improved goods and services. Because they can spread rapidly, with little cost and minimal skills required for usage, ICTs create a solid background for social and economic gains. They enable significant reduction in information asymmetries, which improves access to economic activities for a multitude of agents, fostering participation, inter alia, in labor market of disadvantaged societal groups.

The adoption of ICTs creates better conditions for education and skills improvement, allows overcoming barriers for disadvantaged groups, brings about empowerment, and paves the way to tap the global market of goods and services. ICTs enhance shifts from traditional to modern forms of conducting business and provide the necessary impetus to usher in an industrial revolution.

Regardless of all the abovementioned facts, information and communication technologies' impact on economies' performance is claimed to exhibit in the long-run perspective, and – in addition – their real impact is limited and hardly quantifiable. Therefore, after almost two decades of rapid diffusion of ICT in the developing world, it becomes imperative to assess the real consequences of adoption of ICTs in economically backward countries. Broad, real-world-based evidence would provide a better understanding of the precise nature of new technologies and their impact on a country's economy and society.

The recent years have witnessed the role of ICTs in influencing the socioeconomic context in many countries. Despite that, in many regions, a significant proportion of the population does not have access to clean water, sanitation, basic health services, infrastructure, and proper education. The mission of this book is to explain how ICTs provide novel opportunities for information interchange and technology transfer and escalate socioeconomic development in the developing world. ICT can be pivotal to building a transparent and all-inclusive society. This being said, integration poses challenges that are not easy to overcome, and so strategic and holistic approaches are needed to realize the full potential of these advancements in technologies to reform governance and transform public agencies and services. The gap is especially wide because policy makers and government agencies view ICT as an add-on technical fix, while ICT specialists fail to speak the mainstream development language. Our thoughts are that policy makers and technology specialists must communicate across the divide and manage the transformations brought about by a new paradigm.

What This Book Offers

This highly valuable book offers the reader a critical look into aspects of ICTs in raising socioeconomic development in underdeveloped countries. It intends to illustrate "success stories" in developing countries in reducing poverty, improving productivity, and addressing climate change issues. It aims to bridge the gap between the disciplines of ICT and economic development, and hence, it argues for the need to merge socioeconomic development with the revolutionary advances in information and communication technologies in order to address development challenges facing poor countries and emerging economies, particularly those concerning basic facilities such as clean water, sanitation, and basic healthcare services. It also builds a case for integrating new technologies into development strategies and governance reforms. It offers a number of frameworks and tools to advance this integration agenda. When properly leveraged, the ICT tools can reduce the cost of public services, enhance access to quality services, and make governing agencies more transparent.

This book comprises five parts.

Part I General and Multiregional Studies: In this part, you will understand why and how ICTs may affect socioeconomic development in economically backward economies and the prerequisites that are required to bring about social and economic escalation. We focus on some of the challenges faced by emerging economies in tackling corruption and the issues encountered in handling and processing heterogeneous, complex, and unstructured data for better decisionmaking. We use case studies to demonstrate how ICT can be a powerful tool to fight corruption and handle big data for implementing better management policies.

Part II Asia: We use Bangladesh as a case study to highlight the role of ICT in strengthening the public sector accounting and introducing more transparency and accountability in the system. You will also gain an insight into how ICT can play a vital role in addressing climate change with particular focus on agricultural adaptation and disaster risk reduction from a community perspective.

Part III Africa and the Middle East: Case studies from Africa and the Middle East are used to evaluate infrastructure deployment in OECD and MENA countries. The section highlights how reconstructing the institutional framework that supports scientific knowledge management systems (SKMS) in developing countries can be a panacea for successful IR innovation. It also throws light on how developing countries can enhance their ICT adoption for development by improving formal institutions and strengthening domestic determinants of ICT adoption.

Part IV Latin America: In this part, we study the role of ICTs, especially the Internet, in three Latin American countries to understand how people can attain the lifestyle they value and how inequalities in this ability or "information richness" can be explained by sociodemographic characteristics that do not depend on the individual's decisions. Evidence from Chile illustrates how ICT can improve communication access and participation in social programs and reinforce preexisting inequalities. We use country-specific information from Chile to show how e-commerce is emerging as a channel to penetrate new markets and opening up new avenues for productivity in the manufacturing and service sector.

Part V Europe: In this part we assess the economic potential of big data industries in Europe and the challenges they face. We use data from Slovenia and Slovakia to understand the common patterns of digital development in developing countries and find that while the levels of efficiency of these industries are high, they are missing some key economic links with other sectors of the economy. We then shift focus to Estonia, which is home to many new ICT startups to understand how ordinary citizens are benefitting from this revolution.

We expect that the book content draws on the insights and contributions of many colleagues and academics in developing countries. Its intended audiences are policy makers and ICT strategists. We also hope that it provides the necessary impetus for a more active communication among government agencies concerned with socio-economic development and ICT strategies to build more inclusive societies in the developing world. We are fully aware that the book tackles only a small sample of issues which are associated with problems of ICT adoption in the developing world and exploiting its full potential. However, we do hope it is an inspiring worldwide study, paving the road ahead for further research.

And last but not the least, we would like to acknowledge the role of the Department of Science & Technology (DST), Ministry of Science and Technology, Govt. of India, India, and the Ministry of Science and Higher Education of the

Government of Poland (MNISW) in making this book possible. This work is catalyzed and supported partially by the Indo-Polish joint research grant funded by the DST and the Ministry of Science and Higher Education (Poland).

New Delhi, India   Harleen Kaur
Gdańsk, Poland   Ewa Lechman
Gdańsk, Poland   Adam Marszk

Contents

Part III   Africa and the Middle East

Part IV   Latin America

Part V   Europe

Part I
General and Multiregional Studies

Chapter 1
Information and Communication Technologies for Economic Development

Identifying the Channels of Impact

Ewa Lechman and Adam Marszk

Abstract This chapter is intended to explain why and how information and communication technologies may affect the process of socio-economic development, especially with regard to economically backward economies. It sheds light on why technological changes constitute prerequisites enabling advancements along the socio-economic development pattern. It is also designed to exhibit the special relevance of information and communication technologies when implemented in developing countries. Additionally it discusses the potential channels through which information and communication technologies may contribute to social and economic development in developing world, with the special focus on the financial systems.

Keywords ICT • Economic development • Social development • Financial markets • Developing countries

> (...) the biggest beneficiary of the Industrial Revolution has so far been the unskilled (Gregory [13], p. 3)

1.1 Introduction

Over last few decades (since 1970s onwards), the world has witnessed, the process of rapid diffusion of new information and communication technologies (ICTs), and undeniably, this process has enforced remarkable changes and structural shifts

This research has been supported by the project no.2015/19/B/HS4/03220 financed by the National Science Centre, Poland.

E. Lechman (✉) • A. Marszk
Faculty of Management and Economics, Gdańsk University of Technology, Gdańsk, Poland
e-mail: eda@zie.pg.gda.pl; amarszk@zie.pg.gda.pl

© Springer International Publishing AG 2017
H. Kaur et al. (eds.), *Catalyzing Development through ICT Adoption*,
DOI 10.1007/978-3-319-56523-1_1

3

going far beyond economic sphere of life. At a time, the process of ICT diffusion radically differs, mainly in terms of speed and geographic coverage, from the process of diffusion of 'old' technologies [14]. As claimed by many, the year 1971 was the turning point as it gave rise to the technological (information) revolution, and hence it determined the emergence of new techno-economic regime [19, 25, 49]. Since then onward, new technologies are profoundly transforming social and economic landscape [27, 40]. The ICT revolution allows for introducing technologies, which are quickly distributable throughout societies and countries. ICTs are claimed to be the general purpose technologies (GPTs) [6] – technologies, which by generating deep structural and qualitative changes, pervasively impact society and economy. Bersnahan and Trajtenberg [6] underline that broad adoption of general purpose technologies fosters radical changes of social norms and structures, which leads to transformation of social systems and ways of doing business, heavily impacting growth of productivity [32] and, at a time, providing solid background for long-term economic growth and development. Importantly to note, these technologies easily overcome geographical, infrastructural and financial constraints and hence may be used by almost everybody regardless of location and income status. That is to say that ICT may be accessed and used by low-income and low-skilled societies, offering them unlimited opportunities to benefit from global information and knowledge flows [40]. Looking back, we may argue that in economically backward countries, advanced technological solutions have been rarely adopted and used. It does not mean, however, that in developing economies, no type of technological progress has ever been introduced. But, importantly to note, that the spread and access to various past technological solutions was extremely limited in poor countries (see, e.g. low electrification rates or negligible access to railway networks). Today, those countries, which are perceived as economically backward, are rapidly heading towards broad deployment of ICT, and this radical change, undoubtedly, is revolutionary and one of the most striking facts in their development paths.

1.2   ICT for Social and Economic Development

Undeniably, new information and communication technologies have triggered profound shifts of societies and economies, allowing for advances in their overall well-being. Today, however, the ongoing information revolution is more deeply changing the global landscape than it was observable in the past.

ICTs become fast available, and, as already stated, the rate of diffusion is extremely high [15]. Importantly to say is that the dynamic process of diffusion of ICT is not limited to the developed economies, but it is also observed in economically backward countries, where the per capita income is low, which lack basic backbone infrastructure, where the majority of society is poorly educated and lives below poverty line [27, 28]. When analyzing the process of ICT diffusion, some characteristic features of the process may be easily observed. These unique features distinguish the process of ICT diffusion from the diffusion of 'old' technologies, and additionally they become of special importance when considering the impact of ICT on long-term economic growth and development. First of all, the adoption of ICT allows for fast growth of social networks [11, 56), which generates economic advantages, like, for instance, economics of scale [38, 20], providing solid foundations for long-term economic growth and development. Dynamic growth of socio-economic networks is predominantly facilitated by the type of technological solution offered by ICT. These are, for instance, wireless networks, which enable direct connections among society members, allowing for information and knowledge flows, regardless the physical location of the agents, diminishing their economic and technological marginalization. Cairncross (2001) [9] writes about the 'death of distance' showing that the geographic distance is no longer a barrier for various types of economic activities, as ICTs become widely adopted and used. Broad adoption of ICT enables fast and, at low cost, flows of knowledge and information [51, 62], which become easily acquirable for all society members who, so far, have been permanently technologically and informational marginalized.

Hanna [27] and Perez [48] indicate that, if considering the developing economies, the process of ICT diffusion deserves special attention for two major reasons.

First, ICT may be easily adopted in all countries regardless their level of economic development, because:

- ICTs are fast installable in regions with poorly developed infrastructure and in those regions which are geographically isolated, permanently suffering from heavy infrastructural underdevelopments. As argued by many, ICTs go far 'beyond geography' and thus allow overcoming physical barriers.
- The costs of adoption and broad use of ICT are relatively low (the marginal cost of adoption of ICT by consecutive users is close to zero – especially in case of wireless technologies), which means that ICT may be acquired even by low-income societies. In economically backward economies, a vast majority of people suffers from material deprivation, while ICT may be easily acquired at relatively low prices.
- ICTs offer technological solutions which may be used even by low-educated, illiterate and unskilled people. This is the main reason why ICTs are claimed to be technologies 'for all'.
- ICTs are fast deliverable, imitable and adoptable, and thus the number of its users grows at high rate, which was not observed in case of the 'old' technologies.

Second, the information and communication technologies may constitute an important determinant of long-term economic growth and development [27], as they allow for unbounded flows of information (reducing the information asymmetries) and access to global markets and mobilize resources – especially labour force, stimulating economic growth.

Through improved access to financial markets (e.g., e-finance and mobile-finance solutions), ICTs allow for greater mobilization of people's savings and provide opportunities to convert them into investments, which, through the banking system channel, may positively affect long-term economic growth and development. ICTs foster greater mobilization of the labour force, enhancing increasing participation in formal labour markets, which in consequence provides a solid fundament for obtaining regular income. Moreover, these changes may shift people from subsistence and extreme poverty, reducing their vulnerability and risk exposure to external shocks.

Growing engagement of people in formal employment creates long-run economic gains and allows eradicating of socio-economic deprivation, which constitutes the first and the most important step through which the ICT potential may be exploited and exhibited in developing countries.

Moreover, the special role of ICT in the process of development of countries is perceived through the educational opportunities that these technologies create. ICTs play a critical role in the socio-economic development process by broadening access to information and all types of knowledge, which improves people's empowerment and their participation in various spheres of life [42, 63]. ICTs allow for eradication of information asymmetries, hence one of the market failures [64], and therefore they enhance the efficiency of resource allocation. Perez and Soete (1988) [57] argue that for many countries, ICTs are the opportunity windows, as they facilitate elimination of multiple barriers disabling entering the pattern of stable economic growth and development. ICT may contribute to overall socio-economic development through improved access to education and knowledge, improved and more effective functioning of healthcare systems or, for instance, e-government solution. ICT may effectively foster increases in human capital and skills, contributing to social cohesion and enhancing empowerment of all social groups.

Many empirical studies demonstrate, however, that unrestricted Internet access remains limited in some of examined countries (especially in low-income economies), but the promising aspect of the latter is that many of these economies are rapidly improving Internet accessibility, which is mainly facilitated by development of wireless networks. As claimed by, inter alia, Hanna [27], Torero and von Braun [60], Unwin [61] or Gruber and Koutroumpis [26], these trends are promising and reveal prospects for the future, providing poorly developed countries with the opportunity to enter a stable socio-economic development pattern.

1.3   ICT for the Development of Financial Systems

Development of the financial system is undeniably an important factor of the economic growth [52]. Even though the number of factors influencing the activities of financial systems has been identified, new technologies (above all ICT) are one of the most significant in both advanced and developing economies [65, 66]. However, as discussed below, the effects of the growing ICT adoption on the financial system may also be negative.

Key channels through which ICT influence financial systems are reduction in the information asymmetry, increase in the information sharing between financial market participants, decrease in the marketing costs and increased market participation [5]. These channels are linked with one of the fundamental features of the financial markets – they are claimed to be 'information markets' [43, 59]. Widely adopted ICTs enable information and data dissemination through which various market failures may be reduced [1, 2, 44]. Due to increasingly more popular usage of the Internet services, including the ones obtained in the high-speed networks, ICTs also enable various market participants to undertake transactions which are not limited by the physical distance, i.e. investing into assets domiciled in distant countries or regions. Such operations may be conducted with shortened time delays [41].

The impact of ICT on the financial systems is not solely positive. There are certain areas where more intensive usage of new technologies may potentially lead to threats for the financial stability, e.g. through increasing the volatility of the financial markets [35] or growing interest in the short-term investments (consequently decreasing focus on the long-term capital uses [58]). According to CFA Institute [12], new technologies may increase fragmentation of the financial markets' liquidity. Another channel, through which ICTs influence financial systems, is the increasing financialization of other, initially nonfinancial markets, including commodities [17, 47]. From the point view of the developing economies, significant threats may result from the varying levels of the ICT adoption between the developing and advanced economies. As a result, the financial exclusion of the countries or regions unable to benefit from the new or improved financial services and products may emerge [50].

Undeniably, modern financial system has become reliant on ICT and financial innovations boosted by new technologies. As a consequence, its complexity has increased, thus hindering proper execution of the supervisory activities by regulators and governments [17, 36].

ICT may also change the features of competition in the finance industry, making it more technology based, with notable example of exchange systems – floor-based exchanges have lost market shares to exchanges with electronic systems (especially among derivative exchanges) as ICTs have diminished some of the entry barriers [22].

The impact of the ICT adoption on the financial system (especially its development) has been verified in a number of empirical studies, yet their results are far from conclusive. Shamim [55] analyzes empirical linkages between increasing ICT penetration and financial markets in 61 economies over the period 1990–2002, formulating the conclusion about the positive impact of ICT on the financial development. Some studies on this topic have concentrated on the developing economies. Among the most recent, Andrianaivo and Kpodar [3] state that adoption of ICTs positively impacted economic growth in a sample of African economies between 1988 and 2007, partially through greater financial inclusion. Sassi and Goaied (2013) [53] as well as Falahaty and Jusoh [24] found that ICTs positively influence financial development in the MENA region. Asongu and Moulin [5] provide results for 53 African countries for 2004–2011, stating that interactions between adoption of ICT and efficiency of private credit bureaus and registries are mixed yet weak – ICTs play very limited role in boosting financial access (one of the elements of financial development).

New technologies have significant impact on the financial services provided by the banking sector. The most notable examples of the services in the banking industry facilitated by ICT are electronic payments, processing of financial transactions through electronic systems, online and mobile retail banking services, mobile applications for banking customers and online services for the corporate clients [18].

Other, well-established example of the ICT adoption in the banking industry is ATMs. It should be underlined that the rate of adoption of the new technologies in the banking industry differs among countries. What is important, though, is that in developing economies often more technologically advanced financial services are used due to leapfrogging and adoption of the most recent solutions. One of the most important examples is the @widespread use of mobile banking services in the developing economies, e.g. in many African countries, where the saturation levels of such services are often higher than in advanced economies, in which traditional banking remains more popular.

Apart from the impact on the range of services offered by the banking companies, ICTs influence also the structure of the financial institutions by allowing increasingly complex task sharing, i.e. with various operations conducted in often physically distant countries. As a result, the largest financial corporations are present in many countries and often move their back offices to locations which enable lowering the costs or increasing the level of services (e.g. in India or Eastern Europe). These changes may be beneficial for the developing countries where such offices are usually opened – they may boost the growth of the local services sector and positively influence its environment, e.g. educational system (large number of highly educated employees is required to provide services for the global financial corporations).

Adoption of new technologies such as ICT is one of the most significant factors which have influenced the development of the financial markets over the last few decades, especially at the end of twentieth and beginning of twenty-first century. Increasing penetration of ICT has transformed the infrastructure of the financial markets, above all in their most dynamic segment, i.e. capital markets. Infrastructure of the financial markets has been defined by Essendorfer et al. ([23], p. 306) as: *innovation that facilitates between-agent (or counterparties) trading and processing, and settlement of securities, commodities and currencies or aggregates data or information from multiple sources to facilitate trading.* Crucial role is played by the introduction and development of fully electronic trading platforms, facilitating algorithmic and high-frequency trading (HFT) with the limited impact of human traders – in case of HFTs computers are responsible for the evaluation of the market data and transactions. The microstructure of the financial markets, especially stock markets, has changed [44]. Costs of the financial transactions as well as the time delays have been decreasing which led to improvements in terms of liquidity and efficiency of the financial instruments' pricing [33].

In case of electronic trading platforms, trading speeds may now even be measured in nanoseconds, i.e. they are much shorter than in case of fully human turnover [36]. However, emergence of the sophisticated algorithmic and HFT systems may also lead to a number of threats for the financial markets, e.g. large and irreversible losses of the markets' participants, lack of adequate control [37] or higher volatility [18]. In 2014, HFT accounted for ca. 50% of all equity trading in the United States, in Europe its share was at ca. 25%, in Japan at ca. 45% which shows its high importance in the advanced economies (in the emerging countries its share was much lower due to, e.g. lower rate of ICT penetration [37]).

Technologically advanced trading platforms are typical for the highly developed economies, yet there are other areas where the impact of ICT on financial markets can be observed, also in developing countries. Adoption of ICT enables more widespread dematerialization of securities, i.e. keeping them as digital record at depositary institution instead of physical form [37]. Dematerialization reduces the cost and duration of transactions as no exchange of physical securities (i.e. printed documents confirming holding the shares or bonds of particular company) is required. Another important benefit is the possibility to use the same trading infrastructure by various market participants (trading infrastructure with the centralized depositary institution).

ICTs are also one of the factors enabling listing of various financial instruments on more than one trading platform. They facilitate transactions between physically distant locations with very limited time delays and are required in the management of exchange rate risk (i.e. changes in the financial result of the transaction resulting from the variations in the prices of currencies) crucial in this type of investments [10, 54]. Such opportunities are particularly important in case of developing economies where costs of transactions in financial markets are usually higher and liquidity as well as pricing efficiency is lower than in advanced economies [8]. It means that adoption of ICT in those financial markets may attract foreign investors and contribute to integrating them into the global financial system.

Apart from the areas discussed above, ICTs have been influencing financial markets through establishment of electronic trading systems which boost the development of the derivative security markets. It has been evidenced, for instance, by introduction of new types of contracts [22] and higher level of the capital markets' integration and globalization [46].

Results of the empirical studies seem to confirm the impact of ICT on the stock markets, both in the advanced and emerging economies. Effects seem to be mostly positive. According to the study by CFA Institute [12], US stock market is critically dependent on new technologies due to its structure (decentralized electronic network). Essendorfer et al. [23] claim that ICTs have created new market ecology on the US stock market by making trading faster and cheaper but also more volatile and fragmented. Hossein et al. [34], in their study for the world's leading capital markets, found that ICT adoption had significant impact on the stock market development (with the exception of the ease of access). Bhunia [7], using the key stock market development indicators, argues that ICT adoption boosted the development of the Indian stock market. Okwu [45] studied stock exchanges in Africa (in Nigeria and South Africa) and stated that ICT adoption is one of the key development factors if transaction capacities are taken into account.

Global financial system has in the recent years undergone a deep and profound transformation. Even though the financial systems of the developing economies have to a varying degree been integrated into the global system, some of the key changes can also be observed in those countries. ICT played a significant role in those developments, especially in the field of financial innovations. They may be claimed to be one of the key factors affecting the spread of innovative financial products, such as exchange-traded funds (or, more broadly, exchange-traded products) which are currently offered and actively traded on the largest developing world financial markets, i.e. China, India, Brazil or Mexico.

Exchange-traded funds (ETFs) are investment funds listed and traded on the stock exchanges in a manner very similar to any other listed securities [17]. ETFs compete with some types of mutual funds (index funds) as well as stock index futures or options [4]. In their most popular form, the aim of ETF is to closely track the prices of the underlying assets (therefore they are considered tools for passive investing). Over the last years, many new types of ETFs have been launched (including active ETFs whose aims are very different from basic ETFs), yet ETFs tracking stock market indexes remain globally the largest category in terms of assets. Their introduction and trading in the financial markets is to a large extent dependent upon the adoption of ICT. Following areas of the potential impact of ICT on the development of the ETF market have been identified in the existing literature [41]:

1. Decreased cost of ETF trading resulting from the adoption of the electronic trading systems.
2. Lower tracking error (deviations of the rates of return of ETFs from the rates of return of the tracked assets) possible due to arbitrage transactions based on access to up-to-date information.
3. More potential for cross-listing of ETFs, i.e. listing on more than one stock exchange or listing of ETFs tracking foreign assets.
4. Increased potential for the development and launch of ETFs from the point of view of the companies which manage such funds – in order to offer ETFs which are able to compete with similar investment choices (such as index funds) and, therefore, gain profits; operational systems of ETF providers must be based on the technologically sophisticated solutions; it applies especially to more complicated types of ETFs, e.g. synthetic ETFs which are managed with the use of derivatives.

Discussion of the impact of ICT on innovative financial products has been presented above with reference to the example of ETFs, yet it may also be applied to other similar financial assets in the category of exchange-traded products (ETPs), for instance, exchange-traded notes (ETNs) or exchange-traded commodities (ETCs). The example of Mexico or China shows that innovative financial products may also be successfully launched in developing economies, partially due to the sufficient level of ICT penetration.

1.4 Summary

Recently observed rapid diffusion of ICT in many developing countries gives rise to questions about how these technologies may affect economic development and whether underdeveloped countries are able to effectively harness the potential that ICT offer [30, 21]. Many scholars argue that near-ubiquitous spread of information and communication technologies offers unprecedented opportunities to take off on the development path (see, for instance, works of Heeks [31], Desai and Potter [16], Hanson and Narural [29] and Khavul and Bruton [39]). However, the most the remarkable impact of ICT on country's overall development can only be confirmed when it converts into growing human opportunities, capabilities and thus wealth.

The very optimistic scenario would be that ICTs will offer a way towards development and growth that will encourage developing countries to climb the ladder and enter a stable development pattern forging ahead economically.

ICTs deeply affect and transform social and economic life, playing an enabling and unlocking role for economic growth and development. There is a causal chain between ICT adoption and a country's ability to enter the pattern of long-term economic development, which finally should allow backward countries to catch up with the best performing economies.

References

1. Aminuzzaman, S., Baldersheim, H., & Jamil, I. (2003). Talking back! Empowerment and mobile phones in rural Bangladesh: A study of the village phonescheme of Grameen Bank. *Contemporary South Asia, 12*(3), 327–348.
2. Andonova, V. (2006). Mobile phones the Internet and the institutional environment. *Telecommunications Policy, 30*(1), 29–45.
3. Andrianaivo, M., & Kpodar, K. (2011). ICT, financial inclusion, and growth evidence from African countries. *International Monetary Fund Working Paper, 11*(73), 3–46.
4. Arnold, M., & Lesné, A. (2015). *The changing landscape for beta replication – Comparing futures and ETFs for equity index exposure.* State Street Global Advisors. 2015.
5. Asongu, S. A., & Moulin, B. (2016). The role of ICT in reducing information asymmetry for financial access. *Research in International Business and Finance, 38*, 202–213.
6. Bresnahan, T. F., & Trajtenberg, M. (1995). General purpose technologies 'Engines of growth'? *Journal of Econometrics, 65*(1), 83–108.
7. Bhunia, A. (2011). An impact of ICT on the growth of capital market – Empirical evidence from Indian stock market exchange. *Information and Knowledge Management, 1*(2), 7–14.
8. Blitz, D., & Huij, J. (2012). Evaluating the performance of global emerging markets equity exchange-traded funds. *Emerging Markets Review, 13*, 149–158.
9. Cairncross, F. (2001). *The death of distance: How the communications revolution is changing our lives.* Boston: Harvard Business Press.
10. Calamia, A., Deville, L., & Riva, F. (2013). Liquidity in European equity ETFs: What really matters? *GREDEG Working Paper Series, 10*, 1–26.
11. Castells, M., Fernandez-Ardevol, M., Qiu, J. L., & Sey, A. (2009). *Mobile communication and society: A global perspective.* Cambridge: Mit Press.
12. CFA Institute. (2012). *Dark pools, internalization and equity market quality.* Charlottesville: Chartered Financial Analysts Institute.
13. Clark, G. (2008). *A farewell to alms: A brief economic history of the world.* Princeton: Princeton University Press.
14. Comin, D., & Hobijn, B. (2011). Technology diffusion and postwar growth. In Daron Acemoglu and Michael Woodford (eds.) *NBER macroeconomics annual 2010* (Vol. 25) (pp. 209–246). University of Chicago Press Volume ISBN: 0-226-00213-6.
15. Comin, D., Hobijn, B., & Emilie, R. (2006). *Five facts you need to know about technology diffusion. No. w11928.* Cambridge: National Bureau of Economic Research.
16. Desai, V., & Potter, R. B. (2013). *The companion to development studies.* Routledge.
17. Diaz-Rainey, I., & Ibikunle, G. (2012). A taxonomy of the 'dark side' of financial innovation: The cases of high frequency trading and exchange traded funds. *International Journal of Entrepreneurship and Innovation Management, 16*(1), 51–72.

18. Diaz-Rainey, I., Ibikunle, G., & Mention, A.-L. (2015). The technological transformation of capital markets. *Technological Forecasting and Social Change, 99*, 277–284.
19. Dosi, G. (1982). Technological paradigms and technological trajectories: A suggested interpretation of the determinants and directions of technical change. *Research Policy, 11*(3), 147–162.
20. Economides, N. (1996). The economics of networks. *International Journal of Industrial Organization, 14*(6), 673–699.
21. Elliott, J. (2012). *An introduction to sustainable development*. Routledge.
22. Ernkvist, M. (2015). The double knot of technology and business-model innovation in the era of ferment of digital exchanges: The case of OM, a pioneer in electronic options exchanges. *Technological Forecasting and Social Change, 99*, 285–299.
23. Essendorfer, S., Diaz-Rainey, I., & Falta, M. (2015). Creative destruction in Wall Street's technological arms race: Evidence from patent data. *Technological Forecasting and Social Change, 99*, 300–316.
24. Falahaty, M., & Jusoh, M. B. (2013). Financial development and information communication technology another look at the evidence from Middle East and North African Countries. In 3rd International Conference on Business, Economics, Management and Behavioral Sciences (ICBEMBS'2013) April (pp. 29–30).
25. Freeman, C., & Louca, F. (2001). *As time goes by: From the industrial revolution to the information revolution*. Oxford: Oxford University Press.
26. Gruber, H., & Koutroumpis, P. (2011). Mobile telecommunications and the impact on economic development. *Economic Policy, 26*(67), 387–426.
27. Hanna, N. K. (2003). *Why national strategies are needed for ICT-enabled development, World Bank Staff Paper*. Washington, DC: World Bank.
28. Hanna, N. K. (2010). *Transforming government and building the information society: Challenges and opportunities for the developing world*. New York: Springer Science & Business Media.
29. Hanson, J., & Narula, U. (2013). *New communication technologies in developing countries*. Routledge.
30. Heeks, R. (1999). *Information and communication technologies, poverty and development*. Manchester, UK: Institute for Development Policy and Management, University of Manchester.
31. Heeks, R. (2010). Do information and communication technologies (ICTs) contribute to development? *Journal of International Development, 22*(5), 625–640.
32. Helpman, E. (1998). General purpose technologies and economic growth. Cambridge, MA: MIT Press.
33. Hendershott, T., Jones, C. M., & Menkveld, A. J. (2011). Does algorithmic trading improve liquidity? *The Journal of Finance, 66*(1), 1–33.
34. Hossein, F. D. A., Fatemeh, F., & Seyed, M. T. (2013). Impact of information technology development on stock market development: Empirical study in the World's leading capital markets. *International Journal of Academic Research in Accounting, Finance and Management Sciences, 3*(1), 382–390.
35. Ilyina, A., & Samaniego, R. (2011). Technology and financial development. *Journal of Money, Credit and Banking, 43*(5), 899–921.
36. Johnson, N., Zhao, G., Hunsader, E., Qi, H., Johnson, N., Meng, J., & Tivnan, B. (2013). Abrupt rise of new machine ecology beyond human response time. *Scientific Reports, 3*, 2627.
37. Kauffman, R. J., Liu, J., & Ma, D. (2015). Innovations in financial IS and technology ecosystems: High-frequency trading in the equity market. *Technological Forecasting and Social Change, 99*, 339–354.
38. Katz, M. L., & Shapiro, C. (1985). Network externalities, competition, and compatibility. *American Economic Review, 75*(3), 424–440.
39. Khavul, S., & Bruton, G. D. (2013). Harnessing innovation for change: Sustainability and poverty in developing countries. *Journal of Management Studies, 50*(2), 285–306.

40. Lechman, E. (2015). *ICT diffusion in developing countries: Towards a new concept of technological takeoff*. Springer.
41. Lechman, E., & Marszk, A. (2015). ICT technologies and financial innovations: The case of exchange traded funds in Brazil, Japan, Mexico, South Korea and the United States. *Technological Forecasting and Social Change, 99*, 355–376.
42. Mansell, R., Avgerou, C., Quah, D., Silverstone, R. (2009). *Information and communication technologies*. Oxford University Press.
43. Morck, R., Yeung, B., & Yu, W. (2000). The information content of stock markets: Why do emerging markets have synchronous stock price movements? *Journal of Financial Economics, 58*(1), 215–260.
44. Nishimura, K.G. (2010). *Electronic trading and financial markets*. Bank of Japan.
45. Okwu, A. T. (2015). ICT adoption and financial markets: A study of the leading stock exchange markets in Africa. *Journal of Accounting and Management, V*(2), 53–76.
46. Panourgias, N. S. (2015). Capital markets integration: A sociotechnical study of the development of a cross-border securities settlement system. *Technological Forecasting and Social Change, 99*, 317–338.
47. Patterson, S. (2012). *Dark pools: High-speed traders, AI bandits, and the threat to the global financial system*. Random House Digital.
48. Pérez, C. (2003). Technological change and opportunities for development as a moving target. In Toye, J. F. J. (ed.) *Trade and development: Directions for the 21st century* Edward Elgar Publishing (p. 100).
49. Perez, C. (2009). Technological revolutions and techno-economic paradigms. *Cambridge Journal of Economics, 34*, 185–202. bep051.
50. Pozzi, F., Di Matteo, T., & Aste, T. (2013). Spread of risk across financial markets: Better to invest in the peripheries. *Scientific Reports, 3*, 1665.
51. Quah, D. (2001). ICT clusters in development: Theory and evidence. *EIB Papers, 6*(1), 85–100.
52. Sahay, R., Cihak, M., N'Diaye, P., Barajas, A., Bi, R., Ayala, D., Gao, Y., Kyobe, A., Nguyen, L., Saborowski, S., Svirydzenka, K., Yousef, S.R. (2015). Rethinking financial deepening: Stability and growth in emerging markets. IMF Staff Discussion Note, 15.
53. Sassi, S., & Goaied, M. (2013). Financial development, ICT diffusion and economic growth: Lessons from MENA region. *Telecommunications Policy, 37*(4), 252–261.
54. Schmiedel, H., Malkamäki, M., & Tarkka, J. (2006). Economies of scale and technological development in securities depository and settlement systems. *Journal of Banking & Finance, 30*(6), 1783–1806.
55. Shamim, F. (2007). The ICT environment, financial sector and economic growth. A cross-country analysis. *Journal of Economic Studies, 34*(4), 352–370.
56. Shapiro, C., & Varian, H. R. (2013). *Information rules: a strategic guide to the network economy*. Boston: Harvard Business Press.
57. Silverberg, G., & Soete, L. (1988). In G. Dosi, C. Freeman, & R. Nelson (Eds.), *Technical change and economic theory* (Vol. 988). London: Pinter.
58. Singh, A. (1997). Financial liberalization, stock markets and economic development. *The Economic Journal, 107*(442), 771–782.
59. Stigler, G. J. (1961). The economics of information. *The Journal of Political Economy, 69*(3), 213–225.
60. Torero, M., & Von Braun, J. (Eds.). (2006). *Information and communication technologies for development and poverty reduction: The potential of telecommunications*. Washington, DC: Intl Food Policy Res Inst.
61. Unwin, P. T. H. (Ed.). (2009). *ICT4D: Information and communication technology for development*. Cambridge: Cambridge University Press.
62. Venables, A. J. (2001). Geography and international inequalities: the impact of new technologies. *Journal of Industry, Competition and Trade, 1*(2), 135–159.
63. Wilson III, E. J. (2004). *The information revolution and developing countries* (Vol. 1). Cambridge, MA: MIT Press Books.

64. Wolf, S. (2001). Determinants and impact of ICT use for African SMEs: Implications for rural South Africa. In *Center for development research* (*ZEF Bonn*). Paper prepared for TIPS Forum.
65. Wurgler, J. (2000). Financial markets and the allocation of capital. *Journal of Financial Economics, 58*(1), 187–214.
66. Yartey, C. A. (2008). Financial development, the structure of capital markets, and the global digital divide. *Information Economics and Policy, 20*(2), 208–227.

Chapter 2
The Impact of ICTs on Women's Economic Empowerment

Dagmara Nikulin

Abstract It is widely argued that ICTs enable the inclusion of low-skilled and traditionally marginalized groups, such as women, people with disabilities, and workers at the base of the pyramid (BoP), in the labor market. In this paper, we investigate the determinants of female participation in the labor market in developing countries with a focus on the impact of the use of ICTs on female labor force participation. We conduct a panel study analysis for 60 developing countries in the time period 2000–2014. Our results confirm that there is rather a positive impact from the use of ICTs on female labor force participation in developing countries. Moreover, we show that gross national income (GNI) per capita, fertility rates, and income inequalities influence to some extent the level of women's engagement in the labor market. Our results are robust against different control variables, as well as different ICT proxies.

Keywords ICTs • Female labor force participation • Panel data • Development level • Income inequalities

2.1 Introduction

Over the past few decades, information and communication technologies (ICTs) have played an important role as a key solution for comprehensive development, poverty elimination, and the empowerment of groups discriminated against in society. One of the important effects of the proliferation of ICTs is the influence on the labor market, both through the creation of new jobs (ICTs as a sector) and making labor markets more inclusive, innovative, flexible, and transparent (ICTs as a tool). The relationship between ICT adoption and labor market outcomes is worth studying, as reflected in numerous studies. On the one hand, it is widely argued that ICTs enable the inclusion of low-skilled and traditionally marginalized groups, such as

D. Nikulin (✉)
Faculty of Management and Economics, Gdańsk University of Technology, Gdańsk, Poland
e-mail: dnikulin@zie.pg.gda.pl

© Springer International Publishing AG 2017   15
H. Kaur et al. (eds.), *Catalyzing Development through ICT Adoption*,
DOI 10.1007/978-3-319-56523-1_2

women, people with disabilities, and workers at the base of the pyramid (BoP), into the labor market [21]. On the other hand, a variety of female labor force participation rates are observed across countries, reflecting differences in economic development, social norms, education levels, and fertility rates. Moreover, labor force participation among women is more varied than among men [26].

In this paper, we examine the influence of ICTs on the labor market in developing countries. The motive for undertaking this research is that there is on the one hand a wide range of literature arguing the positive effect of ICTs on female participation in the labor market and on the other hand statistics showing rather stable levels of female labor force participation in developing countries over the last 15 years, despite rapid changes in ICT indicators. Therefore, the main goal of this study is to examine if and how ICTs shape and change work with regard to the female labor force in the labor market. From our point of view, it is interesting to investigate the determinants of female participation in the labor market in developing countries. To do this, we conduct a panel study analysis for 60 developing countries over the time period 2000–2014.

In our article, we contribute to the relevant literature by examining the relationship between the use of ICTs and the level of the female labor force. As a response variable, we use the female labor force participation rate (as the percentage of the female population aged 15+), modeled as an international labor office (ILO) estimate. As explanatory variables, we employ two different ICT indicators, such as mobile cellular telephone subscriptions per 100 inhabitants and percentage of individuals using the Internet. In this way, we compare the influence of different ICT measures on women's economic empowerment.

Our results confirm that the use of ICTs exerts a positive influence on female labor force participation in developing countries. Moreover, we find that gross national income (GNI) per capita, fertility rates, and income inequalities influence the level of women's engagement in the labor market. Our results are robust against different control variables, as well as different ICT proxies. The remainder of the article is as follows. The second section addresses the role of ICTs in the labor market and in particular in the process of women's empowerment. The third section is devoted to the description of the data and the methodology. In the fourth section, we show and discuss our results. The last section concludes.

2.2   ICTs, the Labor Market, and Women's Empowerment

In the literature, the most popular approach to determining the female labor force participation rate is based on the U-shaped hypothesis [5], according to which the female labor force participation rate is higher in poor countries, slightly lower in middle-income countries and greater in highly developed countries [16]. It is important to remember that the female labor supply should be considered both as a driver and an outcome of a country's development. Moreover, the analysis of women's labor force participation seems to be multifaceted. The empowerment of women may be driven simply by poverty (especially in less-developed countries) but also by women's increasing educational attainment and work opportunities created in modern countries [26]. Analyzing the drivers of female labor force participation in poor countries, we observe push factors, which force women to work, in contrast to well-developed countries, where pull factors draw women into the labor market [13].

At the same time, a considerably greater variation is found in the labor force participation of women than men across developing countries. This variation is driven by a wide variety of economic factors. The study of the determinants of women's economic participation is complex, and many researchers state that the involvement of women is associated with economic, sociodemographic, and cultural factors [23]. There are several factors that influence female labor force participation. First of all, despite the common claim that women's empowerment and economic development are closely interrelated, economic development alone is insufficient to enable significant progress in women's empowerment [7]. Some empirical studies show rather weak evidence on the pure influence of changes in gross domestic product (GDP) per capita on the evolution of female labor force participation [26]. Moreover, some research results show that rising urbanization causes a fall in women's engagement in the labor market as they are withdrawn from the agricultural labor market [26]. The other important factor influencing female labor force participation addressed in the literature is educational attainment, which also shows a U-shaped curve. Moreover, educational level determines the quality of employment through an increase in the reservation wage [26] and therefore is predominantly considered an investment in education [20]. Besides this, a range of social determinants are considered determinants of female labor force participation, such as marriage, fertility, women's role outside the household, and household and spousal characteristics.

Moreover, the role of the quality of female employment is often discussed in analyzing the determinants of female labor force participation. It is therefore crucial to understand and investigate the nature of women's jobs, especially in developing countries where employment is often a last resort to prevent poverty rather than a means of self-development. Due to the implementation of ICTs, the creation of better and more qualified jobs becomes possible. However, Dell'Anno and Solomon [6] argue that the benefits of the influence of ICTs on business performance are greater for highly skilled workers. This leads to the assumption that the effect of ICT adoption is greater in more developed countries.

During the past decade, the international community has focused considerable efforts on strategies to help the people of the world's poorest countries share in the benefits of globalization and escape the trap of poverty [19]. Against this background, it seems increasingly important to examine the role played by ICTs in improving people's level and quality of life [14–16]. In this section, we describe the effects of using ICTs on the labor market and in particular on employment opportunities. The literature suggests that these effects should be analyzed in a complex manner. Three major drivers that enhance the role of ICTs in the labor market can be distinguished: greater connectivity, the digitization of the economy, and the globalization of skills [21]. Greater connectivity means that due to the use of ICT technology, mostly the Internet, people have more opportunities to find a job, and employers have more opportunities to find the right workers. For instance, according to the McKinsey Global Institute, in developing countries, the use of mobile Internet tools influences the productivity of certain types of work [21]. The second driver, the digitization of the economy, is strictly related to the contemporary nature of work, which has been reshaped, as relationships between workers and between workers and employers. Moreover, digitization creates work that is not joined to location and is disaggregated across space and time. Nowadays, through telecommuting and outsourcing, workers can cooperate globally no matter where they live. Moreover, some ICT tools are widespread and available even for small entrepreneurs, which facilitates international collaboration. The third driver is the globalization of skills, which can be observed in the global chain of production processes. The global share of labor creates an opportunity for high-skilled workers from developing countries to obtain well-paid jobs. The implementation of ICT tools is a core factor in inclusion in global value chains, next to knowledge of foreign languages.

The effects of ICTs on the labor market are complex as the impact of ICT on employment can be considered both positive and negative. The negative influences concern job losses and work displacement due to the automatization and transformation of jobs [21]. However, it is primarily the positive effects of ICT proliferation, especially in developing countries, that are discussed in the literature. Therefore, in this section we focus on the positive outcomes of ICT for the labor market.

In general, the impact of ICTs can be considered in terms of ICT as a sector and ICT as a tool. The most obvious effect of ICT adoption is the direct creation of jobs in the ICT sector through the production of ICT and the intensive use of ICT. However, from a broad perspective, ICTs help to make labor markets more inclusive, innovative, flexible, and transparent [21], and thus ICTs can also be considered a tool used in labor market processes. In this sense, every country is touched by ICT, and in the labor market, there are clear implications for productivity and labor. In other words, ICTs empower workers and not only those hired in the ICT sector [21]. In particular, ICTs are helpful in enabling workers to find jobs and employers to find skilled workers as they make it possible to overcome social, cultural, and physical barriers in the labor market [21]. In this way, the labor market has become more transparent and efficient. Moreover, ICTs support new forms of employment, e.g., by creating opportunities for online contracting (working online) [21]. It is important to note that online contracting covers jobs performed not only for larger firms but also SMEs and is related not only to ICT jobs but also to non-ICT work. Another form of ICT-enabled work is microwork. Microwork involves dividing a large task into smaller micro-tasks, which can be performed by individuals regardless of geographical distance [21].

The interaction between ICT adoption and women's empowerment has been described widely in the literature. A growing body of studies shows that the impact of ICTs is increasingly related to women's empowerment, both in economic and social and cultural respects. It is argued that ICTs allow women to transform knowledge and information into innovative products and services [1, 4, 17] and increase the flexibility of their participation in the labor supply, e.g., through facilitating distance work and flexitime [8]. Moreover, ICTs help in creating women's leadership and participation in community and economic development [2]. Most previous research, based mainly on national case studies, has indicated that ICTs increase employability, and thus women's empowerment can be advanced [3, 9–12, 18, 22–24, 27].

In general, empirical research concerning the effects of ICTs on women's empowerment has been based on case study methodology. Predominantly, there is evidence of a positive influence of ICT adoption on the labor market. In addition, numerous initiatives have been undertaken to empower women through the use of ICTs [25]. However, although the interaction between ICT adoption and women's economic empowerment has been described widely in the literature, there is still a lack of international comparisons confirming or rejecting the hypothesis of a positive influence of ICTs on the labor market.

2.3 Data and Methodology

Our data set contains panel data from 2000 to 2014 for 60 developing countries, which are strongly balanced. As a response variable, we use a female labor force participation rate, which is calculated as the proportion of female aged 15 and older who are economically active.[1] As explanatory variables, we employ different ICT indicators, such as mobile cellular telephone subscriptions per 100 inhabitants and percentage of individuals using the Internet. In this way, we can compare the influence of different ICT technologies on women's economic empowerment. Moreover, to ensure the robustness of our results, we use several control variables. Based on existing knowledge concerning the determinants of female labor force participation, we choose the following outcomes as control variables: GNI per capita, the fertility rate, the population sex ratio, the ratio of urbanization, and the GINI index as a measure of income inequality. All data are drawn from 19th edition of the World Telecommunication/ICT Indicators database and the World Development Indicators database. Table 2.1 reports the summary statistics for all the data used in the empirical analysis.

We conduct a random-effects GLS regression with the use of panel data for 60 developing countries over the time period 2000–2014. We have chosen a random effect model because we assume that the differences across analyzed countries have some influence on the dependent variable. Moreover, as an advantage of the use of random effect model, we can include time invariant variable (GINI coefficient), which also seems to be significant while explaining the variability of female labor force participation rate. In this way, we assume random heterogeneity for countries over time and across countries.

---

[1] The female labor force participation rate is modeled according to Key Indicators of the Labour Market provided by International Labour Organization.

Table 2.1 Descriptive statistics

Variable	Mean	Std.Dev.	Min.	Max.
lfpf	54.39533	20.10276	13.0000	88.8
mcts	34.70828	36.36511	0.0000	149.0691
iui	7.596558	10.39419	0.0000	56.8
GNI	1108.917	914.9262	80.0000	4490.0000
WFR	4.097187	1.5316	1.085	7.738
PF	50.14627	1.111045	46.26004	53.78802
UP	50.14627	1.111045	46.26004	53.78802
GINI	39.97569	7.712084	24.55	60.79

Source: Authors' own elaboration

Data description: *lfpf* female labor force participation rate, *mcts* mobile cellular telephone subscriptions per 100 inhabitants, *iui* percentage of individuals using the Internet, *GNI* gross national income (GNI) per capita, *WFR* fertility rate, *PF* percentage of females in population, *UP* urban population as percentage of total population, *GINI* coefficient

2.4   Results

In this section, we conduct panel regressions to examine the determinants of female participation in the labor market and in particular to investigate the association between women's empowerment in the labor market and the use of ICTs. Ceteris paribus, we expect the female participation rate to be positively correlated with the use of ICTs and the percentage of females in the population and negatively correlated with the fertility rate and the urban population rate. In case of the control variable GNI per capita, the direction of influence for female participation in the labor market seems to be problematic; however, according to the U-shaped curve, in developing countries, the sign should be negative. Table 2.2 presents the results of the panel data estimation. As the ICT indicator can be described in several ways, we first use the statistics for the percentage of individuals using the Internet as an ICT proxy.

The results presented in Table 2.2 confirm our initial expectations concerning the determinants of the female labor force participation rate. We conduct five regressions with different control variables as explanatory variables. Analyzing each of the five models, we observe a positive, statistically significant influence of the use of ICTs on female participation in the labor market. Moreover, the results of the estimations indicate that the female labor force participation rate is dependent on GNI per capita in a negative manner. Thus, in developing countries, an increase in income is correlated with lower engagement of women in the labor market. The reason for this is that women are no longer forced to work to prevent poverty, as widely reported in the literature. Similarly, the participation of women in the labor market will be higher if there is greater income inequality in a given economy. Moreover, our results confirm that women's empowerment in the labor market is also related to female fertility in that a higher fertility rate causes lower participation in the labor market. We find no statistically significant result for the influence of the ratio of females in the total population.

Table 2.2 Panel data estimation results (I)

Dependent variable: female labor force participation rate					
	(1)	(2)	(3)	(4)	(5)
iui	0.0043[a]	0.0135[a]	0.0108[a]	0.0110[a]	0.0113[a]
	(0.0015)	(0.0031)	(0.0034)	(0.0034)	(0.0034)
GNI		−0.0295[a]	−0.02978[a]	−0.0306[a]	−0.0320[a]
		(0.0089)	(0.0090)	(0.0091)	(0.0092)
WFR			−0.0693[b]	−0.0691[b]	−0.0712[a]
			(0.0308)	(0.0309)	(0.0310)
PF				−0.1421	−0.1309
				(0.3475)	(0.3495)
GINI					0.8531[a]
					(0.2340)
R-squared	0.0175	0.1327	0.0209	0.0147	0.1411
Observations	879	821	821	821	812
Wald chi2 test	8.83 (0.03)	19.55 (0.0001)	24.72 (0.000)	24.79 (0.0001)	37.80 (0.000)

Source: Authors' own elaboration
All panel regressions include a country random effect. Standard errors are reported in parentheses. In all regressions a constant is also included but not reported
[a]1% confidence level
[b]5% confidence level

Although we observe a positive impact from the determinants analyzed on the female labor force participation rate, we should interpret the results obtained with caution. First of all, we should be aware of the potential underreporting of data and therefore the fact that data on women's participation rates may not accurately reflect women's work. Moreover, as reported in Table 2.2, the estimated models are fitted rather weakly to the empirical values. The reason for this seems to be twofold. Firstly, the female labor force participation rates in the given countries are rather stable over the period of analysis. Secondly, we observe a significant increase in ICT measures over this time period in the developing countries analyzed. Based on the above, it would be impossible to indicate a good fit for the models estimated. Consequently, we point out two important findings. On the one hand, we indicate the positive impact of ICTs technologies on women's empowerment, but on the other hand, the power of the influence is rather scarce. Therefore, our results are very helpful in understanding the role of ICTs in women's empowerment, as they show moderate relation between those variables. We argue that there is no simple shift between the increase in ICT technologies usage and the growth of female labor force participation. The problem is more complex and no simple conclusions should be drawn. However, bearing in mind the differences between the countries analyzed, we stand by the conclusions drawn above.

In the next stage, to ensure the robustness of our results, we conduct further regressions with the use of another ICT proxy: mobile cellular telephone subscriptions per 100 inhabitants (mcts). Table 2.3 presents the estimates of five models, which include different control variables.

Table 2.3 Panel data estimation results (II)

Dependent variable: female labor force participation rate					
	(1)	(2)	(3)	(4)	(5)
mcts	0.0036[a]	0.0132[a]	0.0130[a]	0.0130[a]	0.0131[a]
	(0.0011)	(0.0022)	(0.0024)	(0.0024)	(0.0024)
GNI		−0.0426[a]	0.0428[a]	0.0417[a]	−0.0427[a]
		(0.0084)	(0.0084)	(0.0085)	(0.0086)
WFR			−0.0098	−0.0050	−0.0096
			(0.0318)	(0.0320)	(0.0322)
PF				0.4801	0.4825
				(0.3716)	(0.3741)
GINI					0.82834[a]
					(0.2346)
R-squared	0.0156	0.1418	0.1494	0.2061	0.1899
Observations	878	822	822	822	813
Wald chi2 test	9.71	36.78	36.84	38.53	51.42 (0.0000)
	(0.0018)	(0.0000)	(0.0000)	(0.0000)	

Source: Authors' own elaboration
All panel regressions include a country random effect. Standard errors are reported in parentheses. In all regressions a constant is also included but not reported
[a]1% confidence level

The results presented in Table 2.3 confirm the previous outcomes from Table 2.2. Irrespective of the ICT proxy used, the directions of impact on determinants of female labor force participation are the same. The only difference is the loss of statistical significance in the case of the control variable women's fertility. Therefore, we argue that the use of mobile cellular telephone access and access to the Internet have a positive influence on the activity of women in the labor market.

2.5 Conclusion

Information and communication technologies (ICTs) have over the past few decades played an important role in the empowerment of groups discriminated against in society, in some contexts including women. It is highlighted that studies on the determinants of women's economic participation are complex as the involvement of women in the labor market is associated with economic, sociodemographic, and cultural factors. In this article, we aim to investigate the determinants of female participation in the labor market in developing countries, with a focus on the impact of ICTs on women's empowerment. Conducting a panel study analysis for 60 developing countries over the period 2000–2014, we show that the female participation rate is in general positively correlated with the use of ICTs measured as the percentage of individuals using the Internet and mobile cellular telephone subscriptions per 100 inhabitants. Moreover, the participation of women in the labor market seems to be higher if there is greater income inequality in a given economy. Bearing in mind that our research scope embraces only developing countries, income inequality is often related to a low level of national income, which is reflected in human poverty.

At the same time, we indicate that examining the determinants of women's engagement in the labor market is a complex task. Numerous case studies are described in the contemporary literature, but the significance of the impact of ICTs on women's empowerment should be argued with caution. Although we find a positive influence of ICTs on the women's labor market, it should be noted that the degree of explanation of the dependent variable provided by the factors used should be considered rather small. It is important to remember that we have observed a significant increase in the use of ICTs in developing countries over the period analyzed. The development of ICTs in recent years has been very rapid, while the female labor force participation rate in developing countries remains rather stable. Thus, it is difficult to explain the changes in women's empowerment over time as significant differences can be observed only across countries. Moreover, we underline that the drivers of women's engagement in the labor market are diverse and also act in different directions. In developing countries, we observe push factors, which force women to work. Our analysis confirms to some extent that in countries with higher GNI per capita, the engagement of women in the labor market is lower. This negative relation could be explained by women leaving the labor market when their work is not necessary to prevent poverty. On the other hand, if ICTs were to create the possibility of obtaining better-paid jobs, women's interest in being active in the labor market would increase. Therefore, there is still a need for further research on the influence of ICTs on women's empowerment, mostly in developing countries. While ICTs can certainly contribute to women's empowerment in the labor market, future studies should pay more attention to the quality of women's jobs.

Bibliography

1. Ambujam, N. K., & Venkatalakshmi, K. (2009). The function of information and technology in empowerment of women. Proceedings 2009 2nd IEEE International conference on computer science and information technology, ICCSIT 2009, 385–387. http://doi.org/10.1109/ICCSIT.2009.5234705
2. Anitha, L., & Sundharavadivel, D. (2012). Information and communication technology (ICT) and women empowerment. *International Journal of Advanced Research in Management and Social Sciences, 1*(4), 143–152.
3. Arun, S., & Arun, T. (2002). ICTs, gender and development: Women in software production in Kerala. *Journal of International Development, 14*(1), 39–50. http://doi.org/10.1002/jid.866.
4. Beyond Access. (2012). Empowering women and girls through ICT at libraries. Retrieved from www.beyondaccess.net
5. Çağatay, N., & Özler, Ş. (1995). Feminization of the labor force: The effects of long-term development and structural adjustment. *World Development, 23*(11), 1883–1894. http://doi.org/10.1016/0305-750X(95)00086-R.
6. Dell'Anno, R., & Solomon, H. O. (2014). Informality, inequality, and ICT in transition Economies. *Eastern European Economics, 52*(5), 3–31. https://doi.org/10.1080/001287755.2014.1004264
7. Duflo, E. (2012). Women empowerment and economic development. *Journal of Economic Literature, 50*(4), 1051–1079. http://doi.org/10.1257/jel.50.4.1051.
8. Goyal, A. (2011). Developing women: Why technology can help. *Information Technology for Development, 17*(2), 112–132. http://doi.org/10.1080/02681102.2010.537252.

9. Hafkin, N., & Taggart, N. (2001). *Gender, information technology, and developing countries: An analytic study* (Vol. 2). Office of Women in Development, Bureau for Global Programs, Field Support and Research, United States Agency for International Development. http://doi.org/10.1093/heapol/2.3.251

10. Huyer, S., & Carr, M. (2002). Information and communication technologies: A priority for women. *Gender, Technology and Development, 6*(1), 85–100.

11. Islam, S. (2015). ICT on women empowerment in South Asia. *Journal of Economic & Financial Studies, 03*(03), 80–90.

12. Kelkar, G., & Nathan, D. (2002). Gender relations and technological change in Asia. *Current Sociology, 50*, 427–441.

13. Klasen, S., & Pieters, J. (2012). *Push or pull? Drivers of female labor force participation during India's economic boom. IZA Discussion paper 6395.* Bonn: Institute for the Study of Labor.

14. Lechman, E. (2014). ICT diffusion trajectories and economic development: Empirical evidence for 46 developing countries. In H. Kaur & X. Tao (Eds.), *ICTs and the millennium development goals* (pp. 19–39). New York: Springer US. http://doi.org/10.1007/978-1-4899-7439-6.

15. Lechman, E. (2015). *ICT diffusion in developing countries: Towards a new concept of technological takeoff.* Switzerland: Springer International Publishing.

16. Lechman, E., & Kaur, H. (2015). Economic growth and female labor force participation-verifying the U-feminization hypothesis. New evidence for 162 countries over the period 1990-2012. *Economics and Sociology, 8*(1), 246–257. http://doi.org/DOI: 10.14254/2071-789X.2015/8-1/19.

17. Levis, M. S. (2011). Working toward women's economic empowerment: Using information and communication technology in developing areas to market traditional crafts. In J. A. Jacko (Ed.), *Human-computer interaction. Users and applications* (pp. 266–274). Berlin Heidelberg: Springer http://doi.org/10.1007/3-540-68339-9_34

18. Njelekela, C., & Sanga, C. (2015). Contribution of information and communication technology in improving access to market information among smallholder farmers: The case study of Kilosa District. *The International Journal of Management Science and Information Technology, 17*, 56–72.

19. Opiyo, R. O., & K'Akumu, O. A. (2006). ICT application in the informal sector: The case of the Kariokor market MSE cluster in Nairobi. *Urban Forum, 17*(3), 241–261. http://doi.org/10.1007/s12132-006-0011-x.

20. Psacharopoulos, G. (1994). Returns to investment in education – A global update. *World Development, 22*(9), 1325–1343.

21. Raja, S., Imaizumi, S., Kelly, T., Narimatsu, J., Paradi-Guilford, C., BanK, W. (2013). Connecting to work, (September), 64. Retrieved from http://www-wds.worldbank.org/external/default/WDSContentServer/WDSP/IB/2013/09/09/000456286_20130909094536/Rendered/PDF/809770WP0Conne00Box379814B00PUBLIC0.pdf

22. Shirazi, F. (2012). Information and communication technology and women empowerment in Iran. *Telematics and Informatics, 29*(1), 45–55. http://doi.org/10.1016/j.tele.2011.02.001.

23. Suhaida, M. A., Nurulhuda, M. S., & Yap, S.-F. (2013). Access to ICT as moderating factor to women's participation in the labor force: A conceptual framework. *International Journal of Trade, Economics and Finance, 4*(4), 197–201. http://doi.org/10.7763/IJTEF.2013.V4.285.

24. Umrani, F., & Ghadially, R. (2003). Empowering women through ICT education: Facilitating computer adoption. *Gender, Technology and Development, 7*(3), 359–377.

25. UNESCO. (2016). *ICTs and the informal economy: UNESCO trains women in E-commerce* UNESCO Office in Dakar. Retrieved on 06.05.2016 from http://www.unesco.org/new/en/education/resources/online-materials/singleview/news/icts_and_the_informal_economy_unesco_trains_women_in_e_comm/

26. Verick, S. (2014). Female labor force participation in developing countries. *IZA World of Labor, 87*, 1–10. http://doi.org/10.15185/izawol.87.

27. Wamala, C. (2012). *Empowering women through ICT* (Vol. 3). Retrieved from http://www.bgwomeninict.org/language/bg/uploads/files/documents__0/documents__a3d32c26f6e-5897fa43d9daf6a5e48f2.pdf.

Chapter 3
Big Data Analytics for ICT Monitoring and Development

Ritu Chauhan, Harleen Kaur, Ewa Lechman, and Adam Marszk

Abstract The expanded growth of information and communication technology has opened new era of digitization which is proving to be a great challenge for researchers and scientists around the globe. The utmost paradigm is to handle and process the explosion of data with minimal cost and discover relevant hidden information in the least amount of time. The buzz word "BIG DATA" is a widely anticipated term with the potential to handle heterogeneous, complex, and unstructured data. We can say that big data has evolved as a monitoring tool for ICT to detect relevant patterns which were previous unknown. This chapter focuses on ICT and big data application in varied application domains. The aim is to design a framework for business data resources which gather at unprecedented pace and derive relevant information with big data analytics for better decision-making. In addition, this chapter discusses a novel framework where big data analytics is utilized as potential decision-making step for relatively better management policies.

Keywords Big data • Information and Communication Technologies (ICT) • Network analysis • Business data analytics • Decision-making

R. Chauhan
Centre for Computational Biology and Bioinformatics, Amity University, Noida, India
e-mail: rituchauha@gmail.com

H. Kaur (✉)
Department of Computer Science and Engineering, School of Engineering Sciences and Technology, Hamdard University, New Delhi, India
e-mail: harleen.unu@gmail.com

E. Lechman • A. Marszk
Faculty of Management and Economics, Gdańsk University of Technology, Gdańsk, Poland
e-mail: eda@zie.pg.gda.pl; amarszk@zie.pg.gda.pl

© Springer International Publishing AG 2017
H. Kaur et al. (eds.), *Catalyzing Development through ICT Adoption*,
DOI 10.1007/978-3-319-56523-1_3

3.1　Introduction

Data exploration has opened newly challenges for information society to develop new ways to handle data. The "Big Data" in information and communication technologies (ICTs) has evolved to provide services and hidden information which can benefit end users. The big data is a widely anticipated paradigm which has the capability to handle complex and heterogeneous nature of data that can be utilized in varied application domains. In this context, big data has been exploratory used in healthcare, agriculture, economic, sensor-based technology, mobile data network, and other ICT data to get insights of data for future decision-making [25].

The overall trend today is to detect hidden and unknown information from big data to explore new ventures. However, traditional technology was insufficient to handle and process such billion bytes of data. Big data provides a complement system to handle complex nature of data and discover hidden facts for future knowledge discovery. We can also say that big data can be leveraged with new advanced technology in ICTs [13]. Moreover, the key challenge faced is to synchronize data from various sources, which otherwise can provide inaccurate results. Hence big data can prove to be a game changer where it can applicably demonstrate the relative facts among the data gathered from various sources for decision-making. Business companies are investing billions of dollars to investigate the cause relationship among customer patterns to increase their profit margins. They need an appropriate technology which can benefit them in terms of minimal cost and delivering accurate patterns. So exploration of data is focused on big data analytics where the competitive situation is to deliver real facts and knowledge from complex data resources.

The potential of new intervene technology is to preprocess the voluminous data and extract information with respect to pace of data gathering. Thus, insights into business consumer behavior are one of the leveraged determinate factors that all leading companies want to acquire in order to attain or retain their customers. The relative factor is to meet the customer needs and determine factors which are capable of retaining customers with big data analytics. So the business market is focused on the use of new ICT-based technology which is big data analytics to overwhelm the need of today's market value.

The customer data gathered from emerging digitization technology comprises of heterogeneous and unstructured data congregated from online, shop, mall, and other sources such as a group of people with different behavioral patterns. Hence, big data can withdraw varied patterns to benefit companies to draw interference to retain their valued customers [8, 37, 40–43]. For example, customers doing online shopping express their views and sentiments while buying the products; if this data is interfaced in a proper way, one can detect behavioral pattern and cost sensitivity of a product. This information can help to monitor clear and broad view of market for decision-making. However, there exists a global shift where the customer older market research is linked with the new likes and dislikes of current customers to determine the competitive nature of products or services and create awareness patterns for organizations to have a clear picture of market so that they can dissemble their products with the growing need of market. This will certainly help them to identify their privilege customers and contribute to the need to align strategies that make them distinctive and benefit their customers' retaining policy. Further, we can say that ICT-based technology can gather data from various resources without the struggle to store the data with predetermined purpose and analyze this information with overwhelming strategies in tune with the needs of a business to fulfill customer needs.

The chapter is organized as follows. The next section presents the background literature review of ICT and big data potential on varied application domains. In Sect. 3.3, we describe the predictive analytics in ICT for discovery of patterns for future decision-making. Then, a novel framework is discussed utilizing big data analytics and decision-making for appropriate future management policies. We finally conclude the chapter summarizing is learning from it.

3.2   Background

Over the last decade, data has been growing at an explosive rate. As data is invariably related with digital explosion and the Internet, the challenge is to invariably utilize algorithmic technology and deploy IT-based tools to deliver known facts from big data. For example, consumer behavior patterns are changing in fast, each time a click on the Internet is recorded for likes and dislikes. The data generated each day is tremendous in nature; further the analysis of such data plays a vital role for future decision-making. Hence, the big data term is a commonly utilized term for unstructured flow of data where the focus is to detect hidden patterns with minimal amount of time. The approach of big data is to provide services in the form of analysis, where new process models can be revealed with potential knowledge network.

The big data in ICT can be illustrated with the ever expanding use of the Internet, mobile phones, electronic health care, geographic information data, scanner data, and other data resources that are applicable to varied application domains [1, 27, 28, 30]. In earlier times, in the traditional-based system, the data was getting collected from specific resources which tended to be manual in nature. However, the advent of the Internet has proved to be a game changer and has opened gates for electronic data system. The growth in ICT has potentially driven the society to digital explosion. For example, traditionally when a customer used to buy products from shopping areas on daily basis, there was never a check on the amount of items bought by a specific customer nor were the items ever categorized on quality and productivity. Further, today's customer behavior is integrated with the Internet buying and selling over the Internet. The data collected is then decodified to understand customer needs across the globe. The information is not just about the customer buying trends but business can also categorize the customer in accordance to their sales in correspondence to their sociodemographic factors. Hence, organizations are earning millions of dollars while retrieving hidden facts and knowledge from complex and heterogeneous nature of data.

We can say that there is a revolution in ICT with big data where small or big organizations' day-to-day functionality is driven by computers [2–8]. The database gathered each day from varied resources, if analyzed or predicted, can deliver true instances for future decision-making. Moreover, business organizations are in era of online operation where everyday several customer and financial data is shared through the Internet. For example, big organizations are compiling their inventory system, financial expenditures, tax fillings, employee personal evaluation, and regulatory activities with online-based portals to analyze the cross-sectional profits and reduce cost to acquire maximum benefit for end users.

Further, we can say that data is being gathered for years, but why there exists more concern for knowledge now? The answer is digitization or ICT where the scope has increased from higher to lower. Obliviously, the Internet has expanded the vision of society, the customer behavior and trends have changed, and mostly all the developed and developing nations have acquired online buying and selling portals, which itself is a global shift to new IT-based interventions. This has led to insights for analytics where the scope is to discover hidden effective and efficient patterns for knowledge discovery.

A major change witnessed is that data has expanded with an exponential rate where the challenge among the researchers and practitioners is to optimize tools which can handle and process such large databases. However, the evolution of ICT has redefined the global scenario; earlier data was gathered in few bytes which could easily be processed or handled by traditional or statistical tools. But, the evolution of Internet or digitization has seen an exponential increase in data from a few bytes to millions of bytes every day. In such cases, we require optimized technology to process, store, and analyze data for effective and efficient knowledge discovery for future decision-making.

For instance, nowadays, the complex and heterogeneous data is available which is recorded from various resources. We can say that data in hospital-based system consists of patient healthcare records, scanned images, and sensor-based data, which comprises of electric cardio gram (ECG), financial data, and location-based data. These databases are distinctive in nature and require huge number of correlations to determine hidden facts and knowledge from the same. For example, if we have the entire database available for each time a patient visits the hospital, it can benefit healthcare practitioners to determine the patient behavior and predict which vaccination can benefit more. Besides, the data can also provide information on what drugs the patient is allergic to and other such facts that can help doctors prescribe medications accordingly. So we require optimized tools which can make correct prediction when dealing with real world data.

Eventually, the socio-behavior is an amazing scale of modernized datasets generated through online consumer buying patterns. Data collectively recorded comprises of varied observations which show most purchased and disliked social network connections, complete shopping history, and other background data. If this data is analyzed, it can provide a wealth of information on customer behavior and benefit the organization to retain their valued customers by bestowing them with great deals and offers in accordance with their likes and dislikes.

Although, big data is a term for any data that is more than a few bytes and is difficult to be handled due to its complex and unstructured features. Certainly, big data poses a significant challenge among the researchers to conceive and reform an approach which can grip varied application domains [14, 15]. The confrontation is analysis, which is the major concern while retrieving some specific patterns from large-amount databases [9–15]. Data analytics is gaining momentum with associated challenges to discover novel facts from large-scale databases.

We can certainly demonstrate that big data is the latest buzz in the market. As we know, data is generated by all companies, but significantly there occurs a global shift for data digitization [24, 27, 29, 32]. Big data offers a constructive way to handle information with lower cost and effectiveness and analyze it for future effective knowledge discovery. Big data reflects concern about volume, variety, and velocity, which are gathered through new ICT interventions. The big data is significantly divided into four categories which are also known as 4Vs:

Volume There is tremendous increase in digitization at all spectrums from varied resources. The data comprises of administrative data, financial data, healthcare data, transaction-based data, socio-networking, organizational data, and other activities involved by end users utilizing ICT-based tools. The traditional tools utilized for computational analysis for volume of data are not viable. Most companies try to store their data for convenient report generation.

Velocity The speed at which data is being generated is explosive. For instance, traffic management data, mobile communication, imaging and sensor-based data, GIS, and streaming-based data tend to be major sources which are being generated at an explosive speed. However, big data and developed ICT tools have brought real-time handling, but certainly there is great expansion of data that requires concerns for gaining knowledge for future discovery. The challenge is to handle big data with vast volume to achieve insight of data with advanced predictive analytics techniques to discover novel hidden patterns. Big data provides a recommended technological domain where the emphasis relies on handling volumes of data.

Variety The growth in ICT and digitization has given rise to a number of sources for gathering data. We can say that data resources may be structured and unstructured due to availability of data in different formats which may include audio, video, text, sensor, imaging, and streaming. To gather information from varied sources to compile to big data, there is considerable requirement of valid assessable tools which can benefit decision-makers for policy making. Hence, big data meets the challenges to handle the data with the unknown resources and predicts the relevant information as and when required.

Veracity As the volume of data is increased with varied data streams, the need is to extract authenticity of data with certain and uncertain sources. The analysis of data must be done keeping in view the sources and the authentication from various resources.

The traditional tools available tend to be unsuited to handle uncertainty among the resources; hence big data analytics produces a viable technology to make decision-making utilizing the heterogeneous nature of data. These technological advances will certainly benefit different application domains to generalize data and discover information which is hidden due to unconventional tools and complex nature of data.

Value Another V is value that is generated with respect to socioeconomic development that occurs due to big data. There are several transaction-based data that are generated during the course of a transaction process which can reveal certain facts for decision-making. For example, if consumer wants to take a loan, during the course of entire verification, the phone calls made, transaction process, and other information can lead to discover information which can benefit decision-makers to relatively identify various facts and knowledge related to the overall process. The subset of data generated during the course of action with socio-behavioral facts which are generated is variably true and can really benefit decision-makers. This improved technology and services can assist to extract value from vast explosion of data to determine actual knowledge. In addition, big data has proven unprecedented development in varied application domains to discover knowledge and hidden facts from varied data streams with high volume, variety, and varsity of data. The knowledge driven out from big data analytics is not informatics but cost-effective; both rural and urban development organizations are utilizing the exceptional powers of big data to improve their services and forefronted use of the same for extraction of information and operational domains to increase time utilization. We can also say that big data is widely opted due to various services provided which includes monitoring and its role for timely delivering the hidden facts which can enhance the future policy making for socio well-being.

3.3   Predictive Analytics for ICT

The growth of ICT offers enormous benefits to developed as well as developing nations for future decision-making. The data captured through ICT is growing at an unprecedented speed to confront researchers and scientists to develop automation tools to discover knowledge from big data. Big data itself intensifies data captured through ICT-based technology. The major source of big data is through ICT which includes Internet, telecommunication, social economic web portals, mobile data, and others. The ICT development has exponentially embarked the growth globally, producing heterogeneous and complex nature of data [21, 24, 26, 31]. In addition, providing policy makers to discovery has new instantiated tools for predictive analytics. Collectively, ICT-based predictive analytics can prove exemplary benefits to gain insights of data for future decision-making.

Big data and ICT go together where data is generated by ICT tools and handled by big data optimization tools to discover hidden knowledge and information. The most remarkable use of predictive analytics is in business processes to determine the outcomes for current models. The technology advances such as predictive analytics with ICT are proving to benefit with less cost and higher efficiency. For example, online web portals Amazon, Snapdeal, Flipkart, Google, Twitter, and others are availing consumer information, both before prior purchases and after purchases [11, 36]. This information proves to be vital to discover the usage patterns with socio-behavioral analysis to predict models for relevant customer to upgrade them to substantial offers. In addition, online web portal data, if analyzed properly, can facilitate to discover risk factors and fraud customers which prove to be set back for companies' growth. This information can widely be anticipated at a global platform to enhance overall net profit for development purposes.

The application of predictive analytics approach can be utilized in healthcare application domain where the data is generated, while patient is admitted during the stay in hospital for a specific cause. Further, the online web databases can be maintained globally to deliver predictive models and improve healthcare cost [19–23]. Specifically, risk scores can be identified, for example, which patient is at risk of disease due to specific drug or chances of survival for definite disease. This will certainly benefit healthcare practitioners with a whole set of information relating to insurance policy, pharmacy genetics, financial services, and fraud detection for future median diagnosis. An algorithmic-based Palo Alto company is among the million dollar companies whose major role is to develop algorithms to determine terrorist's threats using communication devices and other related data.

Further, big data analytics also has provision to detect the socio-behavior of patient to discover fraud patients in respect to financial constraints. Similar approach can also be utilized to discover user behavior for credit card handling. The customer financial accounting data may be investigated by banks based on scoring and transactions to enquire about the rational status of user or to determine whether the user pertains to an effective account or not. These policies, when implemented with backbone of predictive data analytics, provide fruitful decision-making for business organizations.

There exist considerable amount of work on predictive analytics using statistical and machine learning platform to discover trends from big data [38]. The widely used techniques for analytics include classification where the emphasis of study relies on discovering patterns in respect to specific class; clustering is mostly utilized when the class is not specific and generates visualized patterns in respect to similarity measurements, for example, if we want to find the similarity between the consumer behavior in respect to socioeconomic features which include age, gender, and location specific, then we can utilize several clustering techniques such as K means, Grid-based, hierarchical, and density-based, as per outcomes required [18, 35, 37, 40]. In addition, association rules are used in empirical studies to relate the consumer buying patterns, in context, for example, if the consumer is buying a shirt what all are the associated other purchases or likes made by him or her. This will help to detect the consumer buying patterns to determine valid offers to retain him or her as the valued customer. In a similar way, outlier detection is widely optimized to discover consumer patterns for credit card fraud detection techniques, where the consumer's financial details are dealt with an onset implemented policy to detect which customer may have high risk factor of defaulting. So, it can benefit a bank organization to investigate the customer and approve or reject credit card accordingly.

3.4   Decision-Making Through ICT and Big Data Analytics

Decision-making is of utmost priority in a management plan to gather maximum profits for stakeholders and organizations. The management plan should be able to encounter all the varied possibilities to enlarge the current scenario with maximum profits to target. The decision predictive analytics should be marked in the management plan to discover trends to get insights of data. As there exist subsisting amount of challenges to understand and deliver services to consumer, there is a constant need to utilize new innovated ICT-based technology, which is able to detect hidden patterns from big data.

A novel decision-making framework is discussed in Fig. 3.1 where ICT-based technological advances can be occupied to discover hidden patterns from big data. The bottom of framework discusses about business data resources which can be gathered at an unprecedented pace, and the nature of data can be heterogeneously collected through logistics, online portal, transactional databases, supply chain management, insurance-based data, consumer data, management data, RFID data, spatial data (location based), and other resources which are high dimensional and unstructured [3, 12, 16, 40]. As we know, the data is in vast volumes; hence, the next question is to extract relevant information from such big data [17]. So application domain relies on what information needs to be extracted as per management plan or identifies the factors which need to be closely related or conferred to gather maximum profit to organization.

Furthermore, the management plan should be attained with previous decisions in correspondence to new decision-making to deliver exact knowledge for future benefits of an organization. The management plan is to rebuild its policies with pertained data analytics for financial risk. After extensive knowledge, the management can decide which all patterns can be extracted during analytics to discover hidden trends which can ensure maximum cost efficiency and provide services to end users. The big data analytics utilize high-end advance technology to deliver nodal factors which can potentially deliver benefits to decision-making bodies [33–35]. After the factors are analyzed, the decision-making body relates various results with ongoing policies and makes changes to management policy with new patterns detected to benefit the stakeholders and consumers for retaining them as valued customers.

The building block of any organization is its management and decision-making team. The decisions should not be hassled with traditional technology as this can generalize data and infer wrong patterns which can highly impact the organizational growth. The new intervened ICT-based technology with big data analytics has opened wide scope and benefited organizations to reap rich dividends. The attainment of predictive analytics from the last decade has opened new ventures for an organization which certainly has revealed to attain them better policy making.

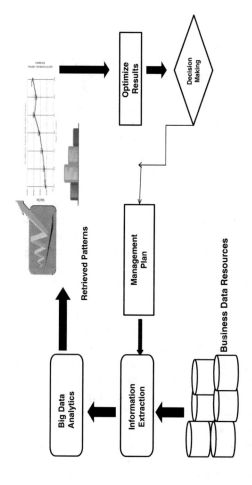

Fig. 3.1 Framework for data analytics in management plan

In addition, big data analytics with business ventures has helped organizations to deliver maximum cost-effective and consumer-retaining policies which are potentially proven to optimize the current scenario. The transition has occurred where decision-making in current management policies has extensively utilized big data to determine factors for extensive growth.

3.5 Conclusion

The current big data has potentially proven beneficial to complement the needs of organizations with prior information to provide insights of data for a channelized decision-making. In particular, the ICT technology is providing challenges to researchers and practitioners to develop new synthesized tools to handle bulk data generated in structured and unstructured formats. In addition, this chapter discusses a novel framework where big data analytics is utilized as potential decision-making step for relatively better management policies.

The main application of ICT is to produce insights of information and to develop utmost technology for analytics to discover hidden information from big data. In particular, ICT has increased the growth of digitization globally, which itself is producing millions of bytes each day. Paramount technological capabilities are required to enhance the digitization and algorithmic powers to attain necessary tools which can handle and process big amount of data. Big data analytics itself is a composite term which has grown in the last few years. More and more organizations are now being forced to adopt big data analytics to remain competitive in the market. Big data researchers are impounding enough efforts to mainstream technology in developing nations so it can benefit all end users with maximum benefits.

Many organizations are working to develop models from data resources with analytics approach for developmental purposes. These organizations are taking advantage of the analytical approach to detect customer patterns for greater understanding of consumer knowledge and incorporating in their product cycle for greater benefits. Big data analytics plays an important role for monitoring of ICT, where it proliferates a constant need to discover hidden facts and knowledge from big data. Certainly, integrating data from various sources is a need of today's time to explore knowledge for future technological interventions.

We can say that environmental organizations, when they share data with hospital-based systems, will be able to generate various causes or alarms which are proving to be cause or prognosis of disease. There exists a constant scope to explore variable factors and technological tools to handle and process big data. Further, we can say as big data moves toward more advance technology, it will assist users and scientists around the globe for knowledge extraction.

Acknowledgments This research work is catalyzed and supported by Indo-Polish joint research grant in bilateral mode DST Ref. No. DST/INT/POL/P-02/2014 funded by the Department of Science and Technology (DST), Ministry of Science and Technology, Govt. of India, New Delhi, India, and the Ministry of Science & Higher Education of the Government of Poland (MNISW), Poland.

References

1. Bakhshi, H., Bravo-Biosca, A., & Mateos-Garcia, J. (2014). *Inside the Datavores: Estimating the effects of data and online analytics on firm performance.* London: NESTA.
2. Brynjolfsson, E., & McAfee, A. (2012, October). Big data's management revolution. *Harvard Business Review, 90,* 61–68.
3. Brynjolfsson, E., Hitt, L. M., & Kim, H. H. (2011). Strength in numbers: How does data-driven decision making affect firm performance? Social Science Research Network (April 22, 2011). Available at SSRN: https://ssrn.com/abstract=1819486 or http://dx.doi.org/10.2139/ssrn.1819486.
4. Burt, R. S. (1992). *Structural holes: The social structure of competition.* Cambridge: Cambridge University Press.
5. García-Muñiz, A. S., & Vicente, M. (2014). ICT Technologies in Europe: A study of technological diffusion and economic growth under network theory. *Telecommunications Policy, 38,* 360–370.
6. Colombo, M. G., Croce, A., & Grilli, L. (2013). ICT services and small businesses' productivity gains: An analysis of the adoption of broadband Internet technology. *Information Economics and Policy, 25*(3), 171–189.
7. Abreu, R. (2013). Big data and Huawei Chile. Presented at the presented at Complexity, Innovation and ICT, UN ECLAC, Santiago, Chile.
8. Boyd, D., & Crawford, K. (2012). Critical questions for big data. *Information, Communication & Society, 15*(5), 662–679. doi:10.1080/1369118X.2012.678878.
9. Brynjolfsson, E., Hitt, L. M., & Kim, H. H. (2011). Strength in numbers: How does data-driven decisionmaking affect firm performance?. SSRN eLibrary. http://papers.ssrn.com/sol3/papers.cfm?abstract_id=1819486
10. Chen, C. L. P., & Zhang, C.-Y. (2014). Data-intensive applications, challenges, techniques and technologies: A survey on big data. *Information Sciences, 275,* 314–347.
11. Choi, H., & Varian, H. (2012). Predicting the present with Google trends. *The Economic Record, 88,* 2–9. doi:10.1111/j.1475-4932.2012.00809.x.
12. García-Muñiz, A. S., & Ramos, C. (2015). Input-output linkages and network contagion in Greece: Demand and supply view. *Applied Econometrics and International Development, 15,* 35–60.
13. Institute of Prospective Technological Studies. (2015). *The 2014 predict report: An analysis of ICT R&D in the EU and beyond.* Seville: Institute of Prospective Technological Studies.
14. Driscoll, K. (2012). From punched cards to "Big Data": A social history of database populism. *Communication, 1*(1), 1. http://scholarworks.umass.edu/cpo/vol1/iss1/4
15. Manyıka, J., Chui, M., Brown, B., Bughin, J., Dobbs, R., Roxburgh, C., & Hung Byers, A. (2011). *Big data: The next frontier for innovation, competition, and productivity.* McKinsey &Company. http://www.mckinsey.com/Insights/MGI/Research/Technology_and_Innovation/Big_data_The_next_frontier_for_ innovation
16. Noormohammad, S. F., Mamlin, B. W., Biondich, P. G., McKown, B., Kimaiyo, S. N., & Were, M. C. (2010). Changing course to make clinical decision support work in an HIV clinic in Kenya. *International Journal of Medical Informatics, 79*(3), 204–210. doi:10.1016/j.ijmedinf.2010.01.002.
17. Fayyad, U. M., Haussler, D., & Stolorz, Z. (1996). KDD for science data analysis: Issues and examples. In *Proceedings of 2nd international conference on knowledge discovery and data mining,* Portland, Oregon (pp. 50–56). AAAI Press, Menlo Park.
18. Koperski, K., Han, J., & Stefanovic, N. (1998). An efficient two-step method for classification of spatial data. In: Proceedings of the 8th symposium on spatial data handling (pp. 45–54). Vancouver.
19. Kolatch, E. (2001). *Clustering algorithms for spatial databases: A survey University of Maryland.* College Park: Department of Computer Science.
20. Kaufman, L., & Rousseeuw, P. J. (1990). *Finding groups in data: An introduction to cluster analysis, Series in applied probability and statistics.* New York: Wiley-Interscience.
21. Kaur, H., Chauhan, R., & Alam, M.A. (2012). SPAGRID: A spatial grid framework for medical high dimensional databases. In *Proceedings of international conference on hybrid artificial intelligence systems,* HAIS 2012, Springer, (Vol. 1) (pp. 690–704).

22. Kaur, H., Chauhan, R., & Alam, M.A. (2010). An optimal categorization of feature selection methods for knowledge discovery. In: Q. Zhang, R. Segall, & M. Cao (Eds.), *Visual analytics and interactive technologies: Data, text and web mining applications* (pp. 94–108). IGI Publishers, USA.

23. Kaur, H., Chauhan, R., & Aljunid, S. (2012). Data mining cluster analysis on the influence of health factors in Casemix data. *BMC Journal of Health Services Research, 12*(Suppl. 1), O3.

24. Robinson, L., Cotten, S. R., Ono, H., Quan-Haase, A., Mesch, G., Chen, W., & Stern, M. J. (2015). Digital inequalities and why they matter. *Information, Communication & Society, 18*(5), 569–582.

25. Smith, M. L., Spence, R., & Rashid, A. T. (2011). Mobile phones and expanding human capabilities. *Information Technologies and International Development, 7*(3), 77.

26. Kleine, D. (2013). *Technologies of choice?: ICTs, development, and the capabilities approach.* Cambridge, MA: MIT Press.

27. Zittrain, J., & Palfrey, J. (2008). Internet filtering: The politics and mechanisms of control. In R. Deibert, J. Palfrey, R. Rohozinski, & J. Zittrain (Eds.), *The practice and policy of global Internet filtering* (pp. 29–56). Cambridge, MA: Massachusetts Institute of Technology Press.

28. Tongia, R., & Wilson III, E. J. (2011). Network theory: The flip side of Metcalfe's law: Multiple and growing costs of network exclusion. *International Journal of Communication, 5,* 17.

29. Barbosa, B., & Amaro, F. (2012). Too old for technology? How the elderly of Lisbon use and perceive ICT. *The Journal of Community Informatics, 8,* 1.

30. Wellman, B., Hasse, A. Q., Witte, J., & Hampton, K. (2001). Does the internet increase, decrease, or supplement social capital? *American Behavioral Scientist, 45*(3), 436–455.

31. Shim, D. C., & Eom, T. H. (2009). Anticorruption effects of information communication and technology and social capital. *International Review of Administrative Sciences, 75*(1), 99–116.

32. McKinsey. (2011). *Big data, the next frontier for innovation, competition and productivity.* New York: McKinsey.

33. Chen, H., Chiang, R. H. L., & Storey, V. C. (2012). Business Intelligence and analytics: From big data to big impact. *Management Information Systems Quarterly, 36*(4), 1165–1188.

34. Beyer, M. A., & Laney, D. (2012). *The importance of 'big data: A definition.* Stamford: Gartner. http://www.gartner.com/technology/research/big-data.

35. Chen, M. S., Han, J., & Yu, P. S. (1996). Data mining: An overview from a database perspective. *IEEE Transactions on Knowledge and Data Engineering, 8*(6), 866–888.

36. Lin, J., & Dmitriy, V. R. (2012). Scaling big data mining infrastructure: The twitter experience. *SIGKDD Explorations, 14*(2), 6–19.

37. Wu, X., Wu, G.-Q., & Ding, W. (2014). Data mining with big data. *IEEE Transactions on Knowledge and Data Engineering, 26*(1), 97–107.

38. Kaur, H., Chauhan, R., & Wasan, S. K. (2015). A Bayesian network model for probability estimation. In Mehdi Khosrow-Pour (Ed.), *Encyclopedia of information science and technology,* 3rd ed, (pp. 1551–1558). Accessed 10 Dec 2014. doi:10.4018/978-1-4666-5888-2. ch148 (2014).

39. Chauhan, R., & Kaur, H. (2015). Big data application in medical domain. In *Computational intelligence for big data analysis: Frontier advances and applications, Adaptation, learning, and optimization* (Vol. 19, pp. 165–179). Switzerland: Springer International Publishing.

40. Chauhan, R., & Kaur, H. (2015). SPAM: An effective and efficient spatial algorithm for mining grid data. *Geo-intelligence and visualization through big data trends. IGI Global, 2015,* 245–263. Web. 9 Sep. 2015. doi:10.4018/978-1-4666-8465-2.ch010.

41. Kaur, H., & Tao, X. (Eds.). (2014). *ICTs and the millennium development goals: A United Nations perspective.* New York: Springer.

42. Lechman, E., & Kaur, H. (2016). *Social development and ICT adoption. Developing world perspective, GUT FME working papers series A, No3 /2016(33).* Gdansk: Gdansk University of Technology, Faculty of Management and Economics, Gdansk, Poland.

43. Lechman, E., & Kaur, H. (2015). *Economic growth and female labor force participation – verifying the U-feminization hypothesis. New evidence for 162 countries over the period* 1990–2012. *Economics & Sociology, 8,* 1.

Chapter 4
The Role of ICT Adoption in Curbing Corruption in Developing Countries

Mohamed Sami Ben Ali and Seifallah Sassi

Abstract Corruption is regarded as a major problem impeding development potentialities, and curbing it is a leading challenge for developing countries. This chapter assesses the possibilities of ICT adoption as a powerful tool for fighting corruption in developing countries that should be recognized by policymakers. We first consider the effects that corruption can have on economic development. Then, we explore the impact of ICT on corruption and particularly how Internet and mobile technologies can be effective in combating corruption. We also highlight the main obstacles and challenges that these countries may face in implementing ICT-based anti-corruption strategies. We address some policy recommendations pertaining to the adoption of ICT strategies in fighting corruption in developing countries.

Keywords Corruption • Bribery • ICT adoption • Developing countries

4.1 Introduction

Many countries display much less growth than they should do. Numerous impediments sand countries' development wheel. In the last three decades, academicians and policymakers have pointed to corruption as the most important of these impediments. For example, [35] considers corruption to be the single greatest restraint on development. Also, [23] describes *corruption as being "one of the most dangerous social ills of any society. This is because corruption, like a deadly virus, attacks the vital structures that make for society's progressive functioning, thus putting its very existence into serious peril."* Given the importance of this phenomenon, national governments implement anti-corruption initiatives by enforcing their laws and strengthening the

M.S.B. Ali (✉)
College of Business and Economics, Qatar University, Doha, Qatar
e-mail: msbenali@qu.edu.qa

S. Sassi
Laboratory of Applied Economics and Finance, Tunis, Tunisia
e-mail: seifallah.sassi@yahoo.fr

© Springer International Publishing AG 2017
H. Kaur et al. (eds.), *Catalyzing Development through ICT Adoption*,
DOI 10.1007/978-3-319-56523-1_4

penalties for corrupt acts. Similarly, many international organizations have declared corruption to be an urgent priority on their agenda. Recently, the nonprofit organization *Global Financial Integrity* reported that corruption deprives the developing economies of some 1000 billion dollars every year; in comparison official development assistance reached $134 billion in 2013 [40]. The importance of fighting corruption is therefore a foreground issue in alleviating poverty and ensuring economic development in these countries. Corruption affects countries at different levels and with different intensity, and the problem seems to be more pronounced in developing countries. Various cultural and institutional factors, mainly persuasive and endemic corruption in some of these countries, are key determinants of these differences.

Corruption can be caused by different sets of economic and noneconomic determinants. Economic factors impacting corruption that have been developed in the literature include variables such as income, which is considered to be the most important determinant of corruption. The most common and obvious fact here is that in rich countries, more resources can be allocated to combating corruption, and therefore a country's corruption level depends in part on its income level. Meanwhile, it has also been documented that high income levels increase corruption [26]. More, corruption's economic determinants include openness to international trade. The literature reports that international trade openness tends to allow more international competition and that this reduces the monopoly power of domestic producers, thus reducing the scope these producers have to influence corrupt officials [1]. Inflation has also been considered in numerous studies to be a main economic determinant of corruption. Obviously, higher inflation induces a deterioration of the purchasing power of salaries, pushing officials to ask for bribes [16, 21, 22]. Numerous other factors are also considered in the literature. For example, the extent to which the administration is centralized influences the country's level of corruption, in the sense that more centralization and monopoly control in the hands of public officials are correlated with greater centralized discretionary powers and therefore higher corruption levels. Moreover, when wages are relatively low, it is likely that officials will tend to increase their demands for bribes. Also, countries with a large public sector tend to have higher corruption levels.

Apart from the economic aspect, corruption is also a noneconomic matter and is determined partly by noneconomic factors. Cultural, social, and institutional dimensions are considered [1, 50, 53]. Recently, academicians and scholars have reported the impact of ICT in curbing corruption. While commitment to fighting corruption has been one of the most urgent problems on most governmental agendas, individual involvement is crucial in this process. On the individual side, access to ICT through personal computer and mobile phones has led to a participatory journalism wave that has helped combat corruption [34]. In this regard, Internet adoption helps remove information asymmetry and to track the outcome of their applications. Internet adoption is also a way to automatize administrative procedures and therefore reduces bureaucracy.

On the governmental side, many initiatives have been considered worldwide to adopt e-government frameworks to combat corruption. E-government improves interaction with businesses and eases access to information [39]. This can help to improve transparency and accountability, decrease or remove information asymmetries, and therefore improve the effectiveness of the public administration. Using ICT is therefore a way to automate administrative processes and develop service delivery points that remove any possibility of human intervention, which helps reduce the possibility of corrupt behavior. As it was clearly stated by Bhatnagar [15] for the banking activity, e-banking removes any agent who can be bribed. Meanwhile, the adoption of e-government makes information and data public, which can improve the behavior of both citizens and officials. Several studies have reported the positive effect of e-government and Internet adoption on curbing corruption [13, 21, 54].

We identify and assess in this chapter the role of ICT in curbing corruption in developing countries. Section 4.2 provides an overview of the harmful effect of corruption on economic development. Section 4.3 sheds light on the importance of fighting corruption and the role that ICT strategies can play in this regard. Section 4.4 presents the main obstacles that hamper the ICT corruption strategies in these countries. Section 4.5 concludes and addresses some policy recommendations pertaining to the adoption of ICT strategies in fighting corruption in developing countries.

4.2   Corruption and Economic Development

A large stratum of literature asserts the negative impact of corruption on economic performance. Corruption prevalence is considered to be a major hinderer of economic development potentialities in poor developing economies, which explains the poor economic performance of some of these countries that experience economic inefficiency and an insecure economic environment [52]. Obviously, corruption needs to be reduced to help realize the Millennium Development Goals [4].

Numerous studies in the literature have considered the negative effect of corruption on economic development. The most common conclusion is the existence of a negative impact of corruption on economic development. In particular, the negative effect of corruption on income has been well established [3, 31, 38] and demonstrated to lower economic activity by as much as 50% at the community level in some developing countries [10], causing at the same time a decrease in a country's standard of living [44]. It should be noted that the cost of corruption for countries is different depending on their level of development and on surges in their national incomes. Indeed, at the early stages of development, income is rather limited and so is the level of corruption. As income level rises, corruption increases. However, as a country reaches a certain level of development, high income levels increase corruption's costs in such a way that corruption is considerably dissuaded [46].

Also, corrupt behavior leads to a diversion of resources to unproductive sectors of the economy such as defense, which give officials more scope for corrupt activities [26]. Rent-seeking activities also reduce tax revenues for the government due to tax evasion and to the emergence of the underground economy [36]. Tax evasion causes a decrease in public investment capacity [33] and in public sector productivity [49]. International investment is also affected by corruption. Prevalence of corruption induces less FDI flows [27]. Furthermore, corruption increases inflation

[12], reduces investment [27] and diverts it away from productive activity [52], deepens income inequality and poverty [26], weakens national institutions [52] and public sector quality [36], and diverts energy from productive economic activities [48]. The overall effect is an adverse one on economic growth potentialities [51].

Countries with pervasive corruption have less efficient public governance, lower competitiveness, and poorer human development [2]. From a human development perspective, the adverse effect of corruption is widely recognized. Corruption reduces availability of goods and increases the cost of basic living as the core social services will be restricted in order to make corrupt gains more available. Second, corruption transfers government expenditure from priority social services to domains which offer more rewards for rent-seeking behavior and where the risk of exposure of corrupt behavior is lower. In fact, corrupt politicians and bureaucrats prefer to allocate governmental funds to large projects or defense contracts, which offer more opportunities for rent-seeking activities, than to build the rural health clinics that are claimed to be a priority [8]. As a result, corruption weakens education and health systems [52].

According to Ben Ali and Saha [11], "*Pervasive corruption and lack of accountability and transparency have been, at different levels, common features of all developing countries.*" We develop in this chapter this strand of thoughts and show how these countries can improve their development potentialities. We particularly consider the role of ICT in curbing countries.

4.3 Adopting ICT as a Control of Corruption Strategy

The literature shows that ICT adoption can be an efficient way to remove barriers that hinder economic development in many countries [41]. Many empirical studies illustrate that ICT have a major role in public management reform [6] since it improve the quality of public service delivery while reducing time and cost [17]. For example, they help people to find jobs and public services in general to function more efficiently [18], helping in the same way in establishing a public engagement and achieving community development [28]. From purely economic point of view, it has been established that ICT adoption improves public productivity [59], efficiency [55], and good governance [9]. In this regard, it has been reported that many governments have reduced their level of corruption in the public sector by improving the effectiveness of their internal work and the relationships with their citizens [14]. Improvement of these relationships can be achieved through the use of ICT in enhancing reform initiatives to reduce corrupt acts and behaviors [47]. By doing so, governments commit themselves to allowing citizens to track and monitor both the progress of their applications and the behavior of officials. The authors stress that the effectiveness of ICT in curbing corruption requires a particular set of social attitudes. For example, increasing citizens' participation can significantly reduce bureaucracy and promote efficiency and transparency [13]. Moreover, citizens' participation and mobilization are a key element for creating pressure on governments and national institutions to improve their accountability and responsiveness to citizens' aspirations. Numerous studies support the finding that ICT are effective anti-corruption tools in developing economies and provide evidence of their ability to enforce the rules and improve transparency [5, 47]. Many other studies report a clear negative relationship between ICT diffusion and corruption [54]. According to Vinod [54], the potentiality of the Internet in curbing corruption is *"promising and obviously vast."* The figures in Appendix A depict that high ICT adoption tends to dissuade corruption in developing countries, since a higher value of CPI is associated with less corruption. This impact remains robust across subsamples of different development levels suggesting that anti-corruption strategies in developing countries should be oriented toward ICT tools.

Specifically, e-government applications have been clearly shown to lead to improvements in transparency, access to information, and accountability, thus enhancing the quality of services delivered to citizens [15, 58, 59]. Its relevance in curbing corruption lies in its ability to enable people to participate and exercise their political and civil rights.

Using an interactive and regularly updated governmental website to communicate with citizens will keep people informed and involved in the government's anti-corruption efforts. According to Andersen [4], *"implementing e-government significantly reduces corruption, even after controlling for any propensity for corrupt governments to be more or less aggressive in adopting e-government initiatives."* Shim and Eom [47] argue that e-government can explain differences in corruption levels between countries better than bureaucratic quality and law enforcement. Relly and Sabharwal [43] show that e-government adoption could help reducing the potential for corrupt acts and empowering citizens by giving them the possibility to monitor and assess government employees and to take corrective actions when needed.

The open government and open data policies that have been adopted in many countries are examples of anti-corruption initiatives which enable and empower people's role in curbing corruption. This viewpoint has been the capstone in the policies of many policymakers and international organizations committed to sustainable development who have embraced the importance of e-government for the fight against corruption [52].

According to Grönlund [25], ICT can be an effective tool in curbing corruption mainly when it is used to automate administrative actions, to identify anomalies and underperformance, to raise awareness by informing the public about their rights and thus prevent arbitrary treatment, to ensure detection of corruption when it is used to monitor networks and individuals, to report and punish violations, to record information about documented cases of corruption, and to promote ethical attitudes. ICT can therefore help to reduce the abuse of power by public officials and monitor their actions and any arbitrary behavior at a low cost. ICT can also be used to report abuses and place administrative complaints through mobile applications, hotlines, and websites.

Internet and mobile technologies are effective tools in reducing the cost of collecting, distributing, and accessing government information [45]. According to Wellman et al. [56], *"the low cost of internet services compared to off-line measures encourages people to use email and blogs to contact their relatives and friends."* Moreover, by connecting isolated and disadvantaged people, ICT build bridges and create better opportunities for these groups [37]. In the end, Internet use improves information access and eases information dissemination, which improves the level of awareness and makes the detection of corruption easier [24]. The Internet offers new opportunities in curbing corruption as it can create instant social interaction and the development of citizens' participation, especially when traditional media are inefficient, controlled by the state or by lobbies, or when there is not enough media coverage. Media freedom is considered to be a useful tool [19] and can assist the public and helping them to avoid or denounce corrupt behavior. Through their participatory role, social media help to share information with the community efficiently, and through their empowering role, they give people a platform to express their thoughts and to broadcast information otherwise unavailable in traditional media. Therefore, they have a democratizing tendency. Social media also allow the sharing of information instantly and in real time and thus save time. Many efforts have been devoted, mainly by nongovernmental organizations, to using social media for fighting corruption. WikiLeaks is the best known example of this.

Mobile technology adoption is also an effective tool in combating corruption by allowing citizens to report corrupt acts and officials. Their effectiveness emerges when scenes of corruption and conversations with official asking for bribes are recorded and documented. As argued by Bailard [7], "*the net effect of the rapid and massive diffusion of mobile phones in Africa will be the reduction of corruption by decentralizing information and communication, thereby shrinking the veil of secrecy that shields corrupt behavior.*" Mobile technology has been used for improving governance and accountability in many developing countries. For example, an Indian initiative was launched in 2008 by the Central Bureau of Investigation to denounce corrupt acts by encouraging citizens to report them using the short messages services (SMS). The idea of this initiative was to establish a list of public employees who needed to be monitored [42]. A similar idea in Pakistan was to require all civil servants dealing with land transfers to include in their submitted transactions the money sum involved and the phone numbers of both the buyer and the seller to undertake all necessary checks. In East Africa, a pioneering initiative has also been launched to use mobile phones for transparency, accountability, and service delivery. For example, Rwanda Government has been using SMS to broadcast urgent and important news, to remind voters of important dates and to ask people to cool down during civil unrest. The access to timely information gives more power to citizens to detect, monitor, and report corrupt behavior and to support governmental efforts in curbing corruption. ICT has also been actively employed by citizens to organize actions, communicate, and raise citizens' awareness during the Arab Spring revolutions.

4.4 Obstacles to Anti-corruption Policies Based on ICT Adoption

It is largely established now that ICT can serve as anti-corruption tools and that their diffusion can assure a sustained culture of transparency. However, many obstacles can hinder their effectiveness. A main obstacle which may restrict the positive impact of ICT is the relative lack of access to these technologies in developing countries. Despite their worldwide expansion, many countries still have no or limited access to information technologies. There may be little availability of computers, poor ICT literacy at government level, lack of Internet access for some population segments, distrusted ICT providers, and unsuitable technological infrastructure.

Filtration of Internet content by government could be considered as a real obstacle to anti-corruption strategies since the amount of accessible information can significantly change. Some countries filter and block websites for security but also political and social reasons, for instance, blocking information linked to human rights and free expression, or on health or religious grounds [60]. For example, the creation of firewalls and filters and blocking of web domains can provide governments with users'-generated content and browsing histories, indicating their social and political beliefs and thus infringing users' personal confidentiality. This of course could reduce potential criminal behavior by controlling Internet surfing but can induce a greater control and central monitoring of the Internet, especially when Internet providers are unable or unwilling to take the required actions to protect the rights of their customers. Many countries, mainly in East Asia, North Africa, the Middle East, and central Africa, have filtered or still limit the Internet access [60]. More than that, some countries, such as Malaysia and Saudi Arabia, established an official systematic Internet filtering as long ago as 1999. For example, Saudi Arabia started with the implementation of an Internet screening and monitoring strategy. A similar monitoring and screening strategy has been implemented in China where citizens were arrested for writings posted on blogs and about 200 of the 2,400 Internet cafes in the country were closed [20].

As regards mobile telephone technology, there is a serious challenge to using it as an anti-corruption tool. There is a risk of SMS interception when the system is not well designed. For example, in China the government has been monitoring and censoring SMS through SMS surveillance centers. The identification of mobile users when governments push telephone services providers to register SIM cards can place the user under surveillance, which could undermine the efficiency of the denunciation of corrupt acts. It is worth noting also that in many developing countries, access to smartphones and mobile applications is rather limited. Mobile broadband technology needs to be developed and improved in terms of capacity, technology, and features in these countries.

Furthermore, the potential of ICT as an effective tool to help in curbing corruption depends on several infrastructural, social and economic factors, and on political willingness to promote deep anti-corruption strategies. Easy access, low costs, and confidentiality are all essential for effective ICT-driven strategies [30]. Another obstacle that could restrict the effectiveness of ICT in curbing inflation is purely juridical. Although legislation allows the use of digital evidence in corruption cases, judges are sometimes reluctant to accept it. Obviously, corrupt acts will continue to occur with impunity in these conditions.

Delivering government services via ICT is cost-efficient for the government and more transparent for citizens. However, sometimes people prefer to access public services directly through governments' representatives in person rather than via Internet and mobile technology. Success with ICT anti-corruption strategies requires that citizens fully join the government's effort. It has been shown that the effectiveness of ICT in curbing corruption has widely divergent results for different nations and cultures. Using five case studies, Heeks [29] shows how ICT diffusion helps to control corruption but also that sometimes it has no effect or can even create new forms of corrupt behavior if some aspects are not regulated, such as organizational and environmental factors. It can privilege government officials who master the operation of ICT [57]. To ensure the effectiveness of anti-corruption strategies is the full involvement of officials [32].

4.5   Conclusions and Policy Recommendations

Corruption has emerged as a serious hindrance to economic development. A number of factors have pushed many countries to consider fighting corruption as a main priority on their agendas. Indeed, recent literature has documented that corruption is associated with fewer development opportunities and has a clear negative impact on income; inflation; public, private, and foreign investment; government revenues; and productivity among others.

Corruption is a complex phenomenon pointing to major failures of institutions. However, legal actions alone cannot be effective in addressing it in developing countries. At the same time, academicians and policymakers have pointed to the role ICT can play in curbing corruption. Mobile phones and the Internet have clearly shown their anti-corruption power in many developing countries. They can be used effectively in decreasing officials' discretion and in promoting transparency and give rise to a participatory journalism. Specifically, e-government applications through open government and open data initiatives have clearly been shown to lead to general improvements in responsibility and transparency.

The relevance of e-government in curbing corruption lies in its ability to keep people participating and exercising their political and civil rights, improve quality delivering, and the governmental governance. Governments in developing countries have to take the required actions in order to support e-government applications and increase citizens' participation by training citizens and officials how to use these applications efficiently. Governments should undertake the necessary advertising campaigns on television and social media to educate the public how to use ICT for anti-corruption purposes.

ICT diffusion strategies should also be supported by a legal framework, administrative and institutional reforms, and a political will to combat corruption. Government bodies and institutions involved in combating corruption must bear in mind that the information and communication technologies for reducing rent-seeking activities can give the possibility in abusing these technologies for corrupt ends. Therefore, governments involved in ICT anti-corruption strategies should assess the risk in using these strategies in public administrations, in order to prevent any abuse of ICT. In this regard, governmental bodies and institutions should be created to collect statistics, date and report any abuses, and respond accordingly.

Appendix A: Corruption and ICT Adoption (Figs. 4.1, 4.2, and 4.3)

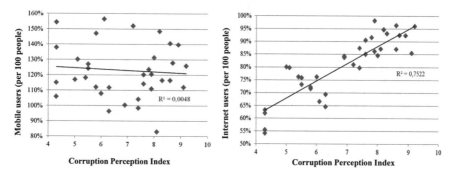

Fig. 4.1 Corruption and ICT adoption in developed economies (2014)

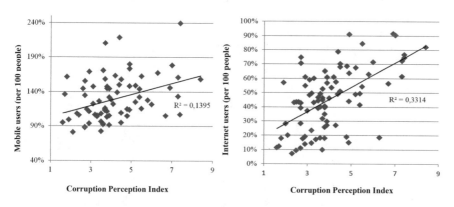

Fig. 4.2 Corruption and ICT adoption in developing economies (2014)

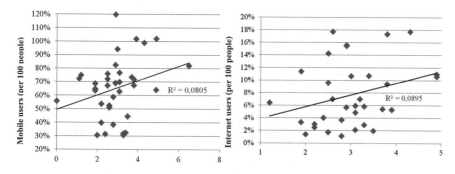

Fig. 4.3 Corruption and ICT adoption in least developed economies (2014) (Source: Authors' calculations. Data was obtained from World Development Indicators and Transparency International)

Appendix B: Countries List

Developed economies		Developing economies					Least developed economies	
Australia	Luxembourg	Albania	Colombia	Indonesia	Mongolia	Sri Lanka	Afghanistan	Madagascar
Austria	Malta	Algeria	Congo, Republic	Iran	Montenegro	St. Kitts and Nevis	Bangladesh	Malawi
Belgium	Netherlands	Antigua Barbuda	Costa Rica	Iraq	Morocco	St. Lucia	Benin	Mali
Bulgaria	New Zealand	Armenia	Cote d'Ivoire	Israel	Namibia	St. Vincent and the Grenadines	Bhutan	Mauritania
Canada	Norway	Aruba	Croatia	Jamaica	Nicaragua	Suriname	Burkina Faso	Mozambique
Cyprus	Poland	Azerbaijan	Dominica	Jordan	Nigeria	Swaziland	Burundi	Nepal
Czech Rep.	Portugal	Bahamas	Dominican Rep	Kazakhstan	Oman	Syrian Republic	Central African Republic	Niger
Denmark	Romania	Bahrain	Ecuador	Kenya	Pakistan	Tajikistan	Chad	Rwanda
Estonia	Slovak Republic	Barbados	Egypt Rep.	Korea, Republic	Panama	Thailand	Comoros	Samoa
Finland	Slovenia	Belarus	El Salvador	Kuwait	Papua New Guinea	Tonga	Congo, Democratic Republic	Senegal
France	Spain	Belize	Fiji	Kyrgyz Republic	Paraguay	Trinidad and Tobago	Djibouti	Sierra Leone
Germany	Sweden	Bolivia	Gabon	Lebanon	Peru	Tunisia	Equatorial Guinea	Solomon Islands
Greece	Switzerland	Bosnia and Herzegovina	Georgia	Libya	Philippines	Turkey	Ethiopia	Sudan
Hungary	UK	Botswana	Ghana	Macao SAR, China	Qatar	Ukraine	Gambia	Tanzania

Iceland	USA	Brazil	Grenada	Macedonia, FYR	Russian Federation	UAE	Guinea	Timor-Leste
Ireland		Brunei Darussalam	Guatemala	Malaysia	Saudi Arabia	Uruguay	Guinea Bissau	Togo
Italy		Cabo Verde	Guyana	Maldives	Serbia	Venezuela	Haiti	Uganda
Japan		Cameroon	Honduras	Mauritius	Seychelles	Vietnam	Lao PDR	Vanuatu
Latvia		Chile	Hong Kong SAR, China	Mexico	Singapore	West Bank and Gaza	Lesotho	Yemen
Lithuania		China	India	Moldova	South Africa	Zimbabwe	Liberia	Zambia

References

1. Ades, A., & Di Tella, R. (1999). Rents, competition and corruption. *American Economic Review, 89*(4), 982–993.
2. Akçay, S. (2006). Corruption and human development. *Cato Journal, 26*(1), 29–48.
3. Alam, M. S. (1995). A theory of limits on corruption and some applications. *Kyklos, 483*(3), 419–435.
4. Andersen, T. (2009). E-government as anti-corruption strategy. *Information Economics and Policy, 21*(2), 201–210.
5. Andersen, K. N., Henriksen, H. Z., Medaglia, R., Danziger, J. N., Sannarnes, M. K., & Enemærke, M. (2010). Fads and facts of e-government: A review of impacts of e-government (2003–2009). *International Journal of Public Administration, 33*(11), 564–579.
6. Asgarkhani, M. (2005). Digital government and its effectiveness in public management reform. *Public Management Review, 7*(3), 465–487.
7. Bailard, C. S. (2009). Mobile phone diffusion and corruption in Africa. *Political Communication, 26*(3), 333–353.
8. Bardhan, P. (1997). Corruption and development: A review of issues. *Journal of Economic Literature, 35*(3), 1320–1346.
9. Basu, S. (2004). E-government and developing countries: An overview. *International Review of Law Computers and Technology, 18*(1), 109–133.
10. Beekman, G., Bulte, E. H., & Nillesen, E. E. M. (2013). Corruption and economic activity: Micro level evidence from rural Liberia. *European Journal of Political Economy, 30*, 70–79.
11. Ben Ali, M. S., & Saha, S. (2016). Corruption and economic development. In M. S. Ben Ali (Ed.), *Economic development in the Middle East and North Africa* (pp. 133–154). New York: Palgrave MacMillan.
12. Ben Ali, M. S., & Sassi, S. (2016). The corruption-inflation nexus: Evidence from developed and developing countries. *The B.E. Journal of Macroeconomics, 16*(1), 125–144.
13. Bertot, J. C., Jaeger, P. T., & Grimes, J. M. (2010). Using ICTs to create a culture of transparency: E-government and social media as openness and anti-corruption tools for societies. *Government Information Quarterly, 27*(3), 264–271.
14. Bhatnagar, S. 2001). *Central vigilance commission website: A bold anticorruption experiment.* World Bank, Washington D. C.
15. Bhatnagar, S. (2003). E-government and access to information. In P. Eigen (Ed.), *Global corruption report* (pp. 24–32). Berlin: Transparency International Press.
16. Braun, M., & Di Tella, R. (2004). Inflation, inflation variability and corruption. *Economics and Politics, 16*(1), 77–100.
17. Breen, J. (2000). At the dawn of e-government: The citizen as customer. *Government Finance Review, 16*(5), 15–20.
18. Brueckner, A. (2005). E-government: Best practices for digital government. *Bulletin of the American Society for Information Science and Technology, 31*(3), 16–17.
19. Brunetti, A., & Weder, B. (2003). A free press is bad news for corruption. *Journal of Public Economics, 87*(7–8), 1801–1824.
20. Dann, G. E., & Haddow, N. (2008). Just doing business, or doing just business: Google, Microsoft, Yahoo!, and the business of censoring China's internet. *Journal of Business Ethics, 79*, 219–234.
21. Elbahnasawy, N. G. (2014). E-government, internet adoption and corruption: An empirical investigation. *World Development, 57*(1), 114–126.
22. Getz, K. A., & Volkema, R. J. (2001). Culture, perceived corruption, and economics. *Business and Society, 40*(1), 7–30.
23. Gire, J. T. (1999). A psychological analysis of corruption in Nigeria. *Journal of Sustainable Development in Africa, 1*, 1–15.
24. Goel, R. K., Nelson, M. A., & Naretta, M. A. (2012). The internet as an indicator of corruption awareness. *European Journal of Political Economy, 28*, 64–75.

25. Grönlund, A. (2010). Using ICT to combat corruption: Tools, methods and results. In C. Strand (Ed.), *Increasing transparency and fighting corruption through ICT: Empowering people and communities* (pp. 7–26). Stockholm: Spider.
26. Gupta, S., Davoodi, H., & Alonso-Terme, R. (2002). Does corruption affect income inequality and poverty? *Economics of Governance, 3*(1), 23–45.
27. Habib, M., & Zurawicki, L. (2002). Corruption and foreign direct investment. *Journal of International Business Studies, 33*(2), 291–307.
28. Hammerman, C. (2005). E-government: Lessons learned in Michigan: Best practices for local e-government. *Bulletin of the American Society for Information Science and Technology, 31*(3), 17–19.
29. Heeks, R. (1998). Information technology and public sector corruption. Information systems for Public Sector Management, Working Paper No.4, Manchester, Institute for Development Policy and Management.
30. Hellström, J. (2008). *Mobile phones for good governance: Challenges and way forward.* Stochkholm University Working Papers, Stockholm.
31. Husted, B. W. (1999). Wealth, culture and corruption. *Journal of International Business Studies, 30*(2), 339–360.
32. Jaeger, P. T., & Matteson, M. (2009). E-government and technology acceptance: The implementation of Section 508 guidelines for e-government websites. *Electronic Journal of E-Government, 7*(1), 87–98.
33. Jain, A. K. (1998). *Economics of corruption.* New York: Kluwer Academic Publishers.
34. Katz, J. E., & Lai, C. H. (2009). News blogging in cross-cultural contexts: A report on the struggle for voice. *Knowledge, Technology, and Policy, 22*(2), 95–107.
35. Kaufmann, D. (1999). *International Herald Tribune, 25*, 02.
36. Lambsdorff, J. G. (2006). Causes and consequences of corruption: What do we know from a cross-section of countries? In S. Rose-Ackerman (Ed.), *International handbook on the economics of corruption* (pp. 3–51). Cheltenham: Edward Elgar.
37. Lin, N. (2001). *Social capital: A theory of social structure and action.* Cambridge: Cambridge University Press.
38. Mauro, P. (1995). Corruption and growth. *The Quarterly Journal of Economics, 110*(3), 681–712.
39. Moon, M. J. (2002). The evolution of e-governance among municipalities: Rhetoric or reality? *Public Administration Review, 62*(4), 424.
40. OECD (2013). OECD working group on bribery: Annual report on activities undertaken in 2012.
41. Piatkowski, M. (2006). Can information and communication technologies make a difference in the development of transition economies? *Information Technologies and International Development, 3*(1), 39–53.
42. Rajaratnam, L. (2008). CBI SMS campaign for anti-corruption. Http://Www.Merinews.Com/Article/Cbi-Sms-Campaign-For-Anti-Corruption/139622.Shtml
43. Relly, J. E., & Sabharwal, M. (2009). Perceptions of transparency of government policymaking: A cross-national study. *Government Information Quarterly, 26*(1), 148–157.
44. Ringen, S. (1991). Households, standard of living, and inequality. *Review of Income and Wealth, 37*(1), 1–13.
45. Roberts, A. (2006). *Blacked out: Government secrecy in the information age.* New York: Cambridge University Press.
46. Saha, S., & Gounder, R. (2013). Corruption and economic development nexus: Variations across income levels in a non-linear framework. *Economic Modelling, 31*(1), 70–79.
47. Shim, D. C., & Eom, T. H. (2009). Anticorruption effects of information communication and technology and social Capital. *International Review of Administrative Sciences, 75*(1), 99–116.
48. Sturges, P. (2004). Corruption, transparency and a role for ICT? *International Journal of Information Ethics, 2*, 1–9.

49. Tanzi, V. (1995). Corruption, arm's-length relationships and markets. In G. Fiorentini & S. Peltzman (Eds.), *The economics of organised crime* (pp. 161–180). Cambridge, MA: Cambridge University Press.
50. Tanzi, V. (1998). Corruption around the world: Causes, scope, and cures. IMF Working Paper No. WP/98/63.
51. Ugur, M. (2014). Corruption's direct effects on per-capita income growth: A meta-analysis. *Journal of Economic Surveys, 28*(3), 472–490.
52. UNDP. (2008). Tackling corruption, transforming lives, accelerating human development in Asia and the Pacific. United Nations Development Program Annual Report.
53. Van Rijckeghem, C., & Weder, B. (2001). Corruption and the rate of temptation: Do low wages in the civil service cause corruption? *Journal of Development Economics, 65*(2), 307–331.
54. Vinod, H. D. (1999). Statistic analysis of corruption data and using the internet to reduce corruption. *Journal of Asian Economics, 10*(4), 591–603.
55. Von Waldenberg, W. (2004). Electronic government and development. *European Journal of Development Research, 16*, 417–432.
56. Wellman, B., Hasse, A. Q., Witte, J., & Hampton, K. (2001). Does the internet increase, decrease, or supplement social capital? *American Behavioral Scientist, 45*(3), 436–455.
57. Wescott, C. (2001). E-government in the Asia Pacific region. *Asia Journal of Political Science, 9*, 1–24.
58. Wong, W., & Welch, E. (2004). Does e-government promote accountability? A comparative analysis of website openness and government accountability. *Governance, 17*(2), 275–297.
59. Yang, K., & Rho, S.-Y. (2007). E-government for better performance: Promises, realities, and challenges. *International Journal of Public Administration, 30*(11), 1197–1217.
60. Zittrain, J., & Palfrey, J. (2008). Internet filtering: The politics and mechanisms of control. In R. Deibert, J. Palfrey, R. Rohozinski, & J. Zittrain (Eds.), *The practice and policy of global internet filtering* (pp. 29–56). Cambridge, MA: Massachusetts Institute of Technology Press.

Chapter 5
Internet, Educational Disparities, and Economic Growth: Differences Between Low-Middle and High-Income Countries

Margarita Billon, Jorge Crespo, and Fernando Lera-López

Abstract This paper examines the influence of educational inequality on the impacts of Internet use on economic growth. We use panel data estimations on a sample of 90 countries from 1995 to 2010. We find that Internet use has a positive impact on growth in both developing and developed countries. Furthermore, we also find that educational inequality negatively influences the impact of Internet use on economic growth, the effect being more significant in developing countries. The results highlight that in addition to the role played by the level of human capital, public policies should take into account the educational distribution to boost Internet use and favor its impacts on economic growth.

Keywords Educational inequalities • Information technologies • Digital divide • Human capital • Economic growth

5.1 Introduction

The literature on the so-called digital divide has highlighted the existence of important inequalities in information and communications technology (ICT) access and use that are usually associated with other within-country social divides, such as human capital endowments [1–3]. In most developing countries, the bulk of Internet

M. Billon (✉)
Department of Economic Structure and Development Economics, Autonomous University of Madrid, Madrid, Spain
e-mail: margarita.billon@uam.es

J. Crespo
Department of Applied Economics, Autonomous University of Madrid, Madrid, Spain
e-mail: jorge.crespo@uam.es

F. Lera-López
Department of Economics, Public University of Navarre, Pamplona, Spain
e-mail: lera@unavarra.es

© Springer International Publishing AG 2017
H. Kaur et al. (eds.), *Catalyzing Development through ICT Adoption*,
DOI 10.1007/978-3-319-56523-1_5

51

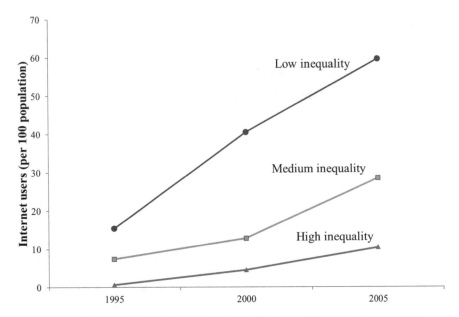

Fig. 5.1 Average diffusion of Internet use by education inequalities at country level (Source: Author's own elaboration from Barro-Lee educational attainment dataset and World Bank Databank. See Sect. 5.4 for details on how education inequalities have been measured. Low education inequality corresponds to countries with Gini <0.125; medium education inequality countries are those with 0.125≤ Gini <0.226; high education inequality countries are those with Gini ≥0.226)

users belong to the most educated sector of the population, whereas the majority lags behind not only in terms of general education but also in terms of Internet skills, creating a gap that may affect the Internet's diffusion [4] and therefore its impacts. In addition, in many less developed countries, lower levels of human capital are associated with greater inequalities in the distribution of education [5]. Figure 5.1 illustrates the Internet diffusion average for three groups of countries according to their educational inequality level. As observed, lower use of the Internet corresponds to countries with higher education inequalities, whereas higher Internet use corresponds to countries exhibiting a lower level of inequalities.

Although the academic literature has investigated the role of education, little attention has been devoted to studying the impacts of educational distribution on ICT's effects on growth. The bulk of studies has focused on the impacts of ICT investments on productivity and growth, in some cases using growth accounting techniques. They have mainly been applied to developed countries and have generally found a positive effect [6–9]. The evidence for developing countries is less extensive and conclusive [10–13]. Other studies within the endogenous growth framework have investigated externalities derived from ICT investments, finding positive effects on the total factor productivity of less developed countries [14] or positive impacts of ICT use on per capita income growth in some countries in Africa [15].

From the academic literature, we also know that together with the crucial role of ICT investments and ICT access, ICT use is a key factor for growth [16, 17]. More specifically, the effective, strategic, and transformative use of ICT may favor participation, empowerment, networking, learning, and innovation processes, which could have significant effects in terms of growth [18, 19].

The transformative use of ICT has commonly been related to more experienced and intensive users and higher levels of education [20, 21]. Furthermore, in addition to the role played by the level of education, Rogers [22] highlighted the need to consider the influence of socioeconomic structure to explain the adoption of innovations. In this sense, the educational distribution within a country may condition the way in which the information and knowledge associated with technology use are disseminated throughout the productive and social system and therefore its impacts.

This chapter seeks to investigate whether educational inequalities influence the effects of Internet use on economic growth using a sample of 90 countries between 1995 and 2010. Unlike previous studies that explore the effects of level of education on ICT use and economic growth, we investigate for the first time the influence of educational inequalities – which are particularly relevant in developing countries – on Internet's effects on growth. We use a panel data approach to take into account specific features of the different countries considered.

The chapter is organized as follows. Following this introduction, Sect. 5.2 provides the theoretical framework of our research. Section 5.3 shows the empirical literature review. Section 5.4 is devoted to presenting the research model. Sections 5.5 and 5.6 show the data methodology and the empirical analysis, respectively. In Sect. 5.7, the main conclusions and discussion are presented, as well as some policy implications of our research.

5.2 Theoretical Framework

Technological progress plays a major role in modern theories of economic growth Since the contributions of Solow [23] and Swan [24] to endogenous growth models proposed by Romer [25], Grossman and Helpman [26], and Aghion and Howitt [27], technology has been considered a key factor for long-run growth. Technological change favors the creation of new products, quality improvement, and heightened efficiency in the use of physical capital and labor. The literature on ICT has highlighted the role played by Internet adoption in facilitating firms' internal and external communication and coordination, lowering transaction costs, and increasing efficiency and productivity [28–31]. Moreover, the Internet also fosters innovation through the development of new products and processes, new business models, and new models of cooperation among firms, impacting economic growth [32, 33]. In addition, the effects of ICT use on growth are also related to the development of new modes of human interaction that may contribute to the creation and diffusion of knowledge.

As Romer [25] pointed out, technology is a non-rival and only partially excludable good. These features favor the diffusion of innovations through individuals and organizations. However, as Keller [34] states, innovations need channels to be assimilated by potential adopters. As general-purpose technologies [35], ICT and the Internet, in particular, facilitate the dissemination of information and the transmission of codified and tacit knowledge [36] throughout productive systems and societies, favoring information networks that may lead to knowledge spill-overs and thus contributing to economic growth [32, 37]. Other approaches also highlight the role played by the creation and diffusion of knowledge flows within local environments and throughout interpersonal interactions as a critical channel for the diffusion of tacit knowledge [38]. However, technology spillovers are not automatic, and cognitive proximity is needed to communicate, understand, assim-ilate, and process new information [39, 40]. The capacity for absorbing, creating, and transmitting new knowledge requires a similar cognitive base to understand and process it effectively [41]. Moreover, along with cognitive proximity, so do relational, social, and technological proximities [42] favor the creation of "cogni-tive spaces." These spaces act as channels that facilitate interactive and collective learning processes [43] which are considered key determinants to guarantee the strategic use of ICT and, therefore, its impacts on growth.

Within this framework, the level of education constitutes an important factor to explaining technology diffusion and its impacts. Several theoretical models [44–46] have demonstrated the importance of human capital to adopt and use new technolo-gies. The diffusion theory also states that individuals with a higher educational level tend to be more prone to accept the risks and uncertainty associated with innova-tions and adopt them faster than people with less education [22]. Early adopters and users of technology show higher levels of education than laggards. Education pro-vides the skills required for using and taking advantage of ICT. Also, heterogeneity models [46] attribute a critical role to disparities in educational levels to explain the differences in diffusion rates [20, 21].

In addition to educational levels, the diffusion theory emphasizes that social structure determines the impacts of technology use more than innovation itself. Differences in educational attainment levels within countries, in other words, edu-cational inequalities, influence the type of communications networks created and the information and knowledge flows that take place among individuals. According to Rogers [22], information and knowledge flows take place among "peers," between "ups" and "ups," on the one hand, and between "downs" and "downs," on the other. In addition, as also mentioned, the dissemination of information and the transmis-sion of codified and tacit knowledge [36] may be related to several cognitive, social, and technological proximities associated with the existing educational structure, with potential impacts on economic growth.

As seen, along with theoretical approaches that stress the role of technology and human capital in economic growth, more modern contributions highlight the rele-vance of collective learning processes as a way to acquire knowledge, considered a key factor for growth. In this context, differences in educational levels within a country, as pointed out by the diffusion theory, may affect ICT use and the associ-ated knowledge flows as well as their potential impact on growth.

5.3 Empirical Literature Review

5.3.1 *Internet Use and Economic Growth*

Empirical evidence on the impacts of Internet use on growth at the country level is still scarce, and although it shows a generally positive relationship, the results are far from conclusive. These results differ considerably depending on the level of development, the period analyzed, and the econometric specifications employed.

Espiritu [47] obtained a positive association between Internet use and economic growth from a sample of 36 developed countries between 1980 and 1999. Baliamoune-Lutz [10] found that some ICT indicators led to a higher per capita income for a sample of 47 developing countries in the period 1998–2000. Using cross-country panel data for 207 countries in the period 1991–2000, Choi and Hoon Yi [48] also detected a very positive and significant effect of Internet use on economic growth. Vu [49] showed the high impact of Internet use on economic growth for a sample of 102 countries in the 1996–2005 period.

The evidence also proves the convenience of taking into account the level of development and the state of the economy, since the results are sensible to them [13, 50]. Meijers [16] captured the positive impact of Internet use on economic growth from a sample of 162 countries in the period 1990–2008, showing that the impact of Internet use on trade is much higher for non-high-income countries, whereas the impact of trade on economic growth is the same for both high-income and non-high-income countries. Yousefi [17] showed that the impact of ICT on economic growth differs across different income groups of countries through a study of 62 countries in the period 2000–2006, playing a major role in the growth of high- and upper-middle-income countries. By contrast, Qiang and Xu [51], conducting a cross-sectional analysis for the period 1980–2009, found a robust economic impact of Internet use only in developing countries.

The literature has also demonstrated that the potential outcomes derived from ICT require complementary investments, such as those associated with human capital [52], which allow us to explore the links between education and ICT.

5.3.2 *Education and ICT Use*

Empirical evidence shows that basic literacy and reading and writing skills are essential to ICT use [3]. Moreover, the transformative use of ICT requires higher levels of education that are also related to the development of specific skills [53]. Furthermore, the skilled labor force is able to use the Internet and other ICTs more efficiently, consequently contributing to increasing firm productivity and performance as well as growth in the long term [12]. Educational achievement is essential for the productive use of ICT in developing countries [54], where the low levels of human capital may constitute a barrier to Internet usage.

The empirical evidence has frequently shown a positive impact of education on ICT diffusion in different countries. Some studies, using national surveys, have verified the important role of education at the personal level. Haight et al. [55] in Canada and Zhu and Chen [56] in China are recent examples. Chinn and Fairlie [57], for a panel of 161 countries, highlighted that educational level is a relevant factor to explain the global digital divide. Demoussis and Giannakopoulos [58], for a sample of European countries, also found that the level of Internet use is positively affected by education. Wunnava and Leiter [59], employing cross-sectional data from 100 countries (developed and developing countries), showed that education has a positive effect on Internet diffusion.

Some studies have focused separately on ICT diffusion in developed and developing countries. Bagchi and Udo [60] analyzed the determinants of ICT adoption in two sets of African countries and countries belonging to the Organization for Economic Cooperation and Development (OECD). The results show that education is more relevant to explaining ICT diffusion in developing countries than in developed ones. Kiiski and Pohjola [61] also emphasized the different roles played by education according to the economic level of the countries. They showed that in OECD countries, education is not a statistically significant factor for Internet diffusion. However, when they employed a bigger sample including non-OECD countries, human capital seemed to be significant in explaining Internet diffusion. Baliamoune-Lutz [10], using a sample of 47 developing countries, also found that ICT diffusion is not associated with education. Nevertheless, more recent studies with bigger samples have pointed out the positive relationship between education and ICT use in developing countries [12, 62].

Other researchers have focused on particular geographical areas. For example, Chong and Micco [63] showed the role of human capital to be one of the most important factors in ICT diffusion in Latin America. Quibria et al. [3], for Asian countries, found that education positively affects computer and Internet use. Ngwenyama et al. [54], investigating some African countries, highlighted the complementarities between ICT and education as well as the need for additional improvements in education to boost the ICT use in those countries.

To sum up, the empirical literature has explored the relationships between ICT and growth and between educational levels and ICT diffusion. However, only some studies have considered the indirect association between educational levels and growth achieved through ICT use [12], while scant attention has been devoted to exploring whether the educational distribution may affect the impacts of ICT.

5.4   Research Model

Along with the effect of Internet use on economic growth, this paper aims to investigate the influence of educational inequalities on the impact that Internet use has on growth. The specific research questions that we attempt to answer are the following:

- Does the Internet have an impact on economic growth?
- Do educational inequalities affect the impact of Internet use on economic growth?

We follow the broadly accepted assumption in economic growth literature that capital accumulation and technology are the main engines of economic growth. From an empirical point of view, we use Barro's [64] approach since it allows us to consider a wide spectrum of explanatory factors of economic growth including technology diffusion. We also take into account the diffusion theory to explore the role of education and its distribution. The proposed empirical growth model includes specific variables to capture the effect of Internet use on economic growth and the joint impact of human capital inequalities and Internet use on growth:

$$\Delta GDP_{i,t-(t+5)} = \beta_1 GDP_{i,t} + \beta_2 I_{i,t-(t+5)} + \beta_3 HK_{i,t} + \beta_4 Exp_{i,t}$$
$$+ \beta_5 Inf_{i,t-(t+5)} + \beta_6 Internet_{i,t-(t+5)} \qquad (5.1)$$
$$+ \beta_7 EducIneq_{i,t} \cdot Internet_{i,t-(t+5)} + u_{i,t}$$

where i denotes countries and t time; $\Delta GDP_{i,t-(t+5)}$ is the 5-year growth of per capita GDP; $GDP_{i,t}$ is the log of per capita income in t (this term is added to allow for conditional convergence; see [64]); $I_{i,t-(t+5)}$ is the log of the 5-year average ratio of gross domestic investment to GDP; $HK_{i,t}$ is the log of human capital; $Exp_{i,t}$ denotes the log of life expectancy; $Inf_{i,t-(t+5)}$ is the 5-year growth in prices; $Internet_{i,t-(t+5)}$ is the log of the 5-year average number of Internet users per 100 people; $EducIneq_{i,t} \cdot Internet_{i,t-(t+5)}$ is the interaction term between educational inequality, measured by the Gini coefficient, and the average number of Internet users; and $u_{i,t}$ is the error term. The inclusion of the interaction term allows us to explore whether the impacts of Internet use on growth depend on educational inequalities. In this sense, the marginal effect of an increase in Internet use would be captured by

$$\frac{\partial \Delta GDP_{i,t-(t+5)}}{\partial Internet_{i,t-(t+5)}} = \beta_6 + \beta_7 \cdot EducIneq_{i,t} \qquad (5.2)$$

So the initial impact of Internet use on growth β_6 would be adjusted by the $\beta_7 \cdot EducIneq_{i,t}$ product.

In accordance with our research questions and the theoretical and empirical literature reviewed, we propose the following main hypotheses.

As already mentioned, given ICT effects in terms of accelerating the diffusion of information, technological know-how, and favoring human interactions, we expect a positive impact of Internet diffusion on growth [47, 49, 51, 59].

H_1: There is a positive impact of Internet use on economic growth.

As previously shown, together with the level of education and according to the diffusion theory, educational structure also influences technology adoption. Along with low levels of human capital, the existence of disparities in educational levels may negatively influence knowledge flows, the dissemination of information and the transmission of codified and tacit knowledge [39–41], and the potential learning processes and impacts on growth.

H_2: Educational inequality negatively influences the impacts of Internet use on economic growth.

The secondary hypotheses derived from the rest of the variables usually included in growth models are the following:

As previously shown, the literature has widely demonstrated the role played by human capital as an engine of economic growth [44, 45, 65].

H_3: Human capital positively impacts economic growth.

Life expectancy has been traditionally included in growth models in line with [64], capturing human capital quality. Life expectancy is usually considered as a proxy for workforce's health [66]. Although the results of life expectancy effects on economic growth are far from conclusive [67], the empirical literature has demonstrated that improvements in population's health may increase human capital, in particular in developing countries [68]. The positive influence of life expectancy is related to the fact that healthier workers are more likely to be more productive [69]. In addition to the productivity gains, life expectancy also may contribute to increase human capital accumulation since expected returns to investment on education are higher [70].

H_4: Life expectancy positively impacts economic growth.

According to the convergence hypothesis in economic growth literature [64], countries per capita GDP should converge to their stationary state. In this sense, their rate of economic growth is inversely related to their distance to their stationary state, so we would expect a negative coefficient for this variable.

H_5: Initial per capita GDP negatively impacts economic growth.

Physical capital is one of the traditional production factors considered in the literature on economic growth [23, 24]. We expect a positive sign for this variable.

H_6: Investment positively impacts economic growth.

Finally, high inflation reduces investment and productivity growth [71], and it is associated with macroeconomic instability [72]. The coefficient for inflation is expected to be negative.

H_7: Inflation negatively affects economic growth.

5.5 Data and Methodology

We use a sample of 90 countries for the 1995–2010 period. We took into account the favorable evolution of Internet use from the 1990s to investigate their impacts on economic growth. Also, following [73] and considering that changes in economic development take time, we calculate growth over a 5-year intervals instead of measuring growth from 1 year to the next. The period selected is also conditioned by human capital data availability. Human capital is measured using the average years of secondary and tertiary schooling for members of the population aged 25 and over and is taken from Barro and Lee [74]. The data for GDP per capita, life expectancy, investment ratio, inflation, and Internet users per 100 people are from World Bank [75]. Educational inequality is computed as a Gini index based on the school attainment data of population aged 25 years and over provided by Barro and Lee [74][1]:

$$G^H = \frac{1}{2\bar{H}} \sum_{i=0}^{3} \sum_{j=0}^{3} \left| x_i - x_j \right| n_i n_j \qquad (5.3)$$

where $\bar{H}$ is the average years of schooling of population, i and j are the different subgroups considered (no schooling, primary education, secondary education, higher education), x_i and x_j are the cumulative average schooling years of each educational level, and, finally, n_i and n_j are the shares of population with an educational i and j level.

Matching both datasets we obtained complete information about all selected variables for 90 countries (52 middle-and low-income countries and 38 high-income countries). Given the lack of data for low-income countries, we grouped middle- and low-income countries together. Table 5.1 shows the descriptive statistics of the variables.

We use a panel data estimation approach because it allows us to consider the existence of specific features of countries that are, generally, unobservable and stable over time (cultural aspects, traditions, legislations, etc.). Otherwise, the estimations would suffer from an omitted variable bias. Moreover, if this unobservable heterogeneity was correlated with one or some of the explanatory variables, the ordinary least-squares estimation would not be consistent (it could even lead us to obtain coefficients whose signs are the opposite of those expected). In order to avoid these problems, we use the fixed-effects (FE) estimator.

Table 5.1 Summary statistics

Variable	Mean	Std. dev.	Minimum	Maximum
$GDP_{i,t-(t+5)}$	0.123	0.111	−0.116	0.580
$I_{i,t-(t+5)}$	3.065	0.200	2.304	3.747
$HK_{i,t}$	0.641	0.532	−0.972	1.823
$Exp_{i,t}$	4.218	0.125	3.731	4.372
$Inf_{i,t-(t+5)}$	0.312	0.400	−0.068	3.540
$Internet_{i,t-(t+5)}$	2.171	1.752	−2.737	4.510
$EducIneq_{i,t}$	0.210	0.149	0.004	0.747

Authors' own calculations

---

[1] This expression is used in Checchi [77].

In addition, the presence of the lagged dependent variable among the regressors in the estimated equation creates endogeneity problems given that this variable is correlated with the error term. As a solution it is necessary to estimate the model using an instrumental variable estimator; specifically, we use the two-stage least-squares estimator (2SLS). However, finding suitable external instruments is a complex task, so we use the lags of the variables as instruments [76]. This is a common practice in estimations that have to tackle endogeneity problems.

5.6   Empirical Analysis

To test our hypotheses, firstly, real GDP per capita growth rate variable is regressed on the selected independent variables for the entire sample. Column (1) in Table 5.2 reports the coefficients of the regression estimated. The results confirm our first hypothesis since Internet use shows a positive and significant influence on economic growth. As for our second hypothesis, the interactive term between the Internet and educational inequality is negative and significant, confirming that the educational distribution negatively influences the effect of Internet use on economic growth. The result indicates that countries with greater differences in the distribution of education may register weaker effects of Internet use on growth than countries with a more homogeneous distribution.

With respect to the traditional variables in Barro's model, neither human capital nor life expectancy is significant (Hypotheses 3 and 4). It should be noted that this result is often obtained when average years of schooling are used in panel data regressions [78, 79]. The results confirm the conditional convergence hypothesis, as the initial per capita GDP coefficient is negative and significant (Hypothesis 5). Finally, investment shows a positive effect on economic growth, while inflation has a negative effect, confirming Hypotheses 6 and 7, respectively.

Secondly, as we are also interested in investigating whether the results may vary when we take into account different development levels, following the World Bank's classification, we divide the sample into two groups. The regressions in Columns (2) and (3) in Table 5.2 show the results obtained for low- and middle-income group and high-income countries, respectively. The answers to our main research questions are the same as that obtained for the total sample. First, in both cases Internet use has a significant and positive impact on economic growth, confirming our first hypothesis. Furthermore, the impact of the Internet seems to be slightly greater in developing countries than in developed countries. Second, the results also provide evidence for our second hypothesis since the interactive term is also significant and has a negative sign for both groups of countries. However, the negative influence of educational inequality on growth is more evident for less developed countries.

Table 5.2 Per capita GDP growth regression models

Variables	(1) Total countries	(2) Low- and middle-income countries	(3) High-income countries
$GDP_{i,t}$	−0.696***	−0.645***	−0.759***
	(.085)	(0.133)	(0.139)
$I_{i,t-(t+5)}$	0.118*	0.162**	−0.026
	(0.061)	(0.062)	(0.178)
$HK_{i,t}$	0.067	0.082	0.070
	(0.097)	(0.098)	(0.135)
$Exp_{i,t}$	0.273	0.315**	0.797
	(0.174)	(0.151)	(0.994)
$Inf_{i,t-(t+5)}$	−0.038**	−0.034**	−0.024
	(0.015)	(0.014)	(0.117)
$Internet_{i,t-(t+5)}$	0.062***	0.055***	0.048***
	(0.009)	(0.011)	(0.017)
$EducIneq_{i,t}$ * $Internet_{i,t-(t+5)}$	−0.176***	−0.161***	−0.203*
	(0.047)	(0.054)	(0.113)
Country dummies	Yes	Yes	Yes
Observations	270	156	114
R^2	0.6765	0.7161	0.6090

(*), (**) and (***) denote significance at the 10%, 5%, and 1% levels, respectively. White's heteroskedasticity-robust standard errors in parentheses

In relation to the rest of the variables in the model, the results vary according to the different country group, probably as a result of their different stage of development. With regard to less developed countries, life expectancy, initial per capita GDP, investment, and inflation are significant and show the expected signs, confirming for this group our Hypotheses 4, 5, 6, and 7, respectively. The results point out the crucial role of investment in economic growth in developing countries. In addition, life expectancy now has a positive and significant impact on economic growth. This finding is consistent with [80], who concluded that the effect of life expectancy on economic growth may in turn be conditioned by life expectancy itself. The higher the life expectancy, the lower its potential effect on economic growth.

In contrast, for developed countries only our main Hypotheses 1 and 2 and the convergence Hypothesis 5 are confirmed. Regarding human capital, we again found a nonsignificant coefficient in line with [78, 79]. Life expectancy seems to be less important for this group of countries as average life expectancy for advanced countries is 74.3 in our sample (64.04 for developing countries). It should be noted that according to Barro [81], the adverse effect of the inflation rate on economic growth is only shown in countries with very high inflation rates (above 10%). He also pointed out the existence of a simultaneity problem between investment and economic growth that cannot be completely solved using investment lagged values as instruments.

5.7 Conclusions and Discussion

This chapter aimed to investigate the effects of Internet use on economic growth and the influence of educational inequalities on the impacts of the Internet on growth. We used a panel data approach to take into account specific features of the different countries considered, using a sample of 90 countries from 1995 to 2010. Within the framework of empirical growth models that consider the role of technology diffusion, results confirm the first hypothesis since we found a positive relationship of Internet use for both the entire sample and for different country groups according to their level of development. The positive relationship seems to be slightly higher among low- and middle-income countries than in high-income countries.

The findings also confirm our second hypothesis. We found that the relationship between educational inequalities and Internet use was negatively related to economic growth for both developed and developing countries, although the results were clearly more significant for developing countries. The contribution is in line with the importance given to educational structure by diffusion theory as a factor that can influence technology adoption and its impacts. Also, the outcomes of the research are in accordance with more recent theoretical approaches that stress the importance of human interactions among individuals who share knowledge bases and cognitive, technological, and social "spaces" that lead to the collective learning processes needed to acquire and process new knowledge considered to be a critical factor for economic development.

These results indicate that along with investments and actions devoted to increasing human capital endowments, specific policy actions are needed to assure a more egalitarian distribution of education. Furthermore, our results reinforce previous studies pointing out that investments in ICT, in particular in developing countries, should be developed with complementary investments in the education infrastructure and programs to reduce human capital inequalities and to boost the effective and productive use of ICT. As Morales-Gómez and Melesse [82] pointed out some years ago, the design of ICT policies should be closely linked with education and training strategies to promote development in developing countries. Then, developing countries might prioritize government initiatives in technology and education to support and increase the access to education and digital literacy and reduce the educational inequalities.

Nevertheless, we should be conscious of the fact that the reduction of educational inequalities in developing countries might require a concerted long-term effort at the national, regional, and local levels. The results of these efforts will be noticeable in the medium and long term. As Barro ([81], p. 3) argued, "physical capital is more amenable than human capital to rapid expansion." Thus, policies to reduce educational inequalities should pursue the improvement of educational systems in developing countries, in particular in rural and remote areas. The integration of ICT-related subjects into all stages of education, particularly at the primary and secondary levels, together with the improvement of the ICT infrastructure in schools (computers, modems, etc.) might contribute not only to reducing the educational inequalities but also to boosting digital literacy and different e-skills, which could contribute to improving productivity and economic development in this type of country. Nevertheless, these efforts to reduce the educational inequality in developing countries are likely to face some challenges, such as the brain drain of highly qualified experts and teachers. This phenomenon has been previously highlighted by other studies [83, 84].[2]

In particular, it might be possible to develop mixed strategies combining educational and ICT programs. These mixed strategies could be developed to target different populations. For example, if younger users are early adopters of more advanced uses of ICT [85], not only the inclusion of ICT subjects in educational programs but also the use of different ICTs as a way to develop basic literacy in students might be interesting. It might also be useful to provide young people with e-skills by offering vocational schooling when these skills are not acquired at school, as undertaken in India [85]. This could improve their job opportunities at the same time as reducing the educational inequalities. Furthermore, organizing literacy courses through the use of computers, for example, to teach adults could reduce the educational inequalities and at the same time increase people's e-skills and abilities. Firms might also be provided with incentives to engage in the development of e-skills training themselves through tax subsidies or tax policies [86]. These incentives could have positive effects on the educational attainments of middle-aged people as well as boosting the productivity improvements within firms.

On the one hand, these efforts might be accompanied by the development of the ICT infrastructure[3] and measures to reduce the cost of usage through subsidies to schools and populations living in rural and remote areas. As 43% of the countries under study have a majority of rural population, it is essential for these measures to be applied in rural areas in particular. Furthermore, to avoid the lack of awareness shown by a great proportion of the population in developing countries, the development of specific applications useful for basic activities in these countries might be necessary. Open-source software could be a good instrument to create online content in people's own languages that support the school-based curriculum and new useful applications in developing countries, considering the local realities of the population. For example, the experience described by Jain et al. [87] among Indian farmers is a good point of reference

---

[2] Brain drain migration has been growing significantly over the last decades, with an increase of 77% in the period 1990–2000, increasing more rapidly than the educational attainments in many developing countries, with negative impacts in these countries [83]. Furthermore, throughout the 1990s, the growth rate of international skilled migration was nearly triple that of unskilled migration, and most of that increase was due to skilled migration from developing to developed countries. The emigration rates in 2000 were three times higher than average for the highly educated and skilled and 12 times higher among emigrants from low-income countries [84].

[3] Satellite networks, wireless infrastructure, and public-private partnerships might reduce the cost of Internet access drastically. In this context, recent initiatives to develop more affordable information and communication systems through satellites to reach rural areas have been implemented in some developing countries (see, e.g., the Ob3 project: http://www.o3bnetworks.com/3222).

for future applications in developing countries, in particular in rural areas. It may also be interesting to develop specific ICT applications (apps) focusing on youth targets that could be used with mobile phones, for example, which are generally more accessible and affordable than computers.

On the other hand, ICT training courses should be developed for teachers in developing countries as well as ICT applications with educational purposes considering the native languages of the population. These measures could help teachers and educational staff to be conscious of ICT's possibilities to improve educational attainment and reduce educational inequalities in developing countries, in particular in rural and remote areas, as previously mentioned.

Finally, our results also reinforce other results that show that the digital divide and the differences in ICT impacts across countries are also related to other social divides associated with differences in development levels. ICT diffusion policies should take into account the characteristics of the economic and social development and coordinate actions with other initiatives to link economic development with ICT diffusion. ICT investments alone might not necessarily lend themselves to development in developing countries if they are not developed together with other initiatives to increase educational and social attainments.[4]

One of the main limitations of the present study is the lack of data, which did not allow us to disaggregate the results to capture the influence of the different stages of development for different groups of developing economies, such as emerging and poor economies. This should be an area for further research when more data are available. It would also be interesting to use additional measures of human capital and educational inequality, different from the Gini index. Although there are several advantages of using this index, such as the fact that it is easy to understand and has many desirable statistical properties, it is not easily decomposable or additive. In addition, it is ever difficult to characterize educational inequality through a single index. Therefore, alternative measures should be considered for further research to capture better the distribution of education in the countries considered.

Acknowledgments Margarita Billon and Fernando Lera-Lopez acknowledge the financial support of the Spanish Ministry of Science (ECO2010-21393-C04-03 and ECO2013-48496-C4-2-R).

---

[4] More details about different measures to promote ICT adoption in developing countries and the relationship with educational, political, and social issues can be found in Keengwe and Malapile [88].

References

1. Billon, M., Marco, R., & Lera-Lopez, F. (2009). Disparities in ICT adoption: A multidimensional approach to study the cross-country digital divide. *Telecommunications Policy, 33*(10), 596–610.
2. Oyelaran-Oyeyinka, B., & Lal, K. (2005). Internet diffusion in sub-Saharan Africa: A cross-country analysis. *Telecommunications Policy, 29*(7), 507–527.
3. Quibria, M. G., Ahmed, S. N., Tschang, T., & Reyes-Macasaquit, M. L. (2003). Digital divide: Determinants and policies with special reference to Asia. *Journal of Asian Economics, 13*(6), 811–825.
4. James, J. (2011). Internet skills in developing countries: How much do we know? *Information Development, 2011*(27), 94–99.
5. Castelló-Climent, A. (2010). Inequality and growth in advanced economies: An empirical investigation. *Journal of Economic Inequality, 8*(3), 293–321.
6. Colecchia, A., & Schreyer, P. (2002). ICT investment and economic growth in the 1990s: Is the United States a unique case? A comparative study of nine OECD countries. *Review of Economic Dynamics, 5*(2), 408–442.
7. Jorgenson, D. W. (2001). Information technology and the US economy. *American Economic Review, 91*(1), 1–32.
8. Oliner, S. D., & Sichel, D. E. (2000). The resurgence of growth in the late 1990s: Is information technology the story? *Journal of Economic Perspectives, 4*(14), 3–22.
9. Stiroh, K. J. (2002). Information technology and the U.S. productivity revival: What do the industry data say? *American Economic Review, 92*(5), 1559–1576.
10. Baliamoune-Lutz, M. (2003). An analysis of the determinants and effects of ICT diffusion in developing countries. *Information Technology for Development, 10*(3), 151–169.
11. Dewan, S., & Kraemer, K. L. (2000). Information technology and productivity: Evidence from country-level data. *Management Science, 46*(4), 548–562.
12. Kottemann, J., & Boyer-Wright, K. (2009). Human resource development, domains of information technology use, and levels of economic prosperity. *Information Technology for Development, 15*(1), 32–42.
13. Samoilenko, S., & Osei-Bryson, K. M. (2011). The spillover effects of investments in telecoms: Insights from transition economies. *Information Technology for Development, 17*(3), 213–231.
14. Seo, H. J., & Lee, Y. S. (2006). Contribution of information and communication technology to total factor productivity and externalities effects. *Information Technology for Development, 12*(2), 159–173.
15. Chavula, H. K. (2013). Telecommunications development and economic growth in Africa. *Information Technology for Development, 19*(1), 5–23.
16. Meijers, H.M. (2012). Does Internet generate economic growth, international trade, or both? Working Paper no. 50 Maastricht Economic and Social Research Institute on Innovation and Technology.
17. Yousefi, A. (2011). The impact of information and communication technology on economic growth: Evidence from developed and developing countries. *Economics of Innovation and New Technology, 20*(6), 581–696.
18. Capello, R., & Spairani, A. (2006). Accessibility and regional growth in Europe. The role of ICTs policies. In G. Vertova (Ed.), *The changing economic geography of globalization* (pp. 192–215). London: Routledge.
19. Hughes, G., Gareis, K., Assis, J., Cornford, J., Richardson, R., & Sokol, M. (2008). TRANSFORM: Benchmarking & fostering transformative use of ICT in EU regions. Report TRANSFORM/Empirica. (EU FP6 – SSA; DG Infso).
20. Geroski, P. A. (2000). Models of technology diffusion. *Research Policy, 29*(4), 603–625.

21. Karshenas, M., & Stoneman, P. (1995). Technological diffusion. In M. Karshenas & P. Stoneman (Eds.), *Handbook of the economics of innovation and technological change* (pp. 265–297). Oxford: Blackwell.
22. Rogers, E. M. (2003). *Diffusion of innovations*. New York: Free Press.
23. Solow, R. (1956). A contribution to economic growth. *Quarterly Journal of Economics, 70*(1), 65–94.
24. Swan, T. W. (1956). Economic growth and capital accumulation economic. *Record, 32,* 334–361.
25. Romer, P. M. (1990). Endogenous technological change. *Journal of Political Economy, 98*(5), 71–102.
26. Grossman, G. M., & Helpman, E. (1991). *Innovation and growth in the global economy.* Cambridge, MA: MIT Press.
27. Aghion, P., & Howitt, P. (1992). A model of growth through creative destruction: Monte Carlo evidence and an application to employment equations. *Econometrica, 60*(2), 323–351.
28. Brynjolfsson, E., & Hitt, L. M. (1998). Beyond the productivity paradox: Computers are the catalyst for bigger changes. *Communications of ACMXLI, 8,* 49–55.
29. Brynjolfsson, E., & Hitt, L. M. (2000). Beyond computation: Information technology, organizational transformation and business practice. *Journal of Economic Perspectives XIV, 4,* 23–48.
30. Brynjolfsson, E., & Hitt, L. M. (2003). Computing productivity: Firm-level evidence. *Review of Economics & Statistics LXXXV,* (4), 793–809.
31. Dedrick, J., Gurbaxani, V., & Kraemer, K. L. (2003). Information technology and economic performance: A critical review of the empirical evidence. *ACM Computing Surveys (CSUR), 35*(1), 1–28.
32. Chu, S. Y. (2013). Internet, economic growth and recession. *Modern Economy, 4,* 209–213.
33. Czernich, N., Falck, O., Kretschmer, T., & Woessmann, L. (2011). Broadband infrastructure and economic growth. *The Economic Journal, 121*(552), 505–532.
34. Keller, W. (2004). International technology diffusion. *Journal of Economic Literature, 42*(3), 752–782.
35. Helpman, E., & Trajtenberg, M. (1996). Diffusion of general purpose technologies. Working Paper no. 5773. National Bureau of Economic Research.
36. Storper, M., & Venables, A. J. (2004). Buzz: Face-to-face contact and the urban economy. *Journal of Economic Geography, 4*(4), 351–370.
37. Bloom, N., Schankerman, M., & Van Reenen, J. (2013). Identifying technology spillovers and product market rivalry. *Econometrica, 81*(4), 1347–1393.
38. Camagni, R., & Capello, R. (2013). Regional innovation patterns and the EU regional policy reform: Toward smart innovation policies. *Growth and Change, 44*(2), 355–389.
39. Boschma, R. (2005). Proximity and innovation: A critical assessment. *Regional Studies, 39*(1), 61–74.
40. Jaffe, A. B. (1986). Technological opportunity and spillovers of R &D: Evidence from firms' patents, profits, and market value. *American Economic Review, 76*(5), 984–1001.
41. Marrocu, E., Paci, R., & Usai, S. (2011). The complementary effects of proximity dimensions on knowledge spillovers. WP CRENoS WP11–21.
42. Basile, R., Capello, R., & Caragliu, A. (2012). Technological interdependence and regional growth in Europe: Proximity and synergy in knowledge spillovers. *Papers in Regional Science, 91*(4), 697–722.
43. Capello, R., & Spairani, A. (2004). The role of collective learning in ICT adoption and use. In H. L. De Groot, P. Nijkamp, & R. R. Strough (Eds.), *Entrepreneurship and regional economic development, a spatial perspective* (pp. 198–224). Cheltenham: Edward Elgar Publishing.
44. Benhabib, J., & Spiegel, M. (2005). Human capital and technology diffusion. In P. Aghion & S. N. Durlauf (Eds.), *Handbook of economic growth, 1A: Handbooks in economics* (Vol. 22, pp. 935–966). Amsterdam: Elsevier & North-Holland.
45. Nelson, R., & Phelps, E. (1966). Investment in humans, technological diffusion, and economic growth. *American Economic Review: Papers and Proceedings, 51*(2), 69–75.

46. Rosenberg, N. (1972). Factors affecting the diffusion of technology. *Explorations in Economic History, 10*, 3–33.
47. Espiritu, A. (2003). Digital divide and implications on growth: Cross-country analysis. *Journal of American Academy of Business, 2*(2), 450–454.
48. Choi, C., & Hoon Yi, M. (2009). The effect of Internet on economic growth: Evidence from cross-country panel data. *Economics Letters, 105*(1), 39–41.
49. Vu, K. M. (2011). ICT as a source of economic growth in the information age: Empirical evidence from the 1996–2005 period. *Telecommunications Policy, 35*(4), 357–372.
50. Roztocki, N., & Weistroffer, H. R. (2011). Information technology success factors and models in developing and emerging economies. *Information Technology for Development, 17*(3), 163–167.
51. Qiang, C. Z., & Xu, L. C. (2012). *Telecommunications and economic performance: Macro and micro evidence*. Washington, DC: World Bank.
52. Ketteni, E., Mamuneas, T., & Stengos, T. (2010). The effect of information technology and human capital on economic growth. *Macroeconomic Dynamics, 15*(5), 595–615.
53. World Bank. (2011). *Approach paper*. Washington, DC: Information & Communication Technologies Sector Strategy.
54. Ngwenyama, O., Andoh-Baidoo, F., Bollou, F., & Morawczynski, O. (2006). Is there a relationship between ICT, health, education and development? An empirical analysis of five West African countries from 1997–2003. *The Electronic Journal on Information Systems in Developing Countries, 23*(5), 1–11.
55. Haight, M., Quan-Haase, A., & Corbett, B. (2014). Revisiting the digital divide in Canada: The impact of demographic factors on access to the Internet, level of online activity and social networking site usage. *Information, Communication & Society, 17*(4), 503–519.
56. Zhu, S., & Chen, J. (2013). The digital divide in individual E-commerce utilization in China: Results from a national survey. *Information Development, 29*(1), 69–80.
57. Chinn, M., & Fairlie, R. (2007). The determinants of the global digital divide: A cross-country analysis of computer and Internet penetration. *Oxford Economic Papers, 59*, 16–44.
58. Demoussis, M., & Giannakopoulos, N. (2006). Facets of the digital divide in Europe: Determination and extent of Internet use. *Economics of Innovation and New Technology, 15*(3), 235–246.
59. Wunnava, P., & Leiter, D. (2009). Determinants of intercountry Internet diffusion rates. *American Journal of Economics and Sociology, 68*(2), 413–426.
60. Bagchi, K., & Udo, G. (2007). Empirically testing factors that drive ICT adoption in Africa and OECD set of nations. *Issues in Information Systems, 8*(2), 45–52.
61. Kiiski, S., & Pohjola, M. (2002). Cross-country diffusion of the Internet. *Information Economics and Policy, 14*, 297–310.
62. Pick, J., & Azari, R. (2008). Global digital divide: Influence of socioeconomic, governmental and accessibility factors on information technology. *Information Technology for Development, 14*(2), 91–115.
63. Chong, A., & Micco, A. (2003). The Internet and the ability to innovate in Latin America. *Emerging Markets Review, 4*, 53–72.
64. Barro, R. J. (1991). Economic growth in a cross section of countries. *The Quarterly Journal of Economics, 106*(2), 407–443.
65. Lucas, R. E. (1988). On the mechanics of economic development. *Journal of Monetary Economics, 22*(1), 3–42.
66. Bloom, D. E., Canning, D., & Sevilla, J. (2004). The effect of health on economic growth: A production function approach. *World Development, 32*(1), 1–13.
67. Acemoglu, D., & Johnson, S. (2007). Disease and development: The effect of life expectancy on economic growth. *Journal of Political Economy, 115*(6), 925–985.
68. Hanushek, E. A. (2013). Economic growth in developing countries: The role of human capital. *Economics of Education Review, 37*, 204–212.

69. Strauss, J., & Thomas, D. (1998). Health, nutrition, and economic development. *Journal of Economic Literature, 36*, 766–817.
70. Bils, M., & Klenow, P. (2000). Does schooling cause growth? *American Economic Review, 90*, 1160–1183.
71. Fischer, S. (1993). The role of macroeconomic factors in growth. *Journal of Monetary Economics, 32*(3), 485–512.
72. Barro, R. J. (2013). Inflation and economic growth. *Annals of Economics and Finance, Society for AEF, 14*(1), 121–144.
73. Rodríguez-Pose, A., & Tselios, V. (2010). Inequalities in income and education and regional economic growth in Western Europe. *The Annals of Regional Science, 44*(2), 349–375.
74. Barro, R. J., & Lee, J. W. (2012). A new data set of educational attainment in the world, 1950–2010. Retrieved 14 Sept 14, 2012, from http://www.barrolee.com
75. World Bank. (2013). *World development indicators database*. Washington, DC: World Bank.
76. Arellano, M., & Bond, S. (1991). Some tests of specification for panel data. *Review of Economic Studies, 58*, 277–297.
77. Checchi, D. (2000). Does educational achievement help to explain income inequality? UNU/WIDER Working papers no. 208.
78. Cohen, D., & Soto, M. (2007). Growth and human capital: Good data good results. *Journal of Economic Growth, 12*, 51–76.
79. Messinis, G., & Ahmed, A. D. (2013). Cognitive skills, innovation and technology diffusion. *Economic Modelling, 30*, 565–578.
80. Zhang, J., & Zhang, J. (2005). The effect of life expectancy on fertility, saving, schooling and economic growth: Theory and evidence. *Scandinavian Journal of Economics, 107*(1), 45–66.
81. Barro, R. J. (1999). *Determinants of economic growth: A cross-country empirical study*. Cambridge, MA: The MIT Press.
82. Morales-Gómez, D., & Melesse, M. (1998). Utilising information and communication technologies for development: The social dimensions. *Information Technology for Development, 8*(1), 3–13.
83. Di Maria, C., & Lazarova, E. (2012). Migration, human capital formation, and growth: An empirical investigation. *World Development, 40*(5), 938–955.
84. Docquier, F., & Marfouk, A. (2006). International migration by educational attainment (1990–2000). In C. Ozden & M. Schiff (Eds.), *International migration, remittances and development* (pp. 151–200). New York: Palgrave MacMillan.
85. Halewood, N., & Kenny, C. (2008). Young people and ICTs in developing countries. *Information Technology for Development, 14*(2), 171–177.
86. Indjikian, R., & Siegel, D. S. (2005). The impact of investment in IT on economic performance: Implications for developing countries. *World Development, 33*(5), 681–700.
87. Jain, L., Kumar, H., & Singla, R. K. (2015). Assessing mobile technology usage for knowledge dissemination among farmers in Punjab. *Information Technology for Development, 21*, 668–676.
88. Keengwe, J., & Malapile, S. (2014). Factors influencing technology planning in developing countries: A literature review. *Education and Information Technologies, 19*(4), 703–712.

Part II
Asia

Chapter 6
Strengthening the Public Sector Accounting Through ICT: The Experience of a Developing Country

Md Salah Uddin Rajib, Md Qutub Uddin Sajib, and Mahfuzul Hoque

Abstract This chapter aims to investigate the performance of public sector accounting (PSA) after introducing the computer-aided mechanism in a developing country, Bangladesh. Transparency and accountability which are assumed as the accelerator for the development of a nation are urged for the PSA for a long time. For poverty alleviation, reformation of PSA in developing countries has been suggested by the donor agencies as well. Different mechanisms have emerged as a consequence for the demand of PSA reformation. As a part of reforming the PSA, Bangladesh has introduced Integrated Budget and Accounting Systems (iBAS), a computer-based network through the country. The iBAS has been introduced with the association of donor agencies. This chapter focuses on the gradual performance of some parts of the PSA (e.g., bill passing, check clearing) to investigate the effectiveness of Information and Communication Technology (ICT) in public sector accounting. The investigation, analysis, and discussion indicate that the iBAS is likely to have positive impacts on strengthening the PSA. Therefore, it is expected that the iBAS can impact favorably on efficient public expenditure. The experience of adopting the iBAS and the structure of the iBAS in Bangladesh have been introduced in the chapter as well.

Keywords Public sector accounting • ICT (Information and Communication Technology) • iBAS (Integrated Budget and Accounting Systems) • Developing country • Bangladesh

M.S.U. Rajib (✉)
Jahangirnagar University, Dhaka 1342, Bangladesh
e-mail: rajibais@juniv.edu

M.Q.U. Sajib
China University of Geosciences (CUG), Wuhan 430074, China
e-mail: qutub.swe.du@gmail.com

M. Hoque
University of Dhaka, Dhaka 1000, Bangladesh
e-mail: mhoque71@gmail.com

© Springer International Publishing AG 2017
H. Kaur et al. (eds.), *Catalyzing Development through ICT Adoption*,
DOI 10.1007/978-3-319-56523-1_6

6.1 Introduction

The concept of New Public Management (NPM) urges the reformation of public sector accounting (PSA) [1]. The concept of NPM was initiated to reform the public sector in the 1980s and 1990s [1]. The term "New Public Management" is introduced by Hood [2]. Broadly, NPM denotes the government policies that aimed to modernize and ensure the efficiency of the public sector. The concept of NPM leads the PSA of different countries to undergo the reformation process for a long time [3–5]. Developing countries are not an exception. Moreover, the surrounding environment of developing countries is under the pressure to reform the PSA. As developing countries are depended on the resources of donor agencies, institutional pressure exists to reform the PSA (e.g., [5]). It is mentioned that to alleviate the poverty, public sector accounting can play a good role through the effective allocation of resources [5–7]. The efficient PSA can ensure the transparency of public expenditure that is urging by different stakeholders. Therefore, since 1980, international organizations (like World Bank, IMF, and donor countries) are raising concern to reform PSA in the developing countries [5].

Accounting's existence and evolution are strongly based on artifacts, things created by humans in order to solve a problem in a specific environment [8, 9]. Information and Communication Technology (ICT) can shape and forms the accounting artifacts as well (see [9]). The relevance of an artifact is determined by its inner environment as well as outer environment [9]. Inner environment indicates the substance and practice of an organization, whereas outer environment means how an organization operates in its surroundings. If inner environment can match outer environment appropriately, or vice versa, the artifact will survive with objectives [10]. Therefore, practice of accounting which is tied with ICT and the demand of stakeholders claim investigation.

This chapter aims to investigate the adoption of ICT in PSA of Bangladesh: its scenario, usage, and impacts. Bangladesh, a South Asian country, is reforming the PSA since the independence in 1971. A number of reformations have been initiated and are executed in PSA of Bangladesh. Most of the reformations have been executed with the associations of donor agencies [11]. As a process of reformation, an integrated reform is ongoing in the public financial management under the banner of "Strengthening Public Expenditure Management Program (SPEM)" since 2007 which is expected to end in 2018. The SPEM is a multi-donor-funded project which is administrated by the World Bank. In the project SPEM, an ICT-based mechanism has been introduced in PSA of Bangladesh named Integrated Budget and Accounting Systems (iBAS) [11]. After the primary introduction of the iBAS in Bangladesh, its problem has been identified, and the iBAS has been modified (iBAS to iBAS++), reintroduced, and re-implemented. Currently, the Office of the Controller General of Accounts (CGA), which is in charge of PSA in Bangladesh, is using the iBAS.

It seems that investigation of ICT adoption in the PSA of Bangladesh can add value for developing countries. As ICT is now recognized as a catalyst of growth and transformation [12], and as there exist a high degree of commonality between accounting and information systems (see [13, 14]), its effectiveness and dissemination experience is worthy to explore. Researchers have agreed that the diffusion of ICT can ensure the development and better governance [15, 16].

The aim of this chapter is fourfold. After disclosing the methodology, theoretical background has been investigated first. Second, introduction, modification, and usage of the iBAS in the PSA of Bangladesh have been discussed. Third, impact of the iBAS has been investigated, and finally a constructive discussion has been drawn.

6.2 Methodology

To conduct the study, theoretical ground has been investigated on whether ICT can play role for accounting. The common ground of ICT and accounting has been focused as well. The role of ICT and PSA in the development of a country has been searched. To get knowledge on the iBAS of Bangladesh, various documents have been collected and analyzed critically. Documents have been collected from the World Bank, the Ministry of Finance (MoF) of Bangladesh, the Office of the Controller General of Accounts (CGA), the Office of the Comptroller and Auditor General (C&AG), and other organizations of Bangladesh which are involved with the PSA. To understand the impact of ICT, 16 months data (from September 2014 to December 2015) of bill passing and check clearing from the local government to the central government of Bangladesh have been analyzed. Time span of data collection have been selected considering the availability and reliability of data. Through the analysis and justification, it has been tried to understand the usage of ICT in PSA, its effectiveness, and probable contribution to the development of a developing country.

It should be noted here that a number of developed countries and developing countries have reformed the PSA. Although the scenario of developing and developed countries are a bit different (e.g., [17]), a growing number of countries are trying to adopt or promise to adopt modified PSA to ensure the transparency [4, 18–20]. Research indicates that intentions and modification path of PSA in developed and in developing countries are different [17, 21, 22]. However, it seems that the ultimate aim of reformation of PSA is to transform the PSA from budgetary or cash basis accounting to accrual basis accounting. But, it has been seen that in developing countries, resources are not adequate to transform the PSA in accrual basis directly. Therefore, gradual developments in infrastructure have been suggested by scholars (e.g., [18–20]). The adoption of the ICT can be seen as an infrastructural change rather than methodological change (cash basis vs accrual basis) of PSA. It should be noted that many countries are not thinking about the accrual basis or alternative standards of accounting to reform the PSA [23]. In this case, ICT can play a significant role to increase the efficiency of PSA regarding the transparency and accountability of accounting. From this notion, in this chapter, the usage of ICT in PSA and its impact has been investigated.

6.3   ICT and PSA: Theoretical Underpinnings

Researchers have mentioned that although accounting and information systems (IS) are different, there exists a high degree of commonality between them [13]. In mainstream research of accounting, it has been mentioned that Information and Communication Technology has impact on the transparency and efficiency of accounting [9, 24]. In previous researches, both the ICT and efficient public sector accounting (PSA) are recognized as a catalyst for the development of a nation [5, 12, 25, 26].

Accounting has been suggested to be used as a tool for promoting good governance and the public interest [27, 28]. Researchers have mentioned that instead of simple financial recording, a broader concept of integrated financial management and stewardship over the effective and efficient use of financial and other resources in all areas of government operations can ensure the accountability [29]. Public accountability is also the focal issue in modern democratic governance. The government must be accountable to public for their acts and omissions, decisions, policies, and expenditures [30]. The concept of accountability is closely related to accounting. At least two features are involved with the term public accountability. First, the term public relates to the openness. The account giving is done in public, i.e., it is open or accessible to citizen [30]. Second, public refers to the public sector. In fact, accountability is usually defined as a social relationship in which an actor feels an obligation to explain and to justify his tasks to other [31, 32]. It seems plausible to say that through the efficient PSA, government can explain and justify its expenditure to the stakeholders. Public sector accountability is urged where there are enforced consequences for ineffective or poorly executed performance, outcomes, or policies (e.g., [26], p. 142). In developing countries, ineffective performance, outcomes, and policies are visible very often [33]. Therefore, developing nations are demanded to perform efficiently from various stakeholders for a long time. It has been agreed that through the efficient PSA, it is possible to ensure the transparency and the efficient use of public expenditure. Therefore, the reformation of PSA is demanded for the development of the developing nations [5].

Like the accounting, ICT is recognized as a catalyst for development and better governance [15]. It has been mentioned in previous researches that ICT can mitigate corruption and enhance the development of a nation. Corruption is defined as an act in which the power of public office is used for personal gain by violating the rules [34]. In many researches, public sector has been recognized as a primary enabler of corruption (e.g., [33, 35]). In the public sector, corruption can drive macroeconomic instability by increasing fiscal deficit which can be created by raising public expenditure and lowering the amount of tax received [36]. Corruption has multidimensional effect on a nation, e.g., discourages investment, alters the composition of government expenditure, limits economic growth, limits mission of reducing poverty, and so on [36, 37]. Very often, corruption impacts on the poorer segment of the population in developing countries and may result in exacerbating income inequality [26]. The country analysis of different international organizations (e.g., World Bank, International Monetary Fund) indicates that corruption intensifies the income inequality and poverty [36, 38]. Researchers have mentioned that by controlling corruption, economic development and competitiveness of the country can be ensured, social condition can be improved, and poverty can be reduced [36]. It has been found that a number of factors induce corruptions in public sector including regulation that creates artificial limitation on goods or services, rigid bureaucratic traditions, lack of transparency, examples of corruption set by leaders, and others [39]. Previous researches find that the efficient usage of ICT can dismantle the enablers of corruptions [26]. ICT in the public sector has been recognized as a mechanism that increases efficiency and transparency and improves accountability in public administration procedures and management to provide better services [15, 25, 40, 41]. ICT (as a mechanism of e-Government) can achieve the thing that is demanded in the concept of NPM.

ICT can play role for PSA. ICT can work as a continuous auditing mechanism in the public sector accounting. Previous researches indicate that the concept of continuous auditing (CA) is not new in accounting and auditing area (see [42]). Positive impact of CA has been noticed by the researchers as well. It is mentioned by the researchers that CA could:

- Change the generation and dissemination of business intelligence by providing real-time reporting of financial results
- Change system assurance by providing artifacts for more efficient and effective independent audits of company financial statement
- Change the design and operation of internal controls by providing artifacts for monitoring transactions and identifying anomalies [9]

It is agreed that CA is normally adopted as a mechanism for monitoring transactions and identifying anomalies.

As both the ICT and accounting are the catalyst of development and as ICT has positive impact on accounting, therefore, it seems plausible to say that the combination of accounting and ICT in PSA can lead the development of developing nations. However, it should be reminded that both the success and failure are seen in the performance of ICT in public sector [43]. A significant number of ICT projects in public sector are ended with disappointing failure [44]. Some empirical researches show that performance of ICT in public sector depends on the intention to use and facilitating conditions of ICT [41]. It has been observed that in spite of strong stakeholders support in emerging economy, ICT projects struggled to meet their objective [45].

6.4   iBAS: Introduction, Modification, and Usage in Bangladesh

6.4.1   Introduction of the iBAS

As it has been mentioned, to ensure the transparency and to cope with the concept of NPM, the government of Bangladesh tempted to reform the PSA. Most of the reformations of PSA have been executed with the association of the donor agencies. PSA of Bangladesh is originated in the mid-1800s, the days of British-occupied India. After the independence in 1971, a number of reformations have been executed in PSA, and a number of reformation initiatives have been taken with the association of donor agencies. Strengthening Public Expenditure Management (SPEMP) is such a multi-donor trust fund program that started in 2007 and expected to end in 2018. The iBAS is introduced under the SPEMP project, and still the iBAS is under the process of development [11]. The SPEMP is funded by UK aid from Department of International Development (DfID), Danish International Development Agency (DANIDA), and European Union, and the project is administrated by the World Bank. The objectives of SPEMP are:

- Strengthen and modernize core institutions of budgeting within the government with particular emphasis on introducing a performance orientation in public financial management
- Enhance demand for better budget outcomes by improving the effectiveness of formal institutions of financial accountability, in particular Comptroller and Auditor General's Office and the financial oversight committee of the parliament

Consisting with the objective of SPEMP, the iBAS is introduced in Bangladesh regarding the public finance management, especially focusing on the infrastructural strength of PSA. The iBAS can be identified as a ICT mechanism that helps to conduct transactions within the government (G2G), between government and business (G2B), and between government and citizen (G2C).

The iBAS was developed from the earlier Transaction Accounting System (TAS). The TAS was based on old technology and was accused of unsuitable functionality and unsustainable technology. The iBAS was primarily considered as the modern replacement of TAS. Initially, iBAS was developed for simple transaction recording systems. During the development of the iBAS, authorities were aimed to add budget module in the same platform of accounting. However, because of traditional view, accounting and budgeting activities were maintained as separate activities.

Normally budget refers to numerical plan under several classifications complying with the chart of accounts. It includes allocation of budget, amendment of the budget, comparison and variance with other data (e.g., actual data or other year's data) relevant to the budget. Accounting refers to recording the transactions against the chart of accounts, managing all the budget-related expenditures, and communicating the reports to the users. Therefore, it appears that there is a linkage and ground for integration between the budget and the accounting. Integration refers to systems where data, entered once, is available to fulfill all functions of that data without the need to enter the same data again for other functions in the one, fully integrated systems [46].

In Bangladesh, the Controller General of Accounts (CGA) office is in charge of accounting wing, and the Ministry of Finance (MoF) is in charge of budgeting divisions. Historically, in Bangladesh, budget and expenditure were seen as separate activities, and the iBAS had been developed accordingly. Therefore, the primary version of Integrated Budget and Accounting Systems (iBAS) fails to integrate the task of budget and accounting. In the iBAS, transaction (accounting) was recorded first and then the decision to add or amend budget was taken. This procedure ultimately divides the budget and accounting systems. However, it should be noted that the preliminary version of iBAS introduced the usage of computer systems and established the reliance on computer that provides a ground for developing more sophisticated computer-based financial management systems and facilities across almost all government finance areas in Bangladesh [46].

6.4.2 Modification of the iBAS

Considering the limitation of the iBAS regarding the integration of budget and accounting, renovation of the software has taken place, and the renovation is continuing for further development. After the reformation, the iBAS++ has taken place of the iBAS.[1] Integration between budget and accounting has given priority in reformation. Continuous assessment, monitoring, performance evaluation, and management are the concern of the iBAS++ to ensure the integration. The flow of accounting data as well as the tasks of iBAS++ has been presented in Fig. 6.1.

Figure 6.1 shows the flow of accounting data in Bangladesh that is currently maintained by the iBAS++. The PSA operates across the country from the local government to the central government. In Bangladesh, the tasks of PSA can be divided into several administrative divisions and level which have been presented in Fig. 6.1. The office of the Controller General of Accounts (CGA) is the central and supreme organization for keeping and maintaining the accounting records for the government of Bangladesh. Figure 6.1 shows that accounting data flows from the local government to the central unit step by step. In Bangladesh, there are 420 Upazila Accounts Offices, 64 District Accounts Offices, 6 Divisional Controller of Accounts, 51 Chief Accounts Officers, 57 Ministries, and a number of Postal Offices, Forest Offices, and Public Health Offices. All these administrations are recording and keeping their accounts and transferring the information to the upper-level administration which aims to transfer the records to the CGA. All these administrations are connected through the iBAS systems.

---

[1] For the next sections of this chapter, iBAS and iBAS++ is used interchangeably.

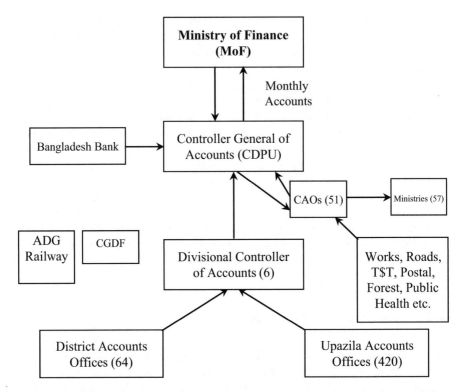

Fig. 6.1 Flow of accounting data in Bangladesh government (Source: various documents of CGA) (where *C&AG* Comptroller and Auditor General, *CGDF* Controller and General Defense Finance, *ADG* Additional Director General, *CAO* Chief Accounts Officer and *CDPU* Central Data Processing Unit)

6.4.3   Usage of the iBAS in the PSA of Bangladesh

At present all the public administration of Bangladesh except the Controller and General Defense Finance (CGDF) and the Additional Director General Railway are connected through the iBAS for accounting purposes. CGDF and the Additional Director General Railways are keeping and maintaining accounts independently. In the iBAS systems, Controller General of Accounts (CGA) is used as the Central Data Processing Unit (CDPU). As it has been mentioned, the key concept to the iBAS design is that data is stored on central database (CDPU) and all entry and reporting is possible to access via a single common user interface. At present all accounting offices under the CGA are fully automated through iBAS.

The responsibility of CGA is to produce monthly and annual accounts for establishing efficient expenditure control and budgetary management. These tasks cannot be ensured efficiently unless Chief Accounts Offices (CAOs), Divisional Controller of Accounts (DCAs), District Accounts Offices (DAOs), and Upazila

Accounts Offices (UAOs) are properly equipped to assume delegated responsibilities [47]. The iBAS is supporting to do this. The accounting data of UAOs, DAOs, DACs, and CAOs move forward to the CDPU through the iBAS.

Upazila Accounts Offices (UAOs) perform a number of accounting activities as routine task. The Upazila Accounts Offices (UAOs) actively participate in the iBAS systems. The Upazila Accounts Offices (UAOs) incorporate monthly accounts in the next following month in the central iBAS with the schedule date specified by CGA. The Upazila Accounts Offices (UAOs) use the iBAS to settle the audit observations which are reported by Chief Accounts Offices (CAOs) and Divisional Controller of Accounts (DCAs) against UAOs. Upazila Accounts Offices settle claims of development expenditure as per authority which is issued by Chief Accounts Offices (CAOs) for the centrally administrated Annual Development Programme (ADP) budget [48]. The Chief Accounts Offices (CAOs) use the iBAS systems as well to monitor the claim of UAOs regarding the ADP budget.

The iBAS helps the preauditing for all accounting administrations including the Upazila Accounts Offices (UAOs). Preaudit is an audit approach where payment vouchers are reviewed by audit staff before final payment is made. Preaudit ensures the internal control and reduces the risk. Accounting and auditing codes are easily useable through the iBAS network to perform the preauditing activities. To make accounting and reporting easy and effective, accounting codes are used. Through accounting codes, user can collect additional data for a transaction which is recorded by using systematic code. Through the efficient use of economic code (coding on the basis of different economic head) and function code (coding on the basis of accounts units), the iBAS has made the accounting data reliable, verifiable, and transparent. The preauditing process of iBAS is interchangeable with the concept of continues audit.

Like the Upazila Accounts Offices (UAOs), District Accounts Offices (DAOs) incorporate monthly accounts in the next following month in central iBAS within the date that has been specified by the Office of the Controller General of Accounts (CGA). The District Accounts Offices (DAOs) use the iBAS to reconcile the preaudit check to settle all the audit observations and claims of development expenditure as CAO imposed the authority on them for the centrally administered ADP budget [49].

Upazila Accounts Offices (UAOs) and District Accounts Offices (DAOs) submit the accounting reports to the Office of the Divisional Controller of Accounts (DCAs). DCAs incorporate monthly accounts of his/her office, monthly accounts of District Accounts Offices (DAOs), and Upazila Accounts Offices (UAOs) under him in the next following month in central iBAS within the schedule date specified by the Office of the Controller General of Accounts (CGA). Divisional Controller of Accounts (DCAs) reconcile preaudit checks of his/her offices as well as of subordinates and reconcile accounts where iBAS plays an important role [50].

In the accounting systems of Bangladesh government, Office of the Chief Accounts Officer (CAO) plays an important role. The Chief Accounts Officer (CAO) acts as the Staff Officer to the Principal Accounting Officer (PAO)/Secretary of Ministry or Division regarding the Accounts and Financial rules [47]. The Chief Accounts Officer (CAO) incorporates monthly account in the next following month in the central iBAS within the schedule date specified by the Office of the Controller

General of Accounts (CGA). The Chief Accounts Officer (CAO) performs some focal activities for Bangladesh government where iBAS plays an important role. For example, the Chief Accounts Officer (CAO) draws management report from iBAS, and the Chief Accounts Officer (CAO) discusses it with the Principal Accounting Officer (PAO). The Chief Accounts Officer (CAO) monitors the trend of collection of revenue and expenditure by iBAS systems, and the Chief Accounts Officer (CAO) advises the Principal Accounting Officer (PAO) on financial discipline. On the basis of information obtained from iBAS, the Chief Accounts Officer (CAO) assists the Principal Accounting Officer (PAO) in preparation of budget estimate and advice on expenditure control. The Chief Accounts Officer (CAO) performs a number of activities like ensuring correctness of balance of the public account; ensuring correctness of accounts of the concerned ministry/division incorporated by Divisional Controller of Accounts (DCA), District Accounts Offices (DAOs), and Upazila Accounts Offices (UAOs); and settling claims of development expenditure and issues authority to DCA, DAO, and UAO for centrally administrated annual development program (ADP) budget [51]. For all these activities, the Chief Accounts Officers (CAOs) take help from the iBAS. The iBAS systems have speeded up the activities of Chief Accounts Officer (CAO) and other administrations through its functions.

As it has been mentioned, the Office of the Controller General of Accounts (CGA) works as the central processing unit of government accounting. It prepares monthly accounts of the government where it uses the data that has been provided by the Chief Accounts Officers (CAOs), Divisional Controller of Accounts (DCAs), District Accounts Offices (DAOs), and Upazila Accounts Offices (UAOs). Through the web page of the Office of the Controller General of Accounts (CGA), it continuously discloses the information of different accounts to the citizen as well. To do these, CGA takes help from the iBAS [47].

The iBAS ensures consistent flow of accounting data to the Central Data Processing Unit (CDPU) at the Controller General of Accounts (CGA). The iBAS with Wide Area Network (WAN) arrangement among Upazila Accounts Offices (UAOs), District Accounts Offices (DAOs), Divisional Controller of Accounts (DCAs), the Chief Accounts Officers (CAOs), and the Central Data Processing Unit (CDPU) is allowing availability of nationwide individual transaction/voucher information and expenditure per budget line to date. At the same time, CGA is disclosing the information publicly through the website of CGA where CGA is taking help from the iBAS continuously. Therefore, it can be mentioned that the iBAS is helping to ensure the accountability of public expenditure.

6.5   Impact of the iBAS: Evidence from Recorded Data

In the previous section of this chapter, it has been seen that the iBAS helps all the accounting administrations of government to keep accounts, and it prompts interaction among them. The iBAS helps to monitor the activities and control the expenditure as well. At the same time, iBAS helps CGA to publish data of accounting publicly.

To assess the effectiveness of the iBAS on the efficiency of public accounting administrations, we collected 16 months data on bill passing and check clearing from the CGA's information technology (IT) team. The IT team of the Office of the Controller General of Accounts (CGA) collected this data randomly from the Chief Accounts Officers (CAOs), Divisional Controller of Accounts (DCAs), and District Accounts Offices (DAOs) to monitor the daily accounting activities and to increase the efficiency of using computer systems. The IT team of the CGA disclosed data from September 2014, and the data is available up to December 2015.

These data have been disclosed publicly. The performance of bill passing and check clearing has been measured by four scales, namely, Excellent, Very Good, Good, and Phone Call. If the bill passing and check clearing are executed within or less than 3 days, it is marked as *Excellent*. If the bill passing and check clearing are executed between 4 and within or less than 5 days, it is marked as *Very Good*. If the bill passing and check clearing are executed between 6 and within or less than 7 days, it is marked as *Good*. If bill passing and check clearing take more than 7 days, it will follow up by the phone call and is marked as *Phone Call*. The activities of bill passing and check clearing are monitored by the iBAS daily, and it marks the performance automatically.

By analyzing the data, we have tried to understand the trends of performance. The trends have been presented in Fig. 6.2. It shows that over the period, performance of bill passing and check clearing is improving. The number of follow up by *Phone Call* is decreasing. Over the period, performance marked as *Excellent* is increasing.

To understand the situation more clearly, we have analyzed the number of maximum days, minimum days, and average days required for bill passing and check clearing over 16 months period. Figure 6.3 shows that over the period, required maximum days and average days for bill passing and check clearing are decreasing.

From Figs. 6.2 and 6.3, it seems plausible to say that the continuous monitoring, feedback, and corrective actions through the iBAS have improved the situation of bill passing and check clearing. As bill passing and check clearing are the tasks of accounting, it also indicates the gradual improvement of the efficiency of PSA of Bangladesh.

6.6   Discussion

The accounting value chain is complex, and it involves a number of practical issues [9]. Therefore, success of the iBAS has to be monitored for a long time to draw conclusions as well as to make it more compatible for the environment of Bangladesh.

From the discussion of the functions of different accounting administrations (UAOs, DAOs, DCAs, CAOs), it appears that iBAS helps to speed up the activities and helps continuous monitoring. In fact, the positive impact of the iBAS on PSA is expected naturally as previous studies show evidence of positive impact of

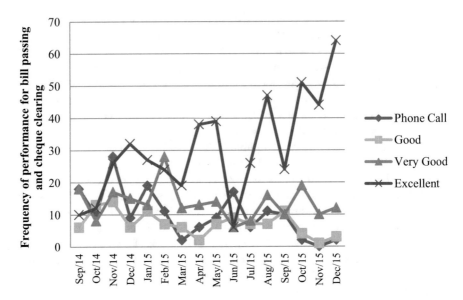

Fig. 6.2 Trends of bill passing and check clearing performance (Source: developed from the data collected from the CGA)

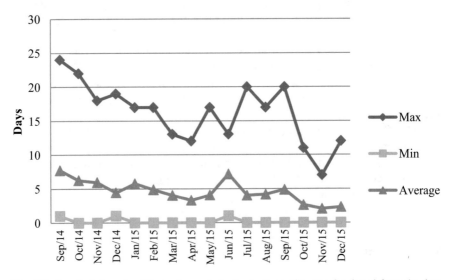

Fig. 6.3 Required days for bill passing and check clearance (Source: developed from the data collected from the CGA)

ICT. Impact of ICT in public sector entities has been investigated by many researches (e.g., [43, 52]). To improve the managerial process in the public sector, the use of ICT has been recommended in many research works [53]. In case of Bangladesh, it seems that both the iBAS and the managerial efficiency of accounting have improved over the time.

The things that the iBAS is providing for the PSA can be justified with the concept of continuous auditing (CA). The iBAS is actually doing the tasks (e.g., preauditing) that are expected from the CA of accounting systems. As it has been mentioned, by reducing interactions with officials, speeding up decisions, reducing human error, and enabling record keeping functions, e-Governance (through ICT) can reduce corruption (see [27]), and it is expected that iBAS will do the same thing for Bangladesh. Not only the internal efficiency but also the public accessibility is ensured through the iBAS which ultimately may enhance the accountability.

Researchers have mentioned that ICT (as a mechanism of e-Governance) expand citizen's access to public information, increase transparency and public accountability, and weaken authoritarian tendencies [26, 54]. Empirical researches indicate that e-Government through ICT can mitigate corruption and can enhance the positive relationship between the citizen and government [55]. iBAS provides public access to information that ultimately supports the accountability. The CGA in Bangladesh is providing information on PSA on the website through the iBAS. Therefore, it seems plausible to say that the iBAS is helping to enrich the accountability in the PSA of Bangladesh.

The overall discussion on the iBAS states that it is helping both for the efficient managerial process and for public accountability regarding the PSA. As it has been found in previous literature, efficient managerial process in public administration and accountability can ensure transparency and work as accelerator for development; it is expected that the iBAS will play the same role for Bangladesh. ICT can play an important role to develop the economy-related factors in the developing nations [26]. The iBAS as a mechanism of ICT is expected to perform similarly The iBAS has helped the Government of Bangladesh (GoB) and the Ministry of Finance (MoF) to make considerable step to move forward to the use of computers and network-based financial systems. It can improve the speed of reporting, can strengthen the control, and can improve the overall performance of public financial management as well as the public sector accounting.

However, it should be noted that ICT does not guarantee the success or development. It is agreed that information technology itself cannot ensure transparency and accountability (e.g., [56]). This statement also is true for the iBAS. ICT projects (as a mechanism of e-Government) are not always the outcome of planned and controlled change management activities [25]. E-Government or ICT projects often emerge from a set of complex relationship which exist between e-Government policies, technological choice and design, and political and institutional environments [25, 57]. The introduction of the iBAS in Bangladesh can be explained from the above statement. There are continuous pressures on Bangladesh from different donor agencies to reform the PSA. Donor agency pressures along with other factors (e.g., technological choice and design and government policies) together have introduced the iBAS in Bangladesh [11]. Therefore, for sustainable success of the iBAS, surrounding environment has to be monitored carefully. Numerous spectacular failures of ICT are seen in the public sector [58–60]. A number of factors have been suggested to consider for the success, namely, needs of users, process, and systems of ICT, levels of uses, lack of choices or forced choice, trust, readiness to usage IT, cost versus quality, and coordination of success. Attention on the citizen engagement has been advised in the public administration as well [61]. Researchers have noticed the interrelationship among ICT, functions of ICT, transparency, accountability, and development in the literature on ICT and development (e.g., [26, 56]). Efficiency of information technology depends also on the planning and design. To reduce the corruption through ICT, concern of transparency and accountability should be integrated into the public service, providing systems from the planning to design phase (e.g., [62]). Reliable and accurate record keeping is identified by researchers as the foundation of transparency (e.g., [26]). Moreover, bureaucratic corruption has to be monitored and controlled carefully. In developing nations, bureaucratic corruption induces from lack of formal rules and regulations, lack of transparency, and other informalities of process [33]. To make the iBAS fruitful for the economic development, all these factors have to be considered.

6.7   Conclusions

The chapter introduces the usage of Information and Communication Technology (ICT) in the PSA of a developing country. It should be noted that the iBAS has improved the structural strength of public sector accounting rather than methods (cash basis vs accrual basis). The introduction and development of the iBAS has improved both the managerial process of PSA and public accountability. It has speeded up the accounting activities among the different public accounting administrations and levels. At the same time, by helping CGA to disclose information publicly, the systems have strengthened the attempt of ensuring public accountability. By helping to conduct interactions within the government (G2G), between government and business (G2B), and between the government and citizen (G2C) simultaneously, the iBAS is serving the multi-facets. Through disclosing the information publicly and ensuring the effective interactions among stockholders, the iBAS is expected to contribute to the efficient public expenditure. And it is agreed that efficient public expenditure can alleviate the poverty. The developing countries, which are suffering from lack of resources to implement accrual basis accounting, can use ICT like the iBAS to enhance the strength of PSA.

For the sake of development and alleviation of poverty, future research can drive to theory building or find better artifacts to bring PSA and ICT together, or it can work on the interconnection between the disciplines.

References

1. Lapsley, I. (1999). Accounting and the new public management: Instruments of substantive efficiency or a rationalising modernity. *Financial Accountability and Management, 15*(3&4), 201–207.
2. Hood, C. (1991). A public management for all seasons. *Public Administration, 69*(Spring), 3–19.
3. Carpenter, V. L., & Feroz, E. H. (2001). Institutional theory and accounting rule choice: An analysis of four US state governments' decisions to adopt generally accepted accounting principles. *Accounting, Organizations and Society, 26*(7/8), 565–596.
4. Harun, H., Van Peursem, K., & Eggleton, I. (2012). Institutionalization of accrual accounting in the Indonesian public sector. *Journal of Accounting and Organizational Change, 8*(3), 257–285.
5. Adhikari, P., Kuruppu, C., & Matilal, S. (2013). Dissemination and institutionalization of public sector accounting reforms in less developed countries: A comparative study of the Nepalese and Sri Lankan central governments. *Accounting Forum, 37*(3), 213–230.
6. Goddard, A. (2010). Contemporary public sector accounting research – An international comparison of journal papers. *The British Accounting Review, 42*, 75–87.
7. Rahaman, A. S. (2010). Critical accounting research in Africa: Whence and whither. *Critical Perspectives on Accounting, 21*(5), 420–427.
8. Hevner, A. R., March, S. T., Park, S. T. J., & Ram, S. (2004). Design science in information systems research. *MIS Quarterly, 28*(1), 75–105.
9. Geerts, G. L., Graham, L. E., Mauldin, E. G., McCarthy, & Richardson, V. J. (2013). Integrating information technology into accounting research and practice. *Accounting Horizons, 27*(4), 815–8840.
10. Simon, H. A. (1996). *The sciences of the artificial* (3rd ed.). Cambridge: MIT Press.
11. Hoque, M., Rajib, M. S. U., & Akter, M. (2016). Development of public sector accounting: Reformation and challenges in Bangladesh. Australia – Bangladesh Research Symposium, Monash Business School, Monash University, Australia.
12. Walsham, G., Robey, D., & Sahay, S. (2007). Forward: Special issue on information systems in developing countries. *MIS Quarterly, 31*(2), 317–326.
13. Hunton, J. E. (2002). Blending information and communication technology with accounting research. *Accounting Horizon, 16*(1), 55–67.
14. Mancini, D., Dameri, R. P., & Bonollo, E. (2016). Looking for synergies between accounting and information technologies. In D. Mancini, R. P. Dameri, & E. Bonollo (Eds.), *Strengthening information and control systems* (pp. 1–12). Switzerland: Springer International Publishing.
15. Heeks, R. (2002). Information systems and developing countries: Failure, success, and local improvisations. *The Information Society, 18*, 101–112.
16. Lechman, E. (2015). *ICT diffusion in developing countries: Towards a new concept of technological takeoff.* Switzerland: Springer International Publishing.
17. Ouda, H. A. G. (2014). Transition requirements of accrual accounting in central government of developed and developing countries: Statistical analysis – with special focus on the Netherlands and Egypt. *International Journal of Accounting and Finance, 4*(3), 261–304.
18. Simpson, Samuel Nana Yaw. (2012). Developments in public sector accounting practices: The Ghanaian experience. In Venancio Tauringana, & Musa Mangena, (Eds.), *Accounting in Africa (research in accounting in emerging economies, volume 12 Part A)* (pp. 209–226). Emerald Group Publishing Limited, UK.
19. Adhikari, P., Kuruppu, C., Wynne, A., & Ambalangodage, D. (2015). Diffusion of the cash Basis International Public Sector Accounting Standard (IPSAS) in Less Developed Countries (LDCs)–the case of the Nepali central government. *The Public Sector Accounting, Accountability and Auditing in Emerging Economies, 15*, 85–108.
20. Yapa, P. W. S., & Ukwatte, S. (2015). The New Public Financial Management (NPFM) and accrual accounting in Sri Lanka. In Kelum Jayasinghe, Nirmala D. Nath, & Radiah Othman,

(Eds.), *The public sector accounting, accountability and auditing in emerging economies (research in accounting in emerging economies, Volume 15)* (pp. 7–50). Emerald Group Publishing Limited, UK.

21. Adhikari, P., Timoshenko, K., & Garseth-Nesbakk, L. (2012). Reforming central government accounting in diverse contexts: A three-country comparison. *International Journal of Public Sector Performance Management, 2*(1), 44–60.

22. Rajib, M. S. U., & Hoque, M. (2016). A literature review on public sector accounting research. *The Jahangirnagar Journal of Business Studies, 5*(1), 39–52.

23. Christiaens, J., Vanhee, C., Manes-Rossi, F., Aversano, N., & Cauwenberge, P. V. (2015). The effect of IPSAS on reforming governmental financial reporting: An international comparison. *International Review of Administrative Sciences, 81*(1), 158–177.

24. James, E. H. (2002). Blending information and communication technology with accounting research. *Accounting Horizons, 16*(1), 55–67.

25. Cordella, A., & Ianncci, F. (2010). Information systems in the public sector: The e-government enactment framework. *Journal of Strategic Information Systems, 19*, 52–66.

26. Mistry, J. J. (2012). The role of eGovernance in mitigating corruption. *Accounting and the Public Interest, 12*, 137–159.

27. Hopper, T., Tsamenyi, M., Uddin, S., & Wickramasinghe, D. (2009). Management accounting in less developed countries: What is known and needs knowing. *Accounting, Auditing & Accountability Journal, 22*(3), 469–514.

28. Neu, D. (2006). Accounting for public space. *Accounting, Organizations and Society, 31*, 391–414.

29. Iyoha, F. O., & Oyerinde, D. (2010). Accounting infrastructure and accountability in the management of public expenditure in developing countries: A focus on Nigeria. *Critical Perspectives on Accounting, 21*(5), 361–373.

30. Bovens, M., Goodin, R. E., & Schillemans, T. (2014). *The Oxford handbook of public accountability. Oxford handbooks* (1st ed.). UK: Oxford University Press.

31. Romzek, B. S., & Dubnick, M. J. (1998). Accountability. In J. Shafritz, D. Krane, & S. W. Deil (Eds.), *International encyclopedia of public policy and administration*. Boulder: Westview Press.

32. Pollitt, C. (2003). *The essential public manager*. London: McGraw-Hill.

33. Mimba, N. S. H., Helden, G. J. V., & Tillema, S. (2007). Public sector performance measurement in developing countries: A literature review and research agenda. *Journal of Accounting and Organizational Change, 3*(3), 192–208.

34. Jain, A. K. (2001). Corruption: A review. *Journal of Economic Surveys, 15*, 72–121.

35. Kaufmann, D., Kraay, A., & Zoido-Lobaton, P. (2000). *Governance matters: From measurement to action, finance and development, 37 (2)*. Washington, DC: International Monetary Fund.

36. Bhargava, V. K., & Bolongaita, E. P. (2004). *Challenging corruption in Asia: Case studies and a framework for action*. Washington, DC: World Bank Publications.

37. Sevensson, J. (2005). Eight question about corruption. *Journal of Economic Perspectives, 13*(9), 19–42.

38. Gupta, S., Davoodi, H., & Alonso-Terme, R. (2002). Does corruption affect income inequality and poverty? *Economics of Governance, 3*(1), 23–45.

39. Tanzi, V. (1998). Corruption around the world: Causes, consequences, scope, and cures. *Staff Papers, 45*(4), 559–594.

40. Dunleavy, P., Margetts, H., Bastow, S., & Tinkler, J. (2006). New public management is dead – long live digital-era governance. *Journal of Public Administration Research and Theory, 16*(3), 467–494.

41. Gupta, B., Dasgupta, S., & Gupta, A. (2008). Adoption of ICT in a government organization in a developing country: An empirical study. *Journal of Strategic Information Systems, 17*, 140–154.

42. Pathak, J., Nkurunziza, S., & Ahmed, S. E. (2007). General theory of cost minimization strategies of continuous audit of databases. *Journal of Accounting and Public Policy, 26*(5), 621–633.
43. Sandeep, M. S., & Ravishankar, M. N. (2014). The continuity of underperforming ICT projects in the public sector. *Information Management, 51*, 700–711.
44. Heeks, R. (2006). *Implementing and managing eGovernment – an international text*. London: Sage Publication.
45. Chaudhuri, A. (2012). ICT for development: Solutions seeking problems? *Journal of Information Technology, 27*(4), 326–338.
46. Pollock, B. (2010). *Bangladesh – Review of iBAS integrated budget and accounting system moving toward 2nd phase of iBAS (iBAS+)*. Washington, DC: World Bank. http://documents. worldbank.org/curated/en/2010/04/16424352/bangladesh-review-ibas-integrated-budget-accounting-system-moving-toward-2nd-phase-ibas-ibas.
47. Office of the Controller General of Accounts (CGA). (n.d.). *Objective and activities*. http://www.cga.gov.bd/index.php?option=com_content&task=view&id=382&Itemid=423. Accessed 3 Feb 2016.
48. Office of the Upazilla Accounts Officer (UAO). (n.d.). *Charter of duties*. http://www.cga.gov. bd/pdf/charter_duties/uao_duties.pdf. Accessed 4 Mar 2016.
49. Office of the District Accounts Officer (DAO). (n.d.). *Charter of duties*. http://www.cga.gov. bd/pdf/charter_duties/dao_duties.pdf. Accessed 7 Mar 2016.
50. Office of the Divisional Controller of Accounts (DCA). (n.d.). *Charter of duties*. http://www. cga.gov.bd/pdf/charter_duties/dca_duties.pdf. Accessed 8 Mar 2016.
51. Office of the Chief Accounts Officer (CAO). (n.d.). *Charter of duties*. http://www.cga.gov.bd/ pdf/charter_duties/cao_duties.pdf. Accessed 9 Mar 2016.
52. Cordella, A., & Bonina, C. M. (2012). A public value perspective for ICT enabled public sector reforms: A theoretical reflection. *Government Information Quarterly, 29*(4), 512–520.
53. Kudo, H. (2010). E-governance as a strategy of public sector reform: Peculiarity of Japanese IT policy and its institutional origin. *Financial Accountability and Management, 26*(1), 65–84.
54. Haque, M. S. (2002). E-governance in India: Its impacts on relations among citizens, politicians and public servants. *International Review of Administrative Sciences, 68*(2), 231–250.
55. Pathak, R. D., Singh, G., Belwal, R., & Smith, R. F. I. (2007). E-governance and corruption-developments and issues in Ethiopia. *Public Organization Review, 7*(3), 195–208.
56. Barata, K., & Cain, P. (2001). Information, not technology, is essential to accountability: Electronic records and public sector financial management. *The Information Society, 17*(4), 247–258.
57. Ylldiz, M. (2007). E-government research: Reviewing the literature, limitations, and ways forward. *Government Information Quarterly, 24*, 646–665.
58. Hackney, R. A., & McBride, N. K. (1995). The efficacy of information systems in the public sector: Issues of context and culture. *International Journal of Public Sector Management, 8*(6), 17–29.
59. Heeks, R., & Bhatnagar, S. (1999). Understanding success and failure in information age reform. In R. Heeks (Ed.), *Reinventing government in the information age: IT enabled public sector reform* (pp. 49–74). London: Routledge.
60. Hazlett, S. A., & Hill, F. (2003). E-government: The realities of using IT to transform the public sector. *Managing Service Quality: An International Journal, 13*(6), 445–452.
61. Dawes, S. S. (2008, December). The evolution and continuing challenges of E-governance. *Public Administration Review, 12*, 586–600.
62. Singh, G., Pathak, R. D., Naz, R., & Belwal, R. (2010). E-governance for improved public sector service delivery in India, Ethiopia and Fiji. *International Journal of Public Sector Management, 23*(3), 254–275.

Chapter 7
Potentials and Challenges of Using ICT for Climate Change Adaptation: A Study of Vulnerable Community in Riverine Islands of Bangladesh

Nuzhat Imam, Md Khalid Hossain, and Toma Rani Saha

Abstract Bangladesh is highly vulnerable to different impacts of climate change. It is argued that ICTs play a vital role in addressing the major challenges related to climate change. ICTs are widely used for communicating the information required for climate change adaptation through raising awareness at the grassroots level, providing access to relevant information, and facilitating learning and sharing of practical knowledge at the community level. Despite its usage, the existing and potential role of ICTs in climate change adaptation in Bangladesh is not notably evident in the literature. The literature hardly presents the potentials and challenges from an empirical perspective where vulnerable community offers the related perspective. Consequently, the paper explores potential uses of ICTs as adaptation tools and the associated challenges, with particular focus on agricultural adaptation and disaster risk reduction from community perspective. The research has been carried out among the climate vulnerable riverine island (*char* land) communities living in four villages of Sirajganj District in Bangladesh. The study reveals how people are getting the benefits of ICTs in adapting to climate change impacts. The study suggests that there are huge untapped potentials of using ICTs in climate change adaptation and proposes an improved governance framework.

N. Imam
Institute of Development Studies (IDS), University of Sussex, Brighton
BN1 9PU, United Kingdom
e-mail: nuzhat.bangladesh@gmail.com

M.K. Hossain (✉)
Oxfam in Bangladesh, Level-8 (Southern Side), RAOWA Complex,
VIP Road, Mohakhali, Dhaka 1206, Bangladesh
e-mail: khalid.shiblee@gmail.com

T.R. Saha
Oxfam in Bangladesh, Level-8 (Southern Side), RAOWA Complex,
VIP Road, Mohakhali, Dhaka 1216, Bangladesh
e-mail: tomasaha.ju@gmail.com

© Springer International Publishing AG 2017
H. Kaur et al. (eds.), *Catalyzing Development through ICT Adoption*,
DOI 10.1007/978-3-319-56523-1_7

Keywords ICT • Mobile phone • Climate change adaptation • Riverine island
• Bangladesh

7.1 Introduction

Due to her geographical location, high density of population, and poverty, Bangladesh is highly vulnerable to natural disasters. Tropical cyclones, floods, and droughts are the main meteorological disasters which affect the environment, ecology, livelihood, and socioeconomic development of the country. Currently, the frequency of disasters associated with all types of major natural hazards is increasing, and disasters associated with hydrometeorological hazards (cyclones, droughts, and floods) are increasing in frequency and at a faster rate than disasters associated with geophysical hazards [29]. According to the recent records, climate change such as the increase of temperature, increase of rainfall and its variability, and sea level rise have caused higher impacts on the environmental and social system. Consequently, Bangladesh is exploring different options to adapt to the changing climate and information and communication technology (ICT) is considered as one of the options.

As already evident, information and communication technology (ICT) plays a vital role for socioeconomic development and addressing the major challenges related to climate change as well as sustainable development. ICTs are widely used for communicating the information required for climate change adaptation through raising awareness at the grassroots level, providing access to relevant information, and facilitating learning and sharing of practical knowledge at the community level [24]. In Bangladesh, ICTs are also used for strengthening the adaptive capacity at local, regional, as well as national level. With increasing availability of ICTs even in rural areas of the country, an exceptional opportunity has been developed to improve the creation, management, exchange, and application of relevant climate change information and knowledge.

Despite its usage, the existing and potential role of ICTs in climate change adaptation in Bangladesh is not very evident in the literature. Majority of the studies on application of ICT tools are focused on the governance aspect of the digitalization of mainly public services [26, 32, 63]. It has been found that so far, climate change governance literature highlights the role of ICTs in climate change adaptation mainly from a conceptual perspective. The literature hardly presents the potentials and challenges in this regard from an empirical perspective where vulnerable community offers the related perspective. Consequently, this chapter explores potential uses of ICTs as adaptation tools and the associated challenges, with particular focus on agricultural adaptation and disaster risk reduction (DRR) from community perspective by carrying out a research among the climate vulnerable riverine island (*char* land) communities living in four villages of Rajapur and Chowhali Upazila of Sirajganj District in Bangladesh.

7.2 Climate Change in Bangladesh

7.2.1 Climate Change Impacts

Bangladesh is highly vulnerable to climate change because of its geographical location, physiographic condition, high density of population, poverty, and dependence on climate-sensitive livelihood sectors [3, 4]. Various natural disasters such as floods, droughts, tropical cyclones, storm surges, and coastal erosion are yearly phenomena of the country causing heavy loss of life and property [10]. The frequency and severity of these natural disasters are increasing and causing higher impacts on the environmental and social system. The Met Office Hadley Centre [40] provided a prediction of future climate conditions of Bangladesh by using the climate model projections from the fourth Assessment Report of the Intergovernmental Panel on Climate Change (IPCC). The report reveals that by 2100, temperature would increase 3–3.5 °C and rainfall would increase by 5–10% over Bangladesh.

In Bangladesh, the frequency of monsoon flood is increasing, and it is predicted that extreme floods like those in 1988 and 1998 would occur more often and environmental damage would be more as a result of climate change [5, 41]. Moreover, it is likely that in future the tropical cyclones will become stronger due to climate change. In South Asia, the tropical cyclones can be 10–20% more powerful if sea surface temperatures rise by 2–4 °C [20]. On the other hand, in recent years, the frequency and severity of droughts has increased in Bangladesh under climate change scenario [55]. A study by Selvaraju et al. [53] revealed that from 1800 to 1900, the numbers of droughts were only five, whereas from 1981 to 2005, four major droughts occurred in Bangladesh. It is also expected that larger area would be affected during droughts and the severity would also increase due to global climate change [34, 55].

Food security in Bangladesh is highly vulnerable to climate change and particularly to the impact of amplified flooding that might be caused by climate change [23, 42]. Besides, high temperature has negative effect on crop production. Studies found that due to temperature rise at higher level, production of *Aman* (rain-fed) rice would be negatively affected [38], and the prospect of growing potato and wheat would be severely affected [35]. Moreover, sea level rise of 1 m combined with a 10% intensification of the present 1-in-100-year storm surge could affect around 23% of Bangladesh's total coastal land area [40]. In addition, higher temperatures along with potential increases in precipitation will create condition for spread of many infectious diseases [54]. Feldacker [25] observed that in Bangladesh, increase of cholera is associated with the increase in sea surface temperature (SST). Increased temperatures in the water bodies could also have negative impact on fisheries [11]. Furthermore, forest ecosystem and biodiversity would be at higher risk due to climate change, such as increased moisture stress in the *Barind* (dryland) and *Madhupur* (large upland area in north central part) Tracts, prolonged flood situations in flood-prone areas, and cyclone and storm surges in coastal area [7].

7.2.2 Climate Change Adaptation

The people at the local level of Bangladesh are adapting themselves through a series of adaptation options for many years [9, 12, 56]. The country has taken several national adaptation strategies at local level. In 2005, Ministry of Environment and Forests (MoEF) prepared Bangladesh National Adaptation Programme of Action (NAPA) to identify priority adaptation projects based on existing coping mechanism [44]. In 2009, MoEF developed the Bangladesh climate change strategy and action plan (BCCSAP) which identified six program areas for climate change adaptation and disaster preparedness [43]. Besides, some components of climate change adaptation are addressed by various sector specific policies [4, 50, 62]. Moreover, the Government of Bangladesh also formed Bangladesh Climate Change Trust Fund (BCCTF) to provide financial resources to advance climate change-related activities. In addition to government, NGOs, CSOs, CBOs, and many voluntary organization and associations have also been engaged in climate change adaptation. Furthermore, a few of the leading research organizations and think tanks in the country such as BCAS, IUCN, BIDS, CNRS, etc. are implementing several climate change adaptation (CCA)- and disaster risk reduction (DRR)-related program, researches, and other activities [58].

To adapt with climate change impact and to reduce the loss and damage, different practices are being carried out in the agriculture sector of coastal areas, such as, floating garden, integrated farming, saline-tolerant crop cultivation, embankment cropping, plant bed raising, dyke cropping at the shrimp farming area, etc. [2, 52, 56]. Moreover, while salinity intrusion is a serious problem for agriculture in coastal areas, Bangladesh Rice Research Institute (BRRI) and Bangladesh Institute of Nuclear Agriculture (BINA) have developed saline-tolerant rice varieties [18], and farmers have started using these varieties [19, 21, 59]. Besides, various non-rice crops such as maize, oil seeds, bean, etc. are also getting popularity in Patuakhali and Satkhira districts to cope with high salinity problem [19, 49].

The people are also taking different adaptation measures to cope with flood and cyclone. Among these practices, flood and cyclone shelters, coastal and flood embankments in the flood-affected and coastal areas, raising of plinth to protect homesteads from the risks of climatic disasters, and tree plantations around homesteads in the flood plains and drought-prone areas are the major effective structural adaptation options in Bangladesh [9, 52]. In the drought-prone areas, people are practicing different traditional approaches for water retention such as excavation of ponds and rainwater preservation in *khari* or canals. They are also practicing alternative livestock and poultry/birds rearing, deep water tube-well facilitated irrigation, etc. [6]. The farmers of drought-prone areas have adopted tillage methods, crop diversification, and various agronomic practices to get maximum yield using available water [30, 39]. Besides, the Union Disaster Management Committee (UDMC), the community members, and the Bangladesh Meteorological Department (BMD) are playing an important role to disseminate early warnings to the people and to identify potential interventions for a successful response and recovery.

7.3 ICT for Climate Change Adaptation

7.3.1 Global Perspective

ICTs play a very crucial role to lessen the various impact of climate change particularly in adaptation and mitigation through exchanging and transferring knowledge and information. People of many developed and developing countries are using ICT services in agriculture, health, early warning, and disaster risk reduction sectors. As for example, India has developed Internet portal to provide online agro-met advice and to provide related information to the farmers. Studies suggest that farmers can increase production by 10% if they have access to good agro-met advisories [14]. Besides, in India, community access to locally relevant knowledge are facilitating through an integrated knowledge-based traditional and new web media, Web 2.0, internet, and mobile phones, helping locals to better adapt within a context of high vulnerability to extreme weather events and food insecurity [32]. In order to adapt to the impact of climate change in agricultural sector, India has already introduced some modern technologies, such as in Haryana, people are using laser-assisted precision land leveling as well as "GreenSeeker" and "leaf color chart" for ensuring best nutrient management. Such site-specific nutrient management technologies are also practiced in Africa and Mexico [22].

Most of the African Countries have identified many new applications of ICTs to adapt to the impact of climate change. In Uganda, Community Knowledge Workers (CKWs) network has been developed which acts as the center for disseminating information to community farmers. On the other hand, Malawi has introduced a community-based Participatory Geographic Information Systems (PGIS) Program to build a centrally located model which can be used to determine current and future water needs [22]. In Burkina Faso, the community radio has become a necessary media service to the community to increase the awareness about the local effects of climate change [36]. In Zimbabwe, ICT services are widely used for early warning systems, urban and rural planning, health services, and education [64]. In Madagascar, participatory videos and digital storytelling are being used to stimulate community debates over climate change issues and raise their concerns to decision-makers and broader audiences [32]. Similarly, Uganda has developed a Rural Communications Development Fund (RCDF) for communicating climate change adaptation-related information [8].

Besides, some countries are developing new technologies to transmit the latest climatic information at the community level. For example, the Philippines has installed about 1,000 automatic weather stations (AWS) to provide short-range forecast and accurate real-time weather information [60]. Kenya and Zambia are using ICT services for early warning in different ways, providing weather-related press releases and transferring information through interaction with media personnel as well as public service announcements through radio and TV channels, Internet and Mobile Apps, and SMS and messaging [57, 60].

7.3.2 Bangladesh Perspective

According to the study of BBS [16], in Bangladesh, 79% of individuals aged 5 years and above are using Internet. In Bangladesh, at the beginning of 2014, the mobile subscriber penetration reached to 40%, and it is expected to grow to 50% by 2020 [28]. The national ICT Policy 2009 provided emphasis on climate change adaptation and disaster management through early warning and geographic information system (GIS) and remote sensing services. For utilizing these services of ICTs, there are a growing number of initiatives for using ICTs for climate change adaptation (CCA) and disaster risk reduction (DRR) both in government and nongovernment sector in Bangladesh [27]. The Government of Bangladesh initiated a range of information and communication technologies for development (ICT4D) projects for rural and remote communities to provide agriculture- and climate-related information [14, 37]. As a part of this, the government established some Union Information and Service Centre (UISC) to ensure the access of rural underprivileged communities to ICT [33]. People living in remote areas are able to access the internet through the union and community centers, and they are getting internet services including videoconferencing and e-commerce services as well as communication hub during disaster and early warnings [26]. Along with the government, some private organizations, mobile phone companies, and NGOs have also started different ICT4D projects all over the country. BRAC, a leading NGO, introduced an ICT4D project, recognized as "*Gonokendra Pathagar*" (People's Central Library) in the rural areas of the country [13].

In Bangladesh, ICTs are used for climate change adaptation in the agriculture sector. Some local NGOs are providing ICT supports for agriculture. A local NGO, Shushilan, has provided ICT-based plant clinics called "plant doctors" in Satkhira. This technology integrated some ICT tools such as mobile phone, GIS and google earth, digital camera, and multimedia as well as suggestions from agricultural experts for ensuring climate resilient agricultural practices [31]. In Khulna, people are using agricultural knowledge management system (AKMS) for getting information about climate-resistant seeds and crops, irrigation, and land preservation [17]. Heeks and Ospina [32] stated that in the southwest region of Bangladesh, people are using ICTs for agricultural adaptation, and they are getting information about saline-tolerant cropping varieties, ecobalanced organic and hydroponic farming, fish cultivation in flooded water bodies, and other climate change adaptation strategies. ComDev is another service in the northwestern drought-prone areas and in the high saline coastal areas to improve the adaptive capacity and to ensure sustainable livelihoods in the agriculture sector of these areas [26]. Beside these, in Bangladesh, GIS and remote sensing technologies are used for developing casualty maps for determining the vulnerability of an area, risk mapping, and storm surge modeling, cyclone forecasting damage assessment, mapping of afforested and deforested areas, and mapping of water resources [48, 51, 63].

7.4   Research Context

The potential of information and communication technology (ICT) in reducing energy use, cutting GHG emissions and supporting adaptation efforts, and helping to build the resilience of communities have been gradually getting momentum in global climate change discourse over the last few years. In November 2013, in Warsaw, Poland the UN Climate Change secretariat launched a new partnership with the Global e-Sustainability Initiative (GeSI) to give emphasis to the important role ICT plays in addressing climate change [61]. Exploring the potentiality of the critical role that ICT can play in putting the world on a low-carbon path and how it can help responding to adaptation challenges has been given importance by the highest level of policy-makers at the UNFCCC [47]. Increasing interest by the governments, NGOs, and private sectors in both developed and developing counties has been noticed in implementing innovative initiatives, largely on mitigation, but also on adaptation [45]. Exploring the linkages between the information technology and sustainable development started in the late 1990s, shifting their focus from broader global environmental issues to CO_2 emissions in the early 2000s. However, these explorations focused mainly on addressing the developed country priorities with regards to climate change [45, 46] which have also been reflected in a prevalent focus on mitigation in relevant literature. However, a growing body of literature at global level indicates the emergence of adaptation priorities of developing contexts and the potential of ICTs [45, 46].

Bangladesh started working on ICTs as a development enabler from the early years of 2000 [1]. In the wake of Digital Bangladesh agenda, there are a growing number of initiatives in using ICTs for climate change adaptation (CCA) and disaster risk reduction (DRR) both in government and nongovernment sector in Bangladesh [46]. Despite the empirical presence, the existing and potential role of ICTs in climate change adaptation in Bangladesh is not very evident in the literature and therefore comprises a very new field of enquiry to be explored further. The priorities and perspectives of climate vulnerable communities should be at the center of this enquiry to get a holistic view of potential of ICTs in addressing the climate change and associated challenges. However, in reality, there is little empirical information on the interplay between use of ICTs and climate change adaptation in climate vulnerable communities in Bangladesh. It is therefore important to explore further on this. The current research has been undertaken to contribute in filling this gap by investigating the role of ICT in adaptation among communities living on the fringe of development parameters and at high climate risk. It is recognized that climate change impacts manifest more severely in developing contexts, increasing existing vulnerabilities, poverty, and resource deprivation.

7.5   Research Design

7.5.1   *Research Sample*

The research has been carried out among the climate vulnerable *char* (Riverine Island) land communities living in four villages of two Unions (Rajapur and Ghorjan) of Sirajganj District of Bangladesh, which are prone to flood and riverbank erosion and where the impacts of climate change are already being felt. People who live in *"chars"* (river islands formed from sedimentation) are extremely vulnerable to natural disasters like flood and riverbank erosion and are also deprived of most of the development facilities because of their physical remoteness. Two of the four study villages are connected with the national power grid, and the rest two villages depend on solar home system for power supply, which offered various dimensions in study findings.

Among the two unions, Rajapur Union of Belkuchi *Upazilla* (sub-district) occupies an area of 6,178 acres with a population of 48,331 [15]. On the other hand, in Ghorjan Union of Chauhali *Upazilla*, the total area occupies an area of 6,993 acres with a population of 18,478 [15]. Like the unions, Chouhali *Upazilla* is larger than Belkuchi, but Belkuchi is more densely populated compared to Chauhali. This is because a large portion of Chauhali is river and always under threat of riverbank erosion. Belkuchi is more developed compared to Chauhali in terms of literacy rate. However, both are lower than the national average. In terms of economic activity, Rajapur Union is more dependent on industrial activities (mainly handloom) and service while Ghorjan Union is more dependent on agriculture. The profile of housing tenancy and drinking water is similar for both the unions, and the coverage of tube-well water availability is quite high. Rajapur Union is connected with the national power grid while Ghorjan depends only on solar power.

As indicated, the rationale for selecting the specific study areas is that the *"char"* community is extremely vulnerable to climatic hazards like flood and river erosion. They lack almost all basic services: water supply, sanitation facilities, hospitals, schools, electricity, transport, police stations, and market access. The study villages have been selected based on the following criteria that these are vulnerable to climatic hazards, some ICT options are available at community level, two of the four villages connected to the national power grid, and the rest two villages dependent on solar home system for power supply. The variation in power supply situation provided the opportunity to compare how it influences the use of ICTs. Moreover, the interpersonal relationship between the researchers and the representatives of the village has been an important consideration to access information and opinion. Besides, the fieldwork locations were convenient enough to enable the researchers to closely observe the situation and verify the data later on if required.

7.5.2   Data Collection and Analysis

In line with "methodological pluralism" as deployed by many other researchers, the study used both qualitative and quantitative techniques. A semi-structured questionnaire was used that consisted of all the relevant questions on the specific information needed for the survey. The group interviews provided in-depth information and enriched the understanding of different groups. Everything that was learnt through the group interviews has been further strengthened through interviews with selected key informants (KII).

The study has been conducted at household (HH) level in Rehaikawlia Village and Teghori Village of Ghorjan Union of Chauhali and Shomeshpur Village and Thakurpara Village of Rajapur Union of Belkuchi of Sirajganj District. There are total 2,085 HH in four villages, of which a representative sample of 100 HH (25 HH in each village), which is around 5% of the total population, have been randomly selected for the quantitative survey for the study.

For the qualitative information, data have been collected through eight group interviews (with male and female of different ICTs users and nonusers of different occupational groups in different villages), 12 KIIs, uncontrolled observations of daily activities of the village dwellers, and review of available secondary literature on socioeconomic condition of the locality. The key informants include ICT service providers and receivers and non-receivers among others.

The data collected from 100 respondents have been processed using the Microsoft Excel Data collected through interview and observation and were analyzed from a sociological perspective and from a holistic view through thematic coding and analysis. At microlevel, appropriate and aptly related indigenous vocabularies and terminology were put into operational meaning.

7.6   Results and Discussion

In this section, the focus is on two key aspects of the results. Firstly, we present the data associated with the role of existing use of ICTs, which is potentially contributing in adapting with the climate change impact on *char* community. Secondly, results related to the challenges and areas of improvement associated with the use of ICTs in adapting to the climate change impacts in *char* are presented.

7.6.1   Potentials of Using ICT for Climate Change Adaptation

Availability of ICT   The predominant available ICTs in the community include mobile phone and its multiple uses including regular phone call, text SMS, voice SMS, transfer of money, and listening to radio, TV, and union level one-stop digital service centers run by the government and development partners (i.e., Union Digital Center and *Char* Digital Center). Mobile phones are found to be the most popular ICT device used by the community. It has been found that almost all the HH in all four villages own at least one mobile phone with some level of disparity based on gender, technological feasibility, and financial ability. Widespread use of mobile phones started in the study villages around 2–3 years back. The Union Digital Centers (henceforth referred as UDC), provide 39 types of ICT services and the Char Digital Centers (henceforth referred as CDC), which are relatively new, provide around 20 types of ICT services. CDCs situated in villages in remote *chars* where UDCs do not reach, have lesser number of services to offer as they are run by NGOs, and do not have the mandate to provide many government services (i.e., issuing birth and death certificates) like UDCs. UDC started working in both the unions 2.5 years ago but started providing information on adaptive agriculture only 1.5 years back. CDC started working in the village 1.5 years back, but it does not provide information on adaptive agriculture yet. Both UDC and CDC provide information on weather forecast and flood early warning. UDC and CDC have active internet facility. However, internet is less available in the villages without regular electricity as dependence on solar and alternatively diesel run generator are beyond their capacity to afford (Fig. 7.1).

Other ICTs like radio and television are available in the study villages with electricity in Rajapur Union for many years. In Ghorjan Union, none in the villagers has TV, as there is no electricity other than solar in 22% of HH. Even those who can afford to buy a solar home system can hardly afford to buy a large enough system to run TV. Few hear radio in mobile phones for recreation but do not like listening to radio much. However, every HH in Rajapur Union, which is connected to power grid, has TV with satellite connections. They watch agricultural programs in different channels but mostly prefer to watch recreational programs. People are well aware

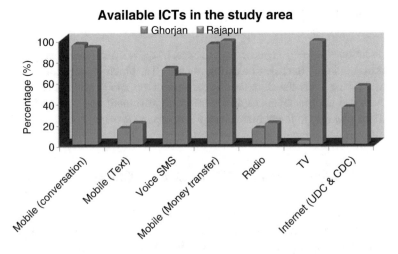

Fig. 7.1 Available ICTs in the study villages of Ghorjan and Rajapur unions

about the money transfer facility through mobile phones and take opportunity of the facility widely through different agents in the villages who usually has shops at the village market or doing it as a business individually. Physical factors like remoteness from the local level administrative centers and availability of regular power supply contributes in disparity in availability of ICT services, which has further contributed at the accessibility of these services along with other denominators.

Accessibility of ICT It is found that access to available ICT services is determined by the awareness about the availability of the services, physical factors, political factors, gender factors, financial factors, and technological factors at different levels. Many people do not access many of the services provided by UDC and CDCs simply because they do not know about it. Physical remoteness of the people living in *chars*, lack of connectivity with the union centers, lower literacy rate in *char* villages, and poor marketing by the service providers play a role here. Political factors linked with physical and economic factors also influence the access. Study villages in Rajapur Union are situated closer to the UDC, and therefore, villagers visit UDC more frequently compared to the villages in Ghorjan Union. The Union Parishad (UP) office of Ghorjan Union as well as the UDC are situated in the mainland while most of the villages of the union are situated in the other side of the river in *char* lands. As reported by the community, the UP office is situated in the mainland, as the UP chair is not willing to come to the *char* everyday crossing the river. Eventually it costs the poor *char* dwellers almost a full day engagement to visit UDC. Therefore, the location of the UDC, which is determined politically, is causing economic stress to the community and eventually influencing the access to the UDC.

Nonliterate people cannot access many ICT services, which can be availed through mobile phones but requires literacy. In many cases, particularly the women, and also men in some cases, can only receive calls but cannot make calls or read and write messages. Voice SMS solves their problem to some extent. Moreover, physical vulnerabilities due to frequent river erosion have made the ICTs less accessible to people even though the services are available to the villagers. Study villages, which are connected to the national power grid (Thakurpara and Shomeshpur), use different ICTs more compared the villages (Rehaikaulia and Teghori) which have to depend on solar power as they have easier access at a cheaper investment. However, in case of mobile phones, financial ability is not found to be a determining factor for accessibility, and even the poorest of the poor can afford or ready to invest on buying a mobile phone. People own more than one mobile phone in the majority of households, particularly in the villages of Rajapur Union, which are connected with the power grid. Every household in the other union also avails mobile phones as they charge their phones through solar power. However, a gender disparity has been observed here. Mostly the adult male members own mobile phones, particularly in households with lesser financial capacity as they cannot afford to buy more than one mobile phones, and it is the head of the household who gets the preference. This impose a restriction on women's access to information. However, women have not reported to have lesser access to other ICT services provided by TV, radio, UDC, and CDC.

ICT for Adapting with Climate Change Impacts The most important adaptation strategies to address climatic hazards like flood, fog, and riverbank erosion as perceived by the community are, respectively, flood early warning (EW) moderating potential damage of flood, improved cropping pattern (to moderate potential damage of crop due to erratic rainfall and temperature), and occupational migration (to moderate potential damage of displacement due to riverbank erosion). The existing ICT services available in the community are already playing a big role in adapting with these hazards. It also helps to address different other development challenges like governance, mobility, lack of capacity, unemployment, etc., which further intensifies the impact of climate change.

The newly introduced flood EW system disseminated through mobile voice SMS, and the weather forecast dissemination mechanism through UDC and CDC are found to be extremely useful for the community living in study villages. They get flood EW with a lead time of 5 days in their mobile phones through voice SMS every day during the rainy season (in between June to September). Twenty-five people including the UP chair and members of each of the study villages get this voice SMS. The messages are designed in a way that makes it easily understandable for the common people. Voice SMS, instead of text SMS, are used for dissemination so that it can reach to everyone, both literate and nonliterate. Majority of people particularly the farmers also go to the UDCs and the CDCs during rainy season to know about the weather forecast so that they can plan for the plantation and cultivation of crops accordingly. Women do not go much to the digital centers, as in the study villages, women are less involved in on-field agricultural activities compared to men. In some cases, people also make phone calls to the operators of digital centers to know about weather forecast. It saves time and ensures the access to the person and information they need.

The system of dissemination of flood EW through voice SMS got introduced in the study villages about 2 years back. Before introduction of the system, people had to depend on indigenous knowledge for forecasting the level of floodwater. The forecast made by Flood Forecast and Warning Center (FFWC) of the government used to be generic for the whole Sirajganj district, which were not precisely applicable at village level due to elevations in land surface. Receiving village specific flood EW with a lead time of 5 days, people take preparations for saving crops, store dry food, make boats (*bhela*) and other arrangements for communication, make portable cooking stove, keep the valuables in a safer place, make room for the poultry in a higher place, and make safer arrangements for the livestock. These DRR activities contribute a lot in reducing the impacts of flood.

The following figures show that how people are using ICTs for reducing their disaster risk. It also helps them in knowing about "relief and rehabilitation" opportunities. Mobile phone (both verbal communication and voice SMS) are found to be most effective medium here. Use of internet through UDC and CDC for knowing about regular weather forecast other than flood EW is also found as playing an effective role. The picture is not significantly different in both study unions even though Ghorjan does not have regular power supply except the fact that the use of TV is almost absent there (Figs. 7.2 and 7.3).

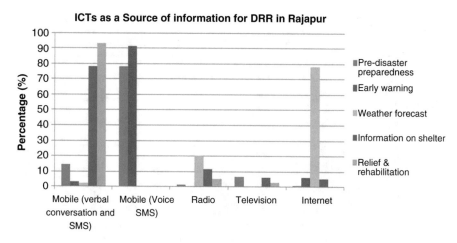

Fig. 7.2 ICTs as a source of information for DRR in Rajapur

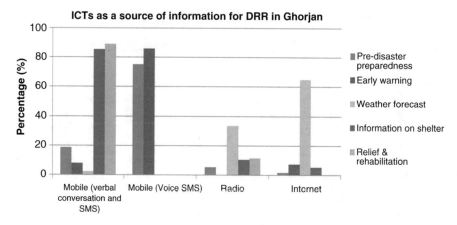

Fig. 7.3 ICTs as a source of information for DRR in Ghorjan

It has been found in the study that UDCs also play a very significant role in informing the farmers on improved and adaptive cropping. The agricultural software used in UDC gives visual guidance to any problem related to agriculture faced by farmers due to flood, fog, and erratic behavior of temperature, rainfall, and seasonal pattern. This software (in the form of mobile application) is also given to the dealers of fertilizer and seed, where farmers go the most. Through using this software, they get clear guidance on which fertilizer or pesticide they need and the amount to be applied. Farmers also communicate with Upazilla Agriculture Extension Officers through mobile phones, which they found to be the most useful medium to reach them as they hardly visit the fields. People go to both UDCs and CDCs to know about weather forecast which is essential for them to decide on different steps of farming (Figs. 7.4 and 7.5).

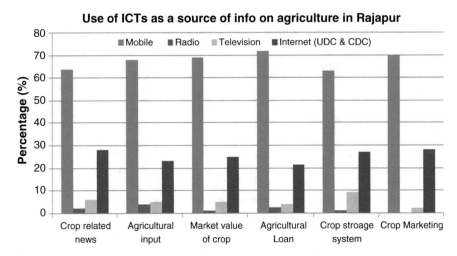

Fig. 7.4 Use of ICTs as a source of information on agriculture in Rajapur

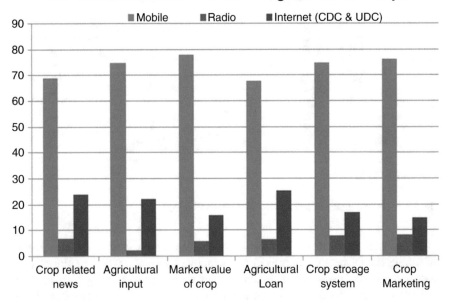

Fig. 7.5 Use of ICTs as a source of information on agriculture in Ghorjan

While riverbank erosion is a major climatic hazard of the study area impacting the community in the form of displacement, community see "planned" occupational migration (both short term and long term) as the most effective way of adapting with this inevitable displacement due to riverbank erosion. ICTs make a significant contribution in the planning process for this occupational migration. Through mobiles phones people get information on different livelihood opportunities in different parts of the country, even in abroad. This also gives them the opportunity to negotiate for better wages. It helps the employers to communicate with the workers they want directly without depending on any intermediary. Money transfer through mobile phones also found to be a "life saver" for the migrant workers and their families. When there were no systems of such transfer of money through mobile phones, it was time consuming and risky and sometimes catastrophic for the family. Use of mobile phones has made it very easy for the migrant families to keep communication with the rest of the families back home which works as a social capital for them. UDCs and CDCs also help people a lot in processing job application and also for processing papers (taking passport size photo, birth registration, checking the authenticity of visa, etc.) for going aboard as migrant workers.

7.6.2 Challenges of Using ICT for Climate Change Adaptation

Villages which are connected with the mainland and less prone to riverbank erosion and which also has power supply from the national power grid face less challenges in using ICTs compared to the other two villages which get eroded almost every year and which have to depend on solar power for their electricity need. However, whatever benefit they are getting through the comparatively limited use of ICTs have proven to be very precious to them. The village, which has to depend on solar power, cannot afford TV, as it requires more power. Charging mobile is also a hassle to them, as they have to go to markets or to other people who have solar home system. In markets, they pay 5 Bangladeshi taka (6 cent) for charging a mobile for once. The CDC in Ghorjan (no electricity) depends on solar power and diesel run generators, which made the services costlier for the villagers compared to UDC and other CDCs in other places with regular electricity connection. This eventually is impacting on the business of the CDC entrepreneur.

The overall economic condition of the villages without regular electricity is more vulnerable compared to the other two study villages with electricity. However, the cost of buying mobile phones does not found to be a problem to any of the study villages compared to the benefit they are getting through it.

Poor network connectivity is a common problem for all the villages and it impacts on using mobile phones as well as internet in UDC and CDC. The situation of the villages in Ghorjan are found to be worst as the nearby mobile tower they had got washed away about a year back in riverbank erosion and the mobile phone company reinstalled the tower in a distant place. Because of poor network, CDC as well as UDCs cannot provide the optimum service to people compared to the capacity they have. But receiving voice SMS in mobile phones on flood EW is not affected by this problem, as the message get stored in the phone memory whenever it gets better network. But it affects on other regular communication.

Illiteracy is also a problem identified in using mobile phones, particularly text SMS; reading dashboard in UDC or CDC. But voice SMS solves this problem.

Those who can read and write help others in disseminating the information they receive through different ICT sources.

There is supposed to be a woman entrepreneur in UDC along with male entrepreneurs. But from the very beginning, it became difficult to sustain female staff. Women are not encouraged to join in UDCs or CDCs. There is a perception that women are less capable of handling technology. The UP Chairman also thinks that a male worker can be utilized for his personal purposes which may not be valid for a woman. Women are also afraid of their security as many types of people; particularly the politicians come to the CDC. However, it is found to be very important to ensure presence of the women service providers for the women who come to take services.

The power politics also play a role in expanding UDCs, as the UP chair wants to control the centre. The way people get services coming to UDCs directly without going to the Chair, makes the UP chairs feeling disempowered.

7.7   Conclusion and Framework

The study reveals that despite some challenges, there are ample of potentials to use ICTs for climate change adaptation in areas vulnerable due to climate change. In this regard, better network for better use of mobile phones and internet, particularly for the people living in remote areas are required to help people getting the optimum benefit of the available ICT services. Mobile phone companies need to act from a social responsibility perspective by setting up accessible mobile tower run by solar energy. This will serve both adaptation and mitigation purpose. UDCs and CDCs must be further strengthened as there are needs for laminating machine, good quality color printer and scanner in UDCs and CDCs. Since there is no UDC in remote areas, it takes a lot of time and working hour of people to go to UDC for any work which is situated in the mainland at Union Paris had premises. While some CDCs are established in remote areas to give the services like UDCs, there are few services which cannot be provided in CDCs like issuing birth certificates, death certificates, etc. as they require endorsement of the UP Chair. But considering the vulnerability of people living in char, there should be some mechanism established which allows people getting these services from CDCs.

Moreover, farmers feel less encouraged to go to CDCs compared to UDCs as they do not have the computer software to give agricultural solutions. The software can be easily accessed by CDCs but it is found that CDC entrepreneurs are not proactive enough to ensure this facility to farmers. Trust and reliability of the information provided through public ICT services is very important so that people feel it is worth investing time and money getting that information. It is also important to provide ICT services according to the need of the people. Mechanisms should be developed in a way that serves the purpose. For example, CDCs have been developed following the model of UDCs to give services to the people living in remote areas. However, the most demanding services like birth registration, death registration (for mutation of

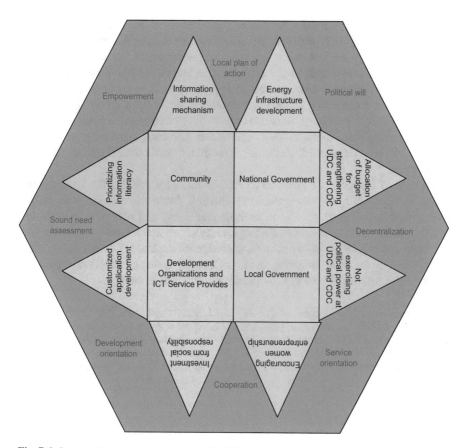

Fig. 7.6 Improved governance framework for ICT use in climate change adaptation

property) cannot be given in CDCs as they require signature from the UP Chair through official procedure. This challenge has impacted on the overall popularity and therefore utilization of the services offered by CDCs.

On the basis of the overall discussion related to the study, an improved governance framework is proposed in this chapter for effective use of ICTs for climate change adaptation. Figure 7.6 shows this improved governance framework which identifies four major groups to act jointly; national government, local government, development organizations and private sector ICT service providers and the community itself.

The framework suggests that while exhibiting political will, national government needs to focus on decentralization and formulating local plan of action. The major areas to work on for the national government would be to build energy infrastructure and to allocate more budget to strengthen the UDCs and CDCs. Local government should increase service orientation and cooperate with actors outside the government. In this regard, current practices of using political power in operating UDCs and CDCs must be avoided and participation of women must be encouraged by the local government representatives. Private sector ICT providers and development organizations should enhance their development orientation and be more efficient in identifying community needs. Their major areas of work should be investment from a social responsibility perspective like setting up mobile tower in remote areas as well as development of customized applications on the basis of community needs. For community, self-empowerment is the key to be a part of this improved governance framework as they need to build their information sharing mechanism to assist each other. Literacy, especially information literacy, must be developed where the community needs to feel the urgency and importance.

In light of the proposed governance framework, we argue that the research may create an opportunity for the population vulnerable due to climate change to analyse their adaptation strategies using ICTs more effectively and may help in exploring other potential uses. The output, findings, observation and lessons of this research are expected to help the policy makers, analyst, national and international organizations, donor agencies for initiating and implementing better, more effective policies, projects and funding for using ICTs in adapting to climate change.

Acknowledgement The authors are grateful to Christian Commission for Development in Bangladesh (CCDB) for the support provided to conduct the study as a part of authors' research responsibilities at CCDB Climate Change Unit. However, the authors are entirely responsible for the comments and interpretations made in this book chapter and by no means should the chapter be treated as a manifestation of CCDB's position or the positions of University of Sussex and Oxfam.

References

1. Access to Information Programme. Prime Minister's Office. (2009). Digital Bangladesh concept note. Available at: http://www.a2i.pmo.gov.bd/sites/default/files/resource_docs/Digital%20Bangladesh%20Concept%20Note_Final.pdf. Accessed on 26 June 2016.
2. Adger, W. N., Nelson, D., & Brown, K. (2007). Adaptation to environmental change: Contributions of a resilience framework. *Annual Review of Environment and Resources, 2007*(32), 395–419.
3. Agrawala, S., Ota, T., Ahmed, A. U., Smith, J., & Aalst, M. V. (2003). *Development and climate change in Bangladesh: Focus on coastal flooding and the Sundarbans. Report no.: COM/ENV/EPOC/DCD/DAC(2003)3/FINAL*. Paris: OECD. Available at: http://www.bip.org.bd/SharingFiles/journal_book/20140128164211.pdf. Accessed on 5 May 2016.
4. Ahmed, A. U. (2004). Adaptation to climate change in Bangladesh: Learning by doing, UNFCCC Workshop on Adaptation, Bonn, 18 June 2004, Available at: https://unfccc.int/files/meetings/workshops/other_meetings/application/pdf/ahsan.pdf. Accessed on 5 May 2016.
5. Ahmed, A.U. (2006). Bangladesh climate change impacts and vulnerability: A synthesis. Climate change cell, Bangladesh Department of Environment. Available at: http://www.preventionweb.net/files/574_10370.pdf. Accessed on 5 May 2016.
6. Ahmed, A. K., & Chowdhury, E. H. (2006). *Final report of "Study on livelihood systems assessment, vulnerable groups profiling and livelihood adaptation to climate hazard and long term climate change in drought prone areas of NW Bangladesh"*. Dhaka: FAO.

7. Ahmed, A. U., Siddiqi, N. A., & Choudhuri, R. A. (1998). Vulnerability of forest ecosystems of Bangladesh to climate change. In S. Huq, Z. Karim, M. Asaduzzaman, & F. U. Mahtab (Eds.), *Vulnerability and adaptation to climate change for Bangladesh*. Dordrecht: Kluwer Academic Publishers. doi:10.1007/978-94-015-9325-0, pp. 93-111.
8. Akoh, B., Bizikova, L. Parry, J., Creech, H., Karami, J., Echeverria, D., Hammill, A., & Gass P. (2011). Africa transformation-ready: The strategic application of information and communication technologies to climate change adaptation in Africa. iisd (International Institute for Sustainable Development). Available at: http://www.digitalopportunity.org/ImageCatalog/strategic-application-of-ict-to-climate-change-adaptation-in-africa.pdf/at_download/file. Accessed on 17 May 2016.
9. Alauddin, S. M., & Rahman, K. F. (2013). Vulnerability to climate change and adaptation practices in Bangladesh. *Journal of SUB, 4*, 25–42.
10. Ali, A. (1996). Vulnerability of Bangladesh to climate change and sea level rise through tropical cyclones and storm surges. *Water, Air, and Soil Pollution, 92*(1), 171–179.
11. Ali, M. Y. (1999). Fish resources vulnerability and adaptation to climate change in Bangladesh. In S. Huq, Z. Karim, M. Asaduzzaman, & Mahtab (Eds.), *Vulnerability and adaptation to climate change for Bangladesh*. Dordrecht: Kluwer Academic Publishers. doi:10.1007/978-94-015-9325-0. 113 – 124.
12. Arfanuzzaman, M., Mamnun, N., Islam, M. S., Dilshad, T., & Syed, M. A. (2016). Evaluation of adaptation practices in the agriculture sector of Bangladesh: An ecosystem based assessment. *Climate, 4*, 11. doi:10.3390/cli4010011.
13. Ashraf, M., & Hoque R. (2016). An illustration of information communication technology (ICT)-mediated innovation-adoption – Implementation in rural Bangladesh. TÉKHNE – Review of Applied Management Studies. *TEKHNE 48*; No. of Pages 7, http://dx.doi.org/10.1016/j.tekhne.2016.04.003.
14. Balaji, V., & Craufurd, P. (2011). Using information and communication technologies to disseminate and exchange agriculture-related climate information in the Indo Gangetic Plains, CCAFS Project Report, CGIAR Research Program on Climate Change, Agriculture and Food Security (CCAFS). Available at: http://iri.columbia.edu/CCAFS/Publications/Balaji.pdf. Accessed on 27 March 2016.
15. BBS. (2012). *Bangladesh statistical yearbook 2012*. Dhaka: Bangladesh Bureau of Statistics, Statistics and Informatics Division, Ministry of Planning.
16. BBS. (2013). ICT use and access by individuals and households. Prepared by, Bangladesh Bureau of Statistics (BBS), Statistics and Informatics Division (SID) and Ministry of Planning. Available at: http://www.bbs.gov.bd/WebTestApplication/userfiles/Image/LatestReports/ICTUseAccessSurvey2013.pdf. Accessed on 27 May 2016.
17. Braun, P., & Islam M. F. (2012). ICTenabled knowledge brokering for farmers in coastal areas of Bangladesh. In R. Heeks & A. V. Ospina (Eds.), *ICTs, climate change and development: Case evidence*. Centre for Development Informatics Institute for Development Policy and Management, SED, Available at: http://agritech.tnau.ac.in/pdf/2015/Book_ICCD_Case_Evidence.pdf. Accessed on 27 May 2016.
18. BRRI. (2012). Achievement of Bangladesh Rice Research Institute – Modern varieties. Available at: http://www.knowldgebank-brri.org. Accessed on 27 Mar 2016.
19. CNRS. (2012). *Piloting some climate resilient development initiatives at char Kajol, Golachipa, Patuakhali – An Innovative Concept of CBA to CC, Second Quarterly Report to UNDP*. Dhaka: CNRS.
20. Cruz, R. V., Harasawa, H., Lal, M., Wu, S., Anokhin, Y., Punsalmaa, B., Honda, Y., Jafari, M., Li, C., & Huu Ninh, N. (2007). Asia. In M. L. Parry, O. F. Canziani, J. P. Palutikof, P. J. van der Linden, & C. E. Hanson (Eds.), *Climate change 2007: Impacts, adaptation and vulnerability, Contribution of Working Group II to the Fourth Assessment Report of the Intergovernmental Panel on Climate Change* (pp. 469–506). Cambridge: Cambridge University Press. Available at: https://www.ipcc.ch/pdf/assessment-report/ar4/wg2/ar4_wg2_full_report.pdf. Accessed on 27 Mar 2016.
21. CSISA. (2012). *Farmers manual on improved rice farming technologies. Cereal Systems Initiative for South Asia in Bangladesh*. Manila: IRRI.

22. Dinesh, D., & Vermeulen, S. (2016). Climate change adaptation in agriculture: Practices and technologies, Presented at Messages to the SBSTA 44 agriculture workshops, Available at: https://cgspace.cgiar.org/bitstream/handle/10568/71051/SBSTA44-Agricultural-practices-technologies.pdf. Accessed on 29 Mar 2016.
23. Douglas, I. (2009). Climate change, flooding and food security in south Asia. *Food Security, 1*, 127–136.
24. FAO. (2010) The role of information and communication technologies for community-based adaptation to climate change, Technical Paper under Communication for Sustain-able Development Initiative. Available at: http://www.fao.org/uploads/media/ap606e_2.pdf. Accessed on 31 Mar 2016.
25. Feldacker, C. B. (2007). Environmental influences on cholera outbreaks in Bangladesh and Vietnam: Implications for prevention and prediction. Paper presented at: APHA 135th Meeting and Expo; November 3–7, 2007; Washington, DC, Available at: https://apha.confex.com/apha/135am/recordingredirect.cgi/id/17192. Accessed on 31 May 2016.
26. Finlay, A., & Adera, E. (2012). Application of its for climate change adaptation in the water sector developing country experiences and emerging research priorities, Apc-201202-Apc-r-en-pdf-134. Available at: https://www.apc.org/en/system/files/ICTs_Climate_Change_Water.pdf, Accessed on 31 Mar 2016.
27. GoB. (2009). National ICT Policy – 2009. Available at: http://www.bcs.org.bd/img/upload/page/11.pdf. Accessed on 31 Mar 2016.
28. GSMA Intelligence. (2014). Analysis: Country overview: Bangladesh, GSMA Mobile for Development Impact, Available at: https://www.gsmaintelligence.com/research/?file=140820-bangladesh.pdf&download. Accessed on 25 May 2016.
29. Guha-Sapir, D., Hargitt, D., & Hoyois, P. (2004). Thirty years of natural disasters 1974–2003: The numbers. Belgium: Presses universitaires de Louvain. 188 pp. Available at: http://www.preventionweb.net/files/1078_8761.pdf, Accessed on 31 Mar 2016.
30. Habiba, U., Hassan, A. W. R., & Shaw, R. (2013). Livelihood adaptation in the drought prone areas of Bangladesh. In R. Shaw, F. Mallick, & A. Islam (Eds.), *Climate change adaptation actions in Bangladesh*. London: Springer.
31. Haq, A. H. R., Bakuluzzaman, M., Dash, M., & Rabi- uzzaman Nandi, R. (2012). An ICTbased community plant clinic for climateresilient agricultural practices in Bangladesh. In R. Heeks & A. V. Ospina (Eds.) *ICTs, climate change and development: Case evidence, Centre for Development Informatics Institute for Development Policy and Management, SED*, Available at: http://agritech.tnau.ac.in/pdf/2015/Book_ICCD_Case_Evidence.pdf. Accessed on 21 May 2016.
32. Heeks, R., & Ospina, A. V. (2012). ICTs, climate change and development: Case evidence, Centre for Development Informatics Institute for Development Policy and Management, SED. Available at: https://www.weadapt.org/sites/weadapt.org/files/legacy-new/knowledge-base/files/54b7f1f376145book-iccd-themes-actions.pdf. Accessed on 31 Mar 2016.
33. Hoque, M., & Sorwar, G. (2014). E-Governance for rural development: A case study on Union Information and Service Centre (UISC) of Bangladesh. In The 18th pacific Asia conference on information systems. Available at: http://aisel.aisnet.org/pacis2014/117. Accessed on 23 May 2016.
34. Huq, S., Ahmed, A. U., & Koudstaal, R. (1996). Vulnerability of Bangladesh to climate change and sea level rise. In T. E. Downing (Ed.), *Climate change and world food security, NATO ASI Series, I 37* (pp. 347–379). Berlin: Springer Verlag.
35. Islam, M. N., Baten, M. A., Hossain, M. S., & Islam, M. T. (2008). Impact of few important climatic parameters on Aman rice production in Mymensingh district. *Journal of Environmental Science and Natural Resources, 1*(2), 49–54.
36. Kalas, P. P., & Finlay, A. (2009). Planting the knowledge seed: Adapting to climate change using ICTs. Building Communication Opportunities (BCO) Alliance. Available at: https://www.apc.org/en/system/files/BCO_ClimateChange.pdf. Accessed on 31 Mar 2016.

37. Karim, M. A. (2010). Digital Bangladesh for good governance. Bangladesh Development Forum. Prepared for Bangladesh Development Forum 2010, Presented at Bangabandhu International Conference Centre, 15–16 February, 2010, Available at: http://www.lcgbangladesh.org/bdf-2010/BG_%20Paper/BDF2010_Session%20VI.pdf. Accessed on 16 July 2016.
38. Karim, Z., Hussain, S. K. G., & Ahmed, A. U. (1999). Climate change vulnerability of crop agriculture. In S. Huq, Z. Karim, M. Asaduzzaman, & Mahtab Vulnerability (Eds.), *Vulnerability and adaptation to climate change for Bangladesh* (pp. 39–54), New Delhi. Springer, doi: 10.1007/978-94-015-9325-0.
39. Mahoo, H. F., Mkoga, Z. J., Kasele, S. S., Igbadun, H. E., Hatibu, N., Rao, K. P. C., & Lankaford B. (2007). Productivity of water in agricultural farmers' perceptions and practices. Int. Water Manage. Insti. (Comprehensive Assessment of Water Management in Agriculture. Discussion Paper 5, Colombo, Sri Lanka. ISBN: 978–92–9090-679-7.
40. Met Office Hadley Centre. (2011). Climate: Observations, projections and impacts, prepared for Bangladesh Met Office, United Kingdom. pp 55–130. Available at: http://www.metoffice.gov.uk/media/pdf/1/q/Bangladesh.pdf. Accessed on 31 Mar 2016.
41. Mirza, M. M. Q. (2002). Global warming and changes in the probability of occurrence of floods in Bangladesh and implications. *Global Environmental Change, 12*(2), 127–138.
42. Mirza, M. M. Q. (2011). Climate change, flooding in South Asia and implications. *Regional Environmental Change, 11*, 95–107.
43. MoEF. (2009). *Bangladesh Climate Change Strategy and Action Plan 2009*. Dhaka: Ministry of Environment and Forest (MOEF), Government of the People's Republic of Bangladesh. 76 p. Available at: http://www.climatechangecell.org.bd/Documents/climate_change_strategy2009.pdf. Accessed on 31 May 2016.
44. MoEF-UNDP. (2005). National Adaptation Programme of Action, Ministry of Environment and Forest (MOEF), Government of the People's Republic of Bangladesh and United Nations Development Programme (UNDP), Dhaka. Available at: http://unfccc.int/resource/docs/napa/ban01.pdf. Accessed on 31 May 2016.
45. Ospina, A., & Heeks, R. (2010). Linking ICTs and climate change adaptation: A conceptual framework for e-resilience and e-adaptation, Centre for Development Informatics Institute for Development Policy and Management, SED, University of Manchester. Available at: http://www.preventionweb.net/files/14900_ConceptualPaper1.pdf. Accessed on 22 June 2016.
46. Ospina, A., & Heeks, R. (2010). Unveiling the Links between ICTs & climate change in developing countries: A scoping study, Centre for Development Informatics Institute for Development Policy and Management, SED University of Manchester. Available from: http://www.fao.org/fileadmin/user_upload/rome2007/docs/ICT%20and%20CC%20ScopingStudy.pdf. Accessed on 23 June 2016.
47. Ospina, A.V., Faulkner, D., Dickerson, K., & Bueti, C. (2014). Resilient pathways: The adaptation of the ICT sector to climate change. ITU, v–vi. Available at: http://www.itu.int/en/ITU-T/climatechange/Documents/Publications/Resilient_Pathways-E.PDF. Accessed on 28 June 2016.
48. Pramanik, M. A. H. (2009). Remote Sensing applications in disasters monitoring in Bangladesh, Geospatial World, September 1, 2009, Available at: http://www.geospatialworld.net/article/remote-sensing-applications-in-disasters-monitoring-in-bangladesh. Accessed on 31 May 2016.
49. Rahman, M. M., & Islam, A. (2013). Adaptation technologies in practice and future potentials in Bangladesh. In R. Shaw, F. Mallick, & A. Islam (Eds.), *Climate change adaptation actions in Bangladesh*. London: Springer.
50. Rahman, A., Rabbani, G., Muzammil, M., Alam, M., Th apa, S., Rakshit, R., & Inagaki, H. (2010). Scoping assessment of climate change adaptation in Bangladesh, Summary Report, Adaptation Knowledge Platform, Bangkok, pp. 24, Available at: http://www.climateadapt.asia/upload/publications/files/4d81c35109ddfScoping_Assessment_on_Climate_Change_Adaptation_in_Bangladesh.pdf. Accessed on 31 May 2016.

51. Rana, M. S., Gunasekara, K., Hazarika, M. K., Samarakoon, L., & Siddiquee, M. (2010). Application of remote sensing and GIS for cyclone disaster Management in coastal area: A case study at barguna district, International Archives of the Photogrammetry, Remote Sensing and Spatial Information Science, Volume XXXVIII, Part 8, Kyoto Japan 2010. Available at: http://www.isprs.org/proceedings/XXXVIII/part8/pdf/JTS64_20100608144600.pdf. Accessed on 21 May 2016.
52. Schaerer C., & Ahmed A. U. (2004). Adaptation to climate change in vulnerable communities: Lessons from practice in southwestern Bangladesh. In A.U. Ahmed, N. Haque (Ed.), *Adaptation to climate change: Knowledge sharing for capacity building*. Proceedings of workshop held on 10 December 2003 at COP 9 Milan. Climate Action Network South Asia (CANSA) and RVCC, Dhaka.
53. Selvaraju, R., Subbiah, A. R., Baas, S., & Juergens, I. (2006). Livelihood adaptation to climate variability and change in drought prone areas of Bangladesh: Developing institutions and options. Asian Disaster Preparedness Centre, Food and Agriculture Organization Of The United Nations: Rome, ISBN .978-925-105602-8, Available at: ftp://193.43.36.93/docrep/fao/009/a0820e/a0820e01.pdf. Accessed on 31 May 2016.
54. Shahid, S. (2015). Probable impacts of climate change on public health in Bangladesh. *Asia-Pacific Journal of Public Health, 22*(3), 310–319.
55. Shahid, S., & Behrawan, H. (2008). Drought risk assessment in the western part of Bangladesh. *Natural Hazards, 46*, 391–413.
56. Shaw, R., Mallick, F., & Islam, A. (2013). *Climate change adaptation actions in Bangladesh*. Tokyo: Springer. doi:10.1007/978-4-431-54249-0.
57. Shilenje, Z.W., & Ogwang B.A. (2015). Review article: The role of Kenya meteorological service in weather early warning in Kenya. *International Journal of Atmospheric Sciences*, Article ID 302076. http://dx.doi.org/10.1155/2015/302076.
58. The Asia Foundation. (2012). A situation analysis of climate change adaptation initiatives in Bangladesh. The Asia Foundation, Bangladesh, pp. 23–38. .Available at: https://asiafoundation.org/resources/pdfs/SituationAnalysisofCCinitiatives.pdf. Accessed on 25 May 2016.
59. UNDP. (2012). *Mid-term evaluation of community based adaptation to climate change through coastal afforestation in Bangladesh*. Dhaka: UNDP.
60. UNDP. (2016). Climate information & early warning systems communications toolkit: UNDP Programme on Climate Information for Resilient Development in Africa, United Nations Development Programme, Environment and Energy, pp 20–53, Available at: http://www.undp.org/content/dam/undp/library/Climate%20and%20Disaster%20Resilience/climate-info-and-ews-communications-toolkit.pdf?download. Accessed on 31 Mar 2016.
61. UNFCCC. (2013). Press release: Showcasing information and communication technology solutions, UN Climate Change Secretariat launches new partnership with GeSI. Available at: https://unfccc.int/files/press/press_releases_advisories/application/pdf/20132111_mfc_ict.pdf. Accessed on 23 June 2016.
62. UO-Oxfam. (2008). *Climate change: As if development mattered* (p. 30). Dhaka: Unnayan Onneshan (UO) and Oxfam GB Bangladesh. (Mimeo), Available at: www.unnayan.org/reports/Climate.Change.Policy.Paper.pdf.
63. Zaman M. A., & Biswas, A. K. M. A. A. (2014). Application of ICT tools for climate change and disaster management in Bangladesh, Proceedings of AFITA 2014. Available at: http://s3.amazonaws.com/academia.edu.documents/35562820/Application_of_ICT_Tools_for_Climate_Change_and_Disaster_Management_in_Bangladesh.pdf?AWSAccessKeyId=AKIAJ56TQJRTWSMTNPEA&Expires=1459663899&Signature=e4RLqccwc7sZ2CJPoLuxB%2FnU9lc%3D&response-content-disposition=attachment%3B%20filename%3DApplication_of_ICT_Tools_for_Climate_Cha.pdf. Accessed on 31 Mar 2016.
64. Zanamwe, N., & Okunoye, A. (2013). Role of information and communication technologies (ICTs) in mitigating, adapting to and monitoring climate change in developing countries, Proceedings of "International Conference on ICT for Africa 2013, February 20–23, Harare, Zimbabwe". Available at: http://ictforafrica.org/attachments/section/4/ict4africa2013_submission_55.pdf. Accessed on 31 Mar 2016.

Part III
Africa and the Middle East

Chapter 8
Evaluation of E-Infrastructure Deployment in OECD and MENA Countries

Jörn Altmann, Almas Heshmati, and Baseem Al-Athwari

Abstract This paper introduces new indices quantifying country's level of e-infrastructure deployment. These indices comprise six components, which include several indicators, and are based on parametric or nonparametric methods. They improve existing indices. Based on index calculations, variations between countries, regions, and over time are analyzed. The data used covers MENA and OECD countries, 2000–2007. Analysis results identified areas, in which countries need improvements, and showed that some MENA countries outperformed some OECD countries. The rankings based on the indices differ only slightly. Additionally, the parametric method-based index produces equally distributed value ranges and shows an overall e-infrastructure improvement over time.

Keywords ICT infrastructure • Indices • E-readiness • Composite index • Principal component analysis • MENA • OECD

8.1 Introduction

The rapid proliferation of information and communication technologies (ICT) has resulted in the introduction of many Internet-based services such as e-business, e-commerce, e-government, and e-learning. As the provision of such services mainly

J. Altmann
Technology Management, Economics, and Policy Program, Department of Industrial Engineering, College of Engineering, Seoul National University,
Gwanak-Ro 1, 08826 Seoul, South Korea
e-mail: jorn.altmann@acm.org

A. Heshmati (✉)
Department of Economics, Sogang University,
K526, 35 Baekbeom-ro, 121-742 Seoul, South Korea
e-mail: heshmati@sogang.ac.kr

B. Al-Athwari
Technology Management, Economics, and Policy Program, College of Engineering, Seoul National University, Gwanak-Ro 1, 08826 Seoul, South Korea
e-mail: baseem_cs@yahoo.com

© Springer International Publishing AG 2017
H. Kaur et al. (eds.), *Catalyzing Development through ICT Adoption*,
DOI 10.1007/978-3-319-56523-1_8

113

depends on the level of the existing ICT-relevant infrastructure (e-infrastructure) in a country, it is clear that an appropriate level of e-infrastructures needs to be in place for a specific service to work successfully. E-infrastructure is the basis for ICT development. Only then, businesses and citizens of a country can benefit from ICT investments.

Despite this fact, e-infrastructure deployment has not been evaluated. Instead, a large number of indices for measuring ICT deployment in a country have been formulated by researchers, governments, and private institutions. These indices, which capture the ICT status, are the technological achievement index (TAI), the networked readiness index (NRI), the digital access index (DAI), the digital opportunity index (DOI), and the ITU ICT development index (IDI). The ICT-deployment indices are unable to fully identify the true extent of e-infrastructure development as their indicators do not reflect the level of the countries' readiness in terms of e-infrastructure.

This study introduces new e-infrastructure indices that quantify the level of e-infrastructure development in a country. The e-infrastructure indices that we introduce cover not only ICT access and ICT use but also all infrastructure areas that are related to ICT development. The indices comprise the following six components: electricity, telecommunication, Internet, processing power, broadcasting, and human capital. Each of those components is generated from a comprehensive set of indicators that are prerequisites for subsequent access and use of information and telecommunication technologies. This composition also provides the possibility of tracking each of the components separately and, therefore, identifies strengths and weaknesses of a country with respect to the e-infrastructure-relevant area specified through the component. It will also help pointing out the source of failure in developing an e-infrastructure and in developing policies for enhancing an ICT-supporting infrastructure.

For the computations of the indices, which are based on parametric methods and nonparametric methods, this study also suggests several improvements for the composition of the indices compared to existing indices.

Furthermore, the paper calculates and analyzes the indices for different countries as well as the index variations between countries, regions, and over time. The data used for the analysis is about Middle East and North Africa (MENA) and OECD countries for the period between 2000 and 2007.

Moreover, the study also measures the efficiency of countries in terms of e-infrastructure development compared with the best practiced e-infrastructure country to show not only the rank but also the distance to the frontier country in e-infrastructure development.

The results show that countries differ significantly in their e-infrastructure development. We also observe some degree of heterogeneity by regional location. Although the majority of OECD countries are ranked higher than MENA countries, the MENA countries, which belong to the Gulf Cooperation Council (GCC), outperformed a few OECD countries.

Our results also show that the two e-infrastructure indices differ only slightly with respect to the results produced. However, the parametric method-based e-infrastructure index produces a more equally distributed value range and shows an expected evolution over the course of 7 years.

The remainder of the paper is organized as follows: First, in Sect. 8.2, a literature review about existing indices for measuring ICT deployment is presented and compared. The framework of the new e-infrastructure indices is given in Sect. 8.3. While Sect. 8.4 describes the data and indicators used in the analysis of the study, Sect. 8.5 introduces the methodologies used in the computation of the e-infrastructure indices. Section 8.6 describes the results of the empirical analysis. In Sect. 8.7, policy recommendations and a discussion on how to improve the e-infrastructure index are given. The paper concludes with a summary of the main findings of the study in Sect. 8.8.

8.2 Literature Review

E-readiness assessments are meant to guide development efforts, providing benchmarks for comparing and gauging the development progress of a country [29]. In many cases, e-readiness is given through indices, which measure various indicators (e.g., the number of telephone lines per 100 people and the percentage of GDP spent on information technology (IT)) that describe the country's situation in information technology. The results are tabulated and ranked. Then, the table can be used to make comparisons between countries and to conduct longitudinal studies for a single country [8]. The ranking of countries indicates the differences between countries.

8.2.1 Definition of Development Indices

Given the implications of the e-readiness assessment, several organizations, academia, and researchers are interested in this type of measure. However, it resulted in many different definitions of readiness. The Economist Intelligence Unit defines e-readiness as the measure of a country's ability to use digital channels for communication, commerce, and government, in order to foster economic and social development [11]. Asia-Pacific Economic Cooperation (APEC) defines e-readiness as the degree to which an economy or community is prepared to participate in the digital economy [4]. CID's[1] readiness for the networked world defines a framework for developing countries to evaluate their e-readiness [7]. It defines the readiness as "the degree to which a community is prepared to participate in the networked world," which measures a community's relative advancement in the areas that are most critical for ICT adoption and most important for ICT applications. Danish [8] defines e-readiness as a measure of the degree to which a country or economy is ready, willing, or prepared to obtain the benefits of information and communication technologies.

---

[1] CID refers to Harvard University's Center for International Development.

8.2.2   Existing ICT Development Indices

A large number of ICT rankings between countries have been prepared by many public and private institutions. The most known indices, on which the rankings are based, are the networked readiness index (NRI), the technology achievement index (TAI), the new indicator of technological capabilities (ArCO), the economist intelligence unit (EIU) e-readiness ranking tool, the UNCTAD ICT development index, the digital access index (DAI), the digital opportunity index (DOI), the ICT opportunity index (ICT-OI), the ITU ICT development index (IDI), telecommunication and broadcasting infrastructure index (TI), and development of telecommunication infrastructure (DTI) suggested by Rudra et al. [30]. Archibugi et al. [6] compute nine internationally well-known technological capability composite indices using the same data and compare their correlation and performance in ranking countries. The indices are used to capture multidimensional nature of technological change and to rank countries based on different sets of indicators. The values of the indicators of technological capabilities are assessed for public policy, company strategies, and economic studies. Although these indices have been developed to measure and rank the e-readiness of countries, they have been developed from different perspectives, use different data, apply different methodologies, and define the e-readiness concept differently; the rankings and findings from different institutions differ from each other. Consequently, some findings seem to be inconsistent with each other. A comparison between these indices including their subindices, methodology, and usage is presented in Table 8.1.

8.2.3   Shortcomings of Existing Indices

Despite the significant efforts and importance of the above indices for measuring ICT development, the e-infrastructure, which is considered as the basis for such development, has not been investigated much. For instance, the most relevant index to this study is the IDI, which has been developed by ITU. The IDI excludes infrastructure supply (e.g., electricity) and does not take into consideration technology convergence of telecommunication and broadcasting and the emergence of new technologies and services (e.g., IPTV, digital terrestrial TV, and WiMAX). Another related piece of work has been developed by Al-Mutawkkil et al. [1]. It focuses on telecommunications and broadcasting infrastructure but excludes the electricity infrastructure. Moreover, most of the existing indices include many factors that are not related to e-infrastructure and, therefore, do not show a realistic state of the ICT-related infrastructure. In another study Lim and Nguyen (2013) [25] compare the weighting schemes in the three traditional, principal component and dynamic factor approaches to summarizing information from a number of component variables and compare their performance. The results show the advantage of dynamic factor approach in capturing both significance and variability of the components.

Table 8.1 Comparison of existing ICT-related indices

Index name	Literature reference	Subindices	Methodology	Perspective/use
Technological achievement index (TAI), 2001/2002	UNDP [32], Desai et al. [9]	Creation of new technology	The methodology used to calculate the TAI is a simple average of the dimensions of the index, which in turn is calculated based on the selected indicators	TAI is a composite measure of technological progress that ranks countries on a comparative global scale
		Diffusion of newest technologies		
		Diffusion of oldest technologies		
		Human skills		
Networked readiness index (NRI), 2003	WEF, INSEAD & infoDev [33]	Environment for IT offered by a given country or community	135 variables were considered available from hard data and an executive opinion survey and narrowed these down to 65 based on a variety of criteria. These 65 variables were grouped into 11 separate micro-indices	It is defined as "the degree of reparation of a nation or community to participate in and benefit from IT developments"
		Readiness of the community's key stakeholders (individuals, businesses, and governments) to use IT		
		Actual use of IT among these stakeholders		
Indicator of technological capabilities (ArCO), 2004	Archibugi and Coco [5]	Creation of technology	The overall technology index (ArCo) has been built upon the equal weighting of the three mentioned categories	It is a more comprehensive indicator of technological capability
		Technological infrastructures		
		Development of human skills		
EIU E-readiness ranking tool, 2008/2009	Economist Intelligence Unit [11, 12]	Connectivity and technological infrastructure	In EIU 2009, over 100 separate criteria, both qualitative and quantitative, are evaluated for each country. The categories and the individual criteria within them (38 indicators and 81 sub-indicators) are weighted according to their assumed importance. The subindices are weighted as follows: connectivity and technology infrastructure 20%; business environment 15%; social and cultural environment 15%; legal environment 10%; government policy and vision 15%; consumer and business adoption 25%	It assessed the world's largest economies on their ability to absorb information and communications technology (ICT) and to use it for economic and social benefit
		Business environment		
		Social and cultural environment		
		Legal environment		
		Government policy and vision		
		Consumer and business adoption		

(continued)

Table 8.1 (continued)

Index name	Literature reference	Subindices	Methodology	Perspective/use
UNCTAD ICT development index, 2005	United Nations Conference on Trade and Development [31]	Connectivity	UNCTAD uses the aggregate index approach with component indices (similar to UNDP's HDI)	It assesses technological development
		Access		
		Policy		
		Usage of telecom traffic		
Digital access index (DAI), 2003	ITU [18]	Infrastructure (fixed telephone subscribers per 100 inhabitants and mobile phone subscribers per 100 inhabitants)	It is based on a methodology that uses goalposts (upper value limits), which were averaged to obtain category scores. Categories were then averaged to obtain the overall index value	It measures the overall ability of individuals in a country to access and use information and communication technologies
		Affordability		
		Knowledge		
		Quality		
		Usage		
ICT opportunity index (ICT-OI), 2007	ITU and Orbicom [20]	Networks	The ICT-OI calculates values for a reference country and reference year, which served as the basis for calculating changes in "infostate" developments	It was less designed as a tool for benchmarking and ranking countries, but rather for tracking country and group differences across time and in relation to each other
		Skills		
		Uptake		
		Intensity		
Digital opportunity index (DOI), 2005	ITU & United Nations Conference on Trade and Development [21]	Opportunity	The methodology used for the DOI was close to that of the DAI, using goalposts and absolute values	The objective of the DOI is to measure "digital opportunity" or the potential of countries to benefit from access to ICT
		Infrastructure		
		Utilization		

Index name	Literature reference	Subindices		Methodology	Perspective/use
ITU ICT development index (IDI), 2009	ITU [19]	ICT infrastructure and access		The IDI uses weighted summation applied to the normalized indicators and subindices	It tracks the digital divide and benchmarks information society developments
		ICT use			
		ICT skills			
Telecommunication and broadcasting infrastructure index (TI), 2009	Al-Mutawkkil et al. [1]	Telecommunications (fixed telephone, mobile phone, Internet)		The TI's three telecommunication infrastructure subindices are calculated using the parametric PCA approach, while the composite (TI) is calculated using nonparametric approach (weighted summation of the subindices)	It analyzes ICT-related infrastructures
		Broadcasting			
Technological capability indices (TCI), 2009	Archibugi et al. [6]	Review 9 indices: Tech WEF, TechRead WEF, TechInnov WEF, GSII EUComm, KIWB, ArCo, TAI UNCTAD, TechAdv UNIDO, and SII EUComm		Compute 9 internationally well-known technological capability composite indices using the same data and compare their correlation and performance in ranking sample countries	The indices are used to capture multidimensional nature of technological change and rank countries based on different sets of indicators. Assess the value of synthetic indicators of technological capabilities for public policy, company strategies, and economic studies

(continued)

Table 8.1 (continued)

Index name	Literature reference	Subindices	Methodology	Perspective/use
TR, PC, and DF indices, 2013	Lim and Nguyen [25]	Compare 3 performance indices: *TR*, traditional, *PC* principal component approach, and *DG* dynamic factor approach	Compare the weighting schemes in the three approaches to summarizing information from a number of component variables	The indices are used to capture multidimensional nature of technological change and rank countries based on different sets of indicators. Assess the value of synthetic indicators of technological capabilities for public policy, company strategies and, economic studies
DTI, 2014	Rudra et al. [30]	Examine the linkage between the development of telecommunication infrastructure (DTI), economic growth, and 4 indicator operations of a modern economy	Employ a panel vector-autoregressive model for detecting Granger causality	Find evidence of bidirectional Granger causality between DTI and economic growth in the long run

The e-infrastructure index that we present in this study is the first to cover all areas of infrastructure required for ICT development. It focuses on measuring the e-infrastructure level with comprehensive coverage of related indicators. The framework and indicators used for calculating the e-infrastructure index will be discussed in more detail in the next section.

8.3 Conceptual Framework for Developing an E-Infrastructure Index

8.3.1 Main Objectives and Conceptual Framework

As the main objective of this study is to develop an index that reflects the level of information technological infrastructure in a country (e-infrastructure index), the provisioning of measures (i.e., indicators) for capturing the level of existing e-infrastructures of a country is the first step. Then, this index together with its indicators can be used by developed countries, as well as developing countries, to benchmark their performance. For example, it can be used by developing countries (e.g., by MENA countries as in our study) to compare their performance with developed countries in the OECD.

The framework for the construction of our e-infrastructure index departs from the basic assumption that any country can be ready to implement any kind of e-services once its e-infrastructure is in place. For example, as the adoption of e-government services mainly depends on specific, technology-relevant infrastructures (e.g., access to PCs that are connected to the Internet), these infrastructures should be in place before the introduction of e-government services. Without that, there will be neither hardly any use of e-government services nor further development of e-government services. Therefore, the index should give an indication of the extent to which a country has advanced in all IT-related infrastructure areas and provide a holistic picture of the state of IT-related developments within the country.

8.3.2 Selection of Indicators for the E-Infrastructure Index

In order to make an e-infrastructure index a useful tool for the quantification of the extent of the level of ICT-related infrastructure, we design our index to be multidimensional and decomposable [27]. Following the above-described framework, the selected indicators should represent all major areas of IT relevance. These six areas (which we will also call components or subindices) of the indices are (1) electricity, (2) telecommunications, (3) Internet, (4) processing power, (5) broadcasting, and (6) human capital. For each of these subindices, a list of potential indicators will be established. However, the selection of indicators was strongly influenced by the availability of data (and the quality of the data) for developing countries. Since the availability of IT-related data in the majority of developing countries is poor, data availability was the main restrictive factor in the selection. The selection impacts only the relevance of a particular indicator for contributing to the main objectives but not the conceptual framework of the e-infrastructure index.

8.4   Data and Indicators

The data was obtained from the Word Development Indicator database 2009, the ITU-World Telecommunication/ICT Indicators 2009, and the UNESCO Institute for Statistics (UIS). These databases cover 20 countries of Middle East and North Africa (MENA) and 27 countries of the Organization for Economic Cooperation and Development (OECD) for the time period 2000–2007.

The electric power consumption per capita (kilowatt per hour per capita) indicator is used as a proxy measure for the electricity subindex. The electricity subindex is important as the lack of electricity (besides problems with existing telecommunication infrastructure) which is one of the problems that developing countries face with regard to ICT development.

The telecommunication subindex is a composite of fixed telephone lines per 100 inhabitants indicator and the mobile cellular telephone subscriptions per 100 inhabitants indicator. As mobile cellular telephony replaces fixed telephony in many countries over time, the joined consideration of both indicators is important. The telecommunication subindex is a key indicator for measuring telephone access and uptake. However, despite the high growth of mobile subscriptions and their role in replacing fixed telephony, fixed lines are a basis for Internet access and for upgrading to broadband Internet access.

The Internet is a vital infrastructure for any country in terms of its ICT development. The Internet subindex is based on a composite of the Internet users per 100 inhabitants indicator and the indicator of the Internet bandwidth of a country per inhabitant. While the first indicator (i.e., the Internet users indicator) measures the availability of Internet access by a country, the second indicator measures the quality of the Internet access. The Internet bandwidth of a country refers to the capacity that backbone operators provide to carry Internet traffic to and from other countries. The Internet bandwidth of a country per inhabitant (in bits/second/inhabitants) is calculated by dividing the amount of bandwidth (in bits/second) by the total population [17].

The processing power subindex concerns the computer access and supercomputing in those countries. For this subindex, we use two indicators: personal computers (PCs) per 100 inhabitants and the sum of the processing power of all supercomputers. However, due to the lack of data about supercomputers, only the indicator of personal computers per 100 inhabitants has been used for the computation of the processing power subindex.

Recently, as a result of convergence of services, Internet access and telecommunication services via broadcasting infrastructure become a common approach. To capture this, three indicators could be used for this subindex (media). The first indicator is the number of television sets per 100 inhabitants. The second and third indicators are the number of cable television subscribers per household indicator and the number of satellite subscribers per household indicator. However, as the selection of indicators takes into account the availability of data in the countries under study, we consider only the first indicator.

For the human capital subindex, the key considerations are two human capital indicators and three ICT skills indicators. The human capital indicators capture the number of engineers and technicians, which are required to install, operate, and maintain ICT. The indicators are the number of technicians per million inhabitants and the science and engineering enrollment ratios at colleges. Despite the availability of simple ICT devices (e.g., mobile devices) that require little reading skills, the use of the Internet requires a fairly complex set of skills, including technological know-how and reasonable fluency in English. The skills indicators are primary school enrollment (in percent gross amount), secondary school enrollment (in percent gross amount), and tertiary school enrollment (in percent gross amount). However, due to the lack of data availability in the countries under study, we had to exclude the first two indicators. The computation of the human capital subindex is only based on the last three indicators.

8.5 Methodology and Model Specification

The methodology used in this study includes two different methods, resulting in the computation of four e-infrastructure indices. The first method computes the e-infrastructure index nonparametrically, following the normalized human development index (HDI). The second method estimates the e-infrastructure index parametrically, using the principal component analysis (PCA). The reason for selecting the two methods is to allow for a more detailed analysis of the proposed e-infrastructure indices by comparing their outcomes. Consequently, we can suggest the most appropriate e-infrastructure index for widespread use.

8.5.1 Nonparametric E-Infrastructure Index

The nonparametric e-infrastructure index is a composite index constructed to aggregate a number of indicators of a certain outcome [15]. Such indices are used for measuring many economic or social phenomena, such as globalization [3, 10, 13, 23, 24], the state of the environment [22], human development [26], and the trajectory of development strategy, technology, and research [5, 14].

The basic of our nonparametric e-infrastructure index is a very commonly used index, the United Nation Human Development Program (UNDP) Human Development Index (HDI). Our index differs from the HDI index as we use a different method of weighting than the traditional approach of equal weighting, which is frequently used in the construction of nonparametric indices. The weights of our nonparametric e-infrastructure index are given based on the square of their normalized values. By using this system of weighting, the differences in the performance of countries, which are ranked closely together, become more obvious. The nonparametric e-infrastructure index is then computed as subsequent aggregation of its indicators and subindices, which is shown with the following equation:

$$\text{npindex}_{ct} = \sum_{J}^{j=1} \left\{ \frac{1}{M} \sum_{M}^{m=1} \left\{ \left(x_{jmct} - x_{jmt}^{\min} \right) / \left(x_{jmt}^{\max} - x_{jmt}^{\min} \right) \right\} \right\}^2 \tag{8.1}$$

where the variables c and t indicate the country and the time period. The variable m is the individual indicator for each subindex j. X_{ct} is the observed value of the individual indicator m in a given year. The variable $X_t^{\min}$ is the minimum, and the variable $X_t^{\max}$ is the maximum values of the indicator across countries in a given year, allowing for year-specific reference points.

8.5.2   Parametric E-Infrastructure Index

This study also adopts a parametric method for computing an e-infrastructure index, using principal component analysis (PCA). PCA is a multivariate technique for reducing multidimensional data sets to lower dimensions. It was originally developed by Pearson [28] and further developed by Hotelling [16]. The method has been employed in many areas including the computation of an environmental index [22] and in the computation of a simple globalization index using trade and financial openness by Agénor [2] and a globalization index by Heshmati [13]. Heshmati and Oh [14] used the method for the computation of the Lisbon development strategy index. Besides, Heshmati et al. [15] used PCA to measure and analyze child well-being in middle- and high-income countries. In short, this method gives a least square solution to the following model:

$$Y_{it} = \sum_{J}^{j=1} \beta_j X_{jit} + E_{it} \tag{8.2}$$

where X_{jit} ($j = 1,2,...,J$) is the indicator score for the year t and the country i. Furthermore, the variable β_j is the factor pattern or eigenvector. The variable E_{it} is the residual.

Unlike the traditional lease squares estimation case, in which the vertical distance to the fitted line is minimized, the PCA minimizes the sum of the squared residuals measured as distances from the point to the principal axis. Furthermore, researchers, who use the PCA methodology, use the first principal component to get at a single omnibus measurement scale. In this study, however, we use a more elaborated approach. We rely on the weighted average of several principal components with eigenvalues greater than 1.0, in order to utilize all the power of the principal components in explaining variations in the data. In the aggregation, the share of variance explained by each component is used as weights.

8.6 Analysis and Empirical Results

The summary statistics of the variables are given in Table 8.2. We observed large variations among the variables that are used for calculating the indices. The distribution of the index components is also not uniform. This is particularly evident for the component electricity, Internet, computer, and broadcasting. It has a large dispersion and has a sample mean higher than the median. In case of the human capital component, the mean and median values almost overlap.

Table 8.2 Summary statistics of e-infrastructure data, 2000–2007

Variable	Number of observations	Mean	Median	Standard derivation	Minimum	Maximum
region	376	2.8723	3	1.105	1	4
year	376	2003.5	2003.5	2.2943	2000	2007
elec	376	7540.4	6398.2	6305.2	135.58	36,853
fixd	376	35.844	42.031	20.866	1.227	74.867
cell	376	64.859	72.309	38.244	0	176.5
intn	376	33.753	29.058	25.831	0.048	86
comp	376	30.714	23.966	25.642	0.195	101.47
band	376	23,821	817.91	386,755	0.179	8.00E + 06
tvse	376	51.675	48.917	33.237	6.443	308.38
prim	376	101.15	101.6	11.69	32.5	128
seco	376	94.571	95.9	24.446	13.7	161.7
tert	376	45.84	49.75	23.602	0.3	94.9

elec electricity consumption per capita (kwh per capita, kilo Watt hour per capita)), *fixd* fixed telephone lines per 100 inhabitants, *cell* mobile subscribers per 100 inhabitants, *intn* Internet users per 100 people, *comp* personal computers per 100 inhabitants, *band* international Internet bandwidth per inhabitant (bits/sec), *tvst* number of TV sets per 100 inhabitants, *prim* primary school enrollment (percent gross), *seco* secondary school enrollment (percent gross), *tert* tertiary school enrollment (percent gross)

8.6.1 Estimation of the E-Infrastructure Indices and Their Subindices

8.6.1.1 Nonparametric E-Infrastructure Index

The nonparametric e-infrastructure index is computed for 47 countries over a time period of 8 years starting from 2000 to 2007, using Eq. 8.1. For this, the ten normalized individual indicators have been calculated. After calculating their square values, the indicators have been aggregated first for each subindex and, then, across all subindices.

Based on the nonparametric index for each of the 47 countries, a ranking of the countries under study has been performed (Table 8.3).

Norway is ranked the highest, followed in decreasing order by Sweden, Denmark, Iceland, and Switzerland.

The highest (lowest) contributing component to a country's rank for electricity is Iceland (Djibouti and Yemen), for telecommunications is Iceland (Djibouti), for processing power is Switzerland (Djibouti), for the Internet is Denmark (Djibouti), for broadcasting media is Norway (Djibouti), and for human capital is Australia (Djibouti). The results also show that most OECD countries are ahead of the MENA countries. The only exceptions are three countries (UAE, Bahrain, and Qatar) that belong to the Gulf Cooperation Council (GCC). They are ranked ahead of several OECD countries.

8.6.1.2 Parametric E-Infrastructure Index

For calculating the parametric e-infrastructure index, the first step is to check the correlation structure of the data and find out whether the indicators are correlated. Only if they are correlated, the principal component analysis (PCA) can reduce the number of individual indicators to a small set while preserving the maximum possible proportion of the total variation in the original data set. If the original variables are uncorrelated, the application of PCA is of no value. The result of the correlation check is given in Table 8.4. It shows the correlation coefficients between the index components.

Table 8.4 shows that the components are positively and, some of them, even significantly correlated. Except for the coefficient value of the tertiary education component and the bandwidth component, which shows a negative correlation (-0.071), all other components show a positive correlation. The highest correlation (0.904) is found between Internet users and personal computers. This is expected, as accessing the Internet is highly dependent on the access to a computer. Similarly, there is a high correlation between fixed telephone lines and personal computers (0.804). This is also expected, as fixed telephone lines remain essential for dial-up connections (especially in developing countries) and DSL connections.

Table 8.3 Country ranking according to the nonparametric e-infrastructure index for the period 2000–2007

Obs	Country	electr	telec	proces	intern	media	human	npindex
1	Norway	0.735	0.536	0.492	0.306	0.915	0.564	3.548
2	Sweden	0.291	0.709	0.782	0.518	0.372	0.636	3.309
3	Denmark	0.051	0.696	0.576	0.704	0.390	0.583	3.000
4	Iceland	1.000	0.760	0.344	0.251	0.109	0.475	2.940
5	Switzerland	0.078	0.756	0.963	0.393	0.144	0.335	2.669
6	USA	0.216	0.456	0.789	0.210	0.379	0.509	2.561
7	Netherlands	0.054	0.526	0.634	0.593	0.211	0.528	2.546
8	UK	0.044	0.668	0.490	0.301	0.506	0.452	2.461
9	Canada	0.350	0.383	0.682	0.248	0.235	0.462	2.360
10	Luxembourg	0.300	0.727	0.558	0.335	0.166	0.223	2.308
11	Finland	0.319	0.518	0.337	0.226	0.221	0.664	2.283
12	Australia	0.139	0.455	0.587	0.161	0.203	0.724	2.269
13	Germany	0.057	0.656	0.393	0.194	0.202	0.423	1.925
14	Austria	0.069	0.534	0.434	0.173	0.176	0.408	1.793
15	South Korea	0.060	0.449	0.396	0.192	0.067	0.591	1.754
16	New Zealand	0.103	0.378	0.324	0.186	0.147	0.586	1.723
17	Belgium	0.084	0.461	0.160	0.260	0.132	0.577	1.674
18	France	0.070	0.485	0.342	0.096	0.187	0.486	1.665
19	Ireland	0.043	0.539	0.348	0.087	0.126	0.467	1.611
20	Japan	0.076	0.373	0.260	0.135	0.305	0.410	1.559
21	Italy	0.036	0.603	0.136	0.088	0.143	0.440	1.445
22	Spain	0.039	0.455	0.099	0.066	0.138	0.543	1.339
23	Israel	0.050	0.584	0.098	0.029	0.046	0.453	1.261
24	Greece	0.029	0.547	0.010	0.018	0.121	0.509	1.233
25	Portugal	0.022	0.481	0.027	0.036	0.072	0.514	1.153
26	Czech Rep.	0.043	0.384	0.072	0.052	0.135	0.340	1.026
27	Bahrain	0.141	0.264	0.039	0.021	0.068	0.370	0.904
28	Hungary	0.015	0.307	0.028	0.046	0.101	0.394	0.890
29	UAE	0.201	0.319	0.059	0.049	0.013	0.216	0.857
30	Qatar	0.255	0.205	0.042	0.024	0.074	0.247	0.847
31	Slovak Rep.	0.029	0.197	0.121	0.068	0.067	0.312	0.796
32	Kuwait	0.260	0.153	0.049	0.018	0.067	0.230	0.777
33	Libya	0.008	0.035	0.000	0.000	0.004	0.493	0.541
34	Saudi Arabia	0.049	0.077	0.018	0.006	0.024	0.287	0.460
35	Lebanon	0.005	0.050	0.012	0.015	0.047	0.283	0.412
36	Oman	0.015	0.046	0.003	0.002	0.167	0.170	0.403
37	Jordan	0.003	0.050	0.003	0.004	0.009	0.288	0.356
38	Tunisia	0.001	0.046	0.002	0.003	0.011	0.272	0.336
39	Iran	0.004	0.045	0.010	0.005	0.006	0.235	0.305
40	Egypt	0.001	0.017	0.001	0.002	0.014	0.270	0.304
41	Palestine	0.002	0.015	0.002	0.001	0.004	0.270	0.293
42	Algeria	0.000	0.025	0.000	0.001	0.006	0.243	0.275

(continued)

Table 8.3 (continued)

Obs	Country	electr	telec	proces	intern	media	human	npindex
43	Syria	0.002	0.017	0.002	0.003	0.006	0.223	0.252
44	Iraq	0.001	0.004	0.027	0.006	0.030	0.112	0.181
45	Morocco	0.000	0.022	0.000	0.005	0.005	0.125	0.157
46	Yemen	0.000	0.001	0.000	0.000	0.037	0.072	0.111
47	Djibouti	0.000	0.000	0.000	0.000	0.000	0.000	0.000

Table 8.4 Correlation matrix

	elect	fixed	cell	inter	compu	broadb	tvse	prim	seco	tert
elect	1									
fixed	0.587	1								
cell	0.505	0.639	1							
inter	0.634	0.784	0.717	1						
compu	0.584	0.804	0.623	0.904	1					
broadb	0.073	0.052	0.117	0.100	0.094	1				
tvse	0.528	0.596	0.501	0.690	0.677	0.023	1			
prim	0.081	0.399	0.265	0.125	0.105	0.006	0.065	1		
seco	0.419	0.689	0.567	0.602	0.556	0.012	0.492	0.459	1	
tert	0.413	0.716	0.545	0.711	0.617	−0.071	0.572	0.257	0.715	1

Table 8.5 Eigenvalues of the correlation matrix

Principal component	Eigenvalue	Proportion	Cumulative
1	5.4765	0.5476	0.5476
2	1.1856	0.1186	0.6662
3	1.0235	0.1023	0.7686
4	0.5564	0.0556	0.8242

As the correlation check revealed a strong correlation, the PCA can be applied. For this, we calculate the eigenvalues, the percentage of variance explained in each component, and the total variance explained by all components. Those values are shown in Table 8.5.

The next step is to identify the number of principal components that should be considered for the analysis without losing too much information. Using Kaiser's criterion (1960) for selecting the number of components, we dropped all components with eigenvalues below 1. Consequently, three principal components should be considered in the analysis of the parametric e-infrastructure index (Table 8.5). Their eigenvalue is greater than one.

The first principal component explains the variance in all the individual indicators (with an eigenvalue of 5.4765) more than all other principal components. The second principal component explains the remaining variance with an eigenvalue of 1.1856 the best. The third principal component has an eigenvalue of 1.0235.

Table 8.6 Eigenvectors of the principal components

	prin1	prin2	prin3	prin4
elect	0.3031	−0.206	−0.0050	0.8309
fixed	0.3808	0.0068	−0.0240	−0.0960
cell	0.3333	0.0224	0.1516	0.1039
Internet	0.3936	−0.1790	−0.0260	−0.0890
compu	0.3759	−0.2100	−0.0350	−0.1160
broadb	0.0327	−0.3210	0.9014	−0.1820
tvse	0.3245	−0.2010	−0.1560	−0.0870
prim	0.1251	0.7599	0.3287	0.1849
seco	0.3372	0.3577	0.0583	−0.0240
tert	0.3467	0.1787	−0.1620	−0.4390

The proportion of total variance explained by these principal components is 0.5476 + 0.1186 + 0.1023 = 0.7686.

The eigenvectors of each principal component are shown in Table 8.6. An eigenvector value, which is larger than 0.3, indicates that an indicator has a significant contribution to the component. Its sign indicates the direction of the contribution. Although each indicator usually plays a significant role to only one principal component, some indicators are explained in two principal components (e.g., primary and secondary school enrollments). To address this, we use a weighted average of the three principal components.

In the computation of the parametric e-infrastructure index, the first three components are aggregated by using their share of variance explanation as weights:

$$
\begin{aligned}
\text{prin123} = \text{prin1}^* \left(0.5476 / 0.7686\right) + \text{prin2}^* \left(0.1186 / 0.7686\right) \\
+ \text{prin3}^* \left(0.1023 / 0.7686\right)
\end{aligned}
\tag{8.3}
$$

The results of the parametric e-infrastructure index calculation for all 47 countries and the ranking of the 47 countries are given in Table 8.7. To simplify the comparison of both indices, the nonparametric e-infrastructure index is listed in Table 8.7 as well. Similar to the nonparametric index, the results show that OECD countries are ahead of the MENA countries with the exception of Israel and Bahrain. They are ranked ahead of several OECD countries.

The ranking based on the result of the parametric method shows Sweden, Norway, Australia, Denmark, and Iceland at the top of the list. This ranking of the top performers shows some slight differences to the ranking of the nonparametric e-infrastructure index. For example, Norway and Sweden swap their positions. Norway is ranked 2nd, while it is ranked 1st according to the nonparametric e-infrastructure index, and Sweden is ranked 1st, while it is ranked 2nd according to the nonparametric e-infrastructure index. The highest difference in position is observed in case of Australia. It has been ranked 12th in the nonparametric e-infrastructure index but is ranked 3rd in the parametric e-infrastructure index.

Table 8.7 Comparison of the nonparametric and the parametric e-infrastructure indices, 2000–2007, 376 observations

Parametric e-infrastructure index			Nonparametric e-infrastructure index		
Rank by prin123	Country	prin123	Rank by npindex	Country	npindex
1	Sweden	1.014	2	Sweden	3.309
2	Norway	0.940	1	Norway	3.548
3	Australia	0.890	12	Australia	2.269
4	Denmark	0.809	3	Denmark	3.000
5	Iceland	0.794	4	Iceland	2.940
6	Finland	0.751	11	Finland	2.283
7	Netherlands	0.728	7	Netherlands	2.546
8	USA	0.582	6	USA	2.561
9	UK	0.578	8	UK	2.461
10	Luxembourg	0.573	10	Luxembourg	2.308
11	Belgium	0.560	17	Belgium	1.674
12	Canada	0.531	9	Canada	2.360
13	New Zealand	0.527	16	New Zealand	1.723
14	Switzerland	0.496	5	Switzerland	2.669
15	South Korea	0.495	15	South Korea	1.754
16	Germany	0.468	13	Germany	1.925
17	France	0.463	18	France	1.665
18	Ireland	0.402	19	Ireland	1.611
19	Austria	0.385	14	Austria	1.793
20	Portugal	0.383	25	Portugal	1.153
21	Spain	0.381	22	Spain	1.339
22	Italy	0.318	21	Italy	1.445
23	Japan	0.296	20	Japan	1.559
24	Israel	0.290	23	Israel	1.261
25	Greece	0.158	24	Greece	1.233
26	Bahrain	0.087	27	Bahrain	0.904
27	Czech Rep.	0.021	26	Czech Rep.	1.026
28	Hungary	−0.062	28	Hungary	0.890
29	Slovak Rep.	−0.151	31	Slovak Rep.	0.796
30	Qatar	−0.190	30	Qatar	0.847
31	UAE	-0.248	29	UAE	0.857
32	Libya	−0.268	33	Libya	0.541
33	Kuwait	−0.348	32	Kuwait	0.777
34	Saudi Arabia	−0.398	34	Saudi Arabia	0.460
35	Tunisia	−0.562	38	Tunisia	0.336
36	Lebanon	−0.608	35	Lebanon	0.412
37	Jordan	−0.612	37	Jordan	0.356
38	Iran	−0.671	39	Iran	0.305
39	Algeria	−0.690	42	Algeria	0.275
40	Syria	−0.693	43	Syria	0.252

(continued)

Table 8.7 (continued)

Parametric e-infrastructure index			Nonparametric e-infrastructure index		
Rank by prin123	Country	prin123	Rank by npindex	Country	npindex
41	Egypt	−0.701	40	Egypt	0.304
42	Palestine	−0.792	41	Palestine	0.293
43	Oman	−0.843	36	Oman	0.403
44	Morocco	−1.029	45	Morocco	0.157
45	Iraq	−1.161	44	Iraq	0.181
46	Yemen	−1.454	46	Yemen	0.111
47	Djibouti	−2.438	47	Djibouti	0.000

$$\text{prin123} = \text{prin1} * (0.5476 / 0.7686) + \text{prin2} * (0.1186 / 0.7686) + \text{prin3} * (0.1023 / 0.7686)$$

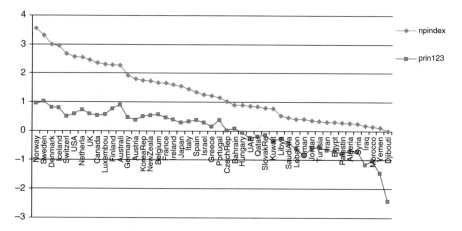

Fig. 8.1 Comparison of nonparametric (npindex) and parametric (prin123) e-infrastructure indices, 2000 and 2007, sorted by npindex in descending order

Comparing the ranking of all countries according to both e-infrastructure indices in Fig. 8.1, the ranking results look similar though. The differences in ranking of each country are little as well as the variation in ranking positions. The nonparametric e-infrastructure index (npindex) is sorted in descending order, providing homogeneously distributed values. It results in almost a linear curve. The parametric e-infrastructure index (prin123) provides very similar values for a large portion of countries, which are ranked in the middle of the list. Irregular differences between the two indices are observed in two cases only, Djibouti and Australia.

In addition to this, both rankings show that the low ranks of some countries are to some extent linked to their economic condition. While poor countries from MENA have low ranks, rich MENA countries (e.g., the Gulf Cooperation Council (GCC) countries) have made remarkable developments. They are not only leading the ranking of MENA countries but they are also higher ranked than a few OECD countries.

8.6.2   Analysis of Heterogeneity in Both E-Infrastructure Indices

Variations in the values of the e-infrastructure indices and their components can be the result of the situation of a country, its geographical location (i.e., regions), and the changes over time. In this section, we will analyze the heterogeneity of countries with respect to these three factors in more detail.

8.6.2.1   Country Heterogeneity in E-Infrastructure Development

The results of the nonparametric e-infrastructure index shows that the performance of countries differs by components (Table 8.8). It also shows that there is no dependency between components, i.e., if a country performed well in one component, it does not mean that it also performs well in another component. An example is Norway, which is ranked 1st, in broadcasting media. It has neither the highest score in electricity (2nd), telecommunication (12th), computers (9th), Internet (6th), nor human capital (8th). With the exception of Iceland, there is no country that gains the highest score in more than one of the six components. However, despite its highest scores in both electricity and telecommunication components, Iceland is only ranked 4th. It shows low performance in the other components (computer 15th, broadcasting media 24th, Internet 9th, and human capital 16th). Denmark, which is ranked 3rd, has the highest Internet score among all countries and a low electricity consumption (22nd).

Among the low-ranked countries, we find that some MENA countries, particularly Gulf countries, perform relatively well in terms of electricity (UAE is 10th, Qatar is 8th, and Kuwait is 7th). Despite their significant improvements in the last few years, especially with respect to mobile and Internet penetration, their low rank is caused by their poor performance in the early years (2000–2003). The other low-ranked countries still have a poor performance in all e-infrastructure components compared with the high-ranked countries.

8.6.2.2   Regional Heterogeneity in E-Infrastructure Development

This analysis is based on grouping the countries by their geographical location and their membership to the OECD. Countries are grouped into four groups: Middle East, North Africa, European, and other non-European OECD countries. Although the OECD group includes countries from different continents, many countries are from Europe. Therefore, we grouped the OECD countries into two groups: European OECD countries and non-European OECD countries. Despite the fact that the non-European OECD countries are from different continents, these countries share similar characteristics, including the level of economic growth and the type of economic system.

Table 8.8 The distribution of the nonparametric index and its decomposition, 2000–2007, 376 observations

Country	electr		telec		proces		intern		media		human		Nonparametric e-infrastructure index (npindex)	
	Rank	Value	Rank	Value	Rank	Value	Rank	Value	Rank	Value	Rank	Value	Rank	Value
Norway	2	0.735	12	0.536	9	0.492	6	0.306	1	0.915	8	0.564	1	3.548
Sweden	6	0.291	4	0.709	3	0.782	3	0.518	5	0.372	3	0.636	2	3.309
Denmark	22	0.051	5	0.696	7	0.576	1	0.704	3	0.390	6	0.583	3	3.000
Iceland	1	1.000	1	0.760	15	0.344	9	0.251	24	0.109	16	0.475	4	2.940
Switzerland	15	0.078	2	0.756	1	0.963	4	0.393	17	0.144	28	0.335	5	2.669
USA	9	0.216	19	0.456	2	0.789	12	0.210	4	0.379	12	0.509	6	2.561
Netherlands	21	0.054	14	0.526	5	0.634	2	0.593	9	0.211	10	0.528	7	2.546
UK	25	0.044	6	0.668	10	0.490	7	0.301	2	0.506	20	0.452	8	2.461
Canada	3	0.350	24	0.383	4	0.682	10	0.248	7	0.235	18	0.462	9	2.360
Luxembourg	5	0.300	3	0.727	8	0.558	5	0.335	15	0.166	40	0.223	10	2.308
Finland	4	0.319	15	0.518	17	0.337	11	0.226	8	0.221	2	0.664	11	2.283
Australia	12	0.139	20	0.455	6	0.587	17	0.161	10	0.203	1	0.724	12	2.269
Germany	20	0.057	7	0.656	13	0.393	13	0.194	11	0.202	22	0.423	13	1.925
Austria	18	0.069	13	0.534	11	0.434	16	0.173	13	0.176	24	0.408	14	1.793
South Korea	19	0.060	22	0.449	12	0.396	14	0.192	29	0.067	4	0.591	15	1.754
New Zealand	13	0.103	25	0.378	18	0.324	15	0.186	16	0.147	5	0.586	16	1.723
Belgium	14	0.084	18	0.461	20	0.160	8	0.260	21	0.132	7	0.577	17	1.674
France	17	0.070	16	0.485	16	0.342	19	0.096	12	0.187	15	0.486	18	1.665
Ireland	26	0.043	11	0.539	14	0.348	21	0.087	22	0.126	17	0.467	19	1.611
Japan	16	0.076	26	0.373	19	0.260	18	0.135	6	0.305	23	0.410	20	1.559
Italy	29	0.036	8	0.603	21	0.136	20	0.088	18	0.143	21	0.440	21	1.445
Spain	28	0.039	21	0.455	23	0.099	23	0.066	19	0.138	9	0.543	22	1.339
Israel	23	0.050	9	0.584	24	0.098	28	0.029	33	0.046	19	0.453	23	1.261

(continued)

Table 8.8 (continued)

Country	electr		telec		proces		intern		media		human		Nonparametric e-infrastructure index (npindex)	
	Rank	Value	Rank	Value	Rank	Value	Rank	Value	Rank	Value	Rank	Value	Rank	Value
Greece	30	0.029	10	0.547	35	0.010	32	0.018	23	0.121	13	0.509	24	1.233
Portugal	32	0.022	17	0.481	31	0.027	27	0.036	27	0.072	11	0.514	25	1.153
Czech Rep.	27	0.043	23	0.384	25	0.072	24	0.052	20	0.135	27	0.340	26	1.026
Bahrain	11	0.141	29	0.264	29	0.039	30	0.021	28	0.068	26	0.370	27	0.904
Hungary	33	0.015	28	0.307	30	0.028	26	0.046	25	0.101	25	0.394	28	0.890
UAE	10	0.201	27	0.319	26	0.059	25	0.049	38	0.013	42	0.216	29	0.857
Qatar	8	0.255	30	0.205	28	0.042	29	0.024	26	0.074	36	0.247	30	0.847
Slovak Rep.	31	0.029	31	0.197	22	0.121	22	0.068	30	0.067	29	0.312	31	0.796
Kuwait	7	0.260	32	0.153	27	0.049	31	0.018	31	0.067	39	0.230	32	0.777
Libya	35	0.008	39	0.035	43	0.000	45	0.000	46	0.004	14	0.493	33	0.541
Saudi Arabia	24	0.049	33	0.077	33	0.018	35	0.006	36	0.024	31	0.287	34	0.460
Lebanon	36	0.005	34	0.050	34	0.012	33	0.015	32	0.047	32	0.283	35	0.412
Oman	34	0.015	36	0.046	38	0.003	41	0.002	14	0.167	43	0.170	36	0.403
Jordan	38	0.003	35	0.050	37	0.003	38	0.004	40	0.009	30	0.288	37	0.356
Tunisia	41	0.001	37	0.046	39	0.002	39	0.003	39	0.011	33	0.272	38	0.336
Iran	37	0.004	38	0.045	36	0.010	36	0.005	41	0.006	38	0.235	39	0.305
Egypt	42	0.001	43	0.017	42	0.001	42	0.002	37	0.014	34	0.270	40	0.304
Palestine	39	0.002	44	0.015	41	0.002	43	0.001	45	0.004	35	0.270	41	0.293
Algeria	44	0.000	40	0.025	44	0.000	44	0.001	43	0.006	37	0.243	42	0.275
Syria	40	0.002	42	0.017	40	0.002	40	0.003	42	0.006	41	0.223	43	0.252
Iraq	43	0.001	45	0.004	32	0.027	34	0.006	35	0.030	45	0.112	44	0.181
Morocco	45	0.000	41	0.022	45	0.000	37	0.005	44	0.005	44	0.125	45	0.157
Yemen	46	0.000	46	0.001	46	0.000	46	0.000	34	0.037	46	0.072	46	0.111
Djibouti	47	0.000	47	0.000	47	0.000	47	0.000	47	0.000	47	0.000	47	0.000

Table 8.9 Mean e-infrastructure indices by region, 2000–2007, 376 observations

Rank	Region	electr	telec	proces	intern	media	human	Nonparametric e-infrastructure index (npindex)	Parametric e-infrastructure index (prin123)
1	Non-European OECD countries	0.278	0.465	0.483	0.198	0.206	0.537	2.166	0.588
2	European OECD countries	0.120	0.539	0.350	0.228	0.226	0.470	1.934	0.461
3	Middle East countries	0.070	0.131	0.026	0.013	0.043	0.247	0.530	−0.546
4	North Africa countries	0.002	0.024	0.001	0.002	0.007	0.234	0.269	−0.948

As expected, both types of e-infrastructure indices show that the non-European OECD countries and the European OECD regions have the highest e-infrastructure scores (Table 8.9). The Middle East region holds the third rank, and the North African region comes out at the bottom of the list.

The non-European OECD region and the European OECD countries differ in the values of the components. For instance, the non-European OECD countries are advantageous in terms of electricity consumption, computers, and human capital, while the European OECD region has a much higher level of telecommunication. In terms of Internet and broadcasting media, they are at a similar level. Despite their progress in the human capital component, the Middle East and North Africa regions still show a relatively low level in all of the other e-infrastructure components. The gap between MENA and the OECD is quite large, as depicted in Fig. 8.2.

Furthermore, given the close relationship between e-infrastructure levels and GDP, most of MENA countries are still lagging behind in terms of e-infrastructure compared with OECD countries. The North Africa region is identified as the least developed region in e-infrastructure. Thus, the low rank of countries is to large extent linked to their economic conditions and their inability to address these issues effectively.

8.6.2.3 Development of E-Infrastructure Over Time

Eight years (2000–2007) is a relatively long period in terms of information and communication technology (ICT) development. ICT technology, infrastructure, and access values may change considerably as a result of the introduction of new technologies, enhanced investments, changes in the market environment, or price cuts. Therefore, the e-infrastructure indices are expected to show large changes over a period of 8 years.

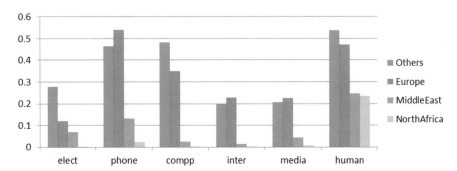

Fig. 8.2 Region heterogeneity of components of the nonparametric e-infrastructure index, 2000–2007

Looking at Fig. 8.3a, in which the indices are normalized at their 2,000 values to ease comparison of their development over time, it can be observed that the parametric e-infrastructure index continuously increased over time. The nonparametric index increased from 2000 to 2001 from 1.000 to 1.016. Afterwards, however, it declined to 0.953 in 2002 and remained at this level until 2005. Then, it declined again to 0.925 in 2007 suggesting 7.5 percent decline in the period. In contrast, the parametric index is continuously increasing from 1.000 in 2000 to 1.604 in 2007, suggesting 60.4% increase during the period studied. The individual country level index development shown in Fig. 8.3b confirms the gap pattern between the two indices. The decline after 2000 is very likely attributed to the global IT bubble. The difference in development of the two indices over time is a result of difference in weights attached to each indicator. Therefore, the parametric e-infrastructure index development is consistent with expectations and, therefore, preferable.

8.6.3 Efficiency in E-Infrastructure Development

In Table 8.10, we report the efficiency of countries in terms of e-infrastructure development. The efficiency of a country is the comparison of the country with the country that has the best-practiced e-infrastructure (i.e., the highest e-infrastructure value). The efficiency measure is in the interval 0 to 1, where 0 is assigned to the country with the lowest score and 1 to the country with the highest score. The measure is computed for the two e-infrastructure indices. It should be noted that the efficiency measure not only shows the rank but also the metric distance to the frontier e-infrastructure and it is easily interpretable as percentage points. Thus, the distance to the best in the e-infrastructure index is quantitatively measured. Concerning the nonparametric e-infrastructure index, Norway is serving as the reference country, while, in the case of the parametric e-infrastructure index, Sweden is the reference country.

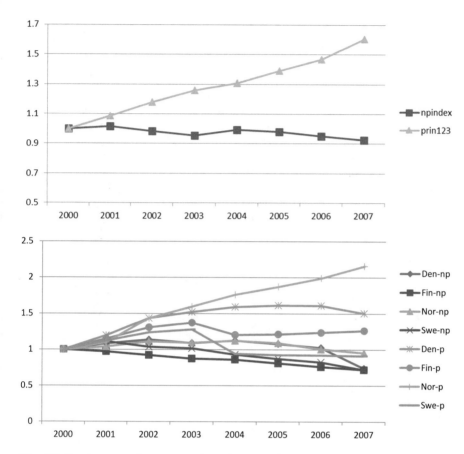

Fig. 8.3 Development of nonparametric and parametric e-infrastructure indices over time: (**a**) normalized at 2000 level and averaged over all countries (npindex and prin123); (**b**) normalized at 2000 level for Scandinavian countries. The nonparametric and parametric indices are indicated with a "np" and "p," respectively

The values of the two efficiencies for each country are shown in Fig. 8.4. In general, both methods show similar performances. Only in a few cases, we observe a significant shift in the position of countries.

We find a wide range of variation in the efficiency among countries. For instance, in the case of the nonparametric index, the efficiency rate of MENA countries is below 50% of the frontier country. It shows that MENA countries perform very poorly compared to the frontier country in terms of e-infrastructure. The efficiency measure for the parametric e-infrastructure index shows that some MENA countries, particularly Bahrain, Qatar, and the UAE, achieve an efficiency of more than 50 performance points (Bahrain 0.7315, Qatar 0.6512, and UAE 0.63). In case of Djibouti, which is placed at the bottom of the efficiency distribution of the two indices, the efficiency is zero.

Table 8.10 Two efficiency measures based on the mean parametric and nonparametric e-infrastructure indices, 2000–2007 (countries are ranked by parametric index), 376 observations

Country	Nonparametric e-infrastructure index (npindex)	Parametric e-infrastructure index (prin123)	Efficiency with respect to the best nonparametric e-infrastructure index	Efficiency with respect to the best parametric e-infrastructure index
Sweden	3.309	1.014	0.9326	1.0000
Norway	3.548	0.940	1.0000	0.9786
Australia	2.269	0.890	0.6395	0.9641
Denmark	3000	0.809	0.8455	0.9406
Iceland	2.940	0.794	0.8286	0.9363
Finland	2.283	0.751	0.6435	0.9238
Netherlands	2.546	0.728	0.7176	0.9171
USA	2.561	0.582	0.7218	0.8749
UK	2.461	0.578	0.6936	0.8737
Luxembourg	2.308	0.573	0.6505	0.8722
Belgium	1.674	0.560	0.4718	0.8685
Canada	2.360	0.531	0.6652	0.8601
New Zealand	1.723	0.527	0.4856	0.8589
Switzerland	2.669	0.496	0.7523	0.8499
South Korea	1.754	0.495	0.4944	0.8497
Germany	1.925	0.468	0.5426	0.8418
France	1.665	0.463	0.4693	0.8404
Ireland	1.611	0.402	0.4541	0.8227
Austria	1.793	0.385	0.5054	0.8178
Portugal	1.153	0.383	0.3250	0.8172
Spain	1.339	0.381	0.3774	0.8166
Italy	1.445	0.318	0.4073	0.7984
Japan	1.559	0.296	0.4394	0.7920
Israel	1.261	0.290	0.3554	0.7903
Greece	1.233	0.158	0.3475	0.7520
Bahrain	0.904	0.087	0.2548	0.7315
Czech Rep.	1.026	0.021	0.2892	0.7123
Hungary	0.890	−0.062	0.2508	0.6883
Slovak Rep.	0.796	−0.151	0.2244	0.6625
Qatar	0.847	−0.190	0.2387	0.6512
UAE	0.857	−0.248	0.2415	0.6344
Libya	0.541	−0.268	0.1525	0.6286
Kuwait	0.777	−0.348	0.2190	0.6054
Saudi Arabia	0.460	−0.398	0.1297	0.5910
Tunisia	0.336	−0.562	0.0947	0.5435
Lebanon	0.412	−0.608	0.1161	0.5301
Jordan	0.356	−0.612	0.1003	0.5290

(continued)

Table 8.10   (continued)

Country	Nonparametric e-infrastructure index (npindex)	Parametric e-infrastructure index (prin123)	Efficiency with respect to the best nonparametric e-infrastructure index	Efficiency with respect to the best parametric e-infrastructure index
Iran	0.305	−0.671	0.0860	0.5119
Algeria	0.275	−0.690	0.0775	0.5064
Syria	0.252	−0.693	0.0710	0.5055
Egypt	0.304	−0.701	0.0857	0.5032
Palestine	0.293	−0.792	0.0826	0.4768
Oman	0.403	−0.843	0.1136	0.4621
Morocco	0.157	−1.029	0.0443	0.4082
Iraq	0.181	−1.161	0.0510	0.3699
Yemen	0.111	−1.454	0.0313	0.2851
Djibouti	0.000	−2.438	0.0000	0.0000

effnpindex = npindex/3.548; effprin123 = (prin123 + 2.438)/(1.014 + 2.438)

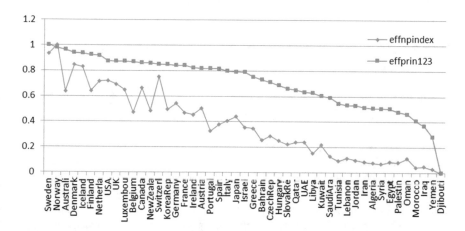

Fig. 8.4 Efficiency based on mean parametric (effprin123) and nonparametric (effnpindex) e-infrastructure indices, 2000–2007, sorted by parametric index in descending order

8.6.4   Comparison Between Different Types of Parametric and Nonparametric Indices

In this section, our nonparametric index, in which each component is given weight by squaring its value, is compared with the human-development-index-type (HDI-type) index, which is based on equal weighting. Besides, our parametric index, which is based on several principal components with eigenvalues greater than 1.0, is compared with the traditional approach that uses only the first principal component. The aim of the comparisons is to see the effect of the new approaches on the ranking of countries.

8.6.4.1   Effect of the New Approach of the Nonparametric E-Infrastructure Indices

Table 8.11 presents the results of our nonparametric index and the HDI-type index. Our method for computing the nonparametric index is compared with the HDI-type index. The nonparametric HDI-type index is based on the ad hoc assignment of weights for the aggregation of the components. For our index, the components are squared before aggregation to give high weights to those with high values. As a result of giving higher weights to the countries with high values, the rank of countries changes compared with those based on the HDI-type index. For instance, among the highest-ranked countries, the Netherlands and Canada swap their positions 5th (6th). The same occurs with Switzerland and the USA 7th (9th). Norway is ranked as the highest in both indices. Iceland, Luxembourg, Sweden, the UK, and Australia keep their positions without change (2nd, 3rd, 4th, 8th, and 10th, respectively). Surprisingly, Portugal and the Slovak Republic swap their positions 27th (31st). Among the MENA countries, the UAE, Kuwait, Saudi Arabia, and Iran keep their positions (ranked 23rd, 33rd, 34th, and 35th, respectively). Also, Iraq, Yemen, and Djibouti keep their ranks at the bottom of the table at 45th, 46th, and 47th, respectively (Fig. 8.5).

8.6.4.2   Effect of the New Approach of the Parametric E-Infrastructure Index

Traditionally, researchers, who use the principal component analysis methodology, use the first principal component to arrive at a single measurement scale. In this study, we computed the index based on the weighted average of the three principal components. In this way, we utilize the explaining power of all significant principal components. The result of the calculation of both indices is shown in Table 8.12.

If we rank countries by the index (prin1) that is based on the first principal component, the rank of some countries is changed significantly compared to our approach. For instance, Luxembourg moved down eight places, from 1st to 9th. That is to be expected because the result of the principal component analysis shows that prin1 does not count the contribution of the international Internet bandwidth indicator and primary enrollment indicator. They were represented in the second (prin2) and third principal component (prin3) but not in the first principal component (prin1). Luxembourg has made a remarkable increase in the international Internet bandwidth indicator (7.5 Mbit/sec per inhabitant in 2007, the highest among all countries) due to the new fiber network deployed by Luxembourg's incumbent operator P&T in 2007 (Fig. 8.6). Another country, which has a lower rank, is Bahrain. It moved down from 18th to 25th. This is also due to the fact that prin1 does not count the contribution of the primary enrollment indicator. Bahrain has the highest value among all the countries surveyed. Countries which decreased in the ranking are Australia, Finland, France, Germany, New Zealand, Korea, Ireland, Spain, Portugal, Qatar, Libya, Iran, Syria, Tunisia, Algeria, and Morocco. Denmark, Italy, Belgium, Egypt, Iraq, Yemen, and Djibouti kept their positions. The remaining countries increased in the ranking.

Table 8.11 Comparison between nonparametric e-infrastructure indices, 2000–2007, 376 observations

Rank by squared components nonparametric index	Country	npindex	Rank by nonparametric index without squaring its components	Country	npindex2
1	Norway	3.038	1	Norway	4.171
2	Iceland	2.588	2	Iceland	3.579
3	Luxembourg	2.517	3	Luxembourg	3.554
4	Sweden	2.364	4	Sweden	3.540
5	Netherlands	2.236	6	Netherlands	3.325
6	Canada	2.225	5	Canada	3.369
7	Switzerland	2.039	9	Switzerland	3.086
8	UK	1.952	8	UK	3.117
9	USA	1.931	7	USA	3.225
10	Australia	1.909	10	Australia	3.042
11	Germany	1.790	13	Germany	2.948
12	Denmark	1.713	12	Denmark	2.962
13	Finland	1.666	11	Finland	3.004
14	France	1.628	14	France	2.800
15	Ireland	1.541	18	Ireland	2.675
16	South Korea	1.540	16	South Korea	2.728
17	New Zealand	1.511	15	New Zealand	2.766
18	Austria	1.449	17	Austria	2.722
19	Italy	1.422	20	Italy	2.600
20	Belgium	1.279	21	Belgium	2.542
21	Spain	1.254	22	Spain	2.400
22	Japan	1.237	19	Japan	2.608
23	UAE	1.202	23	UAE	2.367
24	Greece	1.175	25	Greece	2.084
25	Bahrain	1.023	24	Bahrain	2.126
26	Israel	1.021	29	Israel	2.002
27	Portugal	0.992	31	Portugal	1.970
28	Slovak Rep.	0.908	26	Slovak Rep.	2.064
29	Qatar	0.890	28	Qatar	2.028
30	Hungary	0.887	30	Hungary	1.999
31	Czech Rep.	0.883	27	Czech Rep.	2.052
32	Kuwait	0.691	32	Kuwait	1.890
33	Saudi Arabia	0.563	33	Saudi Arabia	1.521
34	Libya	0.543	37	Libya	1.125
35	Iran	0.451	35	Iran	1.192
36	Lebanon	0.392	34	Lebanon	1.215
37	Jordan	0.368	38	Jordan	1.115

(continued)

Table 8.11 (continued)

Rank by squared components nonparametric index	Country	npindex	Rank by nonparametric index without squaring its components	Country	npindex2
38	Tunisia	0.359	39	Tunisia	1.036
39	Algeria	0.338	42	Algeria	0.901
40	Egypt	0.338	41	Egypt	0.941
41	Oman	0.332	36	Oman	1.178
42	Syria	0.318	40	Syria	0.958
43	Palestine	0.250	45	Palestine	0.766
44	Morocco	0.195	44	Morocco	0.772
45	Iraq	0.190	43	Iraq	0.821
46	Yemen	0.084	46	Yemen	0.462
47	Djibouti	0.000	47	Djibouti	0.017

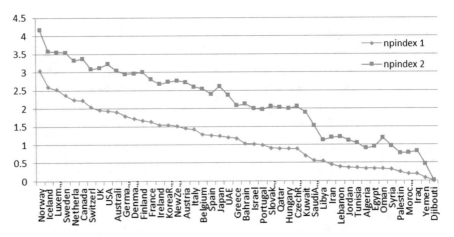

Fig. 8.5 Nonparametric e-infrastructure indices, 2000–2007, sorted by npindex 1 in descending order

8.7 Discussion and Implications

8.7.1 Guidelines for Improving the Index

There is a growing amount of literature on the measurement of e-readiness across countries such as e-government, e-commerce, and other ICT developments. However, the e-infrastructure, which is considered as the basis for such development, is not investigated much.

Table 8.12 Comparison between parametric e-infrastructure indices, 2000–2007, 376 observations

Rank by prin123	Country	prin123	Rank by prin1	Country	prin1
1	Luxembourg	2.226	9	Luxembourg	1.276
2	Norway	1.257	1	Norway	2.497
3	Australia	1.042	8	Australia	1.308
4	Netherlands	1.008	4	Netherlands	1.466
5	Iceland	0.950	3	Iceland	1.604
6	Sweden	0.888	2	Sweden	1.618
7	Denmark	0.849	7	Denmark	1.309
8	Finland	0.779	10	Finland	1.268
9	France	0.737	16	France	0.929
10	Germany	0.735	12	Germany	1.080
11	New Zealand	0.735	14	New Zealand	1.045
12	USA	0.714	6	USA	1.321
13	Canada	0.707	5	Canada	1.325
14	South Korea	0.704	15	South Korea	0.957
15	UK	0.681	11	UK	1.180
16	Ireland	0.672	18	Ireland	0.865
17	Italy	0.669	17	Italy	0.885
18	Bahrain	0.652	25	Bahrain	0.337
19	Spain	0.629	22	Spain	0.723
20	Switzerland	0.591	13	Switzerland	1.066
21	Belgium	0.564	21	Belgium	0.781
22	Austria	0.536	19	Austria	0.853
23	Portugal	0.474	27	Portugal	0.294
24	Japan	0.443	20	Japan	0.818
25	Greece	0.437	23	Greece	0.523
26	UAE	0.423	24	UAE	0.446
27	Israel	0.379	29	Israel	0.252
28	Qatar	0.313	31	Qatar	0.201
29	Czech Rep.	0.227	28	Czech Rep.	0.281
30	Hungary	0.174	26	Hungary	0.311
31	Slovak Rep.	0.165	30	Slovak Rep.	0.203
32	Saudi Arabia	−0.010	33	Saudi Arabia	−0.289
33	Kuwait	−0.123	32	Kuwait	−0.092
34	Libya	−0.152	35	Libya	−0.585
35	Iran	−0.167	38	Iran	−0.676
36	Syria	−0.316	42	Syria	−0.958
37	Tunisia	−0.390	39	Tunisia	−0.765
38	Algeria	−0.392	41	Algeria	−0.893
39	Jordan	−0.444	37	Jordan	−0.641
40	Egypt	−0.475	40	Egypt	−0.860
41	Lebanon	−0.485	34	Lebanon	−0.584
42	Oman	−0.662	36	Oman	−0.618

(continued)

Table 8.12 (continued)

Rank by prin123	Country	prin123	Rank by prin1	Country	prin1
43	Morocco	−0.726	44	Morocco	−1.174
44	Palestine	−0.894	43	Palestine	−1.036
45	Iraq	−0.932	45	Iraq	−1.242
46	Yemen	−1.294	46	Yemen	−1.558
47	Djibouti	−2.261	47	Djibouti	−2.137

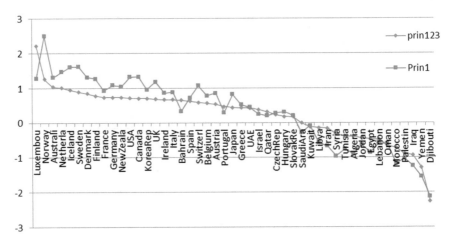

Fig. 8.6 Parametric e-infrastructure indices, (weighted and first principal component based), 2000–2007, sorted by weighted index (prin123) in descending order

This study serves as a major first step toward establishing a proper composite e-infrastructure index. The e-infrastructure index covers all of the related infrastructure components, including electricity, telecommunication, Internet, processing power, broadcasting, and human capital. A breakdown of the index into major components provides the possibility to track each component separately and to identify the strengths and weaknesses of each country in different e-infrastructure areas.

Despite the significant effort made in the construction of the e-infrastructure index, several essential improvements are still possible. One improvement can be achieved by using recent data (i.e., data for the years 2008 and later).

As a consequence of the unavailability of data, especially for MENA countries, particular indicators such as fixed-line broadband Internet subscribers, mobile broadband Internet subscribers, cable television subscribers per households, home satellite antennas, technicians, and engineers were excluded from the study. These additional factors were believed to be relevant and important for creating the e-infrastructure index. With the addition of these indicators, we would have been able to observe the level of e-infrastructure development more accurately.

Using our indices, it would be interesting to investigate how the land size of a country and the size of the urban population impact e-infrastructure development. It is easier to speed up the development of e-infrastructure in a country with a small area and high urban population compared to a large country with scattered populations in rural areas.

It would be also interesting to use our indices to observe the impact of a country's willingness to spend money on the level of the e-infrastructure of the country.

8.7.2 Policy Recommendations

The two types of the multidimensional e-infrastructure indices, parametric and non-parametric, serve as important tools to measure the level of e-infrastructure development among countries and regions and provide useful information about the strengths and weaknesses of the countries in different technological infrastructure areas. The e-infrastructure index can help policy makers with the opportunity to point out the source of the failures they encounter when they are developing their e- infrastructure and allow them to adapt and develop policies for enhancing it accordingly. Based on the results of the study, it should be noted that:

1. The indicators of the e-infrastructure indices showed their significant contribution in determining the level of e-infrastructure development. These indicators have to be focused well in the national policy of all countries. Moving toward developing its e-infrastructure, the government should allocate a significant share or proportion of their annual budget to invest on these indicators.
2. For a country to exploit the potential of ICT, there is a need for the availability of e-infrastructure. Therefore, a country should not only invest in ICT but rather in all technological infrastructure areas that are prerequisites for subsequent access and use of ICT. Based on the results presented by the e-infrastructure indices, many countries in the MENA region suffer from a lack of the basic infrastructure (i.e., electricity) needed to build a solid e-infrastructure base. Therefore, these countries should increase their investments to provide solutions to the basic problems, which are still considered an obstacle for ICT uptake.
3. It is clear that MENA countries still lag behind in the provision of e-services as a result of their poor e-infrastructure. Despite the significant improvements in different areas of e-infrastructure, especially in mobile and Internet penetrations, MENA countries need to increase their investments in the development of their e-infrastructure. Early investment in the provision of that infrastructure can potentially bring faster and more radical changes in the future of the socioeconomic development of these countries.
4. The results show that MENA countries have made a significant improvement in mobile technology. Of course, this is related to the strong relationship between market liberalization and mobile diffusion. Open competition between mobile companies has played a significant role in the dramatic mobile penetration growth in MENA countries. In order to achieve the same growth in the Internet, MENA countries should duplicate this policy with regard to the Internet sector,

which is currently monopolized by the government. The policy should focus on motivating the private sector to invest in e- infrastructure development.

5. Internet quality and connectivity are a vital piece of infrastructure for any country with regard to its ICT development. Therefore, countries should invest in developing their international Internet bandwidth as a crucial backbone infrastructure. Without the necessary international Internet bandwidth, access to the resources of the Internet remains slow and expensive.

6. The e-infrastructure index shows that one of the key factors that impacts or limits e-infrastructure development is the lack of computers. Computer penetration is still very low in MENA countries because many people still cannot afford to buy computers. Therefore, the government should initiate programs to support computer use through the distribution of low-price computers to allow more people to gain access to computers. Also, import taxes on ICT goods should be reduced.

8.8   Conclusion

In this study, we developed and presented two composite indices that quantify the level of e-infrastructure of a country. The e-infrastructure indices are composed of six main components: electricity, telecommunication, Internet, processing power, broadcasting, and human capital. Each component is composed of one or more indicators. We have also suggested several improvements for the composition of the indices.

The first index is the nonparametric e-infrastructure index. It is based on the normalized human development index. Unlike the human-development-index-based indices, in which weights are assigned on an ad hoc basis, our index components were given weights based on the square of their normalized values. The second index is the parametric e-infrastructure index. The weights of this index are estimated using the principal component analysis.

Despite the different methods in the index computation, the outcome of the indices differs only slightly. For example, the country ranking based on the e-infrastructure indices shows that the high-ranked countries share similar patterns in various index component distributions. For the majority of countries, their two indices ranks differ only slightly.

Besides, based on these two e-infrastructure indices, we analyzed the heterogeneity of the e-infrastructure between countries, regions, and over time. Hereby, we put a special focus on Middle East and North Africa (MENA) countries and OECD countries. The results show heterogeneity by region (i.e., economic region). For instance, the non-European OECD countries as an economic region perform quite well in comparison with other regions including the European OECD countries region, Middle East, and North Africa. The low rank of some countries is to some extent linked to their economic condition. Given the close relationship between e-infrastructure level and their GDP, poor countries from MENA have low ranks but some MENA countries, which belong to the Gulf Cooperation Council (GCC), outperformed a few OECD countries.

With respect to country heterogeneity, the results show that the high-ranked countries share similar patterns in various index component distributions. However, we found no evidence to suggest that if a country is performing well in one component, it will also perform well in other components.

The analysis over the time period of 8 years (2000–2007) showed that the two indices develop differently. The nonparametric index shows a decreasing pattern while the parametric index an increasing pattern. This is consistent with our expectations. The difference is attributed to the estimated weight heterogeneity assigned to different indicators in the parametric case. Therefore, the parametric e-infrastructure index is preferable.

References

1. Al-Mutawkkil, A. A., Heshmati, A., & Hwang, J. (2009). Development of telecommunication and broadcasting infrastructure indices at the global level. *Telecommunications Policy, 33*(3–4), 176–199.
2. Agénor, P. R. (2003). Does globalization hurt the poor? World Bank, Unpublished manuscript.
3. Andersen, T. M., & Herbertsson, T.T. (2003). Measuring globalization. *IZA Discussion Paper*, 817, Bonn.
4. APEC. (2000). E-commerce readiness guide, Electronic Commerce Steering Group, available at: www.ecommerce.gov/apec. Accessed 20 Sept 2010.
5. Archibugi, D., & Coco, A. (2004). A new indicator of technological capabilities for developed and developing countries (ArCO). *World Development, 32*(4), 629–654.
6. Archibugi, D., Denni, M., & Filippeti, A. (2009). The technological capabilities of nations: The state of art of synthetic indicators. *Technological Forecasting and Social Change, 76*(7), 917–931.
7. CID. (2006). Readiness for the networked world – a guide for developing countries. http://www.readinessguide.com.
8. Danish, D. (2006). E-readiness for developing countries: Moving the focus from the environment to the users. *The Electronic Journal of Information Systems in Developing Countries, 27*(6), 1–14.
9. Desai, M., Fukuda-Parr, S., Johansson, C., & Sagasti, F. (2002). Measuring the technology achievement of nations and the capacity to participate in the network age. *Journal of Human Development, 3*(1), 95–122.
10. Dreher, A. (2005). Does globalization affect growth? empirical evidence from a new index, University of Konstanz Department of Economics, Unpublished Manuscript.
11. Economist Intelligence Unit. (2008). E-readiness rankings 2008: Maintaining momentum. A white paper.
12. Economist Intelligence Unit. (2009). The 2009 E-readiness.
13. Heshmati, A. (2006). Measurement of a multidimensional index of globalization. *Global Economy Journal, 6*(2): Paper 1.
14. Heshmati, A., & Oh, J. (2006). Alternative composite Lisbon development strategy indices: A comparison of EU, USA, Japan and Korea. *The European Journal of Comparative Economics, 3*(2), 133–170.
15. Heshmati, A., Tausch, A., & Bajalan, C. (2008). Measurement and analysis of child well-being in middle and high income countries. *The European Journal of Comparative Economics, 5*(2), 227–286.
16. Hotelling, H. (1933). Analysis of a complex of statistical variables into principal components. *Journal of Educational Psychology, 24*, 417–441. and 24: 498–520.

17. ITU. (2010). *Partnership on measuring ICT for development, core ICT indicators*. International Telecommunication Union. Retrieved from http://www.itu.int/en/ITU-D/Statistics/Pages/coreindicators/default.aspx.
18. ITU. (2003). World Telecommunication Development Report 2003: Access Indicators for the Information Society. 7th edition.
19. ITU. (2009). *Measuring the information society: the ICT development index*. International Telecommunication Union.
20. ITU. (2007). *Measuring the information society: ICT opportunity index and world telecommunication/ICT indicator*. International Telecommunication Union.
21. ITU & United Nations Conference on Trade and Development. (2007). World Information Society Report 2007. Beyond World Summit on the Information Society.
22. Kang, S. M. (2002). A sensitivity analysis of the Korean composite environmental index. *Ecological Economics, 43*, 159–174.
23. Kearney A.T. Inc. & The Carnegie Endowment for International Peace. (2002). Globalization's last hurrah? *Foreign Policy, 128*, 38–51.
24. Kearney A.T. Inc. & The Carnegie Endowment for International Peace. (2003). Measuring globalization: who's up, who's down? *Foreign Policy*, January/February, 60–72.
25. Lim, G.C., & Nguyen, V.H. (2013). Alternative weighting approaches to computing indexes of economic activity, Journal of Economic Surveys. 29(2), 287–300.
26. Noorbakhsh, F. (1998). The human development index: Some technical issues and alternative indices. *Journal of International Development, 10*, 589–605.
27. OECD - Organization for Economic Cooperation and Development (2008). In *Handbook on construction composite indicator: Methodology and User Guide*. European Commission, Joint Research Centre, OECD publication, ISBN: 9789264043466.
28. Pearson, K. (1901). On lines and planes of closest fit to systems of points in space. *Philosophical Magazine, 6*(2), 559–572.
29. Purcell, F., & Toland, J. (2004). Electronic commerce for the South Pacific: A review of e-readiness. *Electronic Commerce Research, 4*(3), 241–262.
30. Rudra, P. P., Arvin, M. B., & Norman, N. R. (2014). Economic growth and the development of telecommunication infrastructure in the G-20 countries: A panel-VAR approach. *Telecommunication Policy, 38*(7), 634–649.
31. United Nations Conference on Trade and Development. (2005). Information and communication technology (ICT) development indices [Online]. Available at: http://unctad.org/en/docs/iteipc20031_en.pdf.
32. UNDP - United Nations Development Programme. (2001). Creating a development dynamic, Final report of the digital opportunity initiative, Human Development Report [Online]. Available at: http://www.undp.org/hdr2001/completenew.pdf.
33. WEF, infoDev & INSEAD. (2003). The Global Information Technology Report. Available at: http://www.infodev.org/articles/global-information-technology-report-2003-2004.

Chapter 9
Model for Constructing Institutional Framework for Scientific Knowledge Management Systems: Nigerian Institutional Repository Innovation Case Applicable to Developing Countries

Samuel C. Avermaria Utulu and Ojelanki Ngwenyama

Abstract This chapter is a part of an inductive reasoning-based longitudinal study that aims to elicit novel barriers of institutional repository (IR) innovation in developing country contexts. The study reported in this chapter is based on qualitative data collected through observation and secondary data from three Nigerian universities. The findings reveal that reconstructing the institutional framework that supports scientific knowledge management systems (SKMS) in developing countries is a panacea for successful IR innovation. The study provides insights that differ from existing ones where scholars assume that IR barriers are only university based.

Keywords Institutional repository • Scientific knowledge management systems • Institutional framework • Open access initiative • Developing countries

9.1 Introduction

The growth of information and communication technology (ICT)-based scientific knowledge management systems (SKMS) such as institutional repository (IR) has been slow in developing countries. This is considered unacceptable given the fact that in the past IR was heralded as a technology that has the potential to promote access to the scientific knowledge required to support development programs in

S.C. Avermaria Utulu (✉)
Systems and Automation Unit, Afe Babalola University Library, Afe Babalola University, Ado-Ekiti, Nigeria

Department of Information Systems, University of Cape Town, Rondebosch, South Africa
e-mail: utulu.samuel@abuad.edu.ng

O. Ngwenyama
Department of Information Systems, University of Cape Town, Rondebosch, South Africa
e-mail: utlsam001@myuct.ac.za; o.ngwenyama@uct.ac.za

© Springer International Publishing AG 2017
H. Kaur et al. (eds.), *Catalyzing Development through ICT Adoption*,
DOI 10.1007/978-3-319-56523-1_9

developing countries. Couple with this is experts' assertion that development initiatives in developing countries must be driven by the scientific and local knowledge produced in local contexts [1] and the presumed role IR can play if this is to be achieved [2]. The indication that developing countries must strive to provide ready and timely access to their scientific knowledge output as a way to promote development also makes the need to improve IR innovation outcomes pertinent [2, 3]. Current situation, however, shows that the performance of SKMS has been poor in developing countries. The inability of developing countries to efficiently and effectively use SKMS to promote access to the scientific knowledge required to support their development programs has taken its toll on open access initiatives, including the IR initiative. It also has negative effects on the outcome of national and regional access-to-scientific-knowledge programs such as the Nigerian Virtual Library Project and DATAD program of the Association of African Universities (AAU) [4]. Although a lot of efforts have been made to ameliorate barrier factors of IR innovation in developing countries [5], including Nigeria, for example [6–8], these barriers still persist.

Conclusions reached in existing assessment of IR innovation have popularized the assumption that IR barriers are mainly university based. In other words, scholars assume that the major barriers that impede IR innovation are those that arise as a result of the inability of university libraries, academics, and university management to manage IR innovation challenges [9, 10]. The consequence of this is that researchers have inadvertently popularized the notion that universities can single-handedly deal with the barriers of IR innovation [6, 11]. Popular notions include the need to create awareness, spur acceptance and utilization, and change scholarly knowledge publication culture that are believed to be acceptable for tenure, promotion, and appointment of academics [12]. Existing studies are therefore characterized by scopes (research subjects and samples) that have to do with phenomena and people that are peculiar to universities [13]. Surprisingly however, our findings reveal novel IR barrier factors, that is, how the institutional framework that supports SKMS in Nigeria constraints IR innovation efforts in the country. This chapter is therefore devoted to explaining how key institutions that are involved in the Nigerian SKMS can be reconstructed to support IR innovation in the country. In Nigeria, for instance, key institutions that are involved in the country's SKMS include Nigerian universities, the National Universities Commission (NUC), Association of Nigerian Universities Vice-Chancellors (ANUV), Tertiary Education Trust Fund (TETFund), and Association of African Universities (AAU).

Our observation shows that these institutions deal with varying, but integrated, aspects of scientific knowledge management that the nonintegration of their responsibilities posed a problem that must be addressed. The chapter shows the kind of integration we propose and confirms its potential to promote IR innovation and other forms of SKMS. It shows how the integration of key institutions can support access to the scientific knowledge required for development in Nigeria and in developing countries with similar SKMS structure. In addition, the study corroborates notions propagated in the information systems in developing countries (ISDC) discipline on how institutional capacity impacts successful IR innovation in developing countries [14, 15]. The remaining parts of the chapter are presented as follows: segment two deals with ICT and development and is followed by segment three which dwells on scientific knowledge production capacity, knowledge divide, and development. The fourth segment deals with the evolution of the open access initiative and its assumed potential as a technology that could support development. Fifth segment deals with how Nigerian SKMS is structured. Sixth segment deals with presentation and discussion of study findings. Segment seven dwells on theoretical elaboration and explanation of the SKMS model and theory that emerged based on the study. Segment eight deals with study conclusion.

9.2   ICT and Development

The term development became popular after the Second World War as a result of the role uneven distribution of economic and political powers played in conflicts that led to the war. Development therefore denotes the level of a country's achievements in terms of its economy, politics, culture, education, information technology (IT), health, environment, and institutions. There are, however, dissenting schools of thought on what constitutes the development of countries around the globe. In contemporary times, development indicators have been subsumed in human development, peace and security, and the environment [16]. It follows that development indicators include basic human needs such as water and sanitation, health, education, shelter, human rights, peace, livelihood, security, safe environment, and finance. Development scholars and experts' interests therefore lie on discussing and measuring the extent to which people are able to attain their natural potentials. They based their arguments on the extent to which people's socio-political, economic, and cultural environment ensure that they achieve their potentials with minimal constraint. Scholars and experts are also interested in proffering measures that will aid governments and citizens to protect and sustain natural environments during the course of their socioeconomic, political, and cultural activities [16].

   In the past decades however, there are four main schools of thought in the scholarly discipline of development. The school that may be considered the earliest among these schools is the modernist development school of thought. Modernist thought elaborates the role of modernization when developing assumptions about development [17]. A second development school is the Marxist development school of thought [18]. The assumptions of this school of thought is dominated by Marxism principles. The school looks at capitalism as the major stimulator of economic crisis. The third development school of thought is the neo-Marxism dependency school of thought. This school of thought lays emphasis on the incursion of capitalism into societies across the globe, particularly poor societies, and how this propels unwarranted dependency of poor countries on rich countries [19]. The fourth development school of thought is the contemporary development school of thought which is normally argued from two fronts, namely, the globalist front and localist or neo-populist front. Like the neo-Marxism dependency development theorists, scholars that support globalist development views rely mainly on postindustrial socio-political, cultural, and economic assumptions. According to the globalist school, central to development is information and communication technology (ICT). Hence, for a country to be adjudged as developed, it must be able to invent or import and diffuse and use ICT to drive its development agenda [20].

The limitation observed in the ways globalist theorists represent local factors when observing and drawing conclusions on global development issues led to the emergence of the localist or neo-populist development school of thought. The neo-populist view was made popular in the mid-1970s as results of its paradigm which was then known as neo-populist thinking [21]. Its tenents are based on putting into primary consideration those societies, people, and individuals that are to be developed. To neo-populist theorists "putting into consideration" implies paying strict attention on people, their culture, situations, contexts, and more importantly their local knowledge when judging a society on the extent to which it has diffused and used ICT for socioeconomic and cultural development. As a consequence of this, development economists' postulation that ICT is fundamental to the development of societies resulted in the emergence of further studies that were concerned with evaluating the impact of ICT on development [22, 23]. The study of ICT and development has therefore become of interest to disciplines such as information systems, information science, human computer interaction, computer science, and communication studies, among others. Information and communication technologies have been heralded by scholars in these disciplines as having the capacity to drive operational efficiency of both public and private organizations [24, 25]. It has also been justified in the literature that ICT has efficiently and effectively impacted on managerial productivity of organizations across the globe. With regard to helping organizations to augment and automate the operations they engage in to attain strategic efficiency, ICT has proven to be of high importance. Every form of organization has found ICT very important to the achievement of their corporate goals.

One primary importance of ICT is that it bridges the gap occasioned by space and time. In other words, ICT has helped people, organizations, and societies to communicate data, information, and knowledge irrespective of how wide apart their physical locations are [26]. By so doing, ICT has unprecedentedly reduced the time it takes to transfer data, information, and knowledge irrespective of the physical locations of the entities concerned. In the recent past, advances in telecommunication and mobile technologies have been recognized in the literature as prime factors that aid development [27, 28]. Every sector of the economy of developing countries has been positively impacted by ICT [29]. With regard to the impact of ICT on SKMS, the literature has revealed how the need to produce, organize, disseminate, and preserve scientific knowledge has resulted into the invention of different types of SKMS (e.g., [30]). These range from ICT advances in scientific knowledge content development like text editing application packages, formula creation application packages, data extraction and trapping (including environmental, marine, and geospatial) packages, and automation packages for scientific knowledge warehouses including laboratories, workshops, and libraries. The wide range of solutions ICT that can be used to deploy resulted to assumptions that developing countries have to look for ways to diffuse and utilize ICT to drive their development goals [15, 31]. However, years of diffusion and use of ICT for diverse purposes and for scientific knowledge management by developing countries seem not to yield expected development outcomes. This is exemplified by the widening of development gap between developing and developed countries. The scenario has resulted into new debates on the actual factors that affect the extent to which ICT impacts the attainment of development goals set by developing countries.

For instance, one of the areas ICT is being diffused and used in developing countries is to support distribution and access to global scientific knowledge through internationalization [32]. Current realities, however, show that there is a wide gap between the scientific knowledge shared and accessed using ICT in developing countries and the actual amount of scientific knowledge produced around the globe. Nonetheless, developing countries have continued to endeavor to use ICT to manage their stock of scientific knowledge as a backdrop of the need to make them available to policy makers and development agents. Yet there is still a clamor on the unavailability of scientific knowledge produced in developing countries to stakeholders. So between 1990 and 2015, a deluge of literature emerged in diverse disciplines. These literature endeavor to explain the factors that determine the extent to which ICT can support access to global scientific knowledge among key stakeholder in developing countries and the factors that determine this [13, 30]. Issues regarding access to global scientific knowledge were therefore assumed to be determined by access to the Internet and the level of investments on computer hardware and software [29]. This results because in real-time and practice the Internet and computer have played vital role in supporting knowledge communication and transfer across the globe. So Internet penetration rate in developing countries, particularly in Africa, grew in an unprecedented rate. For instance, in Nigeria Internet penetration growth rate between 2000 and 2016 grew exponentially to 52% of the country's population. This spurred the use of computers and the Internet in universities and research institutes in the country. It resulted in a number of studies that debated availability of computers and the Internet and their effects on teaching, learning, and research in Nigeria [32, 33]. This trend was also replicated in other developing countries [34–36]. Stakeholders therefore started to evaluate universities in developing countries based on the extent to which they were able to use ICT to achieve acceptable standards of learning, teaching, and research [32].

As a result of this development, reports in the literature indicate that individuals, corporate organizations, intergovernmental organizations, and governments contributed to the growth of ICT investment in developing countries [37]. Despite attempts made by developing countries to diffuse and use ICTs as indicated by the number of computers available to individuals and organizations and Internet penetration growth rate, targeted development goals were still not reached. In reality, there are still persisting needs for mass education, discharge of healthcare services to rural areas, and dissemination of knowledge to support economic activities, particularly in rural areas, among other needs [38]. In places where development goals were reached, the time frame with which the goals were reached normally does not match with projected time frame. This scenario is more profound when it comes to using ICT to support scientific knowledge management. A good example is the scenario in Nigeria where training on IR was organized for Nigerian universities by the National Universities Commission (NUC) in 2010. The plan was that the training will empower all Nigerian universities to deploy IR in no time. However, as of now, only 13 of the 143 university degree awarding institutions have deployed IR in Nigeria. Issues that concern the failure of developing countries to meet with projected time frame resulted into a deluge of studies. Most of the studies revealed that power supply, cost of ICT, and capacity to diffuse and use ICT by universities are the major factors that hinder ICT use for productive scientific knowledge management in developing countries. See, for instance, conclusions reached in studies done by [7, 8]. While the factors identified in existing studies are important to ongoing debates on ICT and development, issues relating to universities' internal capacity came to the fore in this study. Findings in the study provide new dimension and insights into how internal capacities of universities in Nigeria impacted IR innovation in the country. These issues are discussed in the next segment.

9.3   Scientific Knowledge Production Capacity, Knowledge Divide, and Development

The question on scientific knowledge production capacity of societies across the globe came to the fore as a result of the advent of the knowledge society. This is a backdrop of the way knowledge was construed in contemporary time. Knowledge denotes the end product of activity(ies) systematically carried out that lead(s) to the collection of valid and reliable data and inferences drawn after the data may have been appropriately analyzed and interpreted. Hence, it is believed that any society that has citizens that are able to coordinate activities that lead to knowledge creation across all the sectors of its economy and who do so actively is a knowledge society [39, 40]. So it follows that societies that are tagged knowledge societies are those that invest in facilities and activities that promote the creation of the knowledge required for taking vital decisions. This is considered important because knowledge is required to take decisions that touch contemporary societies' sociocultural, political, and economic lives. Given this new way of viewing what constitutes knowledge in contemporary societies, stakeholders started to construct indices with which societies can be categorized to those that are knowledge societies and those that are not.

The following criteria are among the popular criteria that were used to determine if a society is a knowledge society or not: information and communication technology (ICT) and connectivity, usable content, infrastructure and deliverability, and human intellectual capability. Attempts have therefore been made by developing countries to use these indices to access the extent to which they have become knowledge societies. For instance, [40] argued that in sub-Sahara Africa, it is only South Africa that can be said to meet to some extent the knowledge society criteria. Statistics that are available on the amount budgeted by governments of most developing countries for research show a wide gap between expenditure on research in developed countries and developing countries. Apart from this, the level of information literacy of citizens in developed countries has also been adjudged to be higher than those of the developing countries. Information literacy has been defined as the ability of an individual to adequately recognize when she/he needs information, how to determine what constitute appropriate and adequate information, how to get the information, and how to appropriately use the information to create the knowledge she/he requires for the taking decisions in question [41]. Knowledge societies are believed to have citizens with high information literacy level, who as a result support their countries' knowledge creation agenda and productivity driven by informed decision making. It follows that for those countries that are characterized as knowledge societies, the aggregate of their citizens' information generation activities contributes to their sociocultural, political, and economic development. So institutional frameworks that support the integration of such countries' scientific knowledge generation infrastructure are not taken for granted. See, for instance, the declaration of the President of the United States of America on information literacy [42].

Given the realities in developing countries, their scientific knowledge production capacity can easily be adjudged to be poor [40]. In most cases, the percentages of national budgets devoted to research and development are too poor to trigger significant sociocultural, political, and economic outcomes [43]. Universities in developing countries are also poorly funded and have been accused to lack the knowledge generation infrastructure [44, 45] and the quantum of quality manpower required to drive large-scale research that is capable of producing relevant knowledge that is needed to aid development [44, 46]. Scholars from developing countries therefore prefer to be employed in developed countries where they can maximize their potentials due to the adequacy of existing research facilities [47]. Consequently, scientific knowledge production capacity of universities in developing countries is influenced by several factors. The factors may include availability of research-friendly environment, brain drain, personnel, funds, and access to the right quality and quantity of scientific research [40, 47]. These factors have been well managed in developed countries as exemplified by the quality and the enormous quantity of research they produce. Given this scenario, issue relating to knowledge divide therefore emerged as one of the problems developing countries encounter in their bid to use ICT, particularly the Internet, to support development. Primarily, knowledge divide was construed based on the quantity and quality of knowledge available to people through the Internet [48]. Before the advent of knowledge divide however, issues that have to do with digital divide dominated discussions held on how developing countries are short changed as a result of the role ICT plays in the achievement of global development goals [49]. The invention and proliferation of personal computers (PCs) ameliorated to some extent, the digital divide menace. Outcomes of programs put in place globally to combat digital divide, for instance, through the deployment of telecenters [28] and intergovernmental organizations' support for ICT acquisition and deployment [50] also contributed to the reduction, to some extent, of the digital divide menace. When the challenges of digital divide were assumed to have been reduced to what was termed "manageable extent," new realities evolved. These realities indicate that eradicating digital divide alone may not solve the problems associated with using ICT to achieve development goals. It was therefore observed that content produced and distributed using ICT is equally important to the use of ICT to support development in developing countries. This resulted to stakeholders' interest on who produces and benefits from the scientific knowledge made available on the Internet [51].

This scenario led to new questions on how best to use ICT to drive development in developing countries. The term knowledge divide was therefore coined to describe the disparity in the quantity and quality of scientific knowledge produced by, and accessible to, developed countries when compared with those of developing countries. Many scholars have suggested that majority of the scientific knowledge available through the Internet are those produced in developed country contexts. See, for instance, [51]. The implication of this according to concerned scholars is that majority of the ideas made available to policy makers, development agents, and governments through ICT-based scientific knowledge outlets do not directly address the situations in developing countries. Some Nigerian scholars, for instance, have outlined the effects of knowledge divide on Nigeria's development programs, for example [7]. The fact that development agents, policy makers, intergovernmental organizations, global development stakeholders, and governments across the globe have come to terms with the notion that development programs implemented in developing countries must be driven by the knowledge generated there also brought to limelight the need to tackle knowledge divide [52]. This therefore led to the efforts made to develop research capacity of scholars in developing countries. Efforts made include those channeled toward increasing their participation in international conferences, workshops, and scholarly meetings where research capacity issues are discussed. For instance, in Nigeria, apart from university-based grants for research, conference attendance, and foreign travels, federal and state governments have programs that are targeted at supporting research, conference attendance, and foreign travels [53]. There are also a number of programs that have been developed to increase the number and quality of scholarly journals published in Nigeria and to ensure that they are included among those available online [54]. These programs also include plans to help scholarly journal publishers to effectively adopt ICT to drive every aspect of the cycle of scientific knowledge production and publishing [55]. It also includes call on journal publishers to serve as media for training emerging scholars [56].

Apart from this, global development initiatives put in place by United Nations practically focus on how to eradicate ignorance in developing countries. Hence, goals set revolved around improving literacy level, promoting education in rural areas and for girls and women, and advising governments on the percentage of national budge that should be dedicated to higher education and research [57]. The inclination to help developing countries to improve its knowledge creation and use capacity is visible in the Millennium Development Goals (MDGs) which has been reinvented to Sustainable Development Goals (SDGs) [58]. It is also visible in New Partnership for Africa Development (NEPAD) strategy to eradicate poverty, ignorance, and starvation in Africa through democratic governance and appropriate global partnership for development. In Nigeria the Kuru Declaration and the national economic empowerment and development strategy of 2005 also paid strong attention on education and expenditure on research and development [59]. Given the role ICT plays in improving access to knowledge, the assumptions about its costs and the barriers associated with access to ICT-based scientific knowledge, the open access initiative was therefore invented to alleviate these barriers. Open access was assumed to be a new antidote for solving the challenges that hamper the free flow of ICT-based scientific knowledge required to support development programs. The role open access plays since its invention and the assumptions of its creators are discussed in the next segment.

9.4   Open Access, Its Challenges and Development

In order for the open access initiative to solve two major problems – cost and context-specific content issues – that affect the use of ICT in developing countries, it was designed to run on cheap technology and free and open source software. Although the open access initiative was invented in the West, the key focus of its inventors was to make developing countries safe from the menace of knowledge divide and to fight commercial publishers' dominant role in the production and distribution of scientific knowledge [60]. The problem of access to scientific knowledge, particularly those produced using public funds as a result of the business model put in place by commercial publishers, had become a global phenomenon. This is because it affects both developed and developing countries in different ways. The problems, however, had more effects on the development agenda of developing countries than it had on developed countries. Open access inventors that were based in the West therefore started to assume that if libraries, scholars, and organizations in developed countries struggle to meet the cost required to purchase and/or access available commercial publisher-based scientific knowledge, how much more would this affect developing countries. Hence, Steve Harnard's seminal work on IR and Antleman's successful use of open access outlet to justify the assumption that open access outlets promote access to scientific knowledge led to a global call for a paradigm shift in the global scientific knowledge management landscape [61]. Consequently, in developed countries stakeholders started to argue that the payment done to acquire scientific knowledge output that was produced using public funds constitutes dual payment and means exploitation used by commercial publishers.

Developing countries, however, developed their own arguments from the perspective of what should constitute globally acceptable scientific knowledge management practice. According to [62], global scientific knowledge require global use and assessment by stakeholders before it can be adjudged as global scientific knowledge value and validity. In other words, if scientific knowledge produced, for instance, in the West is not available for use in developing countries and in effect, for assessment, then such scientific knowledge may not be adjudged as having global value and validity. This therefore means that while developed countries enjoyed the advantage of having the capacity to produce the vast majority of scientific knowledge available globally, the fact that the scientific knowledge they produce do not receive the required global peer use and assessment also constitutes a challenge that stakeholders should be mindful of [62].

Given these scenarios therefore, the Budapest Declaration on open access was signed by several countries that believe that the open access initiative has the potential to eradicate problems of scientific knowledge circulation across the globe. The Budapest Declaration formalized the call for free and equitable access to global scientific knowledge. The Declaration led to two major radical changes in the scientific knowledge management landscape. First, it led to the invention of open access journals. Second, it resulted into a new scientific knowledge publishing paradigm scholars referred to as self-archiving [61]. The open access journal was designed to have all the characteristics of the paper and online-based commercial publishers' closed access journals. In other words, open access journals could perform essential functions which have been exclusively reserved for commercial publishers' closed access journals. These functions include: registration of scientific knowledge output, processing (editing, designing, and printing) scientific knowledge output, disseminating scientific knowledge output, and preserving scientific knowledge output for posterity. Two major characteristics, however, distinguished open access journals from those of the commercial publishers' closed access journals. These are, namely, free and no access cost and availability of publications to users on the first day of its publication [60, 63]. In other words, open access journals promise to reduce to the bearest minimum, the time between when scientific knowledge is produced and the time it is made available to users.

The self-archiving paradigm allows scholars to post their scholarly knowledge products online. It is based on the use of websites owned by individuals or those owned by organizations, such as universities, that scholars have affiliation with [61, 64]. Hence, websites owned by individuals and organizations became platforms for self-archiving scientific knowledge output. The self-archiving paradigm over time evolved into the IR model in which universities, and later other research institutions, deploy IR-based platforms where they collect scientific knowledge output of their communities and make them available free of charge on the Internet. Given the nature of open access journals and IR, stakeholders assumed that they will speedily aid the eradication of knowledge divide. It was also conceived that open access journals and IR will make developing countries to have equal access to the global scientific knowledge output they need to support their development programs [8]. Disappointingly, the adoption of open access journals in developing countries has not been as dramatic as one would expect [8]. In fact, most open access journals are published by organizations and individuals in developed countries. This also meant that majority of the papers published in open access journals were authored by authors in developed country contexts and primarily on issues that concern developed countries; see, for instance, [65].

Many factors have been identified that slow the adoption of open access journals in developing countries. Primary among them is the cost of publication. The open access journal initiative requires that authors should pay publication fees. The agreement is that open access journal publishers are expected to offset the cost of publishing from publication fees paid by authors so as to be able to make publications freely available to the public. Interestingly, open access journals are relatively cheaper to publish when compared to paper-based journals. However, its cost to authors, particularly those in developing country, is too expensive. Charges of most open access journals are done using currencies such as the US dollars, British pound sterling, and Eurozone euro whose values are far beyond currencies used in most developing countries. Apart from this, rigidity and poor institutional capacity have made the transition from closed access journals to open access journals very cumbersome in developing countries [6]. Acceptance of open access journals as appropriate outlet for disseminating scientific knowledge and to determine tenure and promotion of academics has been very slow in developing countries. Open access journals have been therefore criticized based on their free access philosophy, the speed of publication, and publication fee payment. It has been said that these features subvert the culture of quality scholarly knowledge publication associated within centuries.

This is also the case with IR penetration in developing countries. Going by practical experiences, stakeholders' assumption that universities in developing countries will see IR as a good opportunity to circulate the scientific knowledge output that are needed to support development has not been validated [3, 62]. Current statistics on the ownership of IR across the globe disappointingly show that developing countries still trail developed countries in the league of those countries whose universities have deployed IR to support access to scientific knowledge. In Nigeria 14 out of 125 universities are enlisted in the OpenDoar directory of existing IR. Currently, the extant literature has provided information leading to theoretical assumptions on the reasons why IR innovation has had poor performance in developing countries [7, 8, 10]. Central to existing theoretical assumptions is that IR barriers are university based. Hence, majority of the studies that have been done and ongoing studies focus on eliciting IR barriers that are connected to universities [6, 13, 11]. This has resulted in a situation in which the research subjects that are studied by IR scholars are mostly limited to librarians and academics and, on few occasions, university management, students, and IT personnel. Conceptual studies ranging from those written about a decade ago to those produced in recent time seem to limit IR phenomena to universities [2, 7, 9, 62]. There is no doubt that these studies have contributed immensely to ongoing debates on how to improve access to the scientific knowledge needed to support development in developing countries. However, the study reported in this chapter provides novel insights that IR barriers are not limited to those barriers inherent in universities. It proposes how to advance IR innovation outcomes in developing countries by reconstructing the institutional framework put in place to support the SKMS.

9.5 Reconstructing Institutional Framework for Scientific Knowledge Management Systems: Nigerian IR Innovation Case

9.5.1 Structure of Nigerian Scientific Knowledge Management Systems

In Nigeria, like in most other countries, universities play pivotal role in the production and distribution of scientific knowledge. Consequently in Nigeria, most universities lay strong emphasis on the need for creativity, research, and innovation [10]. Apart from universities, Nigeria has a long-standing culture of establishing and maintaining specialized research institutes. Disciplines of the humanities and languages, management and social sciences, and sciences and technology all have government-owned and government-funded research institutes. These research institutes are treated the same way universities are treated, except for the fact that they are not allowed to admit students and are not accredited by the NUC. Nigerian research institutes, however, have strong affinity with Nigerian universities. They work collaboratively together on research that are of national interest. Consequently, institutions that are part of the Nigerian scientific knowledge production and management system that are identified in this study include Nigerian universities, NUC and ANUV. Government-established funding agencies such as the Petroleum Trust Fund (PTF) and TETFund also constitute a significant part of the scientific knowledge management structure in Nigeria. TETFund initiates programs that it funds based on the mandate given to it by government. TETFund, however, funds projects only in federal- and state-owned universities. Private universities do not benefit from their programs. However, major outlets used to disseminate research output in Nigeria are journals, conference proceedings, textbooks, reports, reference materials, compendium, and electronic sources such as websites, portals, databases, and, in the recent time, blogs. Nigeria's scientific knowledge management systems get input from foreign journals, proceedings, textbooks, reports, references, etc. The system relies primarily on electronic sources to access the materials published offshore.

In the recent past, open access sources are being harnessed and form a crucial part of the Nigerian SKMS. A couple of open access journals are published in Nigeria, while most universities in the country are making frantic effort to innovate IR. Major players in the bid to ensure that Nigeria universities innovate IR are the universities, NUC, and Association of Nigerian Universities Vice-Chancellors. The Association of African Universities (AAU) also collaborates with the ANUV to train stakeholders on IR innovation as a way to support its Database for Africa's Theses and Dissertations (DATAD) project. The DATAD project was initiated to collect electronic theses dissertation, of all member universities across Africa. TETFund funds research, conference attendance and foreign travels, and journal publishing done by Nigerian universities and scholars [66]. In a nutshell, institutions involved in the Nigerian SKMS deal in scientific knowledge production, dissemination, funding, and process coordination.

9.5.2 The Study, Study Site, and Study Investigation

The study aims to explain the barriers of IR innovation in universities in Nigeria as a way to provide other developing countries with explanations on IR innovation success factors. The study was done through empirical observation of IR innovation efforts made by three universities in Nigeria. The universities are made up of two privately owned universities and one publicly owned (federal government) university. The two privately owned universities are, however, at different stages of their IR innovation. While one has plans to present a proposal for IR innovation through its university library to its university management, the other one has no plans for IR innovation. The publicly owned university, however, has an IR that is listed in the OpenDoar directory of IR. Qualitative data was collected through the following methods: observation, analyzing texts and documents, and informal discussions held with a few staff of the universities. Two secondary data sources, official letters and internal memos, were triangulated with data got through observation and discussions. The data analysis technique that was used in the study is thematic data analysis [67, 68] using the Atlas.ti software. Themes regarding the barriers of institutional repository were identified and explained. Theoretical elaboration was done after research findings were presented as a means of building new theories of barriers of IR.

9.6 Findings and Discussing of Findings

9.6.1 Scientific Knowledge Production Capacity

The three universities studied are relatively young universities when compared to more established Nigerian universities. Hence, a good number of the academic staff of the universities are doctoral students in older federal- and state-owned Nigerian universities. This meant that the extent to which academics employed in the universities were involved in independent research is limited. This is mainly because of their commitment to their PhD research and indicates that the capacity of academics to carry out large-scale research in the universities is limited. Also, majority of students in the universities are undergraduate students. The universities have very few postgraduate students who are enrolled for master degrees. The demography of academics and students in the case universities hampers their scientific knowledge production capacity. For instance, one of the staff we discussed with during the observation commented that "if we deploy IR where are we going to get the contents to deposit in it. Research activities here are not on top gear." During a discussion with another staff, he complained that the quality of undergraduate research is "not something we will want to put out there on the Internet...it could discredit our struggle for quality." There were also complains about inadequacy of facilities such as power supply, access to the Internet, and access to databases of recent publications in scientific journals. One academic staff in one of the universities commented that "...you saw our library, it is not even enough for hundred students talkless of accommodating staff." Another academic staff who recently returned from a postdoctoral research study abroad complained that "I have to buy my own data plans [mobile phone subscription based Internet access] to be able to use the Internet. This did not mean that I have access to required materials. No database here to access publications for my research." Given the situations observed in the case universities, it is logical to conclude that scientific knowledge production capacity of the three universities is very low. Based on our findings, scientific knowledge production capacity of the universities studied was hampered by year of establishment, demography of staff and students, access to the Internet, and Internet-based scholarly resources.

9.6.2   Digital and Knowledge Divide

The digital and knowledge divide menace seem to have shifted from unavailability of computers to lack of access to Internet technology. Observation shows that most academics in the three case universities have self-purchased laptops of different grades and models. Most of them also have self-purchased Internet data plans with which they access the Internet. However, through observation and discussions held during the course of the study, we gathered that academics have issues with Internet connectivity and speed and access to required scientific knowledge contents. One of the academics we discussed with complained that "I have a data plan [Internet access plan] that I purchased from ...[one of the mobile phone service providers] but it never works. You pay and end up having nothing." During a discussion with another academic staff, she complained that "I pay ₦ 1,500:00 [about $4:00] to my university for Internet access, for over three months now I have not had any access, yet they deduct the money for Internet every month." On another instance, one of the academics made a confession of how they manage the knowledge divide situation: "for us in the sciences, we call our friends abroad to send papers to us. Even if you go on the Internet you never get any meaningful thing." Through observation done in the three case university libraries on availability of Internet-based scientific knowledge resources, we were able to determine that availability of scientific knowledge through the Internet was poor. None of the university library had fee-based electronic databases for scientific publications. They only have access to free databases such as HINARI, AGORA, and OARE. Most Google Scholar searches done returned materials published in open access journals and other free access sources. Good as this is, it also shows a gap in the kind of scientific knowledge academics that have access in the case universities. While it was possible for respondents to use their laptops and mobile phones to access the Internet, poor Internet connectivity and lack of relevant contents constituted the digital and knowledge divides that plagued the case universities, respectively.

9.6.3   Open Access Adoption Challenges

The level of awareness of open access initiative, particularly IR initiative, differs in the three case universities. In the two case private universities, although existed before the case public university, their open access awareness level was lower. While the public university has an IR that has been listed in the OpenDoar, the two private universities had no IR and have not yet made any formal plans on IR innovation by the time this study started. The situation in one of the private universities is profound; its university librarian claimed that he has heard about IR in the past but has no plan to initiate its innovation. In this particular university, only one of about 15 professional cadre library staff in the university library had a good knowledge of IR. This particular staff claimed that he worked with a private organization that deals with ICT solutions before he was employed in the university library. In the second private university library, IR awareness was high, but formal IR plans had not been made. Other pressing needs such as automation of library operations were given precedence over IR innovation.

The university librarian there indicated that "for now we can't talk about IR. What we urgently need is to have the university provide resources for our automation project." The publicly owned university that has innovated its IR, however, has daunting challenges. Because the IT unit of the university handled the IR innovation project before librarians were employed at the inception of the university, librarians refused to take over the IR project. One of the librarians there complained that "the IR project was the business of the library in the first place, why is it that it is now that they want us to inherit what we did not start." Consequently, we observed that the university's IR has not been well populated with enough publications despite the fact that it has been listed in the OpenDoar. It has also not enjoyed adequate publicity within the university, since this is one of the primary areas where librarians' services are required when it comes to IR projects. When the university librarian was asked about the university's IR project, he simply put: I don't know anything about it, go and ask the IT." The IT director complained that "the library has refused to take over the running of the IR. It is really making it very difficult for us to progress." The internal crisis between IT and university library continues to constitute a barrier to IR use in the university. Given this revelations, internal organizational capacity seems to play very vital role in IR innovation. The fact that IT unit was given the mandate to carry out IR innovation instead of the university library constituted a barrier of IR innovation in the university.

9.6.4 Institutional Framework

The secondary data collected during the course of the study show that the NUC has organized a couple of training on IR for Nigerian universities. However, NUC invites only librarians and IT personnel to represent universities in these free training workshops. Through discussions with some staff member of the university library, it was gathered that NUC is of the opinions that the two major players in universities with regard to IR innovation are librarians and IT personnel. Consequently, academics are conspicuously omitted in workshops NUC organized on IR innovation techniques. Notions put forward by librarians indicate that this scenario may have resulted because NUC did not take its time to find out those that constitute primary IR innovation stakeholders in universities. The NUC also did not find out from universities about those they felt were primary stakeholders in IR innovation. This scenario contributes to the low level of IR awareness and acceptance among academics in the case universities. Although the ANUV encourage each member vice-chancellor to discuss, encourage and provide resources for IR innovation in their universities, a gesture that seems to be a primary way key institutions communicate with universities on IR innovation.

Findings from discussions held with some librarians revealed that the only place vice-chancellors discuss IR innovation is during the university management meeting. This is considered not enough because university management meetings are only opened to principal university administrators such as deputy vice-chancellors, registrars, bursars, and university librarians. Our observation shows that moves made by vice-chancellors to acquaint their universities with IR innovation end up at the top management level and are mainly based on flimsy discussions on required resources for IR innovation. In addition to this, an IR workshop jointly organized by ANUV and the AAU also adopted NUC's technique of inviting only librarians and IT personnel. Given that AAU liaised with ANUV, who constantly work hand in hand with the NUC to organize workshops, those invited were consequently limited to librarians and IT personnel. The AAU was definitely influenced by ANUV and NUC to adopt existing invitation and participation protocol. This also meant that stakeholders such as academics, students, researchers, etc., that are important to IR innovation were left out of discussion concerning IR innovation in Nigerian universities.

With regard to TETFund, memo sent to universities from TETFund and contents of legislative act that set up TETFund indicate that TETFund has been mandated by government to fund research proposals, attendance of international conferences, foreign travel for research, and journal publishing in Nigeria. TETFund was established as an intervention agency under the TETFund Act of 2011. As stated in its website (www.tetfund.gov.ng), TETFund mandate includes "the responsibility for managing, disbursing and monitoring the education tax to public tertiary institutions in Nigeria." Collaboration between TETFund, NUC, ANUV, and Nigerian universities has the potential to lead to policy regime which will facilitate a situation in which the scientific knowledge output of every research proposal funded by TETFund would be compulsorily deposited in the author's university IR. This is also applicable to papers presented in conferences attended by Nigerian participants that were sponsored by TETFund. The presumed policy regime would have been instrumental in making journals published using fund interventions from TETFund open access journals. This development has the potential to help Nigerian universities to have more open access journals and in effect, more research papers deposited in their IR. Based on our observation, the major reason why TETFund has not initiated plans that have the potentials to aid IR innovation is because TETFund seems to be ignorant of its potential to support IR innovation in Nigeria. It primarily assumes that disbursing and keeping records of funds meant for tertiary institutions are all it is established to do. Collaboration between TETFund and other IR innovation stakeholders would have been instrumental in making TETFund to realize an equally important mandate. Hence, most journals published with funds from TETFund are largely paper based and are without any form of online presence. Those that have online presence rely primarily on the African Journal Online (AJOL) project. Access to their contents as a result remains largely low and further deepens the knowledge divide syndrome and the extent to which scientific knowledge produced in Nigeria are made available to the global scientific knowledge community.

9.7 Theoretical Elaboration of Study Findings

9.7.1 Theoretical Elaboration of Study Findings

In the library and information science (LIS) discipline where most of the studies done on IR innovation were carried out, factors identified to be crucial to IR innovation include awareness, availability, and accessibility [10]. These factors have also been used in the LIS discipline to assess other forms of online information resources. Awareness, availability, and accessibility of scientific knowledge, however, led to the evolution and proliferation of IR as a way of supporting the availability and accessibility of online information resources [8]. Since the turn of the twenty-first century, global development programs have been refocused to Africa and the development of other developing countries. The role scientific knowledge plays and the setback it access and use suffers because of digital and knowledge divide have been well underscored in the literature [48–50]. The dominant assumption for the development of developing countries is therefore summed up in the fact that global scientific knowledge should be made readily and time available and accessible to developing countries. This resulted into the transfer and diffusion of the Internet and mobile technologies in developing countries. The Internet has therefore been instrumental in making the open access initiative to spread to and within developing countries.

While cost of technology acquisition has been identified as major barrier factor [8], other factors such as organizational and institutional capacity to innovate Internet-based SKMS [14] and environmental factors – power supply, adequate infrastructure, dominant beliefs, etc. – have also been identified [7, 69]. In the ISDC field, Internet and environmental factors such as cost, capacity to innovate, power supply, dominant organizational beliefs, etc., were believed not to be the only dominant barrier factors. Barrier factors external to organizations, particularly institutional framework that can facilitate empowerment and collaboration of key institutions, have been underscored [15, 31]. The assumption that was generated as a result of this logic is that developing countries need institutional capacity that will facilitate the understanding of SKMS innovation requirements. This is to say that developing countries need to know how key institutions can collaborate in order for them to be able to put into check the intricacies of SKMS innovation [7]. The ISDC discipline has also proved that the evolution of both internal and external capacities required for SKMS innovation can be more meaningfully understood if assessed as a process and not as a state [15]. This therefore indicates that the development of both internal and external SKMS innovation capacities is progressional. This assumption therefore led to the following propositions derived based on the findings of this study and insights available in the extant literature: *SKMS innovation in developing countries should focus on understanding how to progress through internal capacity building to external capacity building in order to ensure institutional collaboration.* This proposition is explained in the next segment of using two models that emerged based on the study findings.

9.7.2   *Emergent SKMS Innovation Model*

The models derived through theoretical elaboration of the study findings is represented in Figs. 9.1 and 9.2. The models indicate the progression processes of IR innovation in developing contexts using examples from Nigeria. See, for instance, Fig. 9.1 below. Figure 9.1 shows two levels of IR innovation. The first level shows internal capacity level, and the second shows cross institutional collaboration level. In other words, the model points out that there are two levels in the building of IR innovation capacity. It further shows three possible progressions that can be adopted by stakeholders to move from internal capacity building (level one) to cross institutional collaboration (level two). Level one explains the ability of universities to manage their internal capabilities, that is, their scientific knowledge production capacity, digital and knowledge divide, and open access adoption challenges. These issues have been addressed in a variety of studies on organizational impact on IS innovation (e.g., [7, 8, 70]. Internal capability of an organization involves its ability to manage organizational and social structures, learning and knowledge management, and the impact ICT may have on the outcomes of activities put in place to manage these factors [70, 71].

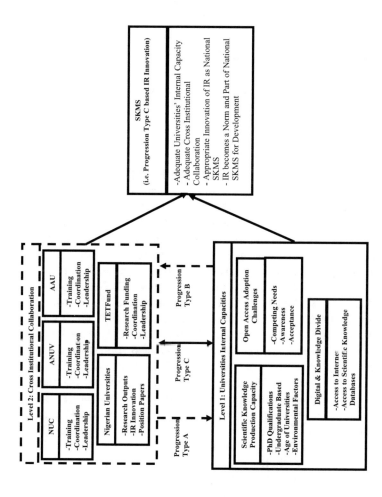

Fig. 9.1 Dynamics of SKMS (IR) innovation

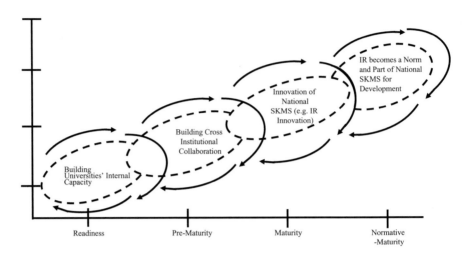

Fig. 9.2 SKMS innovation capacity level

Level two has to do with the ability of national SKMS to be able to identify key institutions and put in place programs that will facilitate their collaboration. This entails making key institutions to know and understand their immediate and extended roles in the successful innovation of SKMS, in the case of this study IR innovation. Although key institutions have constitutionally determined mandates, the model derived in this study indicates that such functions can be aligned with SKMS needs in order for the nation to be able to derive maximal benefits from these institutions. The example derived in this study is that TETFund should insist that every research that is funded by it must be deposited in the IR deployed by authors' universities and that the journals it funds should be open access journals. It is important to note that the progression is not sequential; in the sense that universities' internal capacities must be built before building collaboration capacity of key institutions. Our intention is to present a process that is interwoven and emergent. Given our intention therefore, practical experiences of each university and those of key institutions become the point through which actions to be taken must be determined. Room should also be given for the use of clues that may be derived through joint practical experiences of universities and/or identified key institutions. This therefore means that dialogue and frequent communication among universities and the key institutions must be ensured.

The model shows three major progression types experienced in Nigeria. The progression types were represented using arrows tagged as progression type a, progression type b, and progression type c. Progression type c is taken to be the ideal progression based on the findings of the study. This is because it represents a progression that is determined by communication and dialogue between university(ies) and key institution(s). The dual-pointed arrow indicates continuous communication and dialogue through which logics of IR innovation is shared. In the case of progression type a, the idea is that the institutions that provide(s) training, funds, leadership, and coordination for IR innovation provide IR innovation logics that do not put into consideration needs that are necessitated by contextual issues in universities. A good example as revealed in the study is the ways those to attend sponsored training we determined. There are also indications that identified key institutions do not consider the role other institutions within the SKMS of Nigeria could play in facilitating the achievement of IR innovation goals. Hence, collaboration among them was absent. Our study shows that the NUC, ANUV, and AAU that have constantly organized IR innovation training have not considered that TETFund could be of help to the country's IR innovation aspirations. In practice, the NUC, ANUV, and TETFund have not come together to reflect on how the different roles they play could synergized to ensure IR innovation success in Nigeria. This results because progression type a is the dominant progression types adopted in Nigeria. The absence of collaboration among identified key institutions resulted in the broken border of the box that housed them in the model shown in Fig. 9.1.

Progression type b represents a scenario in which IR innovation logics are communicated to key institutions by university(ies). Considering the nature of key institutions identified and the study, the transfer of IR innovation logics from universities to key institutions are done through knowledge spillover. In other words, most of the information key institutions have on IR innovation experiences of universities are those that are brought to them by principal officers of universities, particularly by vice-chancellors. Given the extent of awareness and acceptance of IR among academics (who by academic culture produce vice-chancellors), it will be logical to say that information provided to key institutions by vice-chancellors may not represent typical experiences of IR innovation in universities. This denotes a likely weak transfer of IR innovation logics and experiences from universities to key institutions who are meant to coordinate, fund, and provide leadership to universities with regard to IR innovation. This is the reason why the arrow that indicates communication between university(ies) and key institution is represented by a broken arrow.

We consider progression type c as the ideal progression. Our assumption is that universities and key institutions must jointly develop a progression strategy that incorporates both internal capacity development and cross institutional collaboration. For instance, universities can through the NUC make TETFund to come up with a policy regime that will ensure that academics that received grants from them become adhere to open access requirements. Conversely, TETFund can also through the NUC advice universities to provide further awareness information to academics in order for them to know more about the open access initiative. This is likely to make academics to see policy regimes put in place, for instance, by TETFund, as policies meant to facilitate national SKMS efforts and not to frustrate their research efforts and to debar them from getting funds from TETFund. If this scenario is enshrined, each university is provided with opportunity to explain its IR innovation challenges to relevant institutions eradicate IR problems, reinvent loose ends intertwined in the IR innovation process, and support appropriate IR innovation plans. Progression type c facilitates a four-step progression subtypes, namely, readiness, prematurity, maturity, and normative progressions. This is represented in Fig. 9.2 below.

As shown Fig. 9.2 the readiness level has to do with the period a university builds its internal capacity and in effects its readiness to innovate IR. A university's readiness involves building its scientific knowledge production capacity, eradicating digital and knowledge divide and promoting its open access adoption plans through the length and breadth of the university. The university then progresses to building collaboration with key institutions such as, in the case of Nigeria, other Nigerian universities, NUC, ANUV, TETFund, and, if need be, AAU. During the progression period, IR innovation will start to take a strong stand within the university. From the prematurity level of both universities and key institutions progress to maturity level where IR innovation has come to be known as notable part of national SKMS. Issues regarding appointment, promotion and tenure, and acceptable publication outlets and practices in connection with IR innovation would have been ironed out. Identified institutions would have deregulation expanded mandate that will make them redefine their roles. This level progresses to the cultural level where IR innovation and use have become the norm, cultural, and taken for granted by universities and the institutions that support it. At this stage IR innovate has become a traditional part they indicates. Consequently, the progressions outlined are therefore taken to be social activities that could be socially constructed. It therefore follows that it will involve the identification, assessment, review, and building of norms, values, and socially negotiated acceptable ways of SKMS innovation.

9.8   Conclusion

The chapter reinforces argument on the fact that both internal factors inherent in organizations and institutional factors inherent in macro-contexts are important to IS innovation. This argument has been restated in this chapter with a sense of commitment to the validity of calls made by stakeholders on the importance of micro-contexts to successful IR innovation. While attention is paid on larger contexts, we note that the technology in question and the contexts of organizations, in our case universities, are very fundamental to how progressions can be made from readiness through prematurity level to the normative level. As shown in the study, each of the universities studied had different contextual challenges that influenced the extent to which their internal capabilities were built to be receptive to IR innovation. The nature of institutions that exist at the micro level also impacts on the ways they are able to initiate programs that are supportive of SKMS. Here national culture comes to bear. The ways organizations display the level of flexibility required to expand its mandate to support equally important missions that are capable of supporting societal development become an issue. TETFund, NUC, ANUV, and AAU are organizations that have strong affinity with government. They have therefore built their organizational logics based on orientations that are similar to those of public organization. Their creativity and ability to align their official mandates with other mandates that are not explicitly expressed in the books remain low. We therefore conclude that frequent communication and dialogue among universities and key institutions that are part of national scientific knowledge structure are important to ensure that they do what is required to support SKMS innovation meaningfully.

References

1. Norbert, F., & Nsouli, S. (2003). *The new partnership for Africa's development (NEPAD): Opportunities and challenges.* International Monetary Fund Working Paper, 1–35. Available at: https://www.imf.org/external/pubs/ft/wp/2003/wp0369.pdf. Accessed 15 Sept 2016.
2. Chan, L., & Costa, S. (2005). Participation in the global knowledge commons: Challenges and opportunities for research dissemination in developing countries. *New Library World, 106,* 141–163.
3. Ifijeh, G. (2014). Adoption of digital preservation methods for theses and dissertations in Nigerian academic libraries: Applications and implications. *The Journal of Academic Librarianship, 40*(3), 399–404.
4. Ani, O. (2005). Evolution of virtual libraries in Nigeria: Myth or reality? *Journal of Information Science, 31,* 67–70.
5. Wyk, B., & Mostert, J. (2011). Toward enhanced access to Africa's research and local contents: A case study of the institutional depository project, University of Zululand, South Africa. *African Journal of Library, Archives and Information Science, 21,* 133–144.
6. Utulu, S., & Akadri, A. (2014). A case of Redeemer's University's adoption of institutional repository using the principle of electronic information management systems. In J. Krueger (Ed.), *Cases on electronic records and resource management: Implications in diverse environments.* Hershey: IGI.
7. Ezema, I. (2013). Local contents and the development of open access institutional repositories in Nigeria university libraries: Challenges, strategies and scholarly implications. *Library Hi Tech, 31,* 323–340.
8. Nwagwu, W. (2013). Open access initiatives in Africa-structure, incentives and disincentives. *The Journal of Academic Librarianship, 39,* 3–10.
9. Pinfield, S. (2015). Making open access work: The 'state-of-the-art' in providing open access to scholarly literature. *Online Information Review, 39,* 604–636.
10. Westell, M. (2006). Institutional repositories: Proposed indicators of success. *Library Hi Tech, 24,* 211–226.
11. Palmer, C., Teffeau, L., & Newton, M. (2008). Strategies for institutional repository development: A case study of three evolving initiatives. *Library Trends, 57,* 142–167.
12. Utulu, S., & Bolarinwa, O. (2009). Open access initiatives adoption by Nigerian academics. *Library Review, 58,* 660–669.
13. Maness, J., Miaskiewicz, T., & Sumner, T. (2008). Using persona to understand the needs and goals of institutional repository users. *D-Lib Magazine, 14.*
14. Sahay, S., & Mukherjee, A. (2015). *Capacity strengthening in a development context: Institutional challenges and approaches.* Proceedings of the 13th International Conference on Social Implications of Computers in Developing Countries, Negombo, Sri Lanka, May.
15. Avgerou, C. (2010). Discourses on ICT and development. *Information Technologies & International Development, 6,* pp 1.
16. Agbu, O., Agwu, F., & Osoata, J. (2004). *Human security development: Nigeria and Ethiopia.* Lagos: Nigerian Institute of International Affairs.
17. Bhambra, G. (2007). *Rethinking modernity: Postcolonialism and the sociological imagination.* New York: Springer.
18. Pathasarathy, B. (1994). Marxist theory of development, the new international division of labour and the third world. *Barkerley Planning Journal, 9*(1), 109–124.

19. Zwingina, J. (1992). *Capitalist development in an African economy: The case of Nigeria.* Ibadan: University Press, Plc.
20. Adams, D. (2013). *Globalization and economic development.* New Delhi: Random Exports.
21. Gore, C. (2000). The rise and fall of the Washington Consensus as a paradigm for developing countries. *World Development, 28,* 789–804.
22. Huq, M. M., Clunies-Ross, A., & Forsyth, D. (2009). *Development economics.* London: McGraw Hill.
23. Bwalya, K. (2014). *Technology development and platform enhancements for successful global E-government design.* Hershey: IGI.
24. Jean, R., Sinkovics, R., & Kim, D. (2008). Information technology and organizational performance within international business to business relationships: A review and an integrated conceptual framework. *International Marketing Review, 25,* 563–583.
25. Ngwenyama, O., Andoh-Baidoo, F., Bollou, F., Morawczynski, O. (2006). Is there A relationship between ICT, health, education and development? An empirical analysis of five west African countries from 1997–2003. *The Electronic Journal of Information Systems in Developing Countries, 23,* 1–11.
26. Zhao, S. (2006). The internet and the transformation of the reality of everyday life: Towards a new analytic stance in sociology. *Sociological Inquiry, 76,* 458–474.
27. Aker, J., & Mbiti, I. (2010). Mobile phones and economic development in Africa. *The Journal of Economic Perspectives, 24,* 207–232.
28. Bailey, A., & Ngwenyama, O. (2013). Toward entrepreneurial behavior in underserved communities: An ethnographic decision tree model of telecenter usage. *Information Technology for Development.* doi:10.1080/02681102.2012.751751.
29. Ehikhamenor, F. (2003). Internet resources and productivity in scientific research in Nigerian universities. *Journal of Information Science, 29,* 107–116.
30. Vasileiou, M., Rowley, J., & Hartley, R. (2012). The e-book management framework: The management of e-books in academic libraries and its challenges. *Library and Information Science Research, 34,* 282–291.
31. Heeks, R. (2010). Do information and communication technologies (ICTs) contribute to development? *Journal of International Development, 22,* 625–640.
32. Olatokun, W., & Utulu, S. (2012). Internationalization of information science education in Nigeria: A review of Africa Regional Centre for Information Science. *International Federation of Library Association (IFLA) Journal, 38,* 166–174.
33. Ani, O., Ngulube, P., & Onyancha, B. (2014). Accessibility and utilization of electronic information resources for research by academic staff at selected Nigerian universities between 2005 and 2012. *International Information & Library Review, 46,* 51–60.
34. Khan, M., Hossain, S., Hasan, M., & Clement, C. (2012). Barriers to the introduction of ICT into education in developing countries: The example of Bangladesh. *Online Submission, International Journal of Instruction, 5*(2), 61–80.
35. Chinn, M., & Fairlie, R. (2010). ICT use in the developing world: An analysis of differences in computer and internet penetration. *Review of International Economics, 18,* 153–167.
36. Oyelaran-Oyeyinka, B., & Adeya, C. (2004). Internet access in Africa: Empirical evidence from Kenya and Nigeria. *Telematics and Informatics, 21,* 67–81.
37. Vu, K. (2013). Information and communication technology (ICT) and Singapore's economic growth. *Information Economics and Policy, 25,* 284–300.
38. Chandra, V., Chandra, R., & Nutchey, D. (2014). Implementing ICT in schools in a developing country: A Fijian experience. In H. Kaur & X. Tao (Eds.), *ICTs and the millennium development goals: A United Nations perspective* (pp. 139–160). New York: Springer.
39. Opoku-Mensa, A. (2007). Information as an economic resource: An Africa perspective. In A. Opoku-Mensa & M. Salih (Eds.), African markets: Information and economic development (pp. 25–42). Addis Ababa: Economic Commission for Africa.
40. Britz, J., Lor, P., Coetzee, I. M., & Bester, B. (2006). Africa as a knowledge society: A reality check. *The International Information & Library Review, 38,* 25–40.

41. Breivik, P., & Gee, E. (2006). *Higher education in the internet age: Libraries creating a strategic edge*. Westport: Greenwood Publishing.
42. Obama, B. (2009). *National Information Literacy Awareness month*. Retrieved August 2, 2016 from https://www.whitehouse.gov/assets/documents/2009literacy_prc_rel.pdf
43. UNESCO. (2010). *Institute of Statistics: Measuring R&D: Challenges Faced by Developing Countries*. Technical Paper No. 5.
44. Osagie, A. (2009). Private universities: Born out of crisis in Nigeria. In A. Osagie (Ed.), *Change and choice: The development of private universities in Nigeria* (pp. 1–18). Benin: Rawel Fortune Resources.
45. Sturges, P., & Neill, R. (1989). *The quiet struggle: Libraries and information for Africa*. London: Mansell Publishing Limited.
46. Erinosho, O. (2013/2014). Transforming Nigeria's universities from local to global centers of learning. *Annals of the Social Science Academy of Nigeria, 18&19*, 3–24.
47. Beine, M., Docquier, F., & Rapoport, H. (2008). Brain drain and human capital formation in developing countries: Winners and losers. *The Economic Journal, 118*, 631–652.
48. Karlsson, S., Srebotnjak, T., & Gonzales, P. (2007). Understanding the North–South knowledge divide and its implications for policy: A quantitative analysis of the generation of scientific knowledge in the environmental sciences. *Environmental Science & Policy, 10*, 668–684.
49. Norris, P. (2001). *Digital divide: Civic engagement, information poverty, and the Internet worldwide*. Cambridge: Cambridge University Press.
50. Steinmueller, W. (2001). ICTs and the possibilities for leapfrogging by developing countries. *International Labour Review, 140*(2), 193–210.
51. Goldsmith, J., & Wu, J. (2006). *Who controls the internet?: Illusions of a borderless world*. Oxford: Oxford University Press.
52. Kanbur, R. (2001). The New Partnership for Africa's Development (NEPAD): An initial commentary. Available at: http://www.arts.cornell.edu/poverty/kanbur/POVNEPAD.pdf. Accessed August 2, 2016.
53. TETFund (2011). TETFund Allocation for the year 2012. Memo written to Nigerian public universities.
54. Aina, L., Alemna, A., & Mabawonku, I. (2005). *Improving the quality of library and information science journals in West Africa: A stakeholders' conference*. Ibadan: Third World Information Services Limited.
55. Alemna, A.. (2005). Improving international visibility of journals. *Proceedings of the Conference held at the Conference Center University of Ibadan, Nigeria*, 7–8 Dec.
56. Utulu, S. (2005). Role of journals in developing emerging scholars in library and information science. *Proceedings of the Conference held at the Conference Center University of Ibadan, Nigeria*, 7–8 Dec.
57. Kaur, H., & Tao, X. (2014). *ICTs and the millennium development goals: A United Nations perspective*. New York: Springer.
58. Oldekop, J., et al. (2016). 100 key research questions for the post-2015 development agenda. *Development Policy Review, 34*, 55–82.
59. Central Bank of Nigeria. (2005). *National Economic Empowerment Strategy: Nigeria*. Abuja: National Planning Commission & CBN.
60. Crow, R. (2002). The case for institutional repositories: A SPARC position paper. Washington, DC: The Scholarly Publishing and Academic Resources Coalition. Available at: www.arl.org/sparc/IR/ir.html. Accessed December 15, 2013.
61. Harnad, S. (2001). The self-archiving initiative. *Nature, 410*(6832), 1024–1025.
62. Utulu, S., & Akadri, A. (2010). *Institutional repositories: The untapped academic goldmine*. Proceedings of Second Professional Summit on Information Science and Technology, Nsukka (Nigeria), 16–23.
63. Foster, F., & Gibbons, S. (2005). Understanding faculty to improve content recruitment for institutional repositories. Online Submission, 11.

64. Kim, J. (2010). Faculty self-archiving: Motivations and barriers. *Journal of the American Society for Information Science and Technology, 61*(9), 1909–1922.
65. Ezema, I., & Onyancha, O. (2016). *Status of Africa in the global open access directories: Implications for global visibility of African scholarly research.* In Fourth CODESRIA conference on electronic publishing: Open Access Movement and the Future of African Knowledge Economy, Dakar, Senegal March
66. Bogoro, S. E. (2015). Sustainability of higher education institutions in Nigeria: challenges and prospects. Being a paper presented, TETFund, Nigeria 2015.
67. Thomas, D. R. (2006). A general inductive approach for analyzing qualitative evaluation data. *American Journal of Evaluation, 27*(2), 237–246.
68. Braun, V., & Clarke, V. (2006). Using thematic analysis in psychology. *Qualitative Research in Psychology, 3*(2), 77–101.
69. Nok, G. (2006). The challenges of computerizing a university library in Nigeria: The case of Kashim Ibrahim Library, Ahmadu Bello University, Zaria. *Library Philosophy and Practice, 8*, 2–9.
70. Halloran, P. (2008). An infrastructure for process improvement, organizational learning, and knowledge management. In A. Koohang & J. Britz (Eds.), *Knowledge management: Theoretical foundations* (pp. 115–155). USA: Informing Science.
71. Nonaka, I., & Takeuchi, H. (1995). *The knowledge-creating company.* Oxford: Oxford University Press.

Chapter 10
Linkages Between Formal Institutions, ICT Adoption, and Inclusive Human Development in Sub-Saharan Africa

Antonio Rodrìguez Andrés, Voxi Amavilah, and Simplice Asongu

Abstract This study empirically assesses the effects of formal institutions on ICT adoption in 49 African countries over the years 2000–2012. It deploys 2SLS and FE regression models (a) to estimate the determinants of ICT adoption and (b) to trace how ICT adoption affects inclusive development. The results show that formal institutions affect ICT adoption in this group of countries, with government effectiveness having the largest positive effects and regulations the largest negative effects. However, while formal institutions generally affect ICT adoption positively, population and economic growth tend to constrain ICT adoption more in low-income countries than middle-income countries. The results further demonstrate that the effects of ICT adoption on development are comparable to those of domestic credit and foreign direct investment. Ceteris paribus, one may conclude that external factors like foreign aid are more limiting to inclusive development than internal factors. This suggests that developing countries, African countries in this specific case, can enhance their ICT adoption for development by improving formal institutions and by strengthening domestic determinants of ICT adoption. Both represent opportunities for further research.

Keywords Formal institutions • ICT adoption • Panel data models • Cross-country analysis

JEL G20 • I10 • I32 • O40 • O55

A.R. Andrés (✉)
School of Business, Universidad del Norte, Barranquilla, Colombia
e-mail: antoniorodriguez@uninorte.edu.co

V. Amavilah
Estrella Mountain College, Phoenix, AZ, USA
e-mail: amavilah@msn.com

S. Asongu
African Governance and Development Institute, Yaoundé, Cameroon

Department of Economics, University of South Africa,
P. O. Box 392 UNISA 0003, Pretoria, South Africa.
e-mail: asongusimplice@yahoo.com

© Springer International Publishing AG 2017
H. Kaur et al. (eds.), *Catalyzing Development through ICT Adoption*,
DOI 10.1007/978-3-319-56523-1_10

10.1 Introduction

In recent years, there has been a major change in thinking about the appropriate role of telecommunications as growth and development enhancers. For instance, it has been stated that the adoption with diffusion of information and communication technologies (ICTs) promotes growth, and growth promotes ICT adoption and diffusion [1–12]. Billón et al. [13]'s study of the patterns and factors affecting ICT adoption[1] found that economic growth, education, and government effectiveness explain high ICT adoption rates positively in developed countries, while in developing countries the age of the urban population and Internet costs affect ICT adoption rates negatively. Kiessling [14] associated ICT adoption in 82 developed and developing countries with economic, financial, and political institutions, as well as with per capita income and education, discovering that institutional effects on ICT adoption varied across countries but that they were comparable in terms of magnitude to those of education and per capita GDP. However, studies like [14] remain few, and even fewer of them address the role of formal institutions in ICT adoption. In this limited sense, [15] are correct that existing models "are not very useful to explain the breadth of technology adoption across countries. Indeed, aggregate diffusion models treat each country as a homogeneous unit, and cannot explain why some countries have a higher probability of adopting in a given year than others" (p. 3). In addition, such models have neglected the "wildfire phenomenon" in the spread of innovations outlined in [16, 17]; (cf. [18–21]). Furthermore, formal comparisons of the relative influences of institutional quality indicators on ICT within developing countries are also missing from existing literature (for instance, [22, 23]).

In this chapter, first, we assess the effects of formal institutions on ICT adoption across 49 African countries. Second, we analyze how ICT adoption affects development in African countries. We concentrate on the two technologies, because among ICTs newer technologies and/or new uses of old technologies have had stronger impacts than others.

We link ICT adoption rates to the quality of formal institutions as predictors under control. Once we have estimated the factors determining ICT adoption, we examine how ICT adoption catalyzes development. Our approach departs from previous studies (cf. [13, 24]) in that its underlying hypothesis is that cross-country differences in institutional quality, and hence in ICT adoption, enhance or limit inclusive development, where formal institutions are measured by the World Bank indicators of governance.

The chapter is organized as follows: Sect. 10.2 describes the empirical model. We characterize key variables and data in Sect. 10.3. Section 10.4 implements the model and presents the results, while Sect. 10.5 concludes the exercise.

---

[1] Wherever the term "adoption" appears in this study, it should be read and understood as "adoption with diffusion." Under conditions of rapid technological change, an ICT that is just adopted may never be diffused, and for this reason we stress ICTs that have been adopted and penetrating the economy as catalysts for inclusive development.

10.2 Empirical Model

To examine the impact of formal institutions on ICT adoption, we estimate the following regression:

$$\text{ICT}_i = \alpha_0^* + \alpha_i^* \text{EconGrowth}_i + \beta_i^* \text{Institutions}_i + \gamma_i^* \text{Controls}_i + \lambda_i + v_i \quad (10.1)$$

where ICT represents the average ICT adoption, measured as cellular (mobile) phone and Internet penetration rates, and EconGrowth is economic growth predicted to promote ICT adoption, a relationship well-documented in the development literature [5, 6, 10, 11, 12]. Institutions are formal institutions, Controls include the educational attainment of the population, expected to affect ICT adoption positively, $\alpha_0^*, \alpha_i^*, \beta_i^*, \gamma_i^*$ are parameters to be estimated, λ are the country-fixed effects, and v is the error term. A short theoretical underpinning of the model is available upon request.

Finally, ICT adoption catalyzes development, where development is characterized as structural change in the economy that is accompanied by measurable improvement in the quality of life of the people. Many times such improvements are measured as positive changes in HDI, real GDP per capita, labor markets (low unemployment, high wages, better working conditions, etc.), financial markets, productivity, competitiveness, poverty reduction, human capital and technological knowledge, globalization, health, and security. In this study we take development to be inequality-adjusted HDI and estimate it as:

$$\text{Development}_i \equiv \text{IHDI}_i = \delta_{0i} + \delta_{1i}\text{ICT}_i^* + \delta_{2i}Z_i + \varepsilon_i \quad (10.2)$$

where δ are coefficients to be estimated, ICT_i^* is estimated from (10.1), Z are the determinants of development not already included in (10.1), and ε is the classical error term. There is a lot on Eq. (10.2) in the literature, see, e.g., [25–29]), and so on.

10.3 Key Variables and Data

10.3.1 Dependent Variables for ICT Adoption (ICT)

Unlike [24] who measure ICT adoption as investment per worker of computer produced domestically and/or imported, here dependent variables are measured as the rates of adoption of mobile phones and Internet per 100 people, i.e., penetration rates. The use of these dependent variables is consistent with recent African knowledge economy literature [30].

10.3.2 Determinants of ICT Adoption

Many factors determined ICT adoption. However, we stress only a few predictors, beginning with formal institutions.

Institutions and Institutional Quality Our key explanatory variable is governance. We define governance as the way in which policy makers are empowered to make decisions and the manner in which policy decisions are formulated and executed. The governance data come from [31] study, and the World Bank.[2] The World Bank indicators capture different aspects of governance as they are constructed from several sources including polls of experts and surveys of residents and entrepreneurs within a country, and they could be grouped into three concepts. The first concept is about the process by which those in authority are selected and replaced (political governance: voice and accountability, and political stability). The second has to do with the capacity of government to formulate and implement policies and to deliver services (economic governance: regulatory quality and government effectiveness). The last deals with the respect for citizens and the state of institutions that govern the interactions among them (institutional governance: rule of law, and control of corruption).

Each indicator normalized to range from -2.5 to 2.5, and with a zero mean and a standard deviation of one, provides a subjective assessment of some aspect of a country's quality of governance. Higher values signal better governance. Despite data aggregation problems, one of the advantages of aggregate indicators is that they are more informative about broad notions of governance. Individual data provides a noisy signal of the broader concept of governance, which is good for statistical significance and not necessarily for economic significance. Although they lack sufficient random variations over time, aggregate indicators used in isolation measure different aspects of the impact of formal institutions on ICT adoption. Poor institutions, for instance, would influence aggregate economic growth by delaying productivity improvements. Productivity is an important channel for the effects of institutions on ICT adoption and hence on economic growth and development.

Other Variables Previous research has used many other explanatory variables. [13], for example, argued that disparities in ICT adoption depend on GDP per capita, population aged 15–64 years old, fraction of GDP that comes from the service sector, foreign trade as a percentage of GDP, population density, urban population size, educational level measured as years of schooling, government effectiveness, income level of the country, dummies for the dominant market structure, and language.

Caselli and Coleman II [24] associated adoption of personal computers with income per worker, and investment per worker is calculated either as investment in the computing power of the country, value of imports of computing goods and services, or the sum of the two. Other variables were the shares of GDP originating from agriculture and manufacturing, government spending as a percentage of GDP, manufactured imports from OECD as well as non-OECD countries, country's structure of property rights, and dummy for language. A notable omission here is human capital.

---

[2] The World Bank data is available at: http://info.worldbank.org/governance/wgi/index.aspx#home.

Kiessling [14]'s examination of the adoption of cellular telephony, Internet, and PC stresses economic, financial, and political institutions, arguing that good economic institutions attract foreign interactions (investment, trade, aid) and are effective tools in devising effective anti-diversion and anticorruption policies. Among macro-economic variables, [14] also included changes in the general price level (CPI). The latter are warranted because cross-country comparison based on common prices is better than those made based on exchange rates; many developing countries have more than one exchange rate running parallel.

Regarding financial institutions the argument is that they either provide free market opportunities or are friendly to the creation and delivery of such opportunities. How good these institutions are is normally reflected in rates of return on private investment, availability of private credit as a sign of the existence of a vibrant entrepreneurial activity, and effective demand for ICTs.[3] Among political institutions, [14] used "an index of political regime characteristics – Polity 2" (p. 39), freedom of press, rule of law, and round off his specification by including education, and income.[4]

10.3.3 Development Dependent Variables

The literature on the link between ICT adoption and development is huge (see, [32–37]). The term of development is one of those things that nearly everyone knows, but no one knows how to measure precisely. Some experts measure development as economic development, approximated by economic (real GDP per capita) growth. In truth development is broader than economic development, which is in turn wider than economic growth. Others measure development as the Human Development Index (HDI). The HDI encompasses real GDP, health (life expectancy), and education (years of schooling). It also has an additional advantage that it can be adjusted for inequalities of income, wealth, poverty, gender, and so on, thereby yielding IHDI. One of IHDI weaknesses is that it is still an index and therefore lacks sufficient variations and may cause some statistical problems in small sample regressions (cf. [38]). IHDI is our preferred option for this study, nonetheless.

10.3.4 Key Determinants of Development

The determinants of development are just as many and complex as development itself. Below are those we considered.

Estimated ICT (ICT*) Among key predictors of inclusive development, we emphasize the role of ICT adoption as estimated in Eq. (10.1). This is just another

---

[3] Note that the existence of entrepreneurs with access to private credit is a key driver of capital formation in a Schumpeterian model – Eq. (10.2) above.

[4] For a description of how the Polity 2 index is calculated, we refer the interested reader to [14]), p. 39ff.

way of acknowledging the importance of formal institutions in development acting through ICT adoption (cf. [38–43]).

Other Development Determinants (Z) From the vast literature, the usual determinants of development would include: geography, foreign trade, foreign aid, foreign direct investment (FDI), remittances, and so on (see, e.g., [44–46]). However, we assume African countries to be geographically homogenous, so that the effects of geographical factors are constant. Even as we do so, we know that development can be measured by its narrower quality-of-life representations like health, participatory democracy, education, privacy and security, innovations, employment, economic performance, and poverty reduction. In such cases determinants of development can be varied. For instance, in [47]), development is represented by "high growth entrepreneurship," which is driven by trade-related intellectual property rights (TRIPS). As the model available as Supplement 1 shows, the results reported in here place a Baumolian-Schmpumpterian emphasis on the entrepreneur as a driver of dynamic development. In fact, according to Schumpeter [53], Becker et al. [54], and Bazhal [55], in a Schumpeterian economy, technological knowledge such as ICT depends on the profit made possible by the risk-taking entrepreneur. The entrepreneur succeeds profitably under an enabling social setting implied by the country's level of development (see, [47], pp. 6–7). An implication of such an approach is that the effects on development of ICT adoption are weak or negative; it does not necessarily imply that adoption rates are low; it could be that entrepreneurship and/or the social organization are somehow reluctant to change.[5] We know that [47]) used real interest rate as a proxy for the cost of capital. However, due to the lack of reliable data on African capital markets, here we use domestic credit as an indicator of the local banking sector and a source of capital for the entrepreneur. The lack of credit constrains the entrepreneur, and without profits ICT adoption is not possible, and without ICT adoption growth and inclusive development are stunted.

10.3.5 Data

To establish a sample of 49 African countries listed at the bottom of Table 10.1, we modify the World Bank country classification in only two groups: low income and middle income. We do so because in the high-income category, there are only two African countries: Equatorial Guinea and Seychelles. The upper middle-income group has only five African countries. This adjustment is defensible because one can argue that these countries are not advanced in terms of ICT. Variable definitions, data, and data relating to ICT adoption (Eq. 10.1) and inclusive development

---

[5]We refer the interested reader to Willian J. Baumol's *The Free-Market Innovation Machine: Analyzing the Growth Miracle of Capitalism*. Princeton/Oxford: Princeton University Press, 2002. However, this great work was not fundamental to our work and therefore we do not include it in our list of cited work.

(Eq. 10.2) are available as supplementary material. Here note again that ICT adoption is measured as Internet penetration rates and mobile penetration rates. Inclusive development is represented by inequality-adjusted HDI (IHDI). The IHDI adjusts HDI for inequality by accounting for the manner in which such achievements are distributed within the population controlling for the mean values of achievements for inequality, where HDI is defined as the average of results in three main areas, notably: (i) knowledge, (ii) decent living standards, and (iii) health and long life. In the African context, as elsewhere in developing countries, control variables for the human development equation would encompass: development assistance, private domestic credit, remittances, and foreign direct investment. The choice of these variables is consistent with recent literature on inclusive development/growth [44–46].

10.4 Empirical Strategy and Results

Our strategy involves estimating Eqs. (10.1 and 10.2). The first regression in both cases is for the entire sample of 49 countries. The second regression focuses on 28 low-income countries, the third on 21 middle-income countries. We use two related estimators: 2SLS and IV FE, corrected for an unknown and unobserved form of heteroscedasticity.

Tables 10.1, 10.2, 10.3, 10.4, and 10.5 present the results. Specifically, Table 10.1 shows 2SLS effects of formal institutions on mobile phone penetration across the full sample of 49 African countries (Panel A) and across the subsamples of 28 low-income (Panel B) and 21 middle-income (Panel C) countries. For all countries formal institutions promote ICT adoption, with the government effectiveness contributing most positively. Considering the 28 low-income and the 21 middle-income countries separately, formal institutions strongly determine ICT adoption in all cases, except for the quality of regulations which undermines ICT adoption in middle-income countries. This is probably because the regulations are not sufficiently tailored toward enhancing ICT adoption. Moreover, the positive effects of corruption control and political governance are not significant for ICT adoption in low-income and middle-income countries, respectively.

Regarding control variables, economic growth and population growth have disadvantaged ICT adoption in this group of countries. The result is reasonable, because if population grows faster than real GDP, then per capita real GDP upon which the calculation of economic growth is based would be low and ICT adoption similarly constrained. Furthermore, if growth does not trickle down to the poor segments of the population, then ICT adoption would not increase. Such a narrative would be consistent with the position that the rich in Africa, as elsewhere, prefer the quality of children to the quantity of children. Therefore the wealthy have fewer children than the poor [48]. Hence, population growth is mostly traceable to the poor segments of the population. This interpretation is buttressed further by the fact that the recent growth resurgence in Africa that began in the mid-1990s has not benefited the poor [49]. In fact, a World Bank report has revealed that extreme

Table 10.1 Mobile phone penetration and governance, Eq. (10.1), 2SLS

| | Dependent variable: mobile phone penetration | | | | | |
| | Political governance | | Economic governance | | Institutional governance | |
	Political stability/ nonviolence	Voice and accountability	Regulation quality	Government effectiveness	Rule of law	Corruption control
Panel A: full sample						
Constant	26.505***	25.298***	27.077***	24.833***	26.146***	20.469**
	(0.001)	(0.003)	(0.002)	(0.003)	(0.002)	(0.012)
Political stability(IV)	6.256***	–	–	–	–	–
	(0.000)					
Voice and accountability (IV)	–	7.841***	–	–	–	–
		(0.000)				
Regulation quality (IV)	–	–	11.064***	–	–	–
			(0.000)			
Government effectiveness (IV)	–	–	–	12.392***	–	–
				(0.000)		
Rule of law (IV)	–	–	–	–	9.810***	–
					(0.000)	
Corruption control (IV)	–	–	–	–	–	10.970***
						(0.000)
Economic growth	–0.402	–0.581**	–0.573**	–0.663***	–0.505**	–0.492**
	(0.107)	(0.022)	(0.023)	(0.008)	(0.046)	(0.048)
Trade openness	0.105**	0.141***	0.146***	0.156***	0.132***	0.153***
	(0.016)	(0.000)	(0.001)	(0.001)	(0.003)	(0.000)
Population growth	–7.197***	–6.584***	–6.485***	–5.079**	–6.473***	–5.517**
	(0.001)	(0.002)	(0.005)	(0.016)	(0.003)	(0.010)
Primary school enrolment	0.148***	0.144***	0.145***	0.150***	0.156***	0.172***
	(0.002)	(0.006)	(0.006)	(0.004)	(0.002)	(0.001)

Adjusted R²	0.226	0.229	0.233	0.244	0.228	0.234
Fisher	13.40***	13.88***	16.69***	14.96***	13.71***	14.97***
Observations	336	336	336	336	336	336
Panel B: low-income countries						
Constant	2.453	5.354	7.781	5.641	5.062	−2.922
	(0.743)	(0.526)	(0.377)	(0.548)	(0.601)	(0.729)
Governance (IV)	5.547***	6.872***	10.803***	8.872***	7.577**	3.742
	(0.001)	(0.005)	(0.000)	(0.004)	(0.025)	(0.301)
Control variables	Yes	Yes	Yes	Yes	Yes	Yes
Adjusted R²	0.172	0.165	0.184	0.162	0.155	0.140
Fisher	10.14***	9.37***	12.42***	10.25***	10.13***	8.13***
Observations	223	223	223	223	223	223
Panel C: middle-income countries						
Constant	54.265*	40.600*	39.309*	38.280*	42.641*	33.900***
	(0.053)	(0.080)	(0.079)	(0.094)	(0.062)	(0.141)
Governance (IV)	5.791	2.915	−0.982*	10.629**	8.660*	12.334***
	(0.127)	(0.468)	(0.051)	(0.039)	(0.054)	(0.006)
Control variables	Yes	Yes	Yes	Yes	Yes	Yes
Adjusted R²	0.186	0.175	0.176	0.201	0.195	0.223
Fisher	6.32***	5.85***	6.73***	6.97***	7.18***	8.69***
Observations	113	113	113	113	113	113

***, **, *: significance levels at 1%, 5%, and 10% respectively. *IV* instrumental variable. Governance (political stability/nonviolence, voice and accountability, regulation quality, government effectiveness, rule of law, and corruption control). For instance, in column 2 of Panel B, governance (IV) represents political stability, while in the last column, governance (IV) denotes corruption control

Table 10.2 Internet penetration and governance, Eq. (10.1), 2SLS

| | Dependent variable: Internet penetration | | | | | |
| | Political governance | | Economic governance | | Institutional governance | |
	Political stability/ nonviolence	Voice and accountability	Regulation quality	Government effectiveness	Rule of law	Corruption control
Panel A: full sample						
Constant	11.095***	10.665***	9.825***	10.304***	11.144***	9.319***
	(0.000)	(0.000)	(0.000)	(0.000)	(0.000)	(0.000)
Political stability (IV)	1.780***	–	–	–	–	–
	(0.000)					
Voice and accountability (IV)	–	2.177***	–	–	–	–
		(0.000)				
Regulation quality (IV)	–	–	0.746	–	–	–
			(0.179)			
Government effectiveness (IV)	–	–	–	2.466***	–	–
				(0.000)		
Rule of law (IV)	–	–	–	–	2.883***	–
					(0.000)	
Corruption control (IV)	–	–	–	–	–	2.944***
						(0.000)
Economic growth	0.068	0.018	0.037	0.007	0.037	0.043
	(0.321)	(0.794)	(0.609)	(0.913)	(0.585)	(0.531)
Trade openness	–0.008	0.001	–0.001	0.003	–0.001	0.005
	(0.348)	(0.840)	(0.912)	(0.760)	(0.895)	(0.608)
Population Growth	–3.074***	–2.888***	–3.234***	–2.739***	–2.865***	–2.626***
	(0.000)	(0.000)	(0.000)	(0.000)	(0.000)	(0.000)
Primary school enrolment	0.019**	0.018**	0.028***	0.022**	0.020**	0.026***
	(0.026)	(0.048)	(0.003)	(0.011)	(0.020)	(0.004)

Adjusted R²	0.252	0 254	0.210	0.214	0.258	0.256
Fisher	9.95***	5 681***	10.00***	10.24***	10.75***	9.85***
Observations	330	330	330	330	330	330
Panel B: low-income countries						
Constant	0.381	−0.112	0.787	1.071	1.491	0.182
	(0.749)	(0.931)	(0.506)	(0.408)	(0.253)	(0.885)
Governance (IV)	0.724***	0.433	1.179**	1.385***	1.477***	1.090*
	(0.001)	(0.244)	(0.022)	(0.001)	(0.001)	(0.050)
Control variables	Yes	Yes	Yes	Yes	Yes	Yes
Adjusted R²	0.088	0.058	0.085	0.089	0.095	0.070
Fisher	6.07***	2.73**	2.73**	4.25***	4.62***	3.94***
Observations	221	221	221	221	221	221
Panel C: middle-income countries						
Constant	18.058***	14.432**	14.585**	14.063**	14.424**	13.0119**
	(0.002)	(3.011)	(0.019)	(0.022)	(0.012)	(0.035)
Governance (IV)	1.744	1.474	−3.640***	−0.326	0.044	1.671
	(0.144)	(0.195)	(0.007)	(0.864)	(0.809)	(0.279)
Control variables	Yes	Yes	Yes	Yes	Yes	Yes
Adjusted R²	0.183	0.180	0.207	0.169	0.176	0.180
Fisher	5.78***	6.05***	5.35***	5.44***	5.83***	5.82***
Observations	109	109	109	109	109	109

***, **, *: significance levels at 1%, 5%, and 10% respectively. IV instrumental variable. Governance (political stability/nonviolence, voice and accountability, regulation quality, government effectiveness, rule of law, and corruption control). For instance, in column 2 of Panel B, governance (IV) represents political stability, while in the last column, governance (IV) denotes corruption control.

Table 10.3 Mobile phone penetration and governance, Eq. (10.1), IV FE

	Dependent variable: mobile phone penetration					
	Political governance	Economic governance			Institutional governance	
	Political stability/ nonviolence	Voice and accountability	Regulation quality	Government effectiveness	Rule of law	Corruption control
Panel A: full sample						
Constant	−58.915***	−77.499***	−70.767***	−101.188***	−82.532***	−54.858***
	(0.000)	(0.000)	(0.000)	(0.000)	(0.000)	(0.001)
Political stability (IV)	−1.091	–	–	–	–	–
	(0.789)					
Voice and accountability (IV)	–	−19.217**	–	–	–	–
		(0.012)				
Regulation quality (IV)	–	–	−15.022*	–	–	–
			(0.059)			
Government effectiveness (IV)	–	–	–	−32.896***	–	–
				(0.000)		
Rule of law (IV)	–	–	–	–	−21.239***	–
					(0.009)	
Corruption control (IV)	–	–	–	–	–	4.747
						(0.461)
Economic growth	−0.655**	−0.565**	−0.662**	−0.481*	−0.672**	−0.671**
	(0.019)	(0.012)	(0.017)	(0.078)	(0.015)	(0.017)
Trade openness	0.039	0.051	0.035	−0.001	0.066	0.048
	(0.686)	(0.596)	(0.715)	(0.984)	(0.497)	(0.628)
Population growth	0.804	1.837	1.238	4.641	2.597	0.068
	(0.839)	(0.640)	(0.753)	(0.238)	(0.513)	(0.986)
Primary school enrolment	0.836***	0.875***	0.855***	0.958***	0.876***	0.840***
	(0.000)	(0.000)	(0.000)	(0.000)	(0.000)	(0.000)

Hausman test	26.23***	32.71***	30.90***	46.70***	33.23***	22.56***
Within R^2	0.154	0.170	0.162	0.204	0.172	0.153
Fisher	10.28***	11.79***	11.11***	14.71***	11.88***	10.39***
Countries	45	45	45	45	45	45
Observations	336	336	336	336	336	336
Panel B: low-income countries						
Constant	−59.305***	−67.618***	−71.693***	−117.286***	−106.260***	−68.206***
	(0.001)	(0.001)	(0.001)	(0.000)	(0.000)	(0.001)
Governance (IV)	−5.702	−11.355	−14.384	−36.718***	−32.822***	−12.576
	(0.157)	(0.151)	(0.104)	(0.000)	(0.000)	(0.102)
Control Variables	Yes	Yes	Yes	Yes	Yes	Yes
Within R^2	0.212	0.212	0.215	0.283	0.261	0.215
Fisher	10.19***	10.20***	11.35***	14.94***	13.36***	10.36***
Countries	29	29	29	29	29	29
Observations	223	223	223	223	223	223
Panel C: middle-income countries						
Constant	−93.280**	−75.570*	−73.832	−96.030**	−81.145*	−123.568***
	(0.045)	(0.096)	(0.116)	(0.040)	(0.082)	(0.009)
Governance (IV)	20.397*	−43.392**	−18.625	−32.938*	4.248	37.581***
	(0.088)	(0.025)	(0.364)	(0.080)	(0.839)	(0.003)
Control variables	Yes	Yes	Yes	Yes	Yes	Yes
Within R^2	0.142	0.162	0.123	0.144	0.115	0.194
Fisher	3.07**	3.57***	2.58**	3.10**	2.40**	4.45***
Countries	16	16	16	16	16	16
Observations	113	113	113	113	113	113

***, **, *: significance levels at 1%, 5%, and 10% respectively. *IV* instrumental variable. Governance (political stability/nonviolence, voice and accountability, regulation quality, government effectiveness, rule of law, and corruption control) poverty has been decreasing in all regions of the world with the exception of Africa where 45% of countries were substantially offtrack from achieving extreme poverty reduction targets [50]. While population and economic growth have restricted ICT adoption, openness to trade and human capital accumulation has had positive effects.

By 2SLS formal institutions also promote ICT adoption measured as Internet penetration rate (Table 10.2). As with cellular (mobile) phone penetration rate, the quality of regulation is inversely correlated with ICT adoption in middle-income countries. Unlike in the full sample, population growth, trade, political stability, and rule of law affect ICT adoption negatively when the sample is disaggregated by income levels. Still, formal institutions generally improve ICT adoption in these countries, although improvements vary by income levels. It is apparent from the results that ICT adoption in Sub-Sahara Africa (SSA) is driven by formal institutions more in low-income countries than middle-income countries. Put in standard economic theory, given formal institutions, the marginal product of ICT adoption increases at an increasing rate in low-income countries, but diminishing returns to ICT adoption appear to set in at middle-income level. Consequently, while both groups of countries gain from ICT adoption, for development the benefits of ICT adoption are greater for poor than for rich countries.

Country Classification by Income Level

Income levels	Countries
Low-income countries ($ 1,045 or less)	Benin, Burkina Faso, Burundi, Central African Republic, Chad, Comoros, Congo, Dem. Rep, Eritrea, Ethiopia, Gambia, The, Guinea, Guinea-Bissau, Liberia, Madagascar, Malawi, Mali, Mozambique, Niger, Rwanda, Sierra Leone, Somalia, South Sudan, Tanzania, Togo, Uganda, Zimbabwe
Middle-income countries ($1,046–12,735)	Angola, Cape Verde, Cameroon, Congo, Rep., Côte d'Ivoire, Djibouti, Egypt, Equatorial Guinea, Gabon, Ghana, Kenya, Lesotho, Mauritania, Mauritius, Morocco, Namibia, Nigeria, São Tomé and Principe, Senegal, Sudan, Swaziland, Zambia

Source: World Bank available at http://data.worldbank.org/about/country-and-lending-groups#Low_income (Accessed on June 2016)

To examine the strengths of the 2SLS results, we ran the Hausman test for endogeneity, and the choice of the IV FE approach was based on that outcome. IV FE results are reported in Tables 10.3 and 10.4. Ceteris paribus, government effectiveness and population growth restrict ICT adoption, all else have positive effects. By income levels the IV FE estimator yields negative institutional effects on ICT adoption except for the corruption indicator. For all 49 countries, corruption, regulation, trade, and population growth assist ICT adoption, and all else have negative effects, although statistically insignificant in most cases. By income levels, political stability and corruption decrease ICT adoption in low-income countries, and ICT adoption is favored by political stability, regulatory quality, and government effectiveness in middle-income countries. The negative effects may be traceable to the fact that formal institutions are a necessary but not a sufficient condition for ICT adoption

Table 10.4 Internet penetration and governance, Eq. (10.1), IVFE

| | Dependent variable: mobile phone penetration | | | | | |
| | Political governance | | Economic governance | | Institutional governance | |
	Political stability/nonviolence	Voice and accountability	Regulation quality	Government effectiveness	Rule of law	Corruption control
Panel A: full sample						
Constant	−1.883	−3.517	−0.998	−4.387	−3.003	−0.535
	(0.552)	(0.306)	(0.767)	(0.233)	(0.406)	(0.866)
Political stability (IV)	0.719	–	–	–	–	–
	(0.357)					
Voice and accountability (IV)	–	−1.023	–	–	–	–
		(0.484)				
Regulation quality (IV)	–	–	1.727	–	–	–
			(0.266)			
Government effectiveness (IV)	–	–	–	−1.459	–	–
				(0.339)		
Rule of law (IV)	–	–	–	–	−0.443	–
					(0.780)	
Corruption control (IV)	–	–	–	–	–	2.842**
						(0.023)
Economic growth	−0.086	−0.078	−0.083	−0.075	−0.084	−0.090*
	(0.107)	(0.144)	(0.120)	(0.163)	(0.116)	(0.090)
Trade openness	0.019	0.020	0.019	0.017	0.020	0.024
	(0.298)	(0.290)	(0.304)	(0.362)	(0.296)	(0.199)
Population growth	1.236	1.365*	1.247	1.479*	1.343*	0.913
	(0.104)	(0.073)	(0.100)	(0.058)	(0.081)	(0.235)

(continued)

Table 10.4 (continued)

	Dependent variable: mobile phone penetration					
	Political governance		Economic governance		Institutional governance	
	Political stability/ nonviolence	Voice and accountability	Regulation quality	Government effectiveness	Rule of law	Corruption control
Primary school enrolment	0.028	0.031	0.026	0.034	0.030	0.032
	(0.235)	(0.187)	(0.258)	(0.151)	(0.205)	(0.169)
Hausman test	20.16***	20.37***	18.15***	19.14***	18.77***	12.75**
Within R^2	0.030	0.028	0.031	0.030	0.027	0.044
Fisher	1.75	1.67	1.83	1.76	1.59	2.64**
Countries	44	44	44	44	44	44
Observations	330	330	330	330	330	330
Panel B: low-income countries						
Constant	−1.144	2.097	−3.274	−6.129**	−5.484*	−0.216
	(0.604)	(0.408)	(0.215)	(0.032)	(0.051)	(0.931)
Governance (IV)	0.996**	0.003	−0.558	−2.027*	−1.799	1.702*
	(0.042)	(0.923)	(0.616)	(0.058)	(0.105)	(0.085)
Control variables	Yes	Yes	Yes	Yes	Yes	Yes
Within R^2	0.071	0.050	0.051	0.068	0.063	0.065
Fisher	2.88**	2.01*	2.05*	2.76**	2.55**	2.63**
Countries	28	28	28	28	28	28
Observations	221	221	221	221	221	221

Panel C: middle-income countries

Constant	3.314	4.188	−0.965	2.796	2.589	−3.807
	(0.782)	(0.725)	(0.935)	(0.817)	(0.828)	(0.757)
Governance (IV)	−1.084	−5.439	9.844**	−0.364	2.788	5.678*
	(0.724)	(0.261)	(0.049)	(0.938)	(0.589)	(0.075)
Control variables	Yes	Yes	Yes	Yes	Yes	Yes
Within R^2	0.049	0.061	0.089	0.048	0.051	0.082
Fisher	0.92	1.16	1.73	0.89	0.95	1.57
Countries	16	16	16	16	16	16
Observations	109	109	109	109	109	109

***, **, *: significance levels at 1%, 5%, and 10% respectively. *IV* instrumental variable. Governance (political stability/nonviolence, voice and accountability, regulation quality, government effectiveness, rule of law, and corruption control)

Table 10.5 ICT and inclusive development, Eq. (10.2), 2SLS, IV FE

Dependent variable: inequality adjusted human development index

	Two-stage least squares				Instrumental variable fixed effects			
Panel A: full sample								
Constant	0.403***	0.402***	0.422***	0.415***	0.436***	0.434***	0.430***	0.427***
	(0.000)	(0.000)	(0.000)	(0.000)	(0.000)	(0.000)	(0.000)	(0.000)
Mobile phone penetration (IV)	0.001***	0.001***	–	–	0.0005***	0.0006***	–	–
	(0.000)	(0.000)	–	–	(0.000)	(0.000)	–	–
Internet penetration (IV)	–	–	0.007***	0.007***	–	–	0.002***	0.002***
	–	–	(0.000)	(0.000)	–	–	(0.000)	(0.000)
Foreign aid	−0.001***	−0.001***	−0.002***	−0.002***	−0.0001*	−0.0001	0.002***	−0.0002
	(0.000)	(0.001)	(0.003)	(0.005)	(0.088)	(0.200)	(0.000)	(0.160)
Private domestic credit	0.001***	0.001***	0.001***	0.001***	−0.00003	0.00009	0.0006*	0.0009**
	(0.002)	(0.001)	(0.000)	(0.000)	(0.925)	(0.799)	(0.102)	(0.020)
Remittances	–	−0.00009	–	−0.0002	–	0.0003	0.0003	0.0001
	–	(0.739)	–	(0.349)	–	(0.338)	(0.053)	(0.792)
Foreign direct investment	–	0.001	–	0.001**	–	0.0005**	–	0.0005**
	–	(0.138)	–	(0.029)	–	(0.025)	–	(0.026)
Hausman test	–	–	–	–	42.48***	38.82***	23.60***	26.45***
Within R²/R²	0.463	0.534	0.434	0.556	0.302	0.363	0.199	0.265
Fisher	94.30***	43.22***	87.75***	64.47***	47.36***	30.19***	26.37***	18.43***
Countries	–	–	–	–	44	39	44	39
Observations	375	308	365	299	375	308	365	399
Panel B: low-income countries								
Constant	0.374***	0.389***	0.381***	0.390***	0.377***	−68.20***	0.370***	0.369***
	(0.000)	(0.000)	(0.000)	(0.000)	(0.000)	(0.001)	(0.000)	(0.000)
Mobile phone penetration (IV)	0.001***	0.001***	–	–	0.0007***	−12.576	–	–
	(0.000)	(0.000)	–	–	(0.000)	(0.102)	–	–

Internet penetration (IV)	–	–	0.010***	0.010***	–	–	0.005***	0.005***
			(0.000)	(0.000)			(0.000)	(0.000)
Control variables	Yes	Yes	Yes	Yes	Yes	Yes	Yes	Yes
Within R²/R²	0.296	0.266	0.236	0.339	0.378	0.440	0.375	0.467
Fisher	48.28***	14.47***	24.25***	28.82***	42.82***	25.24***	41.29***	27.21***
Countries	–	–	–	–	28	24	28	24
Observations	242	189	237	184	242	189	237	184
Panel C: middle-income countries								
Constant	0.494***	0.472***	0.514***	0.492***	0.531***	0.511***	0.523***	0.501***
	(0.000)	(0.000)	(0.000)	(0.000)	(0.000)	(0.000)	(0.000)	(0.000)
Mobile phone penetration (IV)	0.001***	0.001***	–	–	0.0004***	0.0004***	–	–
	(0.000)	(0.000)			(0.000)	(0.000)		
Internet penetration (IV)	–	–	0.005***	0.005***	–	–	0.001**	0.001**
			(0.000)	(0.000)			(0.019)	(0.035)
Control variables	Yes	Yes	Yes	Yes	Yes	Yes	Yes	Yes
Within R²/R²	0.382	0.546	0.399	0.582	0.253	0.314	0.147	0.191
Fisher	25.31***	27.96***	34.24***	44.13***	12.91***	9.09***	6.29***	4.49***
Countries	–	–	–	–	16	15	16	15
Observations	133	119	128	115	133	119	128	115

***, **, *: significance levels at 1%, 5%, and 10% respectively. *IV* instrumental variable

when country-specific effects are considered. It is also important to note that the findings in Tables 10.1 and 10.2 hold only when we control for simultaneity, while those in Tables 10.3 and 10.4 stem from controlling for both simultaneity and unobserved heterogeneity. A broad implication here is that while formal institutions could enhance the adoption of ICT in SSA, policy makers still need to take into account country-specific institutional arrangements in determining ICT adoption outcomes. A corollary explanation is that the weight of countries with negatively skewed government quality variables significantly influences the outcome of all countries, leading to unexpected signs of the estimated coefficients. Consequently, while the significance of such results may be questionable from the statistical viewpoint, the results are nonetheless important from the economic perspective. They suggest that formal institutions are critical to ICT adoption, in both positive and negative ways.

The findings in Table 10.5 are about the effects of ICT adoption on inclusive development estimated by the 2SLS (columns 2–5) and by the IV FE (columns 6–9) methods. In the full sample, ICT adoption strongly affects inclusive human development. The effects of ICT adoption on development are comparable to those of private domestic credit availability and foreign direct investment. The fact that foreign aid limits inclusive human development is consistent with conclusions of [51]) in Africa. Moreover, positive effects of private domestic credit and foreign direct investment are also in accordance with recent inclusive growth/development literature on developing countries [44, 45, 52]. Clearly, ICT adoption increases inclusive development, and the propensity to do so is higher in low-income countries than in middle-income countries. Just as clearly, the evidence shows that holding ICT adoption constant, there is competition between domestic factors and forces tending to increase development and external factors and forces pulling in the opposite direction.

10.5 Conclusion

We have argued in the chapter that ICT adoption is a catalyst for inclusive development of developing countries. We scrutinized data for 49 African countries to support our argument. Using 2SLS and IV FE strategies, first we examined the impact of formal institutions on ICT adoption and found them strong at both the aggregate and disaggregated levels, with government effectiveness having the largest positive effects and regulations the biggest negative effects. Overall formal institutions appear more important to ICT adoption in low-income countries than in middle-income countries, suggesting increasing returns to ICT adoption in low-income countries and constant or diminishing returns in middle-income countries. Population and economic growth tend to constrain ICT adoption with low-income countries more negatively affected than middle-income countries.

Next we have assessed how estimated ICT adoption catalyzes development. Here the results are unambiguously clear that ICT adoption has strong and statistically significant effects on inclusive development on average. However, the results indicate that the positive effects on inclusive development of ICT adoption compare well to those of domestic private credit and foreign direct investment. Given positive ICT adoption impacts, we conclude that it is the external factors like foreign aid rather than internal factors like the availability of credit which hinder inclusive development in these countries. Again, average ICT adoption rate is higher in low-income countries than middle-income countries, which seems to suggest an inverted-U relationship between ICT adoption rate and income level (Eq. 10.1). According to Eq. (10.2), although their average ICT adoption rate is lower, middle-income countries gain more from ICT adoption for their inclusive development than low-income countries. This result might arise due to the nature of the formal institutions in these countries, as well as the analysis of ICT disparities that can be influenced by other variables limiting development.

The policy implications of the results suggest the need for improvements in formal institutions and the strengthening of domestic sources of ICT adoption and inclusive development. Doing so may require less stress on external factors like foreign aid, and that too would carry an opportunity cost. For future research there remains a need to broaden the sample to include more or all developing countries and to fine-tune both the modeling and estimation techniques.

Acknowledgments We thank the editor and one anonymous reviewer for constructive comments on earlier drafts of the paper.

Supplementary Material for the Editor

Supplement 1: The Theory Behind the Model

We assume a basic Schumpeterian model in which the economic activity is described as:

$$Y_i = \left(A_i^{\alpha_i} S_i^{\beta_i} X_i^{\gamma_i} \right) \exp\left(\mu_i \right) \tag{10.3}$$

where, Y_i is the real GDP of the ith economy, in Schumpeter's terminology A_i (technology, including ICT) and S_i (socioeconomic setting, including institutions) are "evolution components", X_i are "growth components", including conventional factors of production, and all variables are dated ([53]; cf. [54, 55]). Central to growth among X_i is capital accumulation, which over time depends on investment (I) equal to savings in a steady state. Savings come from profit (π) made possible by technological change and the socioeconomic setting surrounding it. The evolution of the socioeconomic environment is a function of resources, technology, and level of development, i.e.:

$$\frac{dK_{it}}{dt} = k\left[\frac{dI_{it}}{dt} = f\left(\pi_i\left(A_i,S_i\right)\right)\right], \frac{dS_{it}}{dt} = s\left(X_{i},A_{i},S_i\right), \pi = \text{profit}. \quad (10.4)$$

A Schumpeterian technological change is discontinuous due to five initiators: (a) introduction of new ideas, requiring technological know-how; (b) introduction of new production techniques for which funds (credit) are essential; (c) discovery of new sources of supply; (d) discovery of new markets; and (e) change in the structure and organization of the industry involved. Thus, in dynamic form Eq. (10.1) is characterized by the Schumpeter-Kondratiev waves (cycles), such that A_i over time is sinusoid, i.e.:

$$A_i\left(t\right) = A_0\exp\left(\varphi t + \cos\left(bt + \psi\right)\right)$$

and $\partial A / \partial t = A_0\left(\varphi - b\right)\sin\left(bt + \psi\right)\exp\left(\varphi t + \cos\left(bt + \psi\right)\right)$, which is consistent with [15] Eqs. (10.3 and 10.4 (p. 6)), but we do not pursue this line of thought further. Instead, from Eq. (10.1) we solve for A_i as:

$$A_i = Y_i^{1/\alpha_i} S_i^{-\beta_i/\alpha_i} X_i^{-\gamma_i/\alpha_i}. \quad (10.5)$$

Dividing both sides of Eq. (10.3) Equation 10.5 by some specific $X_i = X_i^*$ such as population or labor (worker), and taking the natural logs on both sides, we get a per capita (per labor, per worker, per head) indicator of adoption with diffusion as follows:

$$\dot{A}_i = \alpha_i^* y_i + \beta_i^* \dot{s}_i + \gamma_i^* \dot{x}_i + \mu_i \quad (10.6)$$

$$\dot{A} = \log\left(\frac{A_i}{X_i^*}\right) = ICT_i; \alpha_i^* = \frac{1}{\alpha}; \dot{y}_i = \text{economic growth};$$

where $\beta_i^* = \frac{\beta_i}{\alpha_i}; \dot{s}_i = \log\left(\frac{S_i}{X_i^*}\right) = \text{economic setting}\left(\text{governance}\right);$

$\gamma_i^* = \frac{\gamma_i}{\alpha_i}; \dot{x}_i = \frac{X_i}{X_i^*} = \text{primary \textit{and} other drivers};$

and μ_i = the random classical error term.

This all shows that in the main document, the ICT equation is the equivalent of 10.(6) Eq. (10.4) above, and the development equation is Eq. (10.1) 10.3.

Supplement 2: A Note on Country Classification by Income Level

The World Bank classifies countries as developing if they are low income ($0–1,045 per capita) and lower middle income ($1,046–4,125 per capita). Countries with upper middle incomes ($4,126–12, 735 per capita) and high incomes ($12,736 or higher) are classified as being developed. The classification is arbitrary. No particular line of reasoning is given for why the cutoff point between "developed" and "developing" is set at $12,735. There is no reason to believe that a country just below the cutoff line cannot be more "developed" than a country just above it. For instance, Equatorial Guinea has a higher average income level than both China and South Africa, but its industrial base and technological structure are miles far behind. This is one of the reasons we modified the World Bank and grouped African countries into two groups: low-income group consisting of 28 countries, and middle-income group made up of 21 countries. This reclassification is consistent with our understanding of both ICT and development in these countries.

Supplement 3: ICT Variable Definitions and Data Sources

Variables	Signs	Definitions	Sources
Mobile phone	Mobile	Mobile phone subscriptions (per 100 people)	WDI
Internet	Internet	Internet subscriptions (per 100 people)	WDI
Telephone	Telephone	Telephone subscriptions (per 100 people)	WDI
Political stability	PolS	"Political stability/no violence (estimate): measured as the perceptions of the likelihood that the government will be destabilized or overthrown by unconstitutional and violent means, including domestic violence and terrorism"	WGI
Voice and accountability	VA	"Voice and accountability (estimate): measures the extent to which a country's citizens are able to participate in selecting their government and to enjoy freedom of expression, freedom of association, and a free media"	WGI
Government effectiveness	GE	"Government effectiveness (estimate): measures the quality of public services, the quality and degree of independence from political pressures of the civil service, the quality of policy formulation and implementation, and the credibility of governments' commitments to such policies"	WGI

(continued)

Variables	Signs	Definitions	Sources
Regulation quality	RQ	"Regulation quality (estimate): measured as the ability of the government to formulate and implement sound policies and regulations that permit and promote private sector development"	WGI
Corruption control	CC	"Control of corruption (estimate): captures perceptions of the extent to which public power is exercised for private gain, including both petty and grand forms of corruption, as well as 'capture' of the state by elites and private interests"	WGI
Rule of law	RL	"Rule of law (estimate): captures perceptions of the extent to which agents have confidence in and abide by the rules of society and in particular the quality of contract enforcement, property rights, the police, the courts, as well as the likelihood of crime and violence"	WGI
GDP growth	GDPg	GDP growth rate	WDI
Trade openness	Trade	Import plus exports of goods and services (% of GDP)	WDI
Population growth	Population	Total population growth (annual %)	WDI
Education	PSE	Primary school enrolment (% of gross)	WDI

WGI World Governance Indicators, *WDI* World Development Indicators, *GDP* gross domestic product

Supplement 4: ICT Summary Statistics

	Mean	SD	Min	Max	Obs
Mobile phone penetration	23.379	28.004	0.000	147.202	572
Internet penetration	4.152	6.450	0.005	43.605	566
Telephone penetration	3.039	5.810	0.005	32.455	565
Political stability	−0.543	0.956	−3.323	1.192	578
Voice and accountability	−0.646	0.737	−2.233	0.990	578
Government effectiveness	−0.771	0.620	−2.450	0.934	577
Regulation quality	−0.715	0.644	−2.665	0.983	578
Corruption control	−0.642	0.591	−1.924	1.249	579
Rule of law	−0.741	0.662	−2.668	1.056	578
GDP growth	4.714	6.322	−47.552	63.379	608
Trade openness	78.177	36.138	20.964	209.874	597
Population growth	2.361	0.948	−1.081	6.576	588
Education	97.446	25.895	32.199	181.700	470

SD standard deviation, *Min* minimum, *Max* maximum, *Obs* observations, *Adj* adjusted

Supplement 5: ICT Correlation Matrix (Uniform Sample Size: 407)

	Governance variables						Control variables				Dependent variables			
	PolS	VA	GE	RQ	CC	RL	GDPg	Trade	Popg	PSE	Mobile	Internet	Telephone	
	1.000													PolS
	0.636	1.000												VA
	0.605	0.740	1.000											GE
	0.538	0.727	0.845	1.000										RQ
	0.614	0.612	0.979	0.649	1.000									CC
	0.767	0.787	0.874	0.772	0.817	1.000								RL
	−0.084	0.018	0.030	−0.025	−0.090	−0.044	1.000							GDPg
	0.253	0.014	0.021	−0.002	−0.014	0.109	0.029	1.000						Trade
	−0.271	−0.250	−0.335	−0.247	−0.309	−0.286	0.157	−0.380	1.000					Popg
	0.255	0.248	0.212	0.217	0.118	0.219	0.083	0.167	−0.172	1.000				PSE
	0.298	0.274	0.293	0.264	0.273	0.274	−0.043	0.259	−0.331	0.288	1.000			Mobile
	0.312	0.325	0.320	0.176	0.342	0.332	−0.002	0.158	−0.414	0.224	0.690	1.000		Internet
	0.470	0.459	0.504	0.286	0.565	0.530	−0.052	0.228	−0.581	0.181	0.479	0.695	1.000	Telephone

PolS Political stability, *VA* voice and accountability, *GE* government effectiveness, *RQ* regulation quality, *CC* corruption control, *RL* rule of law, *GDPg* GDP per capita growth rate, *Popg* population growth, *PSE* primary school enrolment, *Mobile* mobile phone penetration, *Internet* Internet penetration, *Telephone* telephone penetration

Supplement 6: IHDI Variable Definitions and Data Sources

Variables	Signs	Definitions	Sources
Inclusive development	IHDI	Inequality-adjusted human development index	UNDP
Mobile phone	Mobile	Mobile phone subscriptions (per 100 people)	WDI
Internet	Internet	Internet subscriptions (per 100 people)	WDI
Telephone	Telephone	Telephone subscriptions (per 100 people)	WDI
Foreign aid	Aid	Total official development assistance (% of GDP)	WDI
Private credit	Credit	Private credit by deposit banks and other financial institutions (% of GDP)	WDI
Remittance	Remit	Remittance inflows (% of GDP)	WDI
Foreign investment	FDI	Foreign direct investment net inflows (% of GDP)	WDI

UNDP United Nations Development Program, *WDI* World Development Indicators, *GDP* gross domestic product

Supplement 7: IHDI Summary Statistics

	Mean	SD	Min	Max	Obs
Inequality-adjusted human development	0.721	3.505	0.129	0.768	485
Mobile phone penetration	23.379	28.004	0.000	147.202	572
Internet penetration	4.152	6.450	0.005	43.605	566
Telephone penetration	3.039	5.810	0.005	32.455	565
Foreign aid	11.687	14.193	−0.253	181.187	606
Private domestic credit	18.551	22.472	0.550	149.78	507
Remittances	3.977	8.031	0.000	64.100	434
Net foreign direct investment inflows	5.332	8.737	−6.043	91.007	603

SD standard deviation, *Min* minimum, *Max* maximum, *Obs* observations, *Adj* adjusted

Supplement 8: IHDI Correlation Matrix (Uniform Sample Size: 324)

Foreign aid	Credit	Remittances	FDI	Mobile	Internet	Telephone	IHDI	
1.000	−0.173	−0.037	0.411	−0.165	−0.196	−0.223	−0.382	Foreign aid
	1.000	−0.084	−0.065	0.514	0.511	0.614	0.529	Credit
		1.000	0.115	−0.050	−0.035	−0.062	−0.027	Remittances
			1.000	0.111	0.072	−0.029	−0.001	FDI
				1.000	0.749	0.504	0.626	Mobile
					1.000	0.669	0.649	Internet
						1.000	0.747	Telephone
							1.000	IHDI

Credit Private domestic credit, *FDI* foreign direct investment, *Mobile* mobile phone penetration, *Internet* Internet penetration, *Telephone* telephone penetration, *IHDI* inequality-adjusted human development index

References

1. Norris, P. (2001). *Digital divide?: Civic engagement, information poverty and the internet worldwide*. Cambridge: Cambridge University Press.
2. Steinmueller, W. (2001). ICTs and the possibilities of leapfrogging by developing countries. *International Labour Review, 140*(2), 193–210.
3. Brynjolfsson, E., & Hitt, L. (2003). Computing productivity: Firm-level evidence. *Review of Economics and Statistics, 85*(4), 793–808.
4. Wallsten, S. (2005). Regulation and internet use in developing countries. *Economic Development and Cultural Change, 53*(2), 501–523.
5. Harggitai, E. (1999). Weaving the western web: Explaining differences in internet connectivity among OECD countries. *Telecommunications Policy, 23*(10–11), 701–718
6. Quibria, M., Ahmed, S., Tschang, T., & Reyes-Macasaquit, M. (2003). Digital divide: Determinants and policies with special reference to Asia. *Journal of Asian Economics, 13*(6), 811–825.
7. Dasgupta, S., Lall, S., & Wheeler, D. (2005). Policy reform, economic growth and the digital divide. *Oxford Development Studies, 33*(2), 229–243.
8. Oxley, J., & Yeung, B. (2001). E-commerce and readiness institutional environment and international competitiveness. *Journal of International Business Studies, 32*(4), 705–723.
9. Robison, K., & Crenshaw, E. (2002). Post-industrial transformations and cyber-space: A cross national analysis of internet development. *Social Science Research, 31*(3), 334–363.
10. Kiiski, S., & Pohjola, M. (2002). Cross-country diffusion of the internet. *Information Economics and Policy, 14*(2), 297–310.
11. Bellock, R., & Dimitrova, D. (2003). An explanatory model of inter-country internet diffusion. *Telecommunications Policy, 27*(3–4), 237–252.
12. Chinn, M., & Fairlie, R. (2007). The determinants of the global digital divide: A cross country analysis of computer and internet penetration. *Oxford Economic Papers, 59*(1), 16–44.
13. Billón, M., Marco, R., & Lera-Lopez, F. (2009). Disparities in ICT adoption: A multidimensional approach to study the cross-country digital divide. *Telecommunications Policy, 33*, 596–610.

14. Kiessling, J. (2007). *Institutions and ICT technology adoption. Department of Economics.* Sweden: Stockholm University.
15. Dekimpe, M. K., Parker, P. M., & Sarvary, M. (2000). Globalization: Modeling technology adoption timing across countries. *Technological Forecasting and Social Change, 63,* 125–145.
16. Amavilah, V.H. (2008). Inhibited (exhibited) spread of innovations. MPRA paper 8993, University Library Munich.
17. Amavilah, V. H. S. (2007). Innovations spread more like wildfire than like infections. Social Science Research Network (SSRN) Working paper No. 99950.
18. Wejnert, B. (2002). Integrating models of diffusion of innovations: A conceptual framework. *Annual Reviews of Sociology, 28,* 297–326.
19. Young, H. P. (2006a). Innovation diffusion and population heterogeneity. Working Paper.
20. Young, H. P. (2006b). The spread of innovations by social learning, Working Paper.
21. Young, H. P. (2009). Innovation diffusions in heterogeneous populations: Contagion, social influence, and social learning. *American Economic Review, 99*(5), 1829–1944.
22. Geroski, P. A. (2000). Models of technology diffusion. *Research Policy, 29*(4/5), 603–625.
23. Rogers, E. M. (1995). *Diffusion of innovations.* New York: The Free Press.
24. Caselli, F., & Coleman II, W. (2001). Cross-country technology diffusion: The case of computers. *American Economic Review, 91*(2), 328–335.
25. Baliamoune-Lutz, M. (2003). An analysis of the determinants and effects of ICT diffusion in developing countries. *Information Technology for Development, 10*(2), 151–169.
26. Detschew, S. (2007). Impact of ICT in the developing countries on the economic growth: Implications derived from theory and empiricism. DiplomaThesis, Technical University of Ilmenau, Germany.
27. Papaioannou, S. K., & Dimelis, S. P. (2007). Information technology as a factor of economic development: Evidence from developed and developing countries. *Economics of Innovation and New Technology, 16*(3), 179–194.
28. Gholami, R., Higón, D. A., Hanafizedh, P., & Emrouznejad, A. (2010). Is ICT the key to development? *Journal of Global Information Management, 18*(1), 66–83.
29. Seo, H. J., Lee, Y. S., & Oh, J. H. (2009). Does ICT investment widen the growth gap? *Telecommunications Policy, 3,* 422–431.
30. Tchamyou, V. S.. (2015). The role of knowledge economy in African business, African Governance and Development Institute Working Paper No. 15/049, Yaoundé.
31. Kaufmann, D., Kraay, A., & Mastruzzi, M. (2010). The worldwide governance indicators: Methodology and analytical issues. World Bank Policy Research Working Paper no. 5430.
32. UNCTAD. (2006). Using ICTs to achieve growth and development. United Nations Conference on Trade and Development TD/B/COM.3/EM.29/2.
33. UNCTAD (2011). Measuring the impacts of information and communication technology for development. United Nations Conference for Trade and Development.
34. UNDP (2008). The role of information communication technologies in achieving the millennium development goals. United Nations Development Programme Mozambique.
35. UNDP (2010). ICT4D and the human development and capability approach: The potentials of information communication technologies. United Nations Development Programme.
36. World Bank (2009). Information communications technologies for development. http://live. worldbank.org/information-communications-technology-development.
37. World Bank (2012). ICT for greater development impact 2012–2015.World Bank Group Strategy: Information & Communication Technology.
38. Binder, M., & Georgiadis, G. (2011). Determinants of human development: Capturing the role of institutions. CESIFO Working Paper No. 3397.
39. Rodrik, D. (2000). Institutions for high-quality growth: What they are, how to acquire them. NBER Working Paper No. W7540.
40. Rodrik, D. (2001). The global governance of trade as if development really mattered. Report submitted to United Nations Development Programme (UNDP).

41. Acemoglu, D., Johnson, S., & Robinson, J. (2001). The colonial origins of comparative development: An empirical investigation. *American Economic Review, 91*(5), 1369–1401.
42. Acemoglu, D., & Robinson, J. (2008). The role of institutions in growth and development. In D. Brady & M. Spence (Eds.), *Leadership and growth*. Washington, DC: World Bank.
43. Rodrik, D., Subramanian, A., & Trebbi, F. (2004). Institutions rule: The primacy of institutions over geography and integration in economic development. *Journal of Economic Growth, 9*(2), 131–165.
44. Anand, R., Mishra, S., & Spatafora, N. (2012). Structural transformation and the sophistication of production, IMF Working Paper No. 12/59, Washington, DC.
45. Mlachila, M., Tapsoba, R., & Tapsoba, S. J. A. (2014). A quality of growth index for developing countries: A proposal. IMF Working Paper No. 14/172, Washington, DC.
46. Asongu, S. A., & Nwachukwu, J. C. (2016a). Mobile phones in the diffusion of knowledge and persistence in inclusive human development in sub-Saharan Africa. *Information Development, 32*(3), 1–14.
47. Hamdan Livramento, I. M., & Foray, D. (2007). Does IPR protection affect high growth entrepreneurship? A cross-country empirical examination. European Policy for Intellectual Property, 2nd Annual Conference of the EPIP Association, Sweden.
48. Asongu, S. A. (2013). How would population growth affect investment in the future? Asymmetric panel causality evidence for Africa. *African Development Review, 25*(1), 14–29.
49. Fosu, A. K. (2015). Growth, inequality and poverty in sub-Saharan Africa: Recent progress in a global context. *Oxford Development Studies, 43*(1), 44–59.
50. Asongu, S. A., & Nwachukwu, J. C. (2016b). The mobile phone in the diffusion of knowledge for institutional quality in sub-Saharan Africa. *World Development, 86*, 133–147.
51. Asongu, S. A. (2014). The questionable Economics of development assistance in Africa: Hot-fresh evidence, 1996–2010. *The Review of Black Political Economy, 41*(4), 455–480.
52. Asongu, S. A., & Nwachukwu, J. C. (2016c). The role of governance in mobile phones for inclusive human development in sub-Saharan Africa. *Technovation, 55–56*, 1–13.
53. Schumpeter, J. A. (2005). Development. *Journal of Economic Literature, XLIII*(1), 108–120.
54. Becker, M. C., Eblinger, H. U., Hedtke, U., & Knudsen, T. (2005). Introduction to development by Joseph A. Schumpeter. *Journal of Economic Literature, XLIII*(1), 110–111.
55. Bazhal, I. (2016). The theory of economic development of J.A. Schumpeter: Key features. MPRA Paper 69883, University Library of Munich, Germany, revised 25 Feb.

Part IV
Latin America

Chapter 11
Inequalities in the Appropriation of Digital Spaces in Metropolitan Areas of Latin America

Roxana Barrantes and Eduardo Vargas

Abstract This study discusses the role of information and communication technologies (ICTs), especially the Internet, in three Latin American capitals in people's ability to attain the lifestyle they value and how inequalities in this ability or "information richness" can be explained by sociodemographic characteristics that do not depend on the individual's decisions. The analysis is conducted using an Information Richness Index that includes information about the three barriers that people face in making significant use of the Internet: access to the Internet, skills for using ICTs, and the ability to function well in digital environments. Econometric estimations show that women, people who are not active in the workforce, and older adults, particularly senior citizens, have lower IRI levels, while each additional year of education and belonging to learning communities have a positive effect on the level a person achieves.

Keywords ICT4D • Open development • Digital inequality • Latin America • Metropolitan cities

11.1 Introduction

In recent years, information and communication technologies (ICTs) have been changing the way we live and relate to one another. The creation of structures and dynamics based on ICTs is not only important for reducing transaction costs and allowing access to a considerable amount of information, but it also is beginning to

R. Barrantes (✉)
Institute for Peruvian Studies, Lima, Peru

Pontifical Catholic University of Peru, Lima, Peru
e-mail: roxbarrantes@iep.org.pe; Barrantes.r@pucp.edu.pe

E. Vargas
Institute for Peruvian Studies, Lima, Peru
e-mail: evargas@iep.org.pe

shape new venues for interaction and integration, where users can participate in a way that was impossible in non-digital spaces [1]. Digital environments thus become potential equalizers and offer an opportunity to accelerate the path toward development and toward freedom for people to choose the kind of lifestyle they have reason to value [2].

In contexts of great inequality, such as Latin America, however, the most vulnerable people tend to suffer different and varied types of exclusion; as a result, compared to those who are wealthier, they are at a serious disadvantage in significant access to and use of digital spaces [3, 4]. According to data from Peru's National Institute of Statistics [5], 52.9% of Peru's urban population does not use the Internet. This group largely belongs to low-income households. Because of gaps in other areas, digital inequality could therefore reinforce the exclusion experienced by the poorest people instead of opening up new opportunities for social inclusion.

The purpose of this chapter is to analyze the degree of appropriation of the Internet and sources of "information inequality" in three Latin American capitals: Buenos Aires, the capital of a high-income country; Lima, the capital of a middle-income country; and Guatemala City, the capital of a country where income is still low. This will provide an overview of Internet appropriation in areas of the region with high teledensity.

Besides analyzing differences in access by individuals, the study will also take a deeper look at the complexity of Internet use. An Information Richness Index (IRI) will be constructed incorporating information about the three barriers that people face in making significant use of the net: Internet access, ICT skills, and the ability to function well in digital environments [6]. The index will provide insight into how effectively people can expand their freedom through Internet use [1]. The data are taken from the "Survey about Internet use: Platforms and open data – 2014," one of the few surveys that has collected detailed, representative information about patterns of Internet access and use in the region.[1]

11.2 Internet, Development, and Inequality

11.2.1 Internet as a Means and an End: Open Development and Information Richness

ICTs, especially the Internet, are significantly changing the way we live and relate to one another. As the "Information and Communication Technologies for Development" (ICT4D) approach indicates, ICTs are a set of tools that are useful and necessary for overcoming the challenges posed by development [10]. The

---

[1] The survey is part of a significant research effort by the DIRSI network, with financial support from IDRC. Analysis of the descriptive statistics for each of the three cities can be found at DIRSI's web page [7–9] (Consulted: 05 July 2016).

Internet significantly reduces transaction costs for accessing information and resources and for establishing communication. It therefore increases the user's ability to make better decisions about consumption, with more information about the prices and quality of products and services, as well as decisions about production, with more information about providers, competitors, and demand [11].

This approach emphasizes the use of these innovations as tools for improving people's quality of life [12, 13]; as a policy development strategy, Castells proposes expanding access to ICTs and the education necessary for using them, to ensure that no one remains unconnected or left behind in the information society [14].

Castells' analysis, however, omits the relational and collaborative nature of the information society and presents ICTs merely as a means to a higher end [14]. This limitation became clearer with the rapid advance in mobile connectivity worldwide and its impact on people's lives and welfare.[2] As Smith et al. [11] argue, based on the ideas of Sen [2], the use of mobile telephones, and even more so of the Internet, affects users' abilities because they change their position with respect to the resources necessary for development. This occurs in at least two ways: first, by increasing access to recent, relevant information and, second, by expanding the possibility of establishing connections among people and of connecting with new people.

As the digital sphere penetrates more intensely into everyday life, ICTs not only become tools, but, as Benkler [16] argues, they also begin to shape new social systems with structures and activities based on information networks. Appropriation of ICTs, and especially of the Internet, allows a new level of interaction among people and institutions, making feasible the implementation and strengthening of three types of networks: social and community networks, economic and labor networks, and political networks [11]. New platforms and venues for integration are being shaped, in which users can participate in a way that is impossible for them outside the Web [1].

It is in this context that, using the contributions of Amartya Sen [2] about the capability approach and development and those of Dorothea Kleine [17] about the role of ICTs as amplifiers of these capabilities, Mathew Smith et al. [14] unify and complement the work of Castells [10] and Benkler [16] to develop a new approach: Open Development. As Smith states, the Internet and the environments that the Web creates constitute a set of tools (a medium) that makes it possible to achieve development, as it allows users to exercise their capabilities more effectively through the significant reduction of transaction costs and improvement of their productive processes and consumption technologies. It also constitutes a venue for transformation and agency (an end), because it establishes conditions that expand people's freedoms by enabling them to create and reinforce social networks; be part of, share, and cooperate with larger communities; and form part of more participatory

---

[2]According to data from the ITU (International Telecommunication Union) for 2015, mobile teledensity in developed countries is 120.6, while in developing countries, it is 91.8. For 2014, in particular, mobile teledensity was 158.7 in Argentina, 102.9 in Peru, and 106.6 in Guatemala [15] (Consulted: 28 September 2015).

processes in which they not only have a voice, but their voice is also heard and used actively [14].[3]

We take that approach to the Internet and its relationship with development to define Information Richness as a person's ability to expand his or her freedom to choose a way of life through the use of ICTs, particularly the Internet, and the environments that they create [2, 6, 14, 17].

11.2.2 Information Inequality

Despite the benefits that stem from using ICTs and participating in the net, great differences or "technological distance" exist in access to and use of the Internet among individuals, families, enterprises, and geographic areas [18–20]. These differences are relevant, because as Robinson [3] states, people who take greater advantage of digital spaces have significant advantages over those who do not in almost all other spaces. As Tongia and Wilson [21] explain, this is because the positive effects of belonging to a network create a feedback loop that can be divided into two components: (i) an intrinsic effect that depends on the size of the network and corresponds to the direct benefits of communication and (ii) a complementary effect (of externalities) associated with goods, services, and interactions that become more available as the network grows – for example, a larger number of applications for an given operating system or a larger supply of specific contents for a community (contents in a particular language or about particular topics).

The existence of these two effects has two consequences for agents' opportunities. First, their existence implies that not belonging to the network has an opportunity cost borne by all people who are excluded from the user community. Second, both benefits (direct and indirect) depend on the size of the user community and the community's growth rate. The gradual inclusion of the group of people who are disconnected from digital spaces means that the user community will become larger and the non-user community will shrink, thus exponentially increasing the opportunity cost borne by those who remain outside of the network; in other words, those who lag farthest behind or are the most excluded eventually face higher costs for remaining outside of the network [21].

This concern is crucial, because as Robinson [3] notes, digital inequality tends to operate along with other preexisting conditions. The differences in the appropriation and intensity of ICT use tend to be associated with inequality in access to resources and rights. It is therefore no coincidence that groups that are socially, politically, and economically marginalized are also segregated within the digital system or are the last to be included, as that environment tends to reproduce patterns that exist in non-

---

[3] Nevertheless, Smith et al. [14] also mention that there is a latent risk in the expansion of digital systems and that development through these systems is not a matter of seeking not unlimited openness, but of seeking openness that is consistent with the expansion of cabilities and with people's development. This implies beginning with development problems and then looking at how "openness" can serve as a means for overcoming them.

digital spaces. The Internet could therefore end up exacerbating certain types of exclusion [3]. In particular, there is evidence that women [22, 23], older adults [24–28], unemployed people or those working in the informal sector [29, 30], and those with less education [31–34] tend to be the groups that lag in the digital space.

11.3 Information Richness and Inequality in Metropolitan Areas of Latin America

Despite evidence about digital divides, little is known about these inequalities in Latin America, and there is even less information that can aid in understanding the situation beyond the dichotomy of access and non-access. The rest of this chapter, therefore, will analyze Information Richness and the sources of "information inequality" in three capital cities in the region: Buenos Aires, the capital of a high-income country; Lima, the capital of a middle-income country; and Guatemala City, the capital of a country where income is still low. Using data from the "Survey about Internet use: Platforms and open data – 2014," conducted by the Regional Dialogue on the Information Society (DIRSI), this chapter provides an overview of Internet appropriation in metropolitan areas of Latin America.

11.3.1 Information Richness Made Operational

Taking an operational approach to a person's level of Information Richness using a single indicator is complicated, because the impacts of ICTs on people's behavior and on the systems in which they operate exceed the boundaries of a single dimension. An economic approach (input-output relationship) generally will have one magnitude as an objective variable, measured in monetary units or volumes. There is no clear consensus about a general framework for analyzing appropriation of and participation in different ICT-based systems and even less about a variable that can measure the different dimensions [35].

Because the purpose of this study is to examine how people use the Internet to attain the lifestyle to which they aspire [17], the strategy developed by Mendonça et al. [6] will be used to create an Information Richness Index that allows this complex dynamic to be incorporated, through three components related to the three barriers to making significant use of the Internet: (i) access, (ii) skills for using it, and (iii) the users' capabilities for functioning fully in spaces created through ICTs. Details of the construction of each component can be found in Appendix 1.

This strategy is especially useful because, as Mendonça notes, it considers that making significant use of ICTs does not consist merely of taking the person to the door (access) or of them being able to open it (skills for use), but also implies that the person is able to cross the threshold, socialise with other agents, and function fully in the environment they find behind that door (capabilities). The incorporation of this third component is a bridge between the index developed by this author and the Open Development approach proposed by Smith et al. [14], because this methodology makes it possible to add information about people's exercise of their freedoms through the use of open platforms, participation in digital spaces, creation of value through relationships with other users and institutions, and achievement of more functionings [2]. The values used in the index, from a minimum of 0 to a maximum of 100, will offer an approximation of how appropriation of the Internet contributes to users' development and will be defined as follows:

$$\text{IRI}_i = 0.5^* \text{AI}_i + 0,25^* \text{SI}_i + 0,25^* \text{CI}_i \qquad (11.1)$$

Where:

RI: Information Richness Index
AI: Access Index
SI: Skills Index
CI: Capabilities Index

The ability to analyze each component separately using the overall measurement will also provide a clearer understanding of the sources of inequality and how they vary depending on the facet observed.

As Eq. (11.1) indicates, the proposed Information Richness Index assigns greater importance to the Access Index. This strategy is chosen because the CI and SI results are limited by access to devices and access to the Internet, respectively. Giving greater weight to access therefore reduces the differences in results between those who do not access the Internet and those who do.

11.3.2 Level of Appropriation in the Three Capitals

Based on analysis of the IRI descriptive statistics, one initial result that stands out is that the levels of Information Richness attained by users in the three cities are concentrated in low values of the distribution. Considering that the highest score possible is 100, it is noteworthy that users, on average, do not take full advantage of the opportunities created by digital spaces, to such an extent that the average score (35.6 points) is only about one-third of the maximum score.

A more detailed look at the components shows that the Access Index (AI) also has low average and median values; this is an initial indication that Internet access (first barrier) remains an important constraint, even when the information comes from capital cities where mobile teledensity indices tend to be high. In Lima in 2012, teledensity was 159.2, while in 2015, mobile teledensity was 158.7 in Argentina and 106.6 in Guatemala (Table 11.1).[4,5]

---

[4] Data taken from OSIPTEL [36] for Lima and from ITU [15] for Argentina and Guatemala

[5] Similarly, in the sample, only 7% of respondents do not have a mobile telephone (13.9% in Buenos Aires, 6% in Lima, and 1.3% in Guatemala City), and 96% have access to some technological device.

Table 11.1 Statistics of components of the information richness index

Index	Mean	Median	Std. dev.	Minimum	25% Perc.	75% Perc.	Maximum
IRI	35.6	38.4	22.1	0	18.3	51.7	97.8
AI	31.3	40.0	24.2	0	20.0	40.0	100
SI	55.8	62.0	27.6	0	33.3	78.3	100
CI	24.1	21.1	22.9	0	0.0	38.9	100

Compiled by authors
Source: Survey about Internet use: Platforms and open data – 2014

In particular, 22.8% of respondents in the sample do not access the Internet. In this group, the proportion of women (61.9%) is considerably higher than men, and the percentage of women who do not connect to the Web (24.6%) is slightly greater than that of men. Older adults constitute a larger part of the group that does not access the Internet (52.7% adults and 32.3% older adults), especially considering that 61.9% of all older adults do not access the Internet. Finally, the results show that about half the group that does not access the Internet is economically inactive (46.7%); specifically, they are people who are dedicated to household tasks, retired, permanently disabled, or people who report that they neither work nor study.

11.3.3 Information Inequality in the Three Capitals

Regarding inequality in the level of Information Richness, first of all, the level of vertical information inequality – the distance between those who take greatest advantage of the Internet and those who use it least – is relatively low, as the Gini index for the IRI is 0.35, close to that of income at Uruguay in 2013 [37]. Nevertheless, the indicator drops to 42.9% (a Gini index of 0.20) when the sample is limited to users who access the Internet; this means that one of the main sources of inequality comes from the existence of a group of people who remain disconnected or isolated from digital spaces [3].

A second approximation of information inequality among people can be obtained from looking at horizontal inequalities [4]. This is done by comparing the levels of Information Richness attained by the different groups. As Table 11.2 shows, there is a highly significant difference of 4.43 points in favor of men, a difference that decreases only slightly (by 1.1 points) when it is calculated for the sample limited to people to access the Internet. Analysis of the values by age group reveals important differences that increase with age; the differences are even greater and significant to the detriment of adults (8.98) and older adults (25.51). Surprisingly, when the differences are calculated for the limited sample, these figures fall consistently, decreasing by 7.4 points (−82%) between adolescents and adults and 18.5 points (−72%) between adolescents and older adults. These variations indicate that the Internet access component is extremely important in explaining Information Richness inequality between age groups; apparently, as Colombo et al. [27] found, once the problem of access is overcome (not only in supply but also in demand), the effect of age as an impediment to appropriation of the Internet is reduced.

Table 11.2 Statistics of components of the information richness index

	Full sample				Limited sample			
	N	Mean	Median	Dif.	N	Mean	Median	Dif.
Total	3465	35.6	38.4		2675	44.9	44.8	
Sex								
Male	1480	38.2	41.5		1179	46.8	46.8	
Female	1985	33.7	35.6	−4.43***	1496	43.5	43.5	−3.3***
Age group								
Adolescents [13, 18]	524	42.6	44.1		493	45.1	44.9	
Youth [19, 29]	891	43.7	46.2	1.09	803	48.2	47.8	3.03***
Adults [30, 59]	1637	33.6	34.1	−8.98***	1221	43.6	43.2	−1.53*
Older adults [+60]	413	17.1	8.3	−25.51***	158	38.2	36.7	−6.98***
Main occupation								
Inactive	967	25.9	24.6		598	39.5	38.0	
Students	529	44.7	45.4	18.77***	503	46.8	46.2	7.36***
Work w/ stable income	1169	41.8	45.0	15.85***	989	48.5	48.2	9.07***
Work w/ variable income	756	32.2	31.5	6.25***	550	42.6	40.9	3.11***
Unemployed	44	36.6	42.8	10.71***	35	45.4	45.6	5.93**

Compiled by authors. Source: Survey about Internet use: Platforms and open data – 2014
Statistical significance: ***$p < 0.01$, **$p < 0.05$, *$p < 0.1$

11.4 Sources of Information Inequality in the Three Capitals

Although explicit inequalities between the different groups are seen in the level of appropriation, it is necessary to determine whether these differences are due to other characteristics of the individuals and their context. It is not enough to analyze only belonging to certain groups and the result obtained in the index; the analysis must include variables that also influence or determine the level of Information Richness. The next section presents econometric estimations that make it possible to identify the existence and sources of these differences.

11.4.1 Determinants of Level of Information Richness

The first approach is based on proving that the differences observed previously do not correspond to differences in other characteristics and do correspond to differences in appropriation between groups. Different estimation models (OLS, probit model and truncated poisson regression model) will be used, as shown in the first panel of Table 11.3.[6]

---

[6] White's correction for heteroscedasticity is used [38].

Table 11.3 Econometric estimations over the IRI and each component

Variables	IRI	Access or non-access to the Internet	N° of devices from which the Internet is accessed (AI)	Skills index	Capabilities index
Modelo de Estimación	OLS	Probit – Marg. effects	Truncated Poisson – incidence rate ratios	OLS	OLS
Sex Female	-2.910***	-0.0253*	0.890***	-3.578***	-0.832
	(0.632)	(0.0153)	(0.0262)	(0.832)	(0.837)
Age group (base = adolescents) Young adults [19, 29]	-1.606	-0.0821**	0.982	-2.397	0.183
	(1.131)	(0.0411)	(0.0504)	(1.584)	(1.566)
Adults [30, 59]	-7.706***	-0.206***	0.852**	-9.548***	0.369
	(1.287)	(0.0381)	(0.0531)	(1.760)	(1.951)
Older adults [+60]	-8.83***	-0.574***	0.615***	-22.12***	-0.791
	(1.590)	(0.0590)	(0.0654)	(2.396)	(3.253)
Principal occupation (base = inactive) Students	1.959	0.0546*	1.128**	2.176	-2.147
	(1.200)	(0.0291)	(0.0610)	(1.598)	(1.531)
Work w/ stable income	3.235***	0.0382*	1.055	2.593**	5.885***
	(0.982)	(0.0206)	(0.0527)	(1.233)	(1.265)
Work w/ variable income	-0.480	-0.0104	0.960	-1.574	2.956**
	(1.021)	(0.0225)	(0.0545)	(1.302)	(1.362)
Unemployed	2.438	0.0267	1.173	0.777	2.093
	(2.959)	(0.0565)	(0.129)	(3.438)	(3.384)

(continued)

Table 11.3 (continued)

Variables	IRI	Access or non-access to the Internet	N° of devices from which the Internet is accessed (AI)	Skills index	Capabilities index
Modelo de Estimación	OLS	Probit – Marg. effects	Truncated Poisson – incidence rate ratios	OLS	OLS
Human capital characteristics					
Years of education	1.725***	0.0241***	1.046***	2.198***	1.412***
	(0.125)	(0.00295)	(0.00735)	(0.175)	(0.229)
Enrolled in educational center?	5.107***	0.0512**	1.067	3.204***	11.28***
	(0.947)	(0.0211)	(0.0432)	(1.173)	(1.151)
Personal assessment of the Internet					
Is the Internet important for being integrated?	4.634***	0.0825***	1.068***	6.035***	2.628***
	(0.487)	(0.0108)	(0.0265)	(0.633)	(0.747)
Characteristics of the household					
Years of education of head of household	0.577***	0.00960***	1.015***	0.743***	0.334**
	(0.109)	(0.00261)	(0.00533)	(0.145)	(0.148)
Log of net spending in Telecom	4.426***	0.0449***	1.239***	5.451***	4.066***
	(0.521)	(0.0116)	(0.0318)	(0.633)	(0.686)
Rate of dependency	6.782***	0.0897***	1.266***	7.487***	3.958**
	(1.416)	(0.0320)	(0.0931)	(1.870)	(1.992)
Female head of household	1.949***	0.0175	1.089***	1.673*	1.632*
	(0.690)	(0.0160)	(0.0353)	(0.885)	(0.890)
Presence of minors inside the household	1.615**	0.0500***	1.080**	0.886	−1.733
	(0.771)	(0.0181)	(0.0409)	(1.000)	(1.061)
Household has a landline	7.331***	0.0894***	1.339***	–	–
	(0.618)	(0.0149)	(0.0465)	–	–

Variables		IRI	Access or non-access to the Internet	N° of devices from which the Internet is accessed (AI)	Skills index	Capabilities index
Modelo de Estimación		OLS	Probit – Marg. effects	Truncated Poisson – incidence rate ratios	OLS	OLS
City (base = Guatemala City)	Buenos Aires	−0.472	0.0572***	0.907***	1.389	1.072
		(0.782)	(0.0149)	(0.0344)	(1.142)	(1.043)
	Lima	3.502***	0.151***	0.980	1.475	2.424**
		(0.756)	(0.0142)	(0.0344)	(0.955)	(1.218)
	Constant	−44.67***	–	0.101***	−35.88***	−36.46***
		(4.021)	–	(0.0214)	(5.573)	(8.242)
Mills ratio	Lambda				4.862	−3.032
					(5.722)	(3.393)
Model adjustment	Observations	3465	3465	2660	3465	3465
	Prob > F	0,000	0,000	0,000	0,000	0,000
	(Seudo)* R-squared	0.433	0.3256*	0.0756*	–	–

Statistical significance: ***$p < 0.01$, **$p < 0.05$, *$p < 0.1$

First, it shows that being a woman has a negative effect on the IRI results, as seen in the test of differences in means. Belonging to older age groups also has a negative effect on the level of Information Richness; the IRI estimation (first panel) shows that both the negative effect and the significance of the estimator increase substantially as the age group increases, with a negative effect of 18.8 points in the index for older adults, compared to younger people.

Regarding occupation, it was found that only having as the main activity being a worker with a stable income (employees, laborers, and foremen) has positive and significant effects on the level of Information Richness, compared to people who are inactive (dedicated to household tasks, retired, permanently incapacitated, or people who report that they neither work nor study).

Finally, regarding an individual's human capital, the results show that the number of years of education received has a positive and highly significant effect on the level of Information Richness that people attain, as shown by Howard et al. [33], Hargittai and Hinnant [31], Helsper and Galacz [32], and May et al. [39]; one additional year of education is estimated to increase the IRI result by 1.7 points. It was also found that being enrolled in an educational institution has a substantial influence on the results of all the indices. These estimations are consistent with previous case studies that highlight the benefits of open educational resources and the learning communities created in educational centers [16].

Although it is useful to identify whether the differences observed can be attributed directly to these sociodemographic characteristics, identifying the ones that are the main sources of these inequalities would make a strong contribution to public policy aimed at closing these gaps. With this in mind, the next sections analyze the effects on each of the components in order to identify the channels of exclusion.

Because there is limited information about people who do not access to devices or the Internet – we can only know if an individual uses the Internet for educational purposes and if the person has accessed the Internet previously – and because the decision to access the Internet and to engage in some online activity can be expected to stem from different decision-making processes [40], two-stage estimations were used. In the first stage, the informant's access or non-access is analyzed (an exercise conducted in the next section) and in the second stage, each component is analyzed conditioned on the informant's access to the Internet or to a device.[7]

---

[7] The estimation strategies chosen for each component are different depending on the nature of the data. For access, a Hurdle model is used, which first estimates a probit model for the access decision with the entire sample, and then a truncated Tobit count model is used to estimate the effect on the dependent variable only for users who access the Internet [41]. For the skills and capabilities components, a Heckman model is estimated in two stages, where the first is the same as in the previous model (probit), with the difference that the information from the latter is included in a second estimation (OLS) through the incorporation of the probabilities of access from the first stage as a new explanatory variable; this corrects for selection bias [42]. For the skills component, selection is based on the use of devices, while for the capabilities component, selection is based on Internet access.

11.4.2   Access: The First Barrier

As mentioned in the preceding sections, access is a very important component for taking advantage of digital environments and communities; it is therefore necessary to analyze the determinants of access to the Web in order to better understand the differences identified in the level of appropriation.

Estimating a probit binary-dependent variable model, as shown in the second panel of Table 11.3, we find that men and women have on average the same probability of accessing the Internet; that is, the differences observed between men and women in the first panel are not driven mainly by the decision to access.[8] We also see that older adults have less probability of access than younger people; in particular, it is estimated that being an older adult decreases the likelihood of accessing the Internet by 57 percentage points compared to adolescents, while being an adult reduces it by only 20 points. Being a student or worker with a stable income also increases the probability of accessing the Internet, compared to the group of inactive persons. Being enrolled in an educational center and each additional year of education also increase the chance of being connected (by 4.7 and 4.78 percentage points, respectively).

11.4.3   Intensity of Access: Beyond a Dichotomous View

Conventional studies of Internet access tend to limit analysis to the decision to access the net. But intensity of access or the ability to be connected at different times and in different places also influences the range of functionings that an individual can have through ICTs. It is therefore interesting to know what characteristics influence a person's ability to stay connected. To address this question, a Hurdle model [41] is estimated in two parts, the first to analyze access to the Internet (analysis conducted in the preceding section and corresponding to the second panel of Table 11.3) and the second to analyze the number of devices from which users access the Internet – the only component of the Access Index.

This estimation shows that women access from 10% fewer devices than men, while older adults access from slightly more than half the number of devices as younger people. The results also show that only students have more accesses than the unemployed (12%), and each additional year of education increases the number of devices from which the user accesses the Internet by a factor of 1.05.

---

[8]Although a significant difference of 10% is seen, it is lost when a logit model is used or when White's correction for heteroscedacity is used [38]; it therefore cannot be stated that the observed effect is robust.

11.4.4 Digital Skills: The Second Barrier

The use of new technologies implies incurring a cost of learning that is necessary for taking advantage of these tools, what Mendonça et al. [6] refer to as the set of skills needed to open the door. The second component of the Information Richness Index seeks to understand the digital skills necessary for doing this. To identify the characteristics that influence the result of the second component, a Heckman model is estimated in two stages [42], where the first stage evaluates access to digital devices and the second stage evaluates the result in the Skills Index (SI).

The estimation shows that women attain 3.6 points less than men in the SI, a difference that could explain the gap observed in the number of devices from which women connect to the Internet. There are no differences between the skills of adolescents and young adults, but there is a difference in favor of younger people compared to adults (9.5) and a much larger one compared to older adults (22.1). Regarding principal occupation, being a student no longer has a significant effect compared to the group of inactive persons; having a job with a stable income, however, has a small but significant positive effect on the Skills Index. There is also no difference between the group of inactive persons and those who are unemployed.

The estimation also shows that education has a positive effect on digital skills, as May et al. [39] note. In particular, it is estimated that each additional year of studies increases the SI by 2.1 points, while being enrolled in an educational center increases this index by 3.2 points.

11.4.5 Digital Capabilities: The Third Barrier

To analyze how Internet use can expand people's ability to choose the lifestyle they value [14], it is necessary not only to analyze access or the set of digital skills but also to evaluate whether the user is able to function fully in digital environments and in the communities he or she finds there [6]. The third component or Capabilities Index (CI) seeks to estimate the user's free functioning and the set of significant activities in which he or she engages in digital environments. As with the analysis of the skills component, a Heckman model is estimated in two stages [42], where the first stage evaluates access to the Internet and the second stage evaluates the result in the Capabilities Index (CI).

The analysis shows no significant difference in scores between women and men; the main sources of inequality, therefore, stem from the gaps in digital skills. Similarly, no significant differences are found between the scores of individuals from different age groups, not even between adolescents and older adults; inequalities are therefore driven by differences in access and in digital skills. With regard to people's main occupation, it is estimated that a worker with a stable income scores 5.9 points higher than an inactive person, while a worker with unstable income has a 2.9-point advantage. No significant differences are found with regard to students or unemployed persons.

Finally, as with the other two components, the estimation shows that education has a positive effect on digital capabilities. It is estimated that each additional year of studies increases the CI by 1.4 points, while being enrolled in an educational center has a fairly high and significant impact on the result, estimated at 11.28 points. This is consistent with the relational aspect of digital environments [16] and the effects of externalities [21] discussed in the first sections.

11.5 Conclusions

Internet penetration is creating a large number of opportunities that can expand people's freedom to attain the lifestyle that they have reasons to value [14]. This is because they not only constitute powerful tools (means) that enable users to exercise their capabilities more effectively and access a larger amount of information, reduce transaction costs, and increase their ability to stay in communication [14] but also because, as Benkler [21] explains, they configure new social systems with structures and activities based on information networks, where users can participate, interact, share, and exercise their freedoms in ways that are not possible in physical space (ends).

Nevertheless, appropriation of ICTs and digital spaces has not been uniform among all people. The existence of digital divides implies that certain groups show lower levels of appropriation and take less advantage of digital spaces that puts them at a clear disadvantage compared to groups that do make significant use of them [3]. This chapter analyzes the sociodemographic characteristics of the people who have the greatest influence in this process in urban areas of Latin America and the sources of information inequality.

To accomplish this, based on studies by Mendonça et al. [6], an Information Richness Index (IRI) is proposed as a way of studying the complexity of the level of appropriation of the Internet. The index incorporates information about the principal barriers that users face in making significant use of the Internet: access, the skills needed to use ICTs, and the user's capabilities for functioning in digital spaces.

The study shows that the degree of appropriation of digital spaces in the Latin American cities studied is still low, averaging 35.6 points out of a maximum of 100. This means that users, on average, do not take full advantage of the opportunities created by digital spaces. Even when the majority of people use a cellular telephone (92.2%) or a technological device (96%), 22.8% of the sample does not connect to the Internet; non-access to the Internet does constitute a problem, therefore, although it is not explained by access to a device.

The results show that inequality mainly stems not from differences between users who take more advantage of the Internet and those who take less advantage, but from inequality between people in specific groups. In particular, being female and being older have a negative effect on the level of Information Richness, while being a worker with a stable income and having more education have positive and highly significant effects on users' level of appropriation.

Regarding inequality between women and men, the results show that the main source of differences lies in digital skills and in the number of devices from which the user accesses the Internet, two variables that are closely related.

Regarding age groups, it is estimated that age has a strong negative effect on both the user's initial access to the net and the number of devices he or she uses for access and on digital skills; older adults are at a severe disadvantage in almost the entire process of appropriation. Nevertheless, no negative effects are seen on the Capabilities Index; this is consistent with the findings of Colombo et al. [27], who postulate that once the problem of access is overcome (not only by supply but also in demand), the effect of age as an impediment to appropriation of the Internet decreases.

Small effects are associated with the person's main occupation; in particular, it is estimated that being a worker with a stable income has a positive effect and that this effect is driven by the skills and capabilities components; these results conform to findings by Navarro [29] about the acquisition of digital skills in established enterprises or in the mature stage and with the relational and community aspect of digital environments developed by Benkler [16]. Belonging to other occupational groups shows no significant effects.

Finally, having more years of education and belonging to educational communities have positive effects on all components and appear to constitute a potent tool for closing the gaps identified in the three capital cities examined in the study.

11.6 Policy Recommendations

These results reveal the urgency of placing greater importance on the needs of the telecommunication sector on the public agenda in the region. First, access is an important problem, even in places where teledensity is high. Government policy must intensively promote access to broadband Internet and the construction of fiber-optic networks throughout the country, to make this service more accessible, of higher quality for citizens, and affordable.

A more aggressive digital literacy strategy is also needed, with efforts focused on reducing the cost of learning and increasing the benefits expected from the use of ICTs [40], to ensure a significant reduction in the percentage of the population that, despite having access to devices, remains sidelined from digital spaces.

The active creation and dissemination of orderly, flexible learning platforms are another effective way of accelerating and facilitating appropriation, which must be exploited; moreover, targeted initiatives that distinguish not only between whether or not people belong to one of these groups (women and men, or young people, and older adults), but which also understand how the incorporation of ICTs helps satisfy particular needs and people's productive processes will have important impacts.

Appendix 1: Construction of the Components of the IRI (Tables 11.4, 11.5, and 11.6)

Table 11.4 Construction of the access index

Access index (AI)		
Number of devices from which you access to the Internet		
Types of devices:	N° of devices:	Score:
Cellular phone (smartphone or mobile)	5 devices	100
Tablet	4 devices	80
Notebook	3 devices	60
PC	2 devices	40
Smart TV	1 device	20
	0 devices	0

Compiled by author

Source: Survey about Internet use: Platforms and open data – 2014

Table 11.5 Construction of the skills index

Skills index (SI)[a]		
Age of use of the device (SI_1)		
Unit of measurement:	N° of months:	Score:
Maximum length of time device has been used (in months)	Does not use devices:	0
	0> N° months >100	N° of months
	N° of months ≥100	100
Number of activities undertaken on the network (SI_2)		
Types of activities	N° of activities	Score:
Surf in the web	8 activities	100
Use social networks	7 activities	87.5
Using chat	6 activities	75
Reviewing electronic mail	5 activities	62.5
Watching or downloading videos	4 activities	50
Listening or downloading music	3 activities	37.5
Playing online games	2 activities	25
Accessing online banking	1 activity	12.5

Compiled by authors

Source: Survey about Internet use: Platforms and open data – 2014

[a]The Skills Index is constructed as follows:

$SI = (SI_1 + 2 \times SI_2) \div 3$

Table 11.6 Construction of the capabilities index

Capabilities index (CI)[a]		
Do you know about programs that can be freely modified on the Internet? (CI₁)		
Answer:	Score:	
Yes	100	
No	0	
Is the Internet your first choice when you are looking for information about one of the following? (CI₂)		
Types of purposes:	N° of purposes:	Score:
Learning activities	3 purposes	100
Labor or business	2 purposes	66.7
Interaction with the government	1 purpose	33.3
When you search for information on the Internet for learning, work or to communicate with the government, how do you find it? (CI₃)		
Alternatives:	Score by affirmative answers:	
Complete (find everything sought)?	$6{,}67 \times$ (N° of affirmative responses)	
Readable and adequate?	5 questions per item (3) = 15 questions	
Is it in large amounts??	$CI_3 \in [0, 100]$	
Is it free?		
Is it updated?		
Educational uses of the net (CI4)		
Types of uses of the net:	N° of uses:	Score:
Taking online courses	3 uses of the net	100
Accessing educational resources (bibliography or databases)	2 uses of the net	66.7
Participating in social networks with educational purposes	1 use of the net	33.3
Work-related uses of the net (CI5)		
Types of network usage:	N° of uses conducted:	Score:
Accessing social networks to look for work	2 uses of the net	100
Participating in social networks for work-related purposes	1 use of the net	50
Uses of the net related to access to public services and exercise of rights (CI6)		
Types of network usage:	Answer:	Score:
Administrative procedures, consultations, complaints, payments, or making appointments in public entities	Yes	100
	No	0

Compiled by authors.
Source: Survey about Internet use: Platforms and open data – 2014
[a]The Skills Index is constructed as follows:
$CI = (CI_1 + CI_2 + CI_3 + CI4 + CI5 + CI6) \div 6$

References

1. Smith, M. L., Elder, L., & Emdon, H. (2011a). Open development: A new theory for ICT4D. *Information Technologies and International Development, 7*(1), iii–iix.
2. Sen, A. (1999). *Development as freedom*. New York: Oxford University Press.
3. Robinson, L., Cotten, S. R., Ono, H., Quan-Haase, A., Mesch, G., Chen, W., & Stern, M. J. (2015). Digital inequalities and why they matter. *Information, Communication & Society, 18*(5), 569.
4. Stewart, F. (2005). *Horizontal inequalities: A neglected dimension of development. WIDER perspectives on global development*. UK: Palgrave MacMillan.
5. Instituto Nacional de Estadística e Informática. https://www.inei.gob.pe/
6. Mendonça, S., Crespo, N., & Simões, N. (2015). Inequality in the network society: An integrated approach to ICT access, basic skills, and complex capabilities. *Telecommunications Policy, 39*, 192–207.
7. Barrantes, R., Agüero, A., & Vargas, E. (2015a). La conectividad urbana en América Latina: Una mirada a Buenos Aires (In Spanish). Dialogo Regional Sobre Sociedad de la Información. Available at: http://dirsi.net/web/web/es/publicaciones/detalle/la-conectividad-urbana-en-america-latina--una-mirada-a-buenos-aires
8. Barrantes, R., Agüero, A., & Vargas, E. (2015b). La conectividad urbana en América Latina: Una mirada a Lima (In Spanish). Dialogo Regional Sobre Sociedad de la Información. Available at: http://dirsi.net/web/web/es/publicaciones/detalle/la-conectividad-urbana-en-america-latina--una-mirada-a-lima
9. Barrantes, R., Agüero, A., & Vargas, E. (2015c). La conectividad urbana en América Latina: Una mirada a Ciudad de Guatemala (In Spanish). Dialogo Regional Sobre Sociedad de la Información. Available at: http://dirsi.net/web/web/es/publicaciones/detalle/la-conectividad-urbana-en-america-latina--una-mirada-a-ciudad-de-guatemala
10. Castells, M. (2011). *The rise of the network society: The information age: Economy, society, and culture* (Vol. 1). Wiley, Oxford, UK.
11. Smith, M. L., Spence, R., & Rashid, A. T. (2011b). Mobile phones and expanding human capabilities. *Information Technologies and International Development, 7*(3), 77.
12. Chahuara, P., & Trelles, J. (2014). *Impactos heterogéneos del acceso a Internet sobre el Bienestar: Evidencia a partir de Microdatos en el Perú (In Spanish)*. Lima: OSIPTEL.
13. Huaroto, C. (2011). Efecto de la Adopción del Internet en la productividad de las MYPES en el Perú (In Spanish). Tesis de Lic., Lima: Pontificia Universidad Católica del Perú.
14. Smith, M. L., Reilly, K. M., & Benkler, Y. (2014). *Open development: Networked innovations in international development*. Boston: MIT Press.
15. Internatiotional Telecommunication Union. https://www.itu.int/en/Pages/default.aspx
16. Benkler, Y. (2006). *The wealth of networks: How social production transforms markets and freedom*. New Haven: Yale University Press.
17. Kleine, D. (2013). *Technologies of choice?: ICTs, development, and the capabilities approach*. Cambridge, MA/Boston: MIT Press.
18. Agostini, C., & Willington, M. (2012). Acceso y uso de internet en Chile: evolución y factores determinantes. *Persona y sociedad, 26*(1), 11–42.
19. Díaz, R., Messano, O. A., & Petrissans, R. (2003). *La brecha digital y sus repercusiones en los países miembros de la Aladi (In Spanish)*. ALADI/SEC/Estudio, 157.
20. World Bank (2002). *Superar la brecha digital en las Américas (In Spanish)*.
21. Tongia, R., & Wilson III, E. J. (2011). Network theory: The flip side of Metcalfe's law: Multiple and growing costs of network exclusion. *International Journal of Communication, 5*, 17.
22. Hargittai, E., & Shafer, S. (2006). Differences in actual and perceived online skills: The role of gender. *Social Science Quarterly, 87*(2), 432–448.
23. Ono, H., & Zavodny, M. (2003). Gender and the Internet. *Social Science Quarterly, 84*(1), 111–121.

24. Barbosa, B., & Amaro, F. (2012). Too old for technology? How the elderly of Lisbon use and perceive ICT. *Journal of Community Informatics, 8*(1), http://ci-journal.net/index.php/ciej/article/view/800/904.
25. Barrantes, R., & Cozzubo, A. (2015). *Edad para aprender, edad para enseñar: el rol del aprendizaje intergeneracional intrahogar en el uso de la Internet por parte de los adultos mayores en Latinoamérica (In Spanish)*. Lima: Pontificia Universidad Católica del Perú.
26. Castellón, L., & Jaramillo, O. (2002). *Las múltiples dimensiones de la brecha digital (In Spanish)*. Reflexiones académicas (Vol. 13).
27. Colombo, F., Aroldi, P., & Carlo, S. (2015). Nuevos mayores, viejas brechas: TIC, desigualdad y bienestar en la tercera edad en Italia (In Spanish). *Comunicar: Revista Científica de Comunicación y Educación, 23*(45), 47–55.
28. Prensky, M. (2001). Nativos digitales, inmigrantes digitales (In Spanish). *On the Horizon, 9*(6):1–6.
29. Navarro, L. (2010). The impact of internet use on individual earnings in Latin America (No. 2010/11). Development Research Working Paper Series.
30. Witte, J. C., & Mannon, S. E. (2010). *The internet and social inequalities*. New York: Routledge.
31. Hargittai, E., & Hinnant, A. (2008). Digital inequality differences in young adults' use of the Internet. *Communication Research, 35*(5), 602–621.
32. Helsper, E., & Galacz, A. (2009). *Understanding the links between social and digital exclusion in Europe. World wide internet. Changing societies, economies and cultures*. Macau: University of Macau.
33. Howard, P. E., Rainie, L., & Jones, S. (2001). Days and nights on the internet the impact of a diffusing technology. *The American Behavioral Scientist, 45*(3), 383–404.
34. Villatoro, P., & Silva, A. (2005). *Estrategias, programas y experiencias de superación de la brecha digital y universalización del acceso a las nuevas tecnologías de información y comunicación (TIC): un panorama regional (In Spanish) vol. 101*. United Nations Publications.
35. Minges, M. (2005). Evaluation of e-readiness indices in Latin America and the Caribbean. Santiago: ECLAC. Available at: http://www.cepal.org/en/publications/31929-evaluation-e-readiness-indices-latin-america-and-caribbean (Consulted: 29 April 2015).
36. Organismo Supervisor de Inversión Privada en Telecomunicaciones. https://www.osiptel.gob.pe/documentos/indicadores-estadisticos
37. World Bank Data. http://datos.bancomundial.org/
38. Greene, W. H. (2003). *Econometric analysis*. India: Pearson Education.
39. May, J. Dutton, V., & Muntakazi, L. (2014). Information and communication technologies as a pathway from poverty: Evidence from East Africa. In Adera, et al. (Ed.), *ICT Pathways to Poverty Reduction: Empirical Evidence from East and Southern Africa* (p. 33–76). Ottawa: International Development Research Centre.
40. Venkatesh, V., Morris, M. G., Davis, G. B., & Davis, F. D. (2003). User acceptance of information technology: Toward a unified view. *MIS Quarterly, 27*, 425–478.
41. Cameron, A. C., & Trivedi, P. K. (2010). *Microeconometrics using stata*. College Station: Stata press.
42. Heckman, J. J. (1979). Sample selection bias as a specification error. *Econometrica: Journal of the Econometric Society, 47*, 153–161.

Chapter 12
Internet Use and Public Programs Participation: Evidence from Chile

Matteo Grazzi and Sebastian Vergara

Abstract The interest for ICT-related issues has notably increased in the last decades, leading to a flourishing of studies on their impact on many dimensions. Despite the consensus about the importance of ICT effects at micro level, there is lack of analysis on the existence, magnitude and direction of these effects. This article aims to contribute to the literature by performing an analysis of the relationship between Internet use and information diffusion at household level in Chile. By using data from National Household Surveys, we estimate the effect of Internet use at household level on the probability of obtaining a scholarship for young students in the household. The results suggest that ICT use is significantly and positively correlated with the probability of primary students to be granted by a scholarship program, illustrating how ICT improves communication access and participation in social programs. Given that ICT diffusion is largely determined by socio-economic dimensions, the results also illustrate how ICT could reinforce pre-existing inequalities. This highlights the need for proactive public policies in addressing the digital divide.

Keywords Internet • Public programs • Scholarships • Chile

The opinions expressed in this article are those of the authors and do not necessarily reflect the views of neither the Inter-American Development Bank nor the United Nations. Remaining errors are authors' exclusive responsibility.

M. Grazzi (✉)
Inter-American Development Bank, Washington, DC, USA
e-mail: matteog@iadb.org

S. Vergara
Department of Economic and Social Affairs, United Nations, New York, NY, USA
e-mail: vergaras@un.org

© Springer International Publishing AG 2017
H. Kaur et al. (eds.), *Catalyzing Development through ICT Adoption*,
DOI 10.1007/978-3-319-56523-1_12

12.1   Introduction

The interest for Information and Communication Technologies (ICT) has notably increased in recent years, leading to a flourishing of studies on their access, use and impact on economic, social, environmental and cultural dimensions. Furthermore, the diffusion of ICTs has been identified as a key driver of economic growth and sustainable development [1], and it is becoming a crucial tool in public administration, business, education, health and environmental areas. Against this backdrop, scholars have made visible progress on identifying various effects at aggregate level, such as on economic growth [2, 3], productivity [4–6], sector structures (e.g. finance and retail sales) and on the aggregate demand of technological items, among others.

More recently, the literature has moved towards analysing micro-effects, both at firm and individual level. Indeed, many effects from ICT usage occur within the household, affecting individual behaviour and decision-making processes. Gaining access to new technologies means to develop new technlological skills, to increase communication efficiency, to change preferences of media pattern used and to diversify the interaction with one's own community, with important consequences across different dimensions. Psychological effects originated by the ability of ICT to influence individual behaviours can also be included. Possible examples are the effect of ICT-mediated communication on individual decisions as well as the use of web forums and global networks for advancing political goals, building social support nets, connecting disparate groups and providing opportunities for a broader influence of organizations, governments and individuals [7].[1] For instance, it has been found that Internet use was associated with a higher probability of voting in the 2000 US election [9].[2] Moreover, a large body of research has highlighted that Internet has become a primary source of information. For example, about 50% of the US citizens have indicated the Internet as their main source of political news [11].

In this perspective, improving access to information is probably the most important effect of ICT diffusion, as a result of the broad range of impacts this could have on everyday life. In particular, Internet users have been found to have great advantages in activities such as price comparison and job seeking. In addition, some studies have shown that consumers can save important amounts by buying goods and services online. For example, it was reported that buying electronics on web platforms generates an average saving of 16% compared to purchasing at listed prices [12]. Similar results are reported in the case of books and CDs [13] and in the case of new cars [14]. At the same time, Internet use is supposed to smooth search and matching processes in several areas, including the job market. Recent economic literature points out that online job search is effective in various aspects. For example, it has been shown that Internet use reduces by approximately 25% unemployment duration

---

[1] For example, many governments are using ICT, particularly E-government tools, in order to strengthen their openness and transparency [8].

[2] However, a similar study evaluated the effect of Internet use on political participation in Belgium, but it cannot establish a clear relation between time spent on the Internet and propensity to participate in public life [10].

[15] and that Internet increases the probability of labour force participation for married women [16]. Other studies show that access to broadband services is associated with higher employment rates, especially in rural and isolated areas [17]. Also, some evidence suggests that employed individuals who use the Internet to search for jobs are more likely to change jobs and to gain a better wage in the transition [18].

Despite the consensus about the importance of a more complete understanding of these dynamics, empirical studies on the effects of ICT diffusion on individual dynamics are still limited. Therefore, many questions remain still unanswered, especially in the context of developing countries. In fact, due to the availability and quality of data, most of the academic research on ICTs has been conducted in developed economies. But it is probably within the context of developing countries where innovative lines of analysis can be found and explored, proposing a renewed perspective on the relation between ICTs and development. ICT can be an important channel for diffusing information about social and economic programs and for promoting the full participation of the community in their implementation. For instance, the Internet can constitute a powerful tool to provide information about scholarship programs and to obtain a more balanced distribution of educational opportunities.

This paper contributes to the ICT literature by analysing the role of Internet use in allocating scholarships among students in Chile. The hypothesis is that the use of the Internet affects positively the probability of being awarded by a scholarship through access to complete and updated relevant information. The empirical exercise uses statistical information from the Chilean National Household Surveys between 2000 and 2009, when Internet access was still limited but increasing rapidly. Thus, the study focuses on the potential information effects in a period where technology was still unevenly distributed across different socio-economic population groups. The article is organized as follows. Section 12.2 shows the main patterns of ICT diffusion in Chile. Section 12.3 displays the empirical analysis and it discusses the main results. Finally, Sect. 12.4 concludes and establishes some further research areas.

12.2   Main Patterns of ICT Diffusion in Chile

In the last decade, the Internet access increased considerably among the Chilean population. In 2000, less than 10% of Chilean households had Internet access, and this figure surged to 30% in 2009 and to more than 65% in 2014 (Fig. 12.1). However, this aggregate picture hides major differences among locations and population groups. As expected, the Internet access is much higher in urban than in rural areas. In 2009, only 7.2% of the rural households had an available Internet connection, compared with 32% of those households located in urban areas. Not surprisingly, the unequal distribution of ICT access among the population is confirmed by analysing the Internet penetration rates by income and education quintiles. In 2009, only 7% and 15% of households in the first and second income quintiles benefit from Internet access, respectively (Fig. 12.2). By contrast, in the fourth and fifth

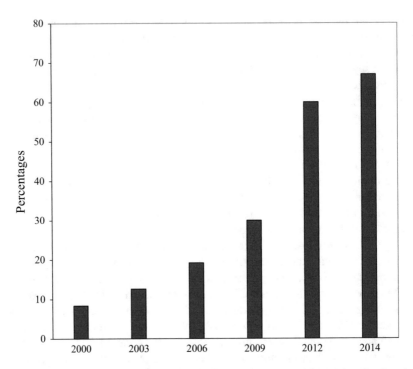

Fig. 12.1 Internet access at household level, 2000–2014 (Source: author's elaboration based on National Household Surveys)

quintiles, more than 42% and 70% of households had Internet access, respectively. Moreover, the differences in the Internet access are not homogeneous along subsequent population segments, and the fifth quintile concentrates the bulk of the Internet penetration. Likewise, the distribution of Internet access by educational quintiles – measured by the average education years of adults in the household – follows a similar pattern across households. In 2009, the Internet access rates in the first and second quintile were 0.7% and 3%, respectively. For the households in the fourth and fifth educational quintiles, penetration rates for Internet reached 18% and 53%, respectively. Thus, to a large extent the access to Internet reflects pre-existing socio-economic inequalities across households.

The type of Internet connection also reflects pre-existing socio-economic inequalities across households. In 2009, the broadband access connection was available only in 5% and 11% of households with an available Internet connection in the first and second income quintiles, respectively. By contrast, these figures reached 35% and 62% in fourth and fifth income quintiles. In addition, differences of Internet use are observed not only across households but also within households. Among households with an available Internet connection, only 40% of the components actually use it, which shows that Internet access does not translate into use [19, 20]. The different population cohorts also play a relevant role. As expected, the Internet use decreases monotonically with age of the population. Indeed, in

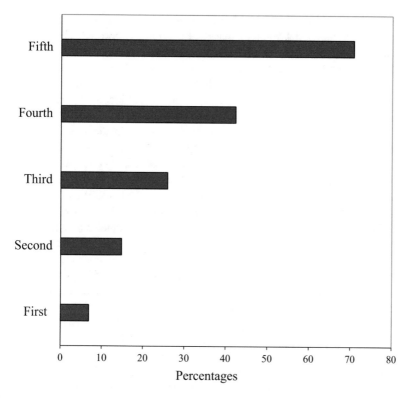

Fig. 12.2 Internet access by income quintiles at household level, 2009 (Source: author's elaboration based on National Household Survey)

2009 more than the 70% of the population aged between 15 and 24 years used the Internet, while only 22% of the population aged between 50 and 59 used the web.

12.3   Empirical Approach and Econometric Results

12.3.1   Empirical Approach

The empirical approach to analyse the determinants of the probability of having a scholarship is based on the following Probit equation:

$$
\begin{aligned}
\Pr\left(\text{Scholarship}_i = 1\right) = \Phi(\alpha + \beta_0^* \text{Income}_j + \beta_1^* \text{Education}_j \\
+ \beta_2^* \text{Family Size}_j + \beta_3^* \text{Rural}_j \\
+ \beta_4^* \text{Head} + \beta_5^* \text{Female}_j \\
+ \beta_6^* \text{Internet}_j)
\end{aligned} \tag{12.1}
$$

where Pr (Scholarship$_i$ = 1) is the probability that the individual i is granted by a scholarship.[3] The Probit model assumes that the error term is normally distributed with mean 0 and variance σ equal to 1, and $\Phi(.)$ corresponds to the cumulative distribution function for a standard normal random variable. In this empirical model, the probability that an individual is granted with a scholarship depends on several variables. The variable *Income* corresponds to the per capita equivalent income of the household,[4] and *Education* corresponds to the household education level measured by the average level of educational years of adults (age ≥ 18). Given that the scholarship system focuses on more vulnerable students, we expect income to be negatively correlated with the probability of having a scholarship. By contrast, the education level of the household can play an important positive role because of the effects on a better access and use of information related to social programs. In addition, it can capture some other unobservable characteristics that can affect positively the probability of obtaining a scholarship, such as parent motivation towards educational achievements.

The variable *Family Size* is the number of individuals in the household and Rural is a dummy variable that controls for the area where the household is located. Meanwhile, *Head* is a dummy variable that takes the value of 1 for households in which the head is a woman. There are several studies that discuss the peculiarities of households having a female head. On one hand, it is generally argued that such households evidence some disadvantages, for example, higher levels of poverty. This is associated to the fact that the head of the household may work less time and that these households generally have lower adult members that generate income. On the other, women are often more attentive about the nutrition and the education of the children, and it is intuitive to expect that students of these households would be more likely to be granted by educational scholarships. *Female* is a dummy variable that takes the value of 1 if the individual is a woman, being the only variable at individual level. The Appendix 12.1 shows basic statistics of explanatory variables, and the Appendix 12.2 displays the correlation matrix.

The main hypothesis to test in this empirical section is that the use of the Internet at household level is positively correlated to the scholarship awarding of primary students living in that household. The Internet might provide advantages in terms of scholarship information, application procedures, updates and in promoting social participation. We specify two different measures on Internet, which is our core variable. The variable *Internet 1* is a dummy variable that takes the value 1 if at least

---

[3] In the case of Chile, the primary scholarship system is complex and covers a wide range of social and economic issues. Indeed, depending on the program, there are several different facilitations that can be provided to students and families, such as monetary payments, food and housing, among others. Basically, the scholarships can be categorized in two main groups. The first group provides a direct pecuniary assistance of free disposal for families. The second group focuses on student reallocation from isolated geographical areas to areas where there are primary schools, nutrition daily provisions and college-study-essentials support.

[4] In order to take into account economies of scale in household consumption and obtain more precise income elasticity, we use an equivalent income measure, which is the total household income divided by the so-called LIS (Luxembourg Income Studies) equivalence scale. It is defined as the square root of the number of household members [21].

Table 12.1 Internet use and scholarship attainment: definition of estimation variables

Variable	Description
Pr (Scholarship = 1)	Primary scholarship attainment. Dummy; 1:yes; 0: no
Household income	Log_n of equivalent household income
Household education	Average of adults education years in the household (age ≥ 17)
Family size	Number of individuals in the household
$Female_i$	Gender variable. Dummy; 1: female; 0: male, at individual level
Rural	Location. Dummy; 1: rural; 0: urban
Head	Head of household is a woman. Dummy; 1:yes; 0:no
Dummy 2009	Dummy variable for the year 2009
Internet 1	Dummy; 1 if at least one adult individual the uses Internet in the household, 0 otherwise
Internet 2	Proportion of individuals within the household that use Internet

Source: Author's elaboration based on Chilean National Household Surveys

one adult in the household uses the Internet. The variable *Internet 2* corresponds to the proportion of individuals within the household that use Internet (see Table 12.1). Thus, with these two variables, we attempt to control for both the Internet use and the Internet use intensity among adults within the household. Finally, we also add municipality fixed effects, to account for different scholarship provision levels.

Therefore, the empirical approach is based on an equation in which the probability for a student of obtaining a scholarship is associated to several household characteristics, like income and education, while the only variable defined at student level is Female. In a general setting, this is likely to create a problem of relevant omitted variable. In particular, the model does not control by individual capabilities that surely affect the probability of obtaining a scholarship, such as academic proficiency. Therefore, the estimation results would be inconsistent and biased. Nevertheless, our focus on primary school greatly reduces this problem. Indeed, the main determinants of the primary scholarship attainment are the household socio-economic characteristics. The statistical information comes from the *National Household Surveys* 2006 and 2009, implemented by *Ministerio de Desarrollo Social*. This survey covers a wide range of social and economic characteristics at individual and household level. Each year the survey covers around 70,000 households (250,000 individuals) and the surveys are statistically representative at national level.

12.3.2 Econometric Results

The econometric results are provided in Table 12.2. We first implement baseline estimations (model 1) and then we sequentially add the core variables (Internet 1 and Internet 2) (model 2 and 4) and Municipalities fixed effects (model 3 and 5). A robust result of the estimations is that the effect of income on the probability of obtaining a scholarship is negative and significant. Thus, students in household with

Table 12.2 Internet and primary scholarship attainment: Probit model estimations

Variables	Model (1)	Model (2)	Model (3)	Model (4)	Model (5)
Household income	−0.077	−0.092	−0.111	−0.091	−0.111
	(3.19)**	(3.82)***	(4.36)***	(3.80)***	(4.34)***
Household education	0.024	0.022	0.023	0.023	0.023
	(3.78)***	(3.51)***	(3.49)***	(3.59)***	(3.58)***
Family size	−0.033	−0.032	−0.034	−0.013	−0.017
	(3.50)***	(3.35)**	(3.44)**	(1.33)	(1.23)
Rural	−0.029	−0.005	0.150	−0.007	0.148
	(0.88)	(0.15)	(4.09)***	(−0.22)	(4.05)***
Female	0.070	0.069	0.071	0.070	0.072
	(1.95)*	(1.91)*	(1.95)*	(1.93)*	(1.98)**
Head	0.101	0.106	0.088	0.094	0.074 (1.69)*
	(2.31)**	(2.41)**	(2.03)**	(2.09)**	
Dummy 2009	0.343	0.360	0.194	0.345	0.232 (1.95)*
	(1.94)*	(1.98)*	(1.96)*	(1.89)*	
Internet 1		0.198	0.224		
		(5.21)***	(5.89)***		
Internet 2				0.813	0.921
				(4.96)***	(5.63)***
Municipalities fixed effects	No	No	Yes	No	Yes
Observations	78,623	78,623	78,623	78,623	78,623

Z-statistics in parenthesis calculated with robust standard errors. *Significant at 10%; **Significant at 5%, ***Significant at 1%

lower income are more likely to be granted by a scholarship. This is consistent with social and redistribution objectives of the young student scholarship programs in Chile, as more disadvantageous students from a socio-economic dimension should be more likely to obtain a scholarship. The level of education in the household also seems to play a relevant role. In fact, students living in more educated households are more likely to obtain a scholarship, on average and *ceteris paribus*. This is consistent with the idea that more educated households are associated to a better and more efficient use of information. Also, a more educated household can have a higher commitment towards educational achievements.

Additionally, there is evidence that students living in households where the head is a woman are more likely to be granted by a scholarship, though its magnitude is small. According to model (5), primary students in a household where the head is a woman are 0.8% more likely to be granted by a scholarship. Meanwhile, the rural location condition displays mixed evidence. This result is not surprising given the scholarship schemes available, with different objective and population targets. Furthermore, the correlation of the location condition with other control variables suggests being cautious about its interpretation.

Our main interest concerns the Internet variables. In the models (2) and (3), the coefficient is positive and significant at 1%. This shows that the students living in a household where at least one adult uses the Internet have higher probability of being granted by a primary scholarship. In terms of magnitude, a student in household with Internet access increases the probability of having a scholarship by 2%. In addition, the estimated coefficients in the models (4) and (5) are also positive and significant at 1%. Thus, the intensity of Internet use among adults within the household is also positively correlated to the probability for a primary student within the household of being granted by a scholarship. Thus, not only the Internet use but also its use intensity within the household is correlated with the individual probability of having a primary scholarship. A key channel that could explain this correlation is having access to improved and updated information through the Internet, particularly about when and how to participate in student scholarship programs.

We acknowledge that it is not possible to interpret this evidence in terms of a causal relationship, so we interpret our results as a correlation. Also, the fact that the scholarship variable is measured at individual level, while the Internet use is measured at household level, might also generate doubts on the relevance of the empirical results. Nevertheless, it should be considered that the main determinants of primary scholarship attainment are actually related to household characteristics. Thus, we think the empirical evidence of such a strong correlation between Internet use and scholarship attainment should not be underestimated. This correlation, controlling by the main socio-economic determinants of scholarship attainment, suggests that the Internet play a role on providing better access to relevant information and promoting greater social participation in public programs.

Nevertheless, the descriptive evidence presented in the section II and evidence from previous studies clearly show that ICT access and usage are largely determined by socio-economic characteristics such as income and education [19, 22]. Thus, more advantageous population groups are more likely to benefit from ICT diffusion. In our case, primary students living in households with Internet access and usage are more likely to be granted by a scholarship, but households with higher education and income are precisely the ones that tend to have more ICT access. Thus, we can expect that the positive effect of ICT diffusion will be concentrated in these households. This illustrates the dual role of ICT. On one hand, ICT promotes social participation and greater access to information with potential large positive effects. However, already advantaged population groups are more likely to benefit more from it.

In sum, this result confirms the role of the Internet in allowing a better access to information and greater social participation. But given that ICT diffusion is not homogeneous across population groups, the benefits will tend to be concentrated in more advantaged population groups. From a public policy perspective, this evidence shows that Internet access and usage can be an important channel for both diffusing information about social and economic programs and promoting the full participation of the community in their implementation. But at the same time it suggests that it is critically important to address the digital divide in order to fully expand its benefits. Therefore, there is a need for proactive and well-designed public policies that could not only promote ICT access but also spread out its benefits across the population.

12.4   Conclusions

The effects of ICT at household and individual level are multiple. Most of the studies at micro level have tried to disentangle this multiplicity of effects by focusing on specific issues. However, the existing literature is far from being complete and exhaustive. There is a lack of empirical analysis on some specific effects, and the dynamic nature of ICT impacts has also been overlooked. In this paper, we contribute to the empirical literature by providing evidence on how ICT diffusion improves access to information and promote social participation in a particular case: scholarships programs for primary students. The evidence presented suggests that primary students in households that use the Internet have larger probability of being awarded by a scholarship, even after controlling by socio-economic characteristics. However, given that ICT diffusion is not homogeneous across population groups, the main benefits from this are expected to be concentrated in more advantageous groups as well. This illustrates both the potential and risks that the ICT diffusion process entails across different dimensions.

Moving forward, it is not certain that observed ICT impacts could persist with the same magnitude and direction found in the existing literature, and there are reasons to suppose that ICT impacts could change along two dimensions: dynamically and cross-sectional. The first simply means that ICT impact could change over time as ICT expands. This hypothesis is supported by the fact that ICT evolves continuously, reaching every year higher levels of sophistication and potentials. If the technological frontier is moving, it is reasonable that its effects will move too. Moreover, variations of ICT impacts over time could simply be given by the taking over of a new generation of ICT users. So far, researches have analysed ICT impact using samples of individuals that approached ICT at a certain stage of their life, but in the future it will be possible to analyse the impacts on the generation born after the beginning of the ICT revolution, whose members have always dealt with ICT since early stages of life. Cross-sectional differences are another possible further extension of the ICT impact literature, given its close connection with the digital divide and digital inequality. For instance, it would be interesting to study possible differences in ICT impacts across different individual characteristics, such as races, educational levels and gender.

The relevance of new technologies in the development path justifies an increasing effort by international institutions, academia and scholars to achieve a better understanding of the ICT diffusion process. Early visions were generally optimistic in considering it as an equalizing factor both at international and at domestic level, but successive scholars have highlighted the risk that ICT might worsen pre-existing inequalities. This is a key area of further research. Considering that ICT have no reason to exist on itself but only on the benefits they have for individuals, it is clear that the research agenda has unavoidable challenges ahead.

Appendix 12.1. Internet and Scholarship Attainment: Basic Statistics of Independent Variables (Estimation Sample; Obs. = 78,623)

Variables	Mean	Stand. error	95% Conf. interval	
Household income	12.0852	0.0036	12.0712	12.1113
Household education	9.9818	0.0051	9.9801	9.9910
Family size	5.0490	0.0074	5.0351	5.0642
Rural	0.3822	0.0020	0.4809	0.4894
Head	0.2213	0.0017	0.2178	0.2249
Female	0.4851	0.0021	0.4809	04894
Internet 1	0.3857	0.0034	0.3702	0.3798
Internet 2	0.1071	0.0005	0.1060	0.1081

Source: Author's elaboration based on Chilean National Household Surveys 2006 and 2009

Appendix 12.2. Internet and Scholarship Attainment: Correlation Matrix of Estimation Independent Variables

Variables	Household	Household education	Family size	Rural	Head	Female	Internet 1	Internet 2
Household income	1							
Household education	0.399*	1						
Family size	−0,138*	0.009*	1					
Rural	−0.186*	−0.274*	−0.003	1				
Head	−0.103*	−0.011*	−0.042*	−0.090*	1			
Female	−0.006	0.000	0.002	0.003	0.003	1		
Internet 1	0.159*	0.137*	−0.037*	−0.172*	−0.004	0.001	1	
Internet 2	0.179*	0.115*	−0.266*	−0.159*	0.041*	−0.000	0.896*	1

Source: Author's elaboration based on Chilean National Household Surveys 2006 and 2009.
*Significant at 5%

Bibliography

1. The World Bank: World Development Report 2016. (2016). *Digital dividends*. Washington, DC: World Bank.
3. Qiang, C.Z., Rossotto, C., Kimura, K. (2009). Economic impacts of broadband. In *Information and communications for development*. Washington, DC: World Bank.
2. Czernich, N., Falck, O., Kretschmer, T., & Woessmann, L. (2011). Broadband infrastructure and economic growth. *The Economic Journal, 121*(552), 505–532.
6. Oliner, S., & Sichel, D. (2000). The resurgence of growth in the late 1990s: Is information technology the story? *Journal of Economic Perspectives, 14*(4), 3–22.
5. Jorgenson, D. W., & Stiroh, K. J. (2000). Raising the speed limit: US economic growth in the information age. *Brookings Papers on Economic Activity, 1*, 125–235.
4. Jorgenson, D. W., & Stiroh, K. J. (1999). Information technology and growth. *American Economic Review, 89*(2), 109–115.
7. Norris, P. (2001). *Digital divide: Civic engagement, information poverty, and the internet worldwide*. New York: Cambridge University Press.
8. Bertot, J. C., Jaeger, P. T., & Grimes, J. M. (2010). Using ICTs to create a culture of transparency: E-government and social media as openness and anti-corruption tools for societies. *Government Information Quarterly, 27*, 264–271.
9. Tolbert, C. J., & Mcneal, R. S. (2003). Unravelling the effects of the internet on political participation? *Political Research Quarterly, 56*(2), 175–185.
10. Quintelier, E., & Vissers, S. (2008). The effect of internet use on political participation an analysis of survey results for 16-year-olds in Belgium. *Social Science Computer Review, 26*(4), 411–427.
11. Caumont, A. (2013). 12 trends shaping digital news. Pew Research Center.
12. Baye, M., Morgan, J., Scholten, P. (2002). Persistent price dispersion in online markets. Working Paper. Indiana University.
13. Brynjolfsson, E., & Smith, M. (2000). Frictionless commerce? A comparison of internet and conventional retailers. *Management Science, 46*(4), 563–585.
14. Zettelmeyer, F., Scott Morton, F., & Silva-Risso, J. (2001). *Cowboys or cowards: Why are internet car prices lower?* Berkeley: Mimeo, UC Berkeley Yale University UCLA.
15. Kuhn, P., & Mansour, H. (2014). Is internet job search still ineffective? *The Economic Journal, 124*(581), 1213–1233.
16. Dettling, L.J. (2013). Broadband in the labour market: The impact of residential high speed internet on married women's labour force participation. Federal Reserve Board Discussion Paper 2013-065.
17. Atasoy, H. (2013). The effects of broadband internet expansion on labour market outcomes. *Industrial & Labuor Relations Review, 66*(2), 315–345.
18. Stevenson, B. (2009). The internet and job search. In D. H. Autor (Ed.), *Studies of labour market intermediation* (pp. 67–86). Chicago: University of Chicago Press.
20. Ono, H. (2005). Digital inequality in East Asia: Evidence from Japan, South Korea and Singapore. *Asian Economic Papers, 4*(3), 116–139.
19. Grazzi, M., & Vergara, S. (2014). Internet in Latin America: Who uses it? … and for what? *Economics of Innovation and New Technology, 23*(2), 327–352.
21. Atkinson, A., Lee, R., & Smeeding, T. (1995). *Income distribution in OECD countries. Evidence from the Luxembourg income study, Social Policy Studies, N. 18*. Paris: OECD.
22. Grazzi, M., & Vergara, S. (2011). Determinants of ICT access. In M. Balboni, S. Rovira, & S. Vergara (Eds.), *ICT in Latin America: A microdata analysis*. Santiago: ECLAC and IDRC.

Chapter 13
E-Commerce and Productivity: Evidence from Chile

Leonardo Ortega, Alison Cathles, and Matteo Grazzi

Abstract The diffusion of e-commerce is deeply changing the way in which business is conducted, by reducing the costs of goods and services to be used in the productive process as inputs and by increasing the access to new markets. However, the relative empirical literature is still limited, and the majority of studies focus on manufacturing firms in developed countries. This paper makes use of a country-representative survey including information for Chilean firms of every size and sector to analyze the impact on firm productivity of e-commerce adoption in the context of a middle-income economy. The results show that e-commerce is associated with higher levels of productivity in both the manufacturing and the service sector, whereas e-buying is the channel that explains this relationship.

Keywords E-commerce • Productivity • Chile

JEL Codes O30 • D24

13.1 Introduction

Early studies launched in the 1980s and 1990s did not find strong empirical evidence to support a positive link between IT investment and firm-level productivity [1]. But since the mid-1990s, a body of literature has amassed that documents the positive impact of IT investment on productivity and economic growth both at the country (e.g., [2–4]) and firm level (e.g., [5, 6]). This suggests that there may be a delay or a time lapse between IT investment and payoff in terms of productivity, at least in developed countries.

L. Ortega (✉) • M. Grazzi
Inter-American Development Bank, Washington, DC, USA
e-mail: lgortega@iadb.org; matteog@iadb.org

A. Cathles
UNU-MERIT, Maastricht University, Maastricht, Netherlands
e-mail: cathles@merit.unu.edu

Most of the research has been conducted in developed countries, and there is still no robust evidence that a strong relationship also exists between productivity and IT investment in developing countries, especially at the firm level [7, 8]. This begs the question of whether developing countries are experiencing the time lag between IT investment and productivity payoffs or whether there is something inherently different about IT investment, adoption, and use in developing countries that yields a different relationship between investment and payoffs. Perhaps the answer lies in some combination of the two, but certainly research regarding possible differences in how ICTs relate to productivity in developing countries is needed. Furthermore, previous research has focused only on the generic adoption and use of ICTs and rarely drills down to the level of a specific application. In particular, several studies have evaluated the impact of Internet adoption on firm performance, but very few have examined the unique impact of various different uses of the Internet, even if they are potentially disruptive, such as e-commerce.

As the Internet has become increasingly pervasive with connections at lower costs and higher velocity, the phenomenon of e-commerce is gaining traction as a game changer that is redefining the marketplace. Today, global e-commerce is estimated to have a value that exceeds $16.2 trillion, and although there are challenges to measuring revenue from e-commerce, available evidence shows remarkable growth over the past decade – and this trend is expected to continue [9]. In the USA, the value of e-commerce shipments in the manufacturing sector increased fivefold from 1999 to 2014 – and – as a percentage of total shipments, it increased from 18% to 60% over the same time period [10]. In US retail, in 2014 the value of e-commerce shipments increased over 20 times the value in 1999 [10].

The diffusion of electronic commerce (e-commerce), defined by the OECD as "the sale or purchase of goods or services conducted over computer networks" ([11], p.72), has provided consumers and businesses with a powerful tool for reducing the cost of transactions while increasing the velocity and quality. Even if it is commonly believed that the development of e-commerce coincided with the development of Internet, in its primordial form, e-commerce has existed for over 60 years, much earlier than Internet. The first application of e-commerce can be dated back to the Berlin airlift in 1948–1949, when the US Army logistics organized a system of semiautomatic ordering of supplies via telex [12]. This inspired first the creation of common electronic formats to facilitate intragroup transactions and later, starting in the late 1970s, the development of national Electronic Data Interchange (EDI) standards. EDI is the transfer of standardized business transactions over some kind of private computer network. Clearly, before the diffusion of the Internet for commercial use, the EDI system was very expensive, because of the high costs of setting up private networks; however, EDI still represents a significant segment of e-commerce. For example, in 2013 the majority of e-commerce sales (69%) in the European Union were conducted through EDI [9]. This may be surprising since the most well-known form of e-commerce is the purchase of goods and services by consumers over the Internet, but e-commerce is a multidimensional concept which includes transactions between different economic agents.

E-commerce includes sales and purchases between businesses (B2B), from businesses to consumers (B2C), between consumers (C2C) (i.e., eBay), and from businesses to the government (B2G). It is tempting to think that businesses would derive most of their profits in e-commerce through e-selling in the form of B2C (business-to-consumer) transactions; however, this does not seem to be the case. The global value of B2B e-commerce in 2013 vastly overshadowed the value of B2C e-commerce (more than $15 trillion of the $16.2 trillion of total e-commerce transaction), albeit the global value was concentrated in very few countries (USA 36 percent; UK 18%; Japan 14%; China 10%) [9].

Considering this picture, this paper intends to look specifically at the impact of e-commerce on firm productivity levels in a developing country, by performing an empirical analysis based on microdata from the Chilean longitudinal firm survey [13–15]. This paper is organized as follows. Section 13.2 provides a brief picture of the relationship between e-commerce and productivity. In Sect. 13.3, we present some stylized facts on the Internet and e-commerce diffusion in Latin America. In Sect. 13.4, the data set used is described, and in Sect. 13.5, we present the econometric model and the main results of the empirical exercise. Section 13.6 concludes.

13.2 E-Commerce and Productivity

Theoretical literature has identified a variety of channels through which e-commerce can benefit enterprises. Clayton and Criscuolo [16] identify two primary mechanisms through which e-commerce can influence the business process: e-commerce can allow firms to access wider markets, through marketing or expanding their customer base, but it can also make business processes more efficient, by allowing cheaper and more targeted material sourcing [16]. Therefore, firms may raise labor productivity by either increasing revenues at no or little additional cost or upping the quantity of materials that contribute to firm output while keeping inputs at a relatively constant level [17]. Moreover, e-commerce can increase effectiveness by enabling firms to gain competitive advantages by improving skills in core competency areas, and it can facilitate tighter integration among key business partners, suppliers, customers, and even competitors [18]. Zwass [19] identified five domains within e-commerce that can initiate (i) more flexible distribution and procurement channels, (ii) enhanced business and customer relations management, and (iii) the introduction of completely virtual or hybrid markets all of which result in amplified collaboration among networks and improvements in complex client support within and across the business ecology [19].

In the early 2000s, scholars came out with different forecasts about the contribution of e-commerce to overall economic output. Input-output analysis was used to predict a large contribution by B2B e-commerce in productivity growth [20]. Others were more cautiously optimistic, for example, Borenstein and Saloner [21] predicted that e-commerce would mimic the effect that other technologies have had on markets and will lead to the expansion of firms' capabilities to create and capture value, spurring the restructuring of many markets, vertical disintegration, and new roles for intermediaries and concluded that despite efficiency gains that could produce overall savings in the economy, e-commerce would not all equally favor all markets [21, 22]. Others favored particular sectors, claiming that e-commerce and resulting productivity gains may depend (at least in part) on the industry sector and results from analysis on e-business surveys imply that the integration of marketing processes can have greater advantages in services than in the manufacturing sector [23]. Still others saw potential for spillovers, cost savings, improved efficiencies, and more fully integrated networks that originate in the service sector electronic systems for supply chain management and enterprise relationship management (ERM) – interestingly – may have positive spillover effects in the manufacturing sector [18]. After all, e-commerce is a network, and network effects do not increase productivity through economies of scale; they are about creating value beyond one single organization. A fax machine in one organization is useless, until a critical mass of fax machines is reached, its potential to affect productivity in the business community cannot be realized [24].

Even if there is general theoretical consensus on the positive impact of e-commerce on firm productivity [23, 25–27], empirical evidence at this respect is scarce and, because of data availability, almost exclusively focused on advanced economies.

Falk and Hagsten [28] published recent evidence from estimations based on a panel of micro-aggregated data for 14 European countries from 2002 to 2010, which revealed that engaging in e-selling (that is B2B and B2C) is increasing, but is not yet widespread in those European countries. Larger and more productive firms tended to be more engaged in e-sales, but the benefits in terms of productivity gains were greater for small or medium firms and stronger for firms in services than in manufacturing. For the whole sample over the whole time period, a 1% increase in the share of firms engaging in e-selling was associated with a 0.1 increase in labor productivity (over a 2-year period). Considering the overall economic climate in Europe during the period under consideration, these results are quite inspiring [28].

To give a sense of the degree to which e-commerce has been found to affect productivity, earlier studies that made use of firm-level data for one or two countries found the following. The usage of information computer networks in manufacturing firms in the USA resulted in a statistically robust increase in labor productivity of about 5% and that more intense the usage (intra-firm) the greater the effect on productivity (up to 7%). In Japan, the usage of information computer networks was associated with a 3% increase in productivity, yet in this case, the intensity of usage did not have a dramatic effect on productivity levels [29]. Business-to-business (B2B) e-commerce is associated with 2% increases in productivity over other firms in Germany and B2B accounted for 85% of e-commerce sales in manufacturing and 65% of e-commerce sales in services [30].

Mitigating factors found in previous studies include complementary investments,[1] innovation activities, skills of employees, ICT infrastructure, and overall levels of

---

[1] Empirical evidence from the literature on ICT invesment suggests that may be a delay or a time lapse between ICT investment and payoff in terms of productivity. Furthermore, adoption alone is not sufficient to take full advantage of the ICTs potential; the embeddness of the technolgy is important – firms need to implement complementary investment, such as those in human capital or

diffusion. Ben Aoun-Peltier and Vicente Cuervo [33] analyze e-commerce adoption and intensity separately using firm-level data from Luxembourg and find that innovating firms equipped with an ICT infrastructure adopt e-commerce, but firms with a greater proportion of employees with degrees use e-commerce more intensively, for both buying and selling [33]. A study that assesses the impact of R&D and e-commerce on productivity in firms in Taiwan finds that the positive impact of e-commerce on the productivity of firms in the same industry is affected by the degree to which technology has diffused in upstream and downstream firms [27]. This concept of the importance of diffusion and integration of e-commerce in upstream and downstream firms as a factor in the ability of a firm to exploit the full potential of e-commerce is particularly important in the context of developing countries where the levels of technological diffusion tend to be less widespread than in developed countries. As with ICTs in general, research suggests that organizational processes need to be developed to accompany e-commerce in order to ingrain adoption and usage into everyday business practices and culture and in order for firms to maximize the benefit that they can derive from e-commerce [19].

Very few studies break out the different effects of e-buying versus e-selling within the context of e-commerce. It appears that e-buying is the much more dominant form of e-commerce [34]. Two studies found that e-buying had a positive impact on productivity, whereas e-selling over the Internet did not have an effect on firm efficiency. The first study was based on data from manufacturing firms in the UK and found that e-buying was positively correlated with increases in productivity of 6% or more [17], and the other study was based on data from manufacturing firms in Spain found that, controlling for other factors, e-buying over the Internet increased efficiency to the tune of 3% gains in productivity [35].

One article by Rincon et al. [36] deviates from these general findings, arguing that the effect of e-buying and e-selling is sector specific. They reach the conclusion that the effect of e-selling and e-buying was roughly equivalent and that both were positively correlated with firm performance. In service sector, however, they find that e-selling has a comparatively greater positive effect on firm productivity than e-buying. In addition, they conclude that the productivity gain is stronger in the service sector than it is in the manufacturing sector. With firms that are in the 1–99% probability distribution of being more likely to trade over the Internet (buy or sell) – those firms in the manufacturing (or production) sector see a 24.4% increase in productivity, while firms in the service sector see a 40% increase in productivity [36].

13.2.1 E-Commerce in Latin America

In general, ICT diffusion and resulting penetration levels in Latin America and the Caribbean (LAC) is much lower than it is in developed countries. In 2014, 46% of individuals are reported as using the Internet in Latin America and the Caribbean

---

organizational change [5, 31, 32], and this may take time.

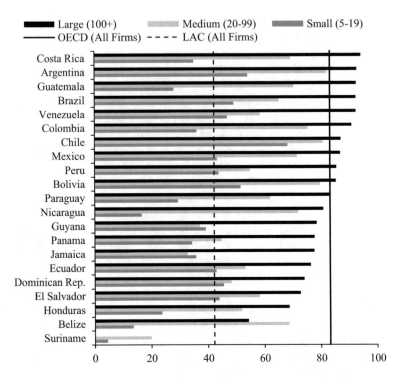

Fig. 13.1 Percent of firms with their own website in 2010 by firm size (Source: World Bank Enterprise Surveys. Notes: Data for Brazil are from 2009)

compared to 82% of individuals in the OECD [37]. Grazzi and Vergara [38] report that in the Latin American countries with the higher Internet penetration and the better connection quality (Brazil, Chile, and Costa Rica), the most used application for the Internet access is communication, information, and entertainment, where on average the share of Internet user that participate in this activities reach 67%, 63%, and 57%, respectively. On the other hand, the least used applications in these countries are purchasing, banking, and government (9%, 15%, and 18%); in Mexico, for example, 80% of Internet users participate in social networking when they are online, but less than 5% use the Internet to make an online purchase [38]. This may be partly due low adoption levels of credit cards [9].

The percentage of large firms in the more advanced economies in the LAC region with their own website is on par with percentages in the OECD, but smaller firms lag behind. Figure 13.1 shows that in Chile, for example, 87% of large firms report having their own website, whereas only 68% of small firms have their own website.

This lack of general ICT diffusion in the region is reflected in the figures relative to e-commerce. In 2013, about 4% of the global total, or an estimated 52 billion dollars were spent in Latin America on B2C e-commerce (compared to 264 billion spent by just the UK, Germany, and France); Latin America is home to 8% of the world's online buyers compared to Europe's 17%, and roughly 30% of Internet users in Latin America have made an online purchase, whereas in Europe, 64% of Internet users have purchased something online [9]. Brazil is the country in the region with the largest B2C market with 14 million buyers spending around $1,000 per year (per buyer). Brazil accounts for 38% of the region's B2C sales and six out of the ten largest Internet retailers in the region; the only other country in the region with an Internet retailer in the top 10 is Chile with SACI Falabella, the third largest Internet retailer operating in the region (the remaining three are US-based retailers).

Chile is also leading the region in UNCTAD's 2014 B2C e-commerce index (see Fig. 13.2). This index is comprised of share of population having mail delivered at home (2012 or latest year available, percent), share of individuals with credit card (15+, 2011 percent), share of individuals using Internet (2013 or latest year available, percent), and the secure servers per 1 million people (normalized, 2013).

Figures 13.1 and 13.2 confirm two important things: (i) that firms may be following the trend of the general population and might be using ICTs but may be using them for less sophisticated types of activities and (ii) that there is a difference in diffusion among differently sized firms. A study that surveyed 83 managers/owners of SMEs in the Bío region in Chile identified organizational readiness as the main discriminator between adopters and non-adopters of e-commerce in Chile. The owners stated that high implementation costs meant that the firm had to be technologically and financially ready and one non-adopting manufacturing firm said that they simply did not have the financial resources to train employees to use e-commerce [39].

13.3 Data

Empirical analysis in this paper is based on microdata from the Chilean longitudinal firm survey [13–15]. This survey captures data for 2007, 2009, and 2013 on 18,885 Chilean formal businesses of any size and sector and is statistically representative at the country level. The questionnaire divides firms into sectors within the economy and size of the business and asks general information about the business, the relationship with the financial investment system, access to the market, knowledge and use of public instruments, innovation in the business, the financial characterization of the business, and the relationship with labor and employment. In addition, the survey includes questions on the level of ICT adoption and the extent of e-commerce. The results from the survey will allow for the analysis of the relationship between e-commerce and productivity across different sectors and firms sizes in Chile. In addition, we will shed some light on the source of that relationship, either through the e-selling or the e-buying.

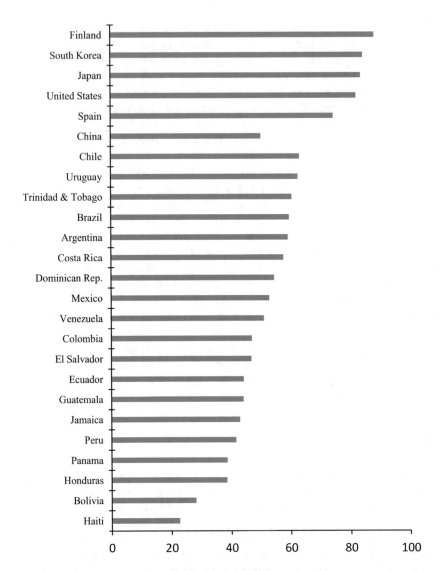

Fig. 13.2 B2C E-commerce index 2014 (Source: UNCTAD, p. 100–103)

Chilean firms in all sectors are dominated by microenterprises (800–2,400 UF[2] in sales) representing on average 45.8% of the sample, whereas the small firms (2,400–25,000 UF in sales) represent the 44.4%. Finally, the medium firms (25,000–100,000 UF in sales) represent 6.5%, and the large firms (100,000 or

---

[2] *Unidad de Fomento* (UF) is a unit of account that is used in Chile to reflect the value of real estate, housing, and secure loans. It is frequently adjusted for inflation to maintain the real value constant. In the ELE survey, the size of a firm is determined by the level of sales in terms of UFs which simplifies the comparison over time.

Table 13.1 ICTs penetration in Chile

Variable	Year	Micro (%)	Small (%)	Medium (%)	Large (%)	Total (%)	Manufacturing sector (%)	Service sector (%)
Broadband connection	2007	39.7	64.0	87.8	88.6	55.1	68.8	53.0
	2009	48.6	67.9	87.5	87.1	60.7	75.4	57.6
	2013	56.8	76.9	93.7	97.8	69.7	81.6	67.1
Website	2007	8.4	20.4	48.7	74.8	18.4	28.9	19.2
	2009	9.3	21.2	52.7	74.9	19.3	29.5	19.6
	2013	20.1	36.1	61.7	84.0	34.1	43.6	36.5
E-selling	2007	0.5	1.2	1.4	3.5	1.0	2.4	1.0
	2009	4.2	6.5	9.5	9.7	5.7	9.8	5.9
	2013	12.7	20.4	27.8	37.3	18.0	29.6	17.2
E-buying	2007	3.7	7.2	13.7	12.8	6.1	7.4	6.3
	2009	5.2	10.4	14.8	14.3	8.3	12.9	7.6
	2013	20.1	35.0	52.5	64.3	30.5	41.5	27.9
E-commerce	2007	3.8	7.9	14.4	15.5	6.7	8.8	6.8
	2009	8.0	12.8	18.9	18.3	11.1	16.8	10.8
	2013	21.3	37.6	54.4	66.6	32.4	44.1	30.0

Source: Own calculations based on ELE

more UF in sales) complete the 3.1%. Regarding to the economic activity, the proportion of firms in the manufacturing sector is far smaller than proportion of firms in the service sector in Chile. The manufacturing sector represent on average 10.9%, whereas the service sector represents 67.3% of firms in the sample.[3]

In Table 13.1 Internet and e-commerce diffusion by firm size and economic sector are presented.[4] As expected, penetration rates have been growing over time, but it varies greatly by firm size. The difference between Internet access rates and e-commerce diffusion rates is striking. Whereas the Internet access varies from 57% in microfirms to 98% in large firms in 2013, the e-commerce penetration varies from 21% to 67%, respectively, in the same year. Although, if we compare the percentage of total firms engaged in e-commerce in developed countries, Chilean firms lag behind. According to Falk and Hagsten [28], the average penetration of e-commerce in 14 countries in Europe exceeds the 45% of the firms, whereas only 32% of Chilean firms adopted the e-commerce [28].

Moreover, the manufacturing sector in Chile seems to be more "technologically ready" than firms in the service sector. This may be due the large proportion of microenterprises in service sector firms, but it may also have something to do with

---

[3] For the purposes of this paper, the service sector will be considered the aggregate of the following more specific service sectors: wholesale and retail, repair of vehicles; hotels and restaurants; transport, storage, and communications; financial intermediation; real estate, renting, and business; and other community, social, and personal type of service.

[4] Penetration rates are calculated as the share of firms with access to Internet or engaged in e-commerce, by firm size.

other firm characteristics. With a higher percentage of firms in the manufacturing sector reporting access to the Internet, broadband, computers, and new computers, it is no surprise that a higher proportion of manufacturing firms are engaging in both e-buying and e-selling.

As for the structure of e-commerce, e-buying occurs much more frequently than e-selling. It seems to indicate a prevalence of B2B model over the B2C model in the country. This may have to do with Internet diffusion levels and usages among the population, which tends to be lower than diffusion among firms (especially larger-sized firms). It could be possible that the logistic platform for the B2B is more developed than for the B2C one. Also, it could be the case that consumers have less access to financial instruments (i.e., credit cards) that are needed to access the e-business which limits the B2C model. This finding is consistent with evidence found in developed countries regarding a greater tendency in business practices toward e-buying that toward e-selling.

13.4   Empirical Approach and Results

The framework for the empirical analysis is an extended Cobb-Douglas production function of the form:

$$Q = AK^{\alpha} L^{\beta} H^{\gamma} \tag{13.1}$$

where the output Q is a function of physical capital K, labor L, and human capital H. A is a technology change term defined as a function of an e-commerce variable, of the form:

$$A = \exp\left(\delta_0 + \delta_1 \text{ECommerce}\right) \tag{13.2}$$

Expressing the variables in per-employee terms, taking logs, and adding an iid error term (e), the equation of labor productivity becomes:

$$Ln\left(\frac{Q}{L}\right) = \delta_0 + \delta_1 \text{ECommerce} + \alpha \ln\frac{K}{L} + \gamma \ln\frac{H}{L} - (\alpha + \beta - \gamma)\ln L + e \tag{13.3}$$

$$Ln\left(\frac{Q}{L}\right) = \delta_0 + \delta_1 \text{Esell} + \delta_2 \text{Ebuy} + \alpha \ln\frac{K}{L} + \gamma \ln\frac{H}{L} - (\alpha + \beta - \gamma)\ln L + e \tag{13.4}$$

Equations 13.3 and 13.4 use different specifications of the e-commerce term, to show joint and separated effects of e-selling and e-buying. eSell and eBuy are defined as dummy variables taking value 1 if the firm sells or purchases on the Internet, respectively. In addition to these factors, we include in any equation a set of controls for observable firm heterogeneity, including the age of the firm, the

Table 13.2 The relationship between e-commerce and productivity in Chile

Dependent variable: log of labor productivity						
	Total		Manufacturing		Service	
E-commerce	0.17***		0.25***		0.12**	
	(0.04)		(0.07)		(0.05)	
E-selling		−0.06		0.13		−0.05
		(0.06)		(0.09)		(0.07)
E-buying		0.20***		0.18**		0.17***
		(0.04)		(0.08)		(0.05)
Age	0.01***	0.01***	−0.01**	−0.01**	0.01***	0.01***
	(0.00)	(0.00)	(0.00)	(0.00)	(0.00)	(0.00)
Age^2	−0.00	−0.00	0.00***	0.00***	−0.00***	−0.00***
	(0.00)	(0.00)	(0.00)	(0.00)	(0.00)	(0.00)
Log of capital per worker	0.05***	0.05***	0.07***	0.07***	0.04***	0.04***
	(0.00)	(0.00)	(0.01)	(0.01)	(0.00)	(0.00)
Log of employees	−0.46***	−0.46***	−0.31***	−0.31***	−0.47***	−0.47***
	(0.03)	(0.03)	(0.05)	(0.05)	(0.03)	(0.03)
Log of share of skilled workers	0.02***	0.02***	0.00	0.00	0.01***	0.01***
	(0.00)	(0.00)	(0.01)	(0.01)	(0.00)	(0.00)
Log of share of exports	0.07***	0.07***	0.06***	0.06***	0.06***	0.07***
	(0.01)	(0.01)	(0.01)	(0.01)	(0.01)	(0.01)
Constant	16.38***	16.39***	15.35***	15.33***	16.36***	16.36***
	(0.11)	(0.11)	(0.22)	(0.23)	(0.14)	(0.14)
Firm size FE	Yes	Yes	Yes	Yes	Yes	Yes
Time FE	Yes	Yes	Yes	Yes	Yes	Yes
Observations	19,612	19,612	2691	2691	12,038	12,038
R-squared	0.549	0.550	0.660	0.660	0.554	0.555

Source: Own calculations based on ELE 1, 2, and 3. Standard errors in parentheses
*$p < 0.10$,**$p < 0.05$,***$p < 0.01$

export conditions, and time and size dummies.[5] The results from the weighted OLS regressions are reported in Table 13.2.[6]

The results seem consistent with the evidence in the developed countries. We find a significant positive relationship between e-commerce and labor productivity. If a firm is engaged in e-commerce, on average, its productivity will be 17% higher than a firm that is not engaged in e-commerce. Also in line with previous evidence, productivity gains seem to derive from e-buying and not from e-selling.

---

[5] Summary statistics of the variables in the regression are presented in Table 13.3 in the Appendix.

[6] We acknowledge this specification may have problems of endogeneity (i.e., the most productive firms engaged more in e-commerce activities). Therefore, we estimated also an IV model using as instruments the age of the manager and the density of e-commerce usage in the same sector of the firm. The results are consistent with the OLS estimation.

Disaggregating by sector, in Table 13.1 we showed that manufacturing firms are more engaged with e-commerce than those in the service sector. The results of the econometric exercise confirm the existence of different dynamics in the two sectors: the coefficients in the two sectors are both highly significant, but the one for manufacturing is twice larger than the one for services (25% vs. 12%). Again, in both sectors we find that the e-buying channel dominates the e-selling in explaining this relationship, and interestingly, when analyzing the different e-commerce channels, this difference between sectors tends to concentrate in the different effect of e-selling. Although not significant, the coefficient in the case of services is negative, while in manufacturing remains positive.

13.5   Conclusions

Over the last half-century, Latin America has failed to catch up with developed countries. Actually, the average income per capita has declined in comparison to the USA, decreasing from 1/4 in 1960 to 1/6 today [40]. There is widespread consensus on the fact that slow productivity growth is at the root of this weak economic performance [41].

Therefore, it is a priority for economies in Latin America to find channels to obtain substantial productivity gains. In this context, a deeper understanding of the potential impacts of e-commerce, which promises to be a very important aspect of private sector businesses in the coming years, is key. In fact, a risk for all empirical analysis is that it is constrained to the availability and the quality of the data. In developing countries, there is often a shortage of available data that are of high quality. The natural tendency then is to turn to evidence from developed countries in the hopes that the results and implications of empirical analysis will have similar applications across different settings. In the case of e-commerce, this could be particularly risky, as most of the existing empirical evidence has been produced in advanced countries.

This paper contributes to this discussion by studying the relationship between e-commerce and productivity using microdata from the Chilean longitudinal firm survey. What the results of this document imply is that firms engaged in e-commerce are substantially more productive than those which are not also in the context of an emerging economy. Nevertheless, this effect seems to be caused only by B2B transactions, while B2C commerce is not found to have a significant impact on productivity. Even if the effect of e-commerce is found to be larger in the case of firms operating in the manufacturing sector, it is relevant also for firms of the services sector.

This is particularly interesting, because not only the service sector employ a significant proportion of the population of the region, but its underperformance is cited as the biggest sectoral culprit in dragging aggregate productivity levels downward [42]. Therefore, any gains that can be realized in that sector could constitute a meaningful opportunity for Latin American economies to reduce the productivity gap with advanced economies.

Appendix (Table 13.3)

Table 13.3 Descriptive statistics, regression variables

Variables	Mean	Median	SD	Min	Max
Labor productivity (millions of pesos)	168	16	2,636	0	164,258
Age of the firm	14	13	12	0	157
Capital (millions of pesos)	6,794	9	101,474	0	8,002,542
Employees	907	33	5,465	1	325,841
Share of skilled workers	22	5	32	0	100
Share of exports	4	2	17	0	100

References

1. Dedrick, J., Gurbaxani, V., & Kraemer, K. (2003). Information technology and economic performance: A critical review of the empirical evidence. *ACM Computing Surveys, 35*, 1–28.
2. Jorgenson, D. W., & Stiroh, K. J. (1999). Information technology and growth. *American Economic Review, 89*(2), 109–115.
3. Jorgenson, D. W., & Stiroh, K. J. (2000). Raising the speed limit: US economic growth in the information age. *Brookings Papers on Economic Activity, 1*, 125–235.
4. Oliner, S., & Sichel, D. (2000). The resurgence of growth in the late 1990s: Is information technology the story? *Journal of Economic Perspectives, 14*(4), 3–22.
5. Bresnahan, T. F., Brynjolfsson, E., & Hitt, L. M. (2002). Information technology, workplace organization, and the demand for skilled labour: Firm level evidence. *The Quarterly Journal of Economics, 117*(1), 339–376.
6. Brynjolfsson, E., & Hitt, L. M. (2003). Computing productivity: Firm-level evidence. *The Review of Economics and Statistics, 85*(4), 793–808.
7. Dewan, S., & Kraemer, K. L. (2000). Information technology and productivity: Evidence from country-level data. *Management Science, 46*(4), 548–576.
8. Pohjola, M. (2001). *Information technology, productivity, and economic growth: International evidence and implications for economic development*. Oxford: Oxford University Press.
9. UNCTAD. (2015). Information economy report. Unlocking the potential of e-commerce for developing countries. United Nations Publication.
10. U.S. Census Bureau (n.d.). http://www.census.gov/estats.
11. OECD. (2011). *OECD guide to measuring the information society 2011*. Paris: OECD.
12. Zwass, V. (1996). Electronic commerce: Structures and issues. *International Journal of Electronic Commerce, 1*, 3–23.
13. ELE Encuesta Longitudinal de Empresas. (2008). Gobierno de Chile and Observatorio Empresas.
14. ELE Encuesta Longitudinal de Empresas. (2012). Gobierno de Chile and Observatorio Empresas.
15. ELE Encuesta Longitudinal de Empresas. (2015). Gobierno de Chile and Observatorio Empresas.
16. Clayton, T., Criscuolo, C. (2002). E-Commerce and business change. *Economic Trends, 583*, 62–69.
17. Criscuolo, C., & Waldron, K. (2003). E-commerce and firm productivity. *Economic Trends, 600*, 52–57.
18. Carayannis, E., Alexander, J., & Geraghty, J. (2001). Service sector productivity: B2B electronic commerce as a strategic driver. *Journal of Technology Transfer, 26*, 337–350.
19. Zwass, V. (2003). Electronic commerce and organizational innovation: Aspects and opportunities. *International Journal of Electronic Commerce, 7*, 7–37.
20. Brookes, M., Wahhaj, Z. (2000). *The shocking economic effect of B2B*. Global Economics Paper No. 37. Goldman Sachs, New York, NY.

21. Borenstein, S., & Saloner, G. (2001). Economics and electronic commerce. *Journal of Economic Perspectives, 15*, 3–12.
22. Luckling-Reiley, D., & Spulber, D. (2000). Business-to-business electronic commerce. *The Journal of Economic Perspectives, 15*(1), 55–68.
23. Goodridge, P., & Clayton, T. (2004). E-business and labor productivity in manufacturing and services. *Economic Trends, 609*, 47–53.
24. Kelly, K. (1998). *New rules for the new economy*. New York: Penguin Group.
26. Colombo, M. G., Croce, A., & Grilli, L. (2013). ICT services and small businesses' productivity gains: An analysis of the adoption of broadband internet technology. *Information Economics and Policy, 25*(3), 171–189.
27. Liu, T. K., Chen, J. R., Huang, C. C. J., & Yang, C. H. (2013). E-commerce, R&D and productivity: Firm-level evidence from Taiwan. *Information Economics and Policy, 25*(4), 272–283.
25. Chen, J.R., Lin, T.K., Huang, C. (2004). Electronic commerce, R&D, externalities, and productivity – an empirical study of Taiwanese Manufacturing Firms. Presented at Asia-Pacific Productivity Conference (APPC), July 14–16.
28. Falk M., Hagsten, E. (2015). E-commerce trends and impacts across Europe. UNCTAD Discussion Paper: UNCTAD/OSG/DP/2015/2 March.
29. Atrostic, B.K., Motohashi, K., Nguyen, S. (2008). Computer network use and firms' productivity performance: The United States vs. Japan. Bureau of the Census, CES 08-30.
30. Bertschek, I., & Kaiser, U. (2004). Productivity effects of organizational change: Microeconometric evidence. *Management Science, 50*, 394–404.
32. Crespi, G., Criscuolo, C., Haskel, J. (2007) Information technology, organisational change and productivity growth: Evidence from UK Firms. CEP Discussion Paper.
31. Bertschek, I., Fryges, H., & Kaiser, U. (2006). B2B or not to be: Does B2B e-commerce increase labour productivity? *International Journal of the Economics of Business, 13*, 387–405.
33. Ben Aoun-Peltier, L., Vicente Cuervo, M.R. (2012). E-commerce diffusion: Exploring the determinants of the adoption and the extent of usage at firm-level. Working paper No. 57, STATEC, Luxembourg.
34. Hollenstein, H., & Woerter, M. (2008). Inter – and intra – firm diffusion of technology: The example of e-commerce, an analysis based on Swiss firm-level data. *Research Policy, 37*, 545–564.
35. Romero, C. Q., & Rodriguez, D. (2010). E-commerce and efficiency at the firm level. *International Journal of Production Economics, 126*, 299–305.
36. Rincon, A., Robinson, C., Vecchi, M. (2005). The productivity impact of e-commerce in the UK, 2001: Evidence from microdata. NIESR WP 257.
37. ITU (n.d.). http://www.itu.int/en/ITU-D/Statistics/Pages/stat/default.aspx
38. Grazzi, M., Vergara, S. (2014). Internet in Latin America: Who uses it? … and for what? *Economics of Innovation and New Technology, 23(4)*, 327–352.
39. Grandon, E., & Pearson, J. M. (2004). E-commerce adoption: Perceptions of managers/owners of small and medium sized firms in Chile. *Communications of the Association for Information Systems, 13*, 81–102. Article 8.
40. IDB. (2016). In M. Grazzi & C. Pietrobelli (Eds.), *Firm and productivity in Latin America and the Caribbean: The engine of economic development*. Washington, DC: Inter-American Development Bank-Palgrave-Macmillan.
41. IDB. (2014). In G. Crespi, F. Fernadez-Arias, & E. Stein (Eds.), *Rethinking productive development: Sound policies and institutions for economic transformation*. Washington, DC: Inter-American Development Bank-Palgrave-Macmillan.
42. IDB. (2010). The importance of ideas: Innovation and productivity in Latin America. In C. Pagés (Ed.), *The age of productivity: Transforming economies from the bottom up. Development in the Americas*. Washington, DC: Inter-American Development Bank-Palgrave-McMillan.

Part V
Europe

Chapter 14
Assessing the Economic Potential of Big Data Industries

Ana Salomé García-Muñiz and María Rosalía Vicente

Abstract Information and communication technologies have made possible that data can be collected and processed at rates previously unseen. It is the big data phenomenon, which holds potential to boost innovation and improve productivity growth.

This chapter attempts to provide some evidence of the strengths and challenges faced by big data industries. Attention is focused on the position that these industries hold within the economic network in terms of their access to information and knowledge. To achieve this aim, network analysis is used over input-output table information. Given the absence of appropriate statistical data for developing countries, attention is paid to two developed countries, Slovenia and Slovakia, which show some common features in their patterns of digital development with some developing countries. Results show that while the levels of efficiency of these industries are high, they are missing some key economic links with other sectors of the economy.

Keywords Big data • Input-output analysis (IO) • Information and communication technologies (ICT) • Network analysis • Structural holes

14.1 Introduction

One of the most relevant features of the past few years has been the explosion in the generation, collection, and diffusion of data. It is the "big data" phenomenon: thanks to information and communication technologies (ICT), data collection is taking place at rates of quantity and speed previously unseen.

A.S. García-Muñiz (✉)
REGIOLab, Applied Economics, University of Oviedo, Oviedo, Spain
e-mail: asgarcia@uniovi.es

M.R. Vicente
Applied Economics, University of Oviedo, Oviedo, Spain
e-mail: mrosalia@uniovi.es

© Springer International Publishing AG 2017
H. Kaur et al. (eds.), *Catalyzing Development through ICT Adoption*,
DOI 10.1007/978-3-319-56523-1_14

As United Nations ([34], p. 2) states "data are the lifeblood of decision-making and the raw material for accountability. Without high-quality data providing the right information on the right things at the right time; designing, monitoring and evaluating effective policies becomes almost impossible."

Within this context, "big data" can open up great possibilities in order "to unlock new sources of economic value" ([32], p.1), to improve citizens' well-being [28], and, furthermore, to address the needs of developing countries [16, 28, 36, 40].[1]

However, the realization of the "big data" opportunities faces some big challenges: not only might countries lack the appropriate infrastructure and skills to deal with these data, but furthermore in some countries, there is little data available about these particular activities in order to evaluate their current situation and assess the potential strengths and weaknesses of the firms and sectors involved. Thus the novelty of the phenomenon and the lack of appropriate statistics hinder the measurement of the social and economic impacts of big data activities.

This is specially the case of developing countries. As United Nations ([34], p. 11) recognizes "too many countries still have poor data (…) and too many issues are still barely covered by existing data." Within this context, the analysis of big data industries in other nations, where there is available and updated information, could offer useful insights for developing countries.

Henceforth, the aim of this chapter is to provide some evidence on the economic importance of big data industries as enablers of the diffusion knowledge and innovation. In particular, we try to assess their position within the economic network and identify strengthens and weaknesses. To achieve this aim, we apply network analysis tools over input-output table information.

Given the lack of appropriate data to carry out such an analysis for developing countries, the attention in this chapter is focused on two developed nations, Slovenia and Slovakia. These two countries have been chosen by three main reasons. In the first place, they have updated information of big data industries which allow making an appropriate analysis of these activities. In the second place, while they are both developed nations, they do not enjoy the levels of wealth of some of the "old" members of the European Union (EU); accordingly, the analysis of big data industries in these countries might provide more useful insights for developing nations than those that could be gathered by studying other more developed nations. Finally, the conditions of the digital economy in Slovenia and Slovakia are similar to those of some developing nations, as shown by the Networked Readiness Index elaborated by the World Economic Forum [42]. In particular, the values of the Network Readiness Index in 2016 for Slovenia (4.7) and Slovakia (4.4) are something akin to the obtained indexes for some developing countries such as Chile (4.6), Kazakhstan (4.5), South Africa (4.2), Trinidad and Tobago (4.1), Turkey (4.4), and Uruguay (4.5),[2] among others [42].

---

[1] United Nations Global Pulse [37] has created the network of innovation labs, Global Pulse, with the aim of taking advantage of the potential of big data for human development, sustainable development, and humanitarian aid.

[2] Chile, Kazakhstan, South Africa, Trinidad and Tobago, Turkey, and Uruguay are all classified as developing nations by the United Nations [35].

The chapter is organized as follows. The next section presents the literature review on the potential of big data for economic development. In Sect. 14.3, we describe the methodology used and, in particular, the tools from network analysis employed. Then, data sources are presented and results commented. We finally draw some concluding remarks.

14.2 Background

As already mentioned, big data has become one of the hottest topics in the business and economics field over the last few years. While data has always been an essential component of economic activity, it was difficult and costly to collect. At the present moment, information and communication technologies allow to collect and produce data at superfast speeds, in very large quantities, and with low costs. According, data has reinforced its role in creating economic value by enabling new ways to spur innovation and productivity growth [22, 23, 26, 28].

Much of the big data is generated within the firm: it is the data coming from firms' daily activities and processes. While this data has been traditionally considered as a side product of firm' main activity, now it has become a key input for the improvement of business' efficiency and productivity.

Some big data is produced outside of the firm. There are companies which main business consists in collecting data and selling it to others. In addition, other big data comes from the public sector which is a major collector and producer of data as an essential element to carry out its public functions [38, 39]. In fact, governments worldwide have started to progressively make their data available to the general public, that is, they are making it open [38, 39].

Essentially there are two main ways in which all this big data can generate value added: data-driven decision-making and data-driven innovation.

On the one hand, managers can use data to improve their decision-making. As McAfee and Brynjolfsson ([22], p. 62) indicate, "because of big data, managers can measure, and hence know, radically more about their business, and directly translate that knowledge into improved decision making and performance" and productivity growth.

On the other hand, big data can be used to innovate. Hence, firms can apply big data to develop new products, services, and processes or to improve the existing ones [23, 26, 28]. In this sense, OECD [26] has identified five key areas for data-driven innovation: (i) the development of new products, by using data as a product or as a key input, (ii) the optimization or automatization of processes, (iii) the improvement of marketing, (iv) the development of new management and organizational practices, and (v) the boost of research and development activities. In fact, the so-called app economy is no other thing that the result of the use of big data to develop new products and services, the apps [27].

Online companies were among the first firms to exploit the potential of big data: they tracked their customers' visits and collected the related data (e.g., the products/services they bought, the links they clicked, the time spent on the website, the products/services checked), in order to know more about their clients and use that information to personalize offers to them.

Nowadays, big data has overcome the boundaries of the online world, and firms from every sector and industry are trying to find ways to take advantage of it and fulfill the potential it offers [23]. Hence, in the last few years, there has been an increasing tendency toward investments in data-related technologies and services across all the sectors of the economy [28]. Specially remarking are firms' investments in data specialists. In fact, one of the key elements for firms to be successful in the use of big data is to have workers with the appropriate skills – much of big data is unstructured and presents different formats and hence requires very high-skilled workforce who are able to process all this data and put it in a comprehensible way. Furthermore, firms need workers who are able to make sense of all this data and extract some economic value from it. Hence, one of the major threats to the big data revolution is the lack of data specialists. Though there is no unique definition on data-related skills, there is some agreement in the literature about the need of personnel with some knowledge in statistics, computer science, and business, who are able to clean and organize large data sets, who know how to use visualization tools, and who can extract business and economic insights from the data [22, 26, 28]. Accordingly, the demand for professionals with such kind of skills has been consistently rising over the last years. Apart from the ICT industries, the economic activities which are hiring more data specialists are insurance and finance, science and research and development, advertising and market research, and the public sector [28].

Within this context, the measurement of the economic effects of big data has become a major issue. Much of the available empirical evidence is based on cases studies in the business literature [22, 32]; meanwhile economic studies which estimate the impact of big data for firms and economic sectors are not many. Nonetheless, their results suggest that firms' use of big data can boost their innovation and productivity growth [1, 3, 31]. In this sense, recent research [3] has shown that companies relying on "data-driving decision-making" show higher performance than rival firms. In particular, they are about 5% more productive than those firms which do not use data so intensively in their decision-making processes [3]. Likewise, Bakhshi et al. [1] find that companies that do an intensive use of online customer data are between 8% and 13% more productive than those with low levels of data use [1]. In the same line, Tambe [31] estimates that firms' investments in data-related technologies (measured by the shares of data specialists in their total workforce) are associated with faster productivity growths. In particular, his results indicate that productivity growth is 3% faster for firms doing such kind of investments, provided that they have already invested in data assets and that they are operating in markets where there is availability of complementary inputs. Specifically, Tambe [31] reports the importance of firms' being able to access labor markets with workers with complementary skills to data investments. It is also worth noticing that there is some other evidence on the particular impact of the use of public big data by firms, that is, the data collected and produced by the public sector and that is becoming progressively available to the public (firms, citizens, institutions). In this sense, Koski [18] found that the free provision of geographical public data was associated with 15% higher annual firm growth compared to countries where this kind of data was priced. Moreover, and as highlighted by Tambe [31], he underlines the importance of complementary inputs for data-driven innovation, i.e., firm's absorptive capacity, ICT use, and external information sources [19].

In spite of all this evidence, it is important to bear in mind that the measurement of the economic impact of big data is not an easy task: on the one hand, and given the relative novelty of this phenomenon, there is no standard framework to address its measurement, and there is a dramatic lack of data to carry out a proper economic analysis, especially in what regards developing countries; on the other hand, many of its benefits are not captured by market transactions [20, 21, 28]. Furthermore, the percentage of firms making use of big data is still very low. For example, European Parliament [11] recalls that only 1.7% of European firms make full use of advanced digital technologies (including data-related ones). For developing economies, such information is not available, but it is very likely to be even lower.

In addition, the studies carried out on the economic impact of big data suffer from some limitations which do not allow to generalize their estimates [28]. In this sense, it is important to take into account that the potential positive effects of big data vary across economic sectors and the successful implementation of data initiatives do depend on the availability of complementary inputs, e.g., high-skilled workforce with abilities related to data processing and analytics [19, 28, 31]. Moreover, these studies suffer from some kind of selection bias as highlighted by OECD [28]: estimations are gathered from samples of high-technology firms located on developed economies (mostly the United States, USA).

Hence, the need for more studies allows to better understand the economic potential of big data activities [28]. This is the aim that the present chapter tries to achieve by providing further empirical evidence on the role of big data industries within the economic network.

14.3 Methodology

The raising importance of big data has gone with growing interests and efforts to quantify its economic impact [5, 25].

It is important to bear in mind that a proper analysis of the economic importance of any industry requires taking into account its role in the diffusion of knowledge and innovation throughout the economy. In the particular case of big data industries, their size in the economy is not much (by now), but their importance relies on the effects derived from its widespread diffusion across the economy. As the Networked European Software and Services Initiative ([25], p. 3) indicates "big data software and services generate value by supporting an innovative eco-system and by enabling completely new solutions that have not been possible before" throughout the full economic network.

In this context, it becomes essential to consider the intersectoral relationships established in the industry network. Input-output (IO) analysis reveals as a very useful tool to achieve this goal, since it details the interdependencies between sectors. Recent studies [14, 15, 29, 30] have incorporated the network theory in the input-output framework in order to capture some qualitative features of the industry network. In this sense, network analysis can bring some novel insights into the potential of new technologies to facilitate knowledge flows and, consequently, to generate new sources of income and wealth. The flow of information and resources between two industries depends not only on their relationship to each other but also on their links to everyone else.

To take account of these features, three network measures have been considered: centrality, technical efficiency, and constraints, the latter two based on Burt' Structural Hole theory [4].

Centrality is a basic feature in the network. Though there is no unique definition, centrality measures aim to identify the key nodes in a network. Many measures of centrality have been proposed along the years. In the present analysis, we will be using the eigenvector centrality [2]. This is a standardized measurement based on the algebraic method of the eigenvector calculation, which takes into account not only the direct relations a sector has but also how well connected are the sectors to which it is connected.

Complementary, and following Burt' Structural Hole theory [4], we can consider the different positions that individuals (sectors) hold within a network in terms of the possibilities they have to access to information and, hence, to knowledge. In particular, some individuals (industries) are better positioned than others. Within this context, relations can be classified as redundant or nonredundant, where nonredundant linkages are characterized by the fact that they give access to more varied and less homogenous information and thereafter they can facilitate innovation. Hence, nonredundant relations imply that competitive advantages can be gained over the others. According to Burt [4], these nonredundant links would be connected by structural holes.

Methodologically, the measurement of nonredundant relations is gathered in the so-called effective size [4]. The effective size (TE) is calculated as:

$$\text{TE}_i = \sum_j \left[1 - \sum_q p_{iq} m_{jq} \right]; q \neq i, j \tag{14.1}$$

where index q refers to those individuals (industries) that are connected to both individuals (industry) i and j, p_{iq} shows the proportion of direct relations, and m_{jq} represents the marginal intensity of individual (industry) j in relation to individual (industry) q. The relative measure of these nonredundant relations is called efficiency index, which is bounded between 0 and 1: values closer to 1 (0) indicate high (low) levels of efficiency, meaning high (low) access to nonredundant relations and thus a good (bad) position in the network in terms of access to information and knowledge.

While the level of nonredundant relations is a basic indicator of an individual's (industry's) position in the economic network, such position can be constrained by the existence of dependences between individuals (industries). When the levels of these dependences are high, the benefits of nonredundant links can be small, even for a high-efficiency industry, as long as it suffered from the non-favorable conditions of those industries it depends on. In order to measure the degree of dependence between individuals (industries), Burt [4] defines a constraint index as:

$$C_i = \sum_j c_{ij} \tag{14.2}$$

where

$$c_{ij} = \left(p_{ij}^* + \sum_q p_{iq}^* p_{qj}^* \right)^2 ; q \neq i, j \tag{14.3}$$

p_{ij}^* is the relative intensity of the relations between i sector and j sector, and $p_{iq}^* (p_{qj}^*)$ are defined analogously.

14.4 Data and Results

In order to analyze the capacity of the big data-related industries for technological diffusion, for enhancing innovation, and for creating new market opportunities, it is essential to work with a homogeneous and widely accepted definition. In 2012, the OECD Working Party on Measurement and Analysis of the Digital Economy (WPMADE) attempted to measure big data-related activities from a National Accounts perspective. With this aim, they defined big data-related industries as those activities which aim was to collect, process, and diffuse digital data ([28], p. 74). Based on the International Standard Industrial Classification of All Economic Activities (ISIC, Rev.4), this definition included the following activities: (5812) publishing directories and mailing lists; (5819) other publishing activities; (6311) data processing, hosting, and related activities; and (6312) web data portals.[3] This is the framework adopted in the present analysis order to study big data industries.

The description of the interindustry relationships of big data-related activities requires the use of input-output table data, provided that there is enough disaggregation at the industry level. In the particular cases of analysis, Slovenia and Slovakia, the latest input-output tables refer to the year 2010 with a level of disaggregation of 64 industries (NACE rev. 2) and 64 products (CPA 2008) [13]. Such disaggregation provides enough information to be able to identify the big data-related industries.

---

[3] The big data-related industries are identified by the codes of the International Standard Industrial Classification (ISIC, Rev. 4).

Table 14.1 Correspondence between ISIC and NACE

ISIC (Rev.4)	Sector IO/NACE 2
5812 Publishing of directories and mailing lists	Sector 37/CPA J58. Publishing services
5819 Other publishing activities	
6311 Data processing, hosting, and related activities	Sector 40/CPA J62 y 63. Computer programming, consultancy, and related services; information services
6312 Web portals	

Source: own elaboration using Eurostat [13] and OECD [28]

Nonetheless, a very careful matching process is necessary in order to find the correspondence between the OECD definition and the information contained in the IO tables: the OECD definition relies on the International Standard Industrial Classification of All Economic Activities (ISIC, Rev.4) which was released in its fourth revision by the United Nations in August 2008; meanwhile, in the European member states, IO tables are based on the Statistical Classification of Economic Activities of the European Community (NACE 2), released in the year 2002. Following the correspondence between the two classifications, ISIC and NACE, we can identify the big data-related industries included in the IO table as those presented in Table 14.1.

It is important to bear in mind that these IO sectors include not only big data-related industries but also some other activities that might not be related to big data. Accordingly, and in order to make a rigorous and proper analysis of the sector, it would be necessary to isolate the part that is strictly related to big data. Henceforth, we have to disaggregate sectors 40 and 37 from the input-output table into the four mentioned big data industries.

However, such task is not free of difficulties due to the lack of appropriate information and different possible disaggregation methods. Some selection variables are then needed to be able to separate big data subsectors from the ones that are not. Moreover, disaggregation has to take place at two levels (rows and columns), since the input-output table is a double-entry table for purchases and sales.

Given that the considered four big data industries belong to the services field, we use data from the annual detailed enterprise statistics for services [12] to identify and isolate big data industries. Specifically, data about the valued added and turnover are used. These two variables allow us to carry out the aforementioned disaggregation by columns and rows, respectively. In particular, the distribution of value added and turnover (see the percentages in Tables 14.2 and 14.3) is assumed to be the same along the particular row and column analyzed; in other words, we assume that the structure of purchases and sales equals the figures of value added and turnover.

Once the big data industries have been identified and their information disaggregated, their position in the economic network is analyzed through the network measures described in the previous section. Hence, efficiency, constraint, and eigenvector levels are calculated for Slovenian and Slovakian economies.

Table 14.2 Value added and turnover. Slovenia 2010 (million EUR)

Big data industries	Value added		Turnover	
(ISIC Rev.4.)	Big data	%	Big data	%
58.12 Publishing of directories and mailing lists	0.5	0.45	1.8	0.51
58.19 Other publishing activities	9.8	8.78	25.3	7.20
63.11 Data processing, hosting and related activities	43.6	9.96	102.8	9.87
63.12 Web portals	10.6	2.42	38.9	3.73

Source: Eurostat [12]

Table 14.3 Value added and turnover. Slovakia 2010 (million EUR)

	Value added		Turnover	
Big data industries (ISIC Rev.4.)	Big data	%	Big data	%
58.12 Publishing of directories and mailing lists	0	0	0.1	0.03
58.19 Other publishing activities	31.2	23.09	83.9	25.94
63.11 Data processing, hosting and related activities	217.8	27.25	324.8	20.05
63.12 Web portals	0.4	0.05	0.9	0.06

Source: Eurostat [12]

Tables 14.4 and 14.5 provide some descriptive statistics of the aforementioned network measures in Slovenia and Slovakia: the mean, the standard deviation, and the correlation coefficients between the network metrics and two key economic indicators, i.e., value added and output at basic prices. Results are presented as a matrix where the elements above the diagonal refer to the four activities identified as big data industries; whereas those below the diagonal correspond to the rest of the economy, that is, the non-big data sectors.

Results for Slovenia show that big data industries have high levels of efficiency (0.802), though they are a bit below the average efficiency for the rest of the economy (0.823). Hence, big data activities, while holding a good position in the economic network and being able to access nonredundant information and knowledge (efficiency in the threshold of 0.8), do not contribute to promote diffusion and innovation throughout the economy as much as other industries.

Moreover, big data industries do not present as many important connections with key sectors as other activities: the values of the eigenvector vector for big data industries (0.075) are below those computed for the rest of the economy (0.107).

Nonetheless, there are some positive features about Slovenian big data industries. A first strong point is that they have, on average, less constrained networks than those of the rest of the economy (note the averages for constraints: 0.119 in the big data sector compared to 0.122 in other industries). The level of constraint points out that big data activities have fewer restrictions and need lower investments in the configuration of their network of relationships than the rest of the productive industries.

In addition, big data industries show stronger correlations with economic indicators. In particular, efficiency is highly correlated with both output and value

Table 14.4 Results of network metrics for the Slovenian productive network: big data industries (above the diagonal) and non-big data industries (below the diagonal)

		Mean (S.D)	Network metrics			Economic indicators	
			Constraint	Efficiency	Eigenvector	Output	Value added
			0.119 (0.016)	0.802 (0.003)	0.075 (0.0015)	330.858 (395.86)	18.738 (22.287)
Network metrics	Constraint	*0.122 (0.058)*	1	0.697 (0.303)	0.114 (0.886)	0.351 (0.649)	0.591 (0.409)
	Efficiency	*0.823 (0.025)*	*−0.099 (0.440)*	1	0.353 (0.647)	0.902* (0.098)	0.816 (0.184)
	Eigenvector	*0.107 (0.061)*	*−0.323*** (0.010)*	*0.470** (0.000)*	1	0.567 (0.433)	0.812 (0.188)
Economic indicators	Output	*1076.109 (1194.31)*	*−0.026 (0.842)*	*−0.039 (0.762)*	*−0.051 (0.685)*	1	0.835 (0.165)
	Value added	*474.818 (532.474)*	*−0.120 (0.349)*	*0.239 (0.059)*	*0.361*** (0.003)*	*0.171 (0.173)*	1

Source: own elaboration

S.D stands for standard deviation. Figures in italics refer to non-big data industries

*, ** , and *** indicate, respectively, that the correlation is significant at the 0.10, 0.05, and 0.01 levels (two-tailed)

Table 14.5 Results of network metrics for the Slovakian productive network: big data industries (above the diagonal) and non-big data industries (below the diagonal) (Source: own elaboration)

		Mean	(S.D)	Network metrics			Economic indicators	
				Constraint	Efficiency	Eigenvector	Output	Value added
Network metrics	Constraint	*0.173*	*(0.079)*	1	−0.163	0.540	0.296	0.370
					(0.837)	(0.460)	(0.704)	(0.630)
	Efficiency	*0.841*	*(0.042)*	−0.015	1	−0.896	−0.291	−0.212
				(0.906)		(0.104)	(0.709)	(0.788)
	Eigenvector	*0.101*	*(0.070)*	−0.207	0.502***	1	0.540	0.503
				(0.106)	(0.000)		(0.460)	(0.497)
Economic indicators	Output	*2314.447*	*(2979.279)*	−0.273**	0.202	0.560***	1	0.993**
				(0.032)	(0.115)	(0.000)		(0.007)
	Value added	*912.090*	*(1174.582)*	−0.341***	0.284**	0.580***	0.823***	1
				(0.007)	(0.025)	(0.000)	(0.000)	

S.D stands for standard deviation. Figures in italics refer to non-big data industries

*, **, and *** indicate, respectively, that the correlation is significant at the 0.10, 0.05 and 0.01 levels (two-tailed)

added (correlation coefficients over 0.8). Such result suggests that efficiency improvements might easily translate into better economic performance, provided that constraints keep their low levels.

Within the big data sector, the low values of the standard deviation computed for the three network metrics indicate that the four considered industries seem to behave quite alike in terms of the level of connections with other activities, the access to nonredundant information, and constraints.

These lower levels of efficiency and centrality of Slovenian big data industries (compared to the rest of economic sectors) might be an indication that investments in research and development (R&D) activities in this sector are not enough as to promote and foster its role in the diffusion of knowledge within the economic network. In fact, the figures of the ICT sector business enterprise R&D (BERD) expenditure (as a share of total BERD)[4] show that Slovenia is below the European average and toward the bottom of the distribution of European countries: in Slovenia the share of the ICT sector BERD was about 10% in the period 2010–2012 compared to the European average of 17% [17].

Some more insights into the elements that potentially weaken Slovenian big data industries (and that explain its lower levels of efficiency) can be gained by looking at the general development of its digital economy. As already commented in the second section of this chapter, the potential of big data industries largely depends on having the right technology (infrastructure) to process and analyze this data but also on having a workforce with the appropriate skills and complementary inputs. Composite indicators such as the Networked Readiness Index of the World Economic Forum [41, 42] and the Digital Economy and Society Index (DESI) developed by the European Commission [8] can help us to assess the availability of these elements, since they summarize the main dimensions of a country's digital development.

In this sense, the values of the Networked Readiness Index show that Slovenia is quite well positioned in the digital economy, ranking 37th over a total of 143 nations [42]. In particular, it stands out in ICT infrastructure, skilled population, and e-business tools. However, "Slovenia does not manage to completely leverage the full economic potential of ICTs for boosting innovation, where it continues to lag behind other EU countries" (World Economic Forum [41], p. 20). In fact, Slovenia ranks 18th among the 28 members states of the European Union according to the Digital Economy and Society Index (DESI) [7, 10]. Nonetheless, it is worth noticing that Slovenia belongs to the so-called catching-up group of countries, since it has been growing at a faster pace than the European average [7, 10].[5]

The strongest elements of Slovenian digital development rely on the use of ICT by firms and its high-skilled population, raking 11th and 9th in these two dimensions (among EU members), respectively. In contrast, its weakest element refers to

---

[4]Given the lack of data of R&D investments in the big data industries, we use as a proxy R&D investments in the ICT sector.

[5]According to the 2016 Digital Economy and Society Index [10], Spain, Italy, Latvia, Romania, and Croatia also belong to the catching-up group of countries within the European Union.

the use of these technologies by its population specially in what regards digital public services and open data: not only the number of egovernment users is low compared to the European average, but also Slovenia is in the last position in its efforts to open its data and reuse it [7, 10]. What we see then is that the Slovenian digital economy is characterized by the existence of a gap between the potential of its human resources and their use of ICT.

Such a gap between potential capacity and actual use might be one of the factors that explain why big data industries show lower levels of efficiency and centrality compared to other economic sectors.

Another element of special concern is its low performance in open data given its clear connection to the big data field. In this sense, it is important to bear in mind that big data is not only being produced in the private sector, but also the public sector is a main producer of it [38, 39]. This public big data can generate economic value by being used by firms either as an input to create new products or services or to improve their decision-making ([24, 33, 38, 39]). In the particular case of Slovenia, its bad peformance in this area signals the high risk of losing all this potential to create new sources of innovation and wealth.

Table 14.5 shows the results of the network analysis for Slovakia. In this country, the average efficiency of big data industries is high (over the threshold of 0.85), and moreover it is over the computed average for the rest of the sectors of the economy. Such result implies that big data activities have access to nonredundant economic links which provide them with more varied and rich information (compared to other economic industries) and, hence, they can facilitate innovation.

However, the results for constraints and centrality measures suggest there might be some limiting factors to the role of big data industries as enablers of innovation and knowledge diffusion. Both measures, constraints and eigenvector, show lower values in big data industries compared to the average of the rest of the economy.

The lower value of the eigenvector indicates that big data industries are missing connections with some important economic sectors. While this lack is attenuated (at least, to some extent) by the access to nonredundant information (we recall that the efficiency score is high and over the average), it might constitute a threat for the future development of the big data industries.

In addition, the level of constraints of big data activities is a bit higher than that of the rest of the economy. This result indicates, on the one hand, that the big data industries show more dependence on other industries than the average and, hence, negative shocks in the economy are likely to have a bigger impact over them (due to its higher dependence); on the other hand, the higher level of constraints points out the establishment of new links and connection requires big data industries more efforts and costs than the average of the other economic sectors.

As to the correlations between the network metrics and the considered economic indicators (output and value added), it is worth mentioning that they are not significant and, furthermore, they do not present the expected signs for the case of big data industries. Such result again points out the idea of the existence of some conditions that limit the potential of big data industries (as already suggested by the lower values of centrality and higher constraints compared to the rest of the economy).

In this sense, if we analyze the pattern of digital development in Slovakia, we can see that it is positioned toward the bottom of the distribution of the European countries, ranking 21th among the 28 member states [6, 9]. In fact, over the last years, its pace of growth has been slower than the European average. Therefore, it has been classified in the cluster of "falling-behind" countries [6, 9].[6]

While the most outstanding dimensions of Slovakian digital development are population' skills together with the take-up of ICT, it shows quite important weaknesses on businesses' integration of digital technology, connectivity, and the offer and use of public services online [6, 9]. This low use of technologies by firms might be the reason that explains the observed score for the centrality network measure: it was below the average indicating that some important connections were missing. Hence it seems that the connections of big data industries tend to be concentrated in some particular sectors of the economy (on which they are quite dependent) and are not able to fully expand to other important sectors due to the lack of appropriate technology and infrastructure. Therefore, the comparatively low use of ICT by enterprises raises a serious concern and threat for such big data activities.

Other important weakness for the development of Slovakian big data industries are related to the defficiencies in Slovakian open data initiatives. From 2015 to 2016, Slovakia's position has deeply worsened, falling seven places from ranking 14th to 21th [9]. This fact also poses a serious threat about the future potential of big data activities in this country.

14.5 Concluding Remarks

Over the last few years, more and more attention has been paid to the opportunities that big data can create for countries' economic competitiveness and growth. Most of the empirical evidence in this field has focused on the most developed countries such as the USA, and much less is known about the state of these activities in other less developed nations mainly due to the lack of appropriate information.

Within this context, this chapter has tried to provide some evidence on strengths and weaknesses of big data industries. Due to the lack of appropriate data to carry out such analysis for developing countries, we have paid attention to two relative recent member states of the European Union, Slovenia and Slovakia. In addition to the availability of updated data on big data industries, their patterns of digital development show some common features with those of some developing countries. Henceforth, the analysis of their big data industries could throw more useful insights for a developing country than that of a high developed nation.

Network analysis tools combined with input-output information have been used to assess the position of big data industries in the network of economic relations and identify their weaknesses and strengths. In particular, we have used centrality, efficiency, and constraint network measures.

---

[6]The other countries that are also falling behind are Bulgaria, Cyprus, the Czech Republic, France, Greece, Hungary, and Poland [6, 9].

Results have shown for Slovenia that the levels of efficiency and centrality of big data industries are a bit below the average of the rest of the economy, indicating that (i) these activities are not contributing to promote diffusion and innovation throughout the economy as much as other industries and (ii) that some important connections are missing. The level of constraints, however, is lower than those suffered in other economic sectors.

In the case of Slovakia, efficiency is above the mean, but centrality is lower. These two results point out that while big data industries are able to access nonredundant information, there are still some key links missing. Moreover, the costs to establish those connections might be high for the big data industries given that they have a higher level of constraints than the rest of the economy.

It is important to bear in mind that the economic analysis of the big data sector is a quite difficult issue to address due to its novelty, the lack of a standard definition, and the shortage of appropriate data. This lack of data is especially severe in those countries which are not the most developed nations. In this sense, it would be essential to have information (for this kind of countries) not only about the proper big data sector but also about the level of ICT skills of the population and, in particular, whether the workforce is qualified enough to deal with big data. The two countries analyzed here are both strong in terms of the skills of their populations. However, that not might the case of many developing countries, a feature that could limit their opportunities to develop data-driven economies.

References

1. Bakhshi, H., Bravo-Biosca, A., & Mateos-Garcia, J. (2014). *Inside the datavores: Estimating the effects of data and online analytics on firm performance*. London: NESTA.
2. Bonacich, P. (1972). Factoring and weighting approaches to clique identification. *Journal of Mathematical Sociology, 2*, 113–120.
3. Brynjolfsson, E., Hitt, L.M., Kim, H.H. (2011) Strength in numbers: How does data-driven decision making affect firm performance? SSRN eLibrary.
4. Burt, R. S. (1992). *Structural holes: The social structure of competition*. Cambridge: Cambridge University Press.
5. Center for Economics and Business Research. (2012). *Data equity: Unlocking the value of big data*. London: Center for Economics and Business Research.
6. European Commission. (2016a). *European digital progress report (EDPR): Slovakia profiles*. Brussels: European Commission.
7. European Commission. (2016b). *European digital progress report (EDPR): Slovenia profiles*. Brussels: European Commission.
8. European Commission. (2016c). *The digital economy and society index (DESI)*. Brussels: European Commission.
9. European Commission. (2016d). *The digital economy and society index 2016: Country profile Slovakia*. Brussels: European Commission.
10. European Commission. (2016e). *The digital economy and society index 2016: Country profile Slovenia*. Brussels: European Commission.
11. European Parliament. (2016). *Resolution of 10 march 2016 on 'towards a thriving data-driven economy'*. Brussels: European Parliament.

12. Eurostat. (2015a). *Annual detailed enterprise statistics for services*. Luxembourg: Eurostat.
13. Eurostat. (2015b). *ESA supply, use and input-output tables*. Luxembourg: Eurostat.
14. García-Muñiz, A. S., & Ramos, C. (2015). Input-output linkages and network contagion in Greece: Demand and supply view. *Applied Econometrics and International Development, 15*, 35–60.
15. García-Muñiz, A. S., & Vicente, M. (2014). ICT Technologies in Europe: A study of technological diffusion and economic growth under network theory. *Telecommunications Policy, 38*, 360–370.
16. Gerdon, S., & Reimsbach-Kounatze, C. (forthcoming). *Data-driven innovation for development*. Paris: OECD.
17. Institute of Prospective Technological Studies. (2015). *The 2014 predict report: An analysis of ICT R&D in the EU and beyond*. Seville: Institute of Prospective Technological Studies.
18. Koski, H. (2011). Does marginal cost pricing of public sector information spur firm growth? Etla Discussion Paper, No. 1260.
19. Koski, H. (2012). The role of data and knowledge in firms' service and product innovation. Etla Discussion Paper, No. 1272.
20. Mandel, M. (2012). *Beyond goods and services: The (unmeasured) rise of the data-driven economy*. Washington, DC: Progressive Policy Institute.
21. Mandel, M. (2013) The data economy is much, much bigger than you (and the Government) think. *The Atlantic*. https://www.theatlantic.com/business/archive/2013/07/the-data-economy-is-much-much-bigger-thanyou- and-the-government-think/278113/.
22. McAfee, A., & Brynjolfsson, E. (2012). Big data: The management revolution. Harvard Business Review, 90, 60–68.
23. McKinsey. (2011). *Big data, the next frontier for innovation, competition and productivity*. New York: McKinsey.
24. McKinsey. (2013). *Open data: Unlocking innovation and performance with liquid information*. New York: McKinsey.
25. Networked European Software and Services Initiative. (2012). *Big data: A new world of opportunities*. White Paper. Networked European Software and Services Initiative.
26. OECD. (2013a). *Exploring data-driven innovation as a new source of growth: Mapping the policy issues raised by big data*. Paris: OECD.
27. OECD. (2013b). *The app economy*. Paris: OECD.
28. OECD. (2015). *Data-driven innovation: Big data for growth and well-being*. Paris: OECD.
29. Semitiel García, M., & Noguera Méndez, P. (2012). The structure of inter-industry systems and the diffusion of innovations: The case of Spain. *Technological Forecasting and Social Change, 79*, 1548–1567.
30. Soofi, A., & Ghazinoory, S. (2011). The network of the Iranian techno-economic system. *Technological Forecasting and Social Change, 78*, 591–609.
31. Tambe, P. (2014). Big data investment, skills, and firm value. *Management Science, 60*, 1452–1469.
32. The Economist. (2010). Data, data everywhere. Special Report on Managing Information. The Economist. February 25.
33. Ubaldi, B. (2013). *Open government data: Towards empirical analysis of open government data initiatives*. Paris: OECD.
34. United Nations. (2014a). *A world that counts. Mobilizing the data revolution for sustainable development*. New York: United Nations.
35. United Nations. (2014b). *World economic situation and prospects 2014*. New York: United Nations.
36. United Nations Global Pulse. (2012). *Big data for development: Challenges & opportunities*. New York: United Nations Global Pulse.
37. United Nations Global Pulse. (n.d.). http://www.unglobalpulse.org/about-new
38. Vickery, G. (2011). *Review of recent studies on PSI re-use and related market developments*. Paris: OECD.

39. Vickery, G., & Wunsch-Vincent, V. (2006). *Digital broadband content: Public sector information and content*. Paris: OECD.
40. World Bank. (2016). *World development report 2016: Digital dividend*. Washington, DC: World Bank.
41. World Economic Forum. (2014). *The global information technology report 2014. Rewards and risks of big data*. Geneva: World Economic Forum.
42. World Economic Forum. (2016). *The global information technology report 2015: Network readiness index*. Geneva: World Economic Forum.

Chapter 15
Is ICT the Solution of the Problem for Estonia?

Tõnis Mets

Abstract The Singing Revolution led to regaining independence after 50 years of Soviet occupation and created a new socioeconomic situation in Estonia in 1991. One of the first steps, of the Estonian government, was a telecommunication concession to the private company Eesti Telekom, in 1992. In 1995–1998, the Estonian government launched the national ICT strategy followed by the e-governance program. Fast economic and welfare growth in 1995–2007 ended with the global crisis, reminding many that linear growth of the economy is not sustainable anymore. Some new trends appeared in the last 8 years: Estonia has become the home of many new ICT startups which soon became global. There are opinions that it is not important for the Estonian economy, and ordinary Estonians will never experience a better living standard from such ICT startups. The chapter, based on data available from the statistics and multiple case studies, tries to find the answer.

Keywords National ICT Program • E-governance • Startups • Globalization

15.1 Introduction

Estonians declared their own state in 1918 and defended their rights of self-determination in the Estonian War of Independence against Soviet Russia and Baltic Germans from 1918 to 1920. Estonia, as well as the other Baltic states, was occupied by Soviet Union in 1940 as the outcome of secret protocols of the Molotov-Ribbentrop Pact [1]. The Singing Revolution led to regaining independence after 50 years of Soviet occupations and created a new socioeconomic situation in Estonia in 1991. The inhabitants of Estonia had great determination with catching up to the standard of living, commensurable to the people of Finland. If Estonia and Finland had been economically on the same level in 1940, then the estimates for Estonia in 1988 indicated per capita household income six times lower than in Finland [2].

T. Mets (✉)
University of Tartu, School of Economics and Business Administration, Tartu, Estonia
e-mail: tonis.mets@ut.ee

© Springer International Publishing AG 2017
H. Kaur et al. (eds.), *Catalyzing Development through ICT Adoption*,
DOI 10.1007/978-3-319-56523-1_15

It had been the consequences of a long period of Russification, Soviet command economy, and suppression of entrepreneurial mind-set, if not to mention, direct terror in the 1940s and 1950s.

In the new beginning, since 1991, the Estonian government, having very limited resources, chose liberal economic policies supporting foreign direct investment. After the "shock" of welfare drop and restructuring of the economy, this policy has facilitated fast growth since 1995, reaching approximately the level of 60% of the European Union's GDP per capita in purchasing power by 2006 (absolute values twice lower) (based on [3]). At the same time, Estonia became famous with its e-governance achievements, including online tax declaration and e-voting in general elections. Fast economic and welfare growth ended in 2007 with the global crisis and big recession reminding many that linear growth with the old structure of the economy is not sustainable anymore. Although Estonia has decided "smart specialization" being further development strategy, there is still a lack of confidence on how to reach that target. There also appeared new initiatives, such as Startup Estonia and widening information and communication technology (ICT) studies on the higher education level. This new situation has raised the question about the role of ICT as well as ICT entrepreneurship. Are these creating new perspectives for socioeconomic development? There are opinions that it is not important for the Estonian economy, and ordinary Estonian people will never experience a better living standard from such ICT startups [4]. This opinion could not be noticed if having no attention from among the public and some politicians. Part of Estonians is more optimistic about the impact of ICT and technology entrepreneurship on the Estonian economy.

Trying to answer the question asked in the title, this chapter makes an attempt to find evidence of the potential for ICT startups in Estonian economy and welfare.

That means also:

- Disclosing ICT framework of socioeconomic transition of Estonia
- Overview of economic outcome of ICT sector in Estonia
- Evaluation of the potential of ICT sector in economic growth
- Disclosing investments into ICT startups
- Analysis of value and jobs created by startups

A short overview of the framework and transformation of Estonian economy and developments of ICT sector is presented in the next two sections. These are followed by analysis of the ICT sector and its startups specifically. Conclusions and recommendations end the chapter.

15.2 ICT Framework for Socioeconomic Development

15.2.1 ICT and Economic Development

Several researchers find ICT investment contributing to economic growth and socio-economic development [5, 6]. But there still is an opinion that "theoretical capabilities to study technology innovation in relation to socioeconomic context" remain weak "about IT-enabled socioeconomic development" ([5], p. 1). Not interfering with this discussion, there are noticed several ways how society is influenced by ICT (author's compilation, partly based on [5]):

- Diffusion/transfer of knowledge (to developing countries) on society and personal levels.
- Social embeddedness perspective of ICT. This is the question about sensemaking and accommodating ICT-based innovations and capability to attend in society by citizens. Partly, a digital divide (e.g., access to the Internet) has seen being a new form of inequality, not only between developed and developing countries but also between different age and income groups in society.
- ICT, as an enabler of economic development, has two sides:

  (a) ICT as a technological basis of socioeconomic development. Partly, besides diffusion and embeddedness that is related to communication and information systems (management). Access to digital communication is seen as an assumption to attend in international trade. ICT is also a source of productivity in traditional industries, and it is an enabler of new businesses in any field. As a result, ICT is an enabler of competitiveness of the country in general.

  (b) ICT, as an economic sector, has a direct as well as indirect impact on society. The direct impact on national income includes highly paid jobs in the ICT industry – production and services and export of both. The indirect impact can be seen in a multiplier effect by the creation of jobs in other tradable and non-tradable sectors (e.g., local services). The potential of this effect is different in different countries, e.g., in the USA and Sweden, the effect can appear between 0.4 and 5 [7, 8].

Adoption of ICT is growing in the knowledge economy, based on new knowledge created by R&D and innovation in wider meaning including social and cultural practice [9]. In addition, the growth of service-based industries is the trend intrinsic to knowledge economies [9]. In particular, small, open economies, like Estonia (or Finland), have their "push" factors, coming from the need to cover R&D expenses, and "pull" factors, related to the attractiveness of bigger international markets [10]. As a result, most of technology, including ICT, startups need to go internationally or even globally at an early stage. Partly, lack of seed capital at the home country and searching for international investments for business development support that trend.

15.2.2   Methodology

A general overview of socioeconomic development in the chapter is based on literature review and the statistical databases of the Statistics Estonia. The main attention
focuses on the influence of ICT on the mode of e-governance, economic growth,
and the creation of new jobs. The empirical part of the chapter analyzes economy
aspects of the ICT sector and its subsectors. Among ICT production and services,
more influential subfields are analyzed. For that, subfields are selected according to
the Estonian Classification of Economic Activities (EMTAK), which is the national
version of the international harmonized NACE classification. The data, available
from the statistical databases of the Statistical Office of Estonia, indicates the share
of ICT sector in sales, value creation, export, and employment comparing with other
areas and economy in general. Less can be found about the contribution of ICT to
other (traditional) sectors, although, supposedly, it could be that the employment of
ICT specialists is much wider than in the specific sector according to EMTAK. That
is the aspect needing further studies.

A particular topic is the contribution of ICT startups into socioeconomic development. This is the aspect not counted in the official statistics. As these startups are
making small share among the total number, nearly 6,000 ICT companies, multiple
case studies are used to map their patterns. For that purposes, the data from web
pages of special startup networks, public media, interviews, and data of the
Commercial Registry are analyzed. A sample selection is based on the Garage48
Hub (http://hub.garage48.org/) [11] and the author's previous studies [10]. The criteria for that is the Estonian origin of the idea, success of the entrepreneurial process, and international business focus of the startup. The companies meeting those
requirements have already been launched and reached the market independently or
successfully (for the founder and investors) led to IPO or merged/acquired by the
new owner (exit). Among 30 Estonian startups with most capital raised, ICT application is the leading technology within 27 of them. A sample for case studies, from
the top 30 startups, is based on the author's better knowledge of new ICT ventures
which are demonstrating a variety of ways on how they contribute to the Estonian
economy and welfare. Altogether five startup cases are selected, representing the
biggest investment (TransferWise), successful exit (GrabCAD; Fits.me), as well as
market success (Click & Grow; Defendec).

15.3   Framework for the Socioeconomic Transition of Estonia

15.3.1   Economic Re-structuration

At the beginning of restored independence, in 1991, Estonia, leaving the old Soviet
command economy and Russian influence, found itself in an absolutely new situation. Market relations had to be established and the economy restructured to the

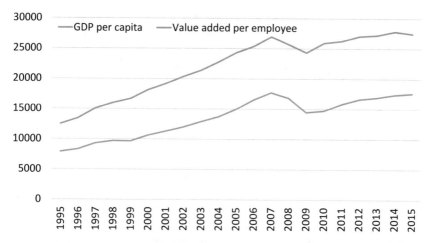

Fig. 15.1 GDP per capita, value added (productivity) per employee in the Estonian economy, EUR in fixed prices (Source: The author based on Statistics Estonia 2016)

market needs. For that, it was necessary to create an environment for entrepreneurship and disconnect own economy from the inflating Soviet ruble. Notwithstanding warning voices of several Western experts in 1992, Estonia introduced its own kroon, which being fixed to the German mark served for stable developments until changing to the euro in 2011. Disconnection of the own economy from the Soviet economic system was not a painless process, although nobody can suppose that the collapse of Soviet Empire could be that in any case. The subsequent decrease of economy lasted 3 years. It was an introduction of the market economy and starting radical reforms and, also, the beginning of a period not only of "shock therapy" for the economic system but also of social shock in the Estonian society.

The first steps were privatization of state enterprises, the return of property expropriated by Soviet system to owners, privatization of state housing to residents, and attraction of foreign direct investments into the economy. The government, led by Mart Laar, also established a flat income tax. These were decisions, creating the legal framework, boosting the entrepreneurial activity of many people. All that activated the economy, GDP started to grow since 1995 with the speed between 4.4% and 10.5% (in fixed prices) per year until 2007 (Fig. 15.1) (the exception was GDP growth 0.3% in 1999 during the "Russian crisis").

1995–1998 was the period of integration within the European Union (EU) and NATO. It was also the period of economic stabilization. Fast economic and welfare growth also continued until 2007, after accession to the EU and NATO in 2004. The global crisis and big recession of the GDP −4.2% in 2008 and −14.1% in 2009 (see Fig. 15.1), but also the unemployment rate reaching 16.9% in 2010, reminded the Estonian government that linear growth with the old structure of the economy is not sustainable anymore. The subsequent growth remained around 2–3% annually, and the level of 2007 was nominally reached again in 2011 (in 2014 at fixed prices).

Estonia, as a small country, has implemented a policy of open economy, which has been described by a high share of export between 26% and 36% of total sales in the last 10-year period. Although Estonian government has selected the goals toward the growth of productivity and smart specialization [3], there is still a lack of confidence about further trajectory.

15.3.2   ICT and E-Governance

One of the first steps of involving international capital into infrastructure development by the Estonian government was a telecommunication concession to the private company, AS Eesti Telekom, in 1992. With this decision, Estonian government prepared modernization and (re)construction of the telecommunication network, the backwardness of which, comparing with developed countries, as inherited from the old system, was approximately 20–30 years. From 1995 to 1998, the Estonian government launched the national ICT strategy (the "Tiger Leap" program). Computer literacy training had already started at schools. Ninety-seven percent of schools were connected to the Internet in 1997 that was followed by the e-governance program; Estonian government's assemblies became paper-free since 2000.

After that, Estonia has developed numerous public e-services including electronic identity card based on that system. The electronic identity card can be used for authentication and signing documents digitally. There is now "one-stop shop" portal (www.eesti.ee) gateway to e-Estonia where the citizen can apply practically for all state services. Among them are, for example, the Electronic Health Registry and e-Prescription. Of particular interest internationally is the e-residency system developed following changes to the residency legislation in 2014 [12]. Electronic ID cards are part of the e-residency system. Many Estonian experiences are benchmarks, not only for developing countries but also, for example, highly developed Japan [13].

The achievements of Estonia, in e-governance and business development, have found wide attention globally. However, Estonia is not ranked in the first positions (mainly 6–28) of any components of a Networked Readiness Index (NRI) by the World Economic Forum [14]. Commenting on the situation, advisor for the Government, Mr. Sikkut, mentions that in part Estonia has left others behind [15]; that means, in several aspects, NRI has no indicator/measurement as of yet.

Besides public e-services, some new trends can be noticed in the last 8 years: Estonia has become the home of many new ICT startups, which will soon become global. Good examples for that have been Regio, Skype, and Fortumo [10]. Now, entrepreneurship training at all educational levels, seed funding, and creation of accelerators for startups have become the policy of the Estonian government. ICT and, particularly, software development-oriented businesses are dominating among the startups [11]. This is calling us about the analysis of the potential of ICT orientation for further welfare development in Estonia.

15.4   Technology Entrepreneurs

15.4.1   ICT Sector in Estonian Economy

The sector is characterized by growing the share of ICT companies from 2.2% in 1995 to 4.9% in 2015, absolute numbers – from 681 to 5,767 for the same period. As, according to the Statistical Office, there are 117,398 registered companies per 1.316 million inhabitants in Estonia (2015), these numbers are impressive. Although absolute numbers and the share of ICT have grown remarkably (Table 15.1, Fig. 15.2) in the last 10-year period, the role of the (ICT) manufacturing sector in value creation remains modest.

The reason behind can be seen in foreign ownership and sub-contract production function of the ICT manufacturing industry in Estonia. Productivity (value added) per employee at 28.7 thousand euro remains lower from the mean 31.95 thousand euros describing the Estonian economy in 2014.

With employment and productivity numbers (8,316 employees and value added per employee 37.0 thousand euro in 2014), programming sector surpasses traditional manufacturing industries, e.g., furniture production (~7,500; 13.7), pulp and paper (~1,400; 26.4), chemical (~4,200; 33.3), clothing (~6,000; 11.0), textile (~3,800; 17.4), gum and plastics (~3,900; 22.1), manufacture of means of transport (~4,300; 21.8), and machinery and equipment (~3,600; 25.8) (author's calculations based on approximate data [16]). The share of export in sales of the manufacturing industry is 67.7%, share in value added −16%, and employment −18.2% [16].

Although the importance of the ICT (manufacturing and service) sector, in export, started to grow after economic recession period 2007–2009 (Fig. 15.2), the (absolute and relative) share of employment in ICT manufacturing industry has decreased in 2005–2014 (Table 15.1). That process may continue in the future, as one could assume from the numbers of employment as well as from lower average added value by the ICT manufacturing sector (Table 15.1).

More productive in value creation is the ICT service sector. Bigger subsectors of that are telecom(munication) and programming (software development). The Estonian telecom sector has been concentrated already between five bigger companies (with over 250 employees) employing 74.6% of the workforce and making 76.2% of sales in the sector. The main share of telecom ownership belongs to foreign corporations. Although these companies are making a good profit (and added value), they are internal market oriented. The market in telecom is not very open anymore.

The software development (as service) sector grows much faster (Table 15.1, Fig. 15.3), employing twice as many people, than telecom. This data does not include software developers working for other sectors and financial institutions. Banks in Estonia have had traditionally large ICT departments. In addition, 15.2% of all Estonian companies, in the statistical profile (6,870 with ten and more employees in 2014), have their ICT specialists (or departments), among them, programmers.

Table 15.1 Main economic indicators of the ICT sector in Estonia

ICT, subsectors	Indicators 2005						Indicators 2014					
	Employment		Added value		Export		Employment		Added value		Export	
	No	%	MEUR	%	MEUR	%	No	%	MEUR	%	MEUR	%
Manufacturing	7159	5.69	82.0	5.35	252.06	7.98	4904	4.60	140.87	5.29	1645.59	22.39
Services	8709	4.24	377.4	11.29	178.40	3.90	15,525	6.80	705.69	11.79	816.33	8.42
Telecom	2966	1.44	251.3	7.52	55.56	1.21	4266	1.87	289.54	4.84	136.75	1.41
Programming	3461	1.68	64.8	1.94	33.44	0.73	8316	3.64	308.05	5.15	251.93	2.60
Total, incl. All ICT subsectors	15,867	3.74	459.4	7.18	430.45	5.26	20,429	4.79	846.57	7.49	2461.92	13.73

Source: The author based on Statistics Estonia 2016, current prices

Remark: The share of ICT manufacturing is as % of manufacturing industry; the share of ICT service(s) is given as % of the service industry in Estonia

Fig. 15.2 The share of ICT (manufacturing and service) sector in Estonian economy, % of total number of employees, sales, and export (Source: The author based on Statistics Estonia 2016)

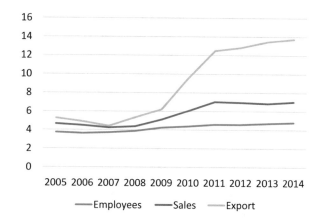

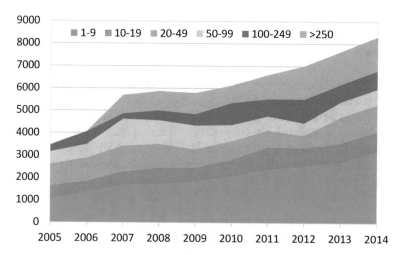

Fig. 15.3 Number of employees by the size of software development companies (Source: The author's extrapolation based on Statistics Estonia and Commercial Registry 2016)

So the total number of employees, in programming, may reach remarkably bigger numbers than directly in the ICT sector statistics.

The companies with the number of employees between one and nine are employing 38.6% of all software developers in 2014. Remarkable is their share 31.3% in value creation and 25.7% in the export of the software sector. This is the group sourcing the number of startups in the field reaching 2,275, employing 3,210 people and involving over 900 on an irregular basis, in 2014. The number of new software businesses is between 130 and 200 last years.

Monthly wages of the software (programming) sector remarkably (1.5 times) surpass the figures of other sectors and the ICT manufacturing sector, particularly (Fig. 15.4).

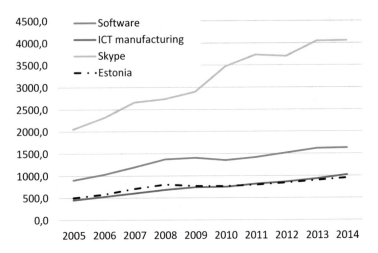

Fig. 15.4 Monthly wages in ICT manufacturing, programming, Skype, and Estonia generally, EUR (Source: The author based on Statistics Estonia and Commercial Registry 2016)

A flagship of Estonian software developers, Skype Technologies (owned by Microsoft Corporation), belongs to top institutions with its wages. Besides direct contribution to the income of employees and taxes for the Estonian state, that is an indicator of the potential of the sector in the indirect creation of new jobs mentioned by Moretti [7]. Growing importance of ICT, in the last 25 years, indicates that Estonia has passed the stages from developing transition economy to developed innovation-driven economy [17].

15.4.2 ICT Startups of Estonian Origin

As mentioned above, up to 200 new software companies are founded every year in Estonia. More public attention among them is paid on startups attracting funding by investors. Funding, from outside the owners' circle, could be considered as an indicator of the magnitude of business potential. The first private venture investors in Estonia appeared in the 1990s [18], but more active investments into ICT startups started after sales of successful IT companies and portals, among them Microlink and Delfi in 2004 and 2005 [11]. A strong impact was from the sale of Skype to eBay in 2005. Estonian engineers, former co-owners of Skype, became investors through their holding company Ambient Sound Investments [19]. Since May 2008, Estonian Development Fund, as a public institution, started investments into new ventures [20], initiating and supporting new innovative businesses and also encouraging private co-funding.

In 2014, the number of startups, receiving outside investment, in the smallest country of the Baltics – Estonia – was 38; neighboring countries with similar

Table 15.2 Summary of startup statistics in the Baltic states 2006–2015

Indicator	Estonia	Latvia	Lithuania
Population, million, 2014	1.31	1.99	2.93
GDP per capita, PPS, USD, 2013	18,722	15,946	18,776
Number of startups	406	220	206
Capital invested into startups, MEUR	262.4	97.7	101.6
Number of new jobs created	2154	450	450

Source: The author based on Funding of Estonian startups [11], Labsoftlatvia: Baltic Startup Scene in Numbers [21], and The GEDI (The Global Entrepreneurship and Development Institute): Profile of Estonian National System of Entrepreneurship [22]

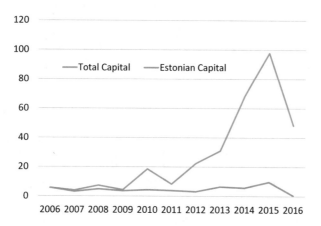

Fig. 15.5 Investments into Estonian startups 2016 QII, MEUR (Source: The author based on [11])

historical backgrounds, Latvia and Lithuania, had 41 and 23, respectively [21]. Comparative data of the three Baltic countries is presented in Table 15.2.

Since 2006, the total number of startups in Estonia was 406, compared to 220 in Latvia and 206 in Lithuania. Evaluation of employment in startups shows 2,154 for Estonia and approximately 900 for Latvia and Lithuania, together [21]. The total amount of raised (accumulated) capital up to August 2015 was €262.4m in Estonia, €97.7m in Latvia, and €101.6m in Lithuania [21]. According to the data of Estonian networks of startups, Garage48 [11], the share of domestic capital is 16.7% in the period until July 2016 (incl.). Usually, Estonian capital combines both – public and private funds. Dynamics of investments into Estonian startups is presented in Fig. 15.5.

Among the top 30 capital raised new ventures, the author has selected five startup cases (Table 15.3) characterizing different development patterns, as mentioned above (expert sampling). They represent the biggest investment (TransferWise), successful exit (GrabCAD; Fits.me), and market success (Click & Grow; Defendec). These startups correspond to the most mature development stages proving their businesses' efficiency [23]. The biggest investment (€95.6m) is counted in TransferWise (Table 15.3) which could only conditionally be considered an Estonian

Table 15.3 Short description of the sample of Estonian startups

Name, founding year	Idea	Rank	MEUR Total	Estonian	Role of ICT	Status	Ownership	Remark
TransferWise, 2011 Kristo Käärmann, Taavet Hinrikus	Crowd-sourced international money transfers	1	95.6	–	Application, innovation of banking	Expanding	TransferWise Ltd., controlled by investors	HQ in London, UK; value >$1 billion
Massi Miliano (Fits.me), 2006 (2010); Heikki Haldre	Virtual fitting room for e-Commerce	4	15.42	2.37	Application, software	Successful exit	Rakuten, Japan Fits.me Holdings Ltd., UK	HQ in London, UK
GrabCAD, 2010; Hardi Meybaum, Indrek Narusk, started as engineers with Futeq, 2007	Engineering platform to share, collaborate in and manage CAD projects	6	11.299	0.269	Open innovation collaboration crowdsourcing platform Integrating CAD technologies	Exit $100M	Stratasys, USA-Israeli	HQ in Boston, USA
Click& Grow (C&G), inventor Mattias Lepp, 2009	Innovative plant growing systems from flowerpots to city farms	17	3.379	0.24	Intelligent houseplant system, software, and chips	Reached global markets	Controlled by investors	HQ in Tartu, Estonia
Defendec (until 2010, Smartdust Solutions OÜ), Jaanus Tamm, Tauri Tuubel, Jürgo-Sören Preden, 2006	SmartDec is an electronic security guard 24/7 in remote locations	21	2.45	2.28	Intelligent virtual wireless sensors' networks and monitoring system	Profit 2014: €0.4M	Controlled by investors and founders	HQ in Tallinn, Estonia

Source: author based on annual reports, [11, 20, 23]

startup because of the founders' Estonian origin and the development unit with 400 people in Estonia. The value of TransferWise, the innovator of banking, was announced over 1 billion USD in 2015 [24], which is the highest valuation for an Estonian startup.

Massi Miliano (Fits.me) belongs to one of the success stories of an Estonian startup, although the value of the deal is not known [20]. It is a good example of the university R&D contribution, based on robotics science, and reaching the global exit. The company's Estonian subsidiary reported global clients/brands (Superdry, Hugo Boss, Mexx, Ecko) and profit since 2013. After the acquisition by Rakuten, a Japanese Internet business corporation, the technology development department of Fits.me remained in Estonia [25].

GrabCAD is the most successful story for Estonians, after Skype. If the business (model) of Skype belonged mostly to foreigners, and Estonians' role was technology, then GrabCAD differs by the fact that the idea and business model both originate from Estonia. As an open innovation platform, it could be considered the biggest revolution in mechanical engineering, after CAD technology. GrabCAD integrates over three million engineers, i.e., more than half of CAD users, and production industry globally. The platform is shortening the product development process and production cycle, radically. The platform development unit has remained in Estonia.

Click & Grow is a startup innovating plant cultivation process starting from an intelligent flowerpot and moving toward smart farm concept for growing plants for food. In that way, the company is integrating different technologies – agriculture and hardware (electronic chips and plastic pots) with software. Compared to traditional agriculture technology, it saves approximately 95% of water usage and needs much less space. Click & Grow has used multiple sources for funding product development, including crowdfunding environment Kickstarter (campaign in 2013). The headquarters (HQ) are still based in Tartu, Estonia.

Defendec, which designs and produces electronic surveillance (security) systems, is another startup integrating software with hardware. Also, its technology is based on high-level university research and patents. The company has its business branch offices in Asia and America. Defendec declared a profit in 2014.

15.4.3   *From the Export of Global Startups to the Export of Smart Products*

Estonian success stories of globalized technology startups have generated the trust of international investors to Estonia as can be seen from the growth of capital inflow (see Fig. 15.5). But the cases also show common patterns describing the entrepreneurial process of Estonian startups.

All these companies started in Estonia and developed their business model in their home country and moved to global market, somehow. But, in the further development of business, in most success cases, the headquarters are moved out of the homeland, and Estonians abandon the ownership and control of the business; new owners are usually big international corporations. In the best cases, part of software/technology development remains in Estonia, creating jobs for programmers and ICT system developers. That means, Estonians are exporting global ideas, which are moving out with the headquarters of startups and only partly support the national welfare, via software sector. Partly, the reason for that comes from the interest of venture capitalists to rapidly earn their investments back. Another side of the problem is a lack of domestic venture/angel capital, which is covering only 16–17% of the need.

There are some identifying signs that this trend could be changed with smart products, but the cases of Click & Grow and Defendec are at the beginning of that process, and there is no confidence that the situation will continue in the future with these businesses. What is important is that these signs exist already. Behind of all these successful startup ideas is ICT competence, which integrated with other technologies, creating new value.

15.5   Discussion and Conclusions

15.5.1   Perspectives for the Ordinary People

Looking for an answer to the question about the contribution of ICT startups into the Estonian economy and welfare of the "ordinary people" specifically, one can meet the multifaceted character of the problem (by "ordinary people" we mean the people not employed as programmers). First, direct contribution in creating new jobs and value added for the Estonian economy is already remarkable. The number of new jobs, 2,154 mainly in ICT startups, as mentioned above, generates approximately a fourth of employment in the software industry. Considering 1.5 times higher wages and the increased productivity of added value per employee contribution of software, (sub-)sector supports society via taxes and consumption of local goods and services. Second, the indirect impact for Estonia has not been studied, as it was done for the USA and Sweden by Moretti and Thulin [7]. This multiplier effect is dependent partly on the direct impact. The indirect impact of creating new (or maintaining existing) jobs for so-called ordinary people is not measured yet. But, considering that median monthly salary in 2014 was a little over 600€ (based on data from Tax and Customs Board), the average salary contribution of software sector (including ICT startups) to the local consumer market exceeds that number more than 2.5 times. That is the factor feeding jobs of "ordinary people" in services' and the consumer market. Another factor is a startup as a customer for local industry. Among the case companies, Defendec and Click & Grow are ordering part of the components for their products from Estonian subcontractors. Finally, although headquarters of successful startups move out of Estonia (sometimes after exit, sometimes – in the business development process), their development branches remain at homeland contributing to Estonian welfare as described above. Is moving out of Estonian startups the best solution for the "ordinary people?" It is the question for government and politicians as well as for researchers and needs their commitment on the topic.

15.5.2   Policy Conclusions

The experience of Estonia has shown that the role of ICT and e-governance is remarkable for creating a competitive advantage of a (small) state. Growing trust among international investors, as well as experts' assessment of entrepreneurial ecosystem and success stories of high technology startups, supports that opinion. But this experience also shows that reaching such results takes 10–15 years from policy measures like the "Tiger Leap" program and wider appearance of its outcomes in socioeconomic development. This is a key for the further trajectory of smart specialization. That means the route for that has been started already. This must be recognized by politicians. That is important because, frequently, decisions are motivated with the argument of budget savings. They do not even discuss whether their decision is about a single expenditure or an investment into the future. In such a way, by closing higher education IT programs in a rural center, politicians deepen inequality between the periphery and the capital city [12]. That inequality is growing in Estonia [26].

Estonia has its startup policy and infrastructure as well as a public foundation for seed capital, which is supporting private initiatives. Now, it appears not to be enough. The question is about the expectations concerning the contribution of startups into the Estonian economy and how ICT could support that in the best way.

References

1. Taagepera, R. (1993). *Estonia: Return to independence*. Boulder: Westview Press.
2. Laar, M. (2004). What we have learned in Estonia about freedom and growth. Paper presented at Conference 'A Liberal Agenda for the New Century: A Global Perspective', 8–9 April, Moscow, http://www.cato.org/events/russianconf2004/papers/laar.pdf
3. Varblane, U., Eamets, R, Haldma, T., Kaldaru, H., Masso, J., Mets, T., Paas, T., Reiljan, J., Sepp, J., Türk, K., Ukrainski, K., Vadi, M., & Vissak, T. (2008). *The Estonian economy current status of competitiveness and future outlooks*. Short Version of the Report. Estonian Development Fund.
4. Hõbemägi, T. (2013). Forbes on Estonia and meaningless statistics, 13.07.2013, http://bbn.ee/Print.aspx?PublicationId=6c1c5e6c-4f34-469f-bf4b-0c712523ceb6
5. Avgerou, C. (2010). Discourses on ICT and development. *Information Technologies and International Development, 6*(3), 1–18.
6. Ulmanis, J., & Kolyshkin, A. (2007). The impact of ICT on the development of Latvia as a new member of the EU. *WSEAS Transactions on Business and Economics, 4*(10), 152–159.
7. Moretti, E. (2012). *The new geography of jobs, Mariner Books*. New York: Houghton Mifflin.

8. Moretti, E., & Thulin, P. (2013). Local multipliers and human capital in the United States and Sweden. *Industrial and Corporate Change, 22*(1), 339–362.
9. Dahlman, C. J., Routti, J., & Ylä-Anttila, P. (2006). *Finland as a knowledge economy: Elements of success and lessons learned.* Washington, DC: World Bank.
10. Mets, T. (2012). Creative business model innovation for globalizing SMEs. In T. Burger-Helmchen (Ed.), *Entrepreneurship – creativity and innovative business models* (pp. 169–190). Rijeka: InTech.
11. Funding of Estonian startups (n.d.). martin@garage48.org.: https://docs.google.com/spreadshe ets/d/1csgtaNSl949AumfOBhwhD_S-o7wc1UIhKZdWUS4Vy-Q/edit?pref=2&pli=1#gid=5
12. Mets, T., & Kelli, A. (2015). Rural development in the digital era: A case of a born-global SME in Estonia. In B. Kotey, T. Mazzarol, D. Clark, T. McKeown, & M. Battisti (Eds.), *SMEs in the digital economy: Surviving the digital revolution* (pp. 50–63). Tilde University Press: Prahran.
13. The Japan Times: Prefectures Begin Mailing 12-digit My Number IDs 2015. http://www. japantimes.co.jp/news/2015/10/23/national/socialissues/prefecturesstartingmailnumberid-numbers/#.V5NZO2h96hd
14. Dutta, S., Geiger, T., & Bruno Lanvin, B. (2015). *The global information technology report 2015.* Cologny: World Economic Forum.
15. Sikkut, S. (2016). E-tiiger Hüppab Endiselt – Teeme Asju Teistmoodi ja Oleme Mõnes Mõttes Liiga Ees. http://arvamus.postimees.ee/3713179/siimsikkutetiigerhuppabendiseltteemeasju-teistmoodijaolememonesmottesliigaees
16. Ministry of Economic Affairs and Communications: Overview of Economy 2014 (2015). https://mkm.ee/sites/default/files/overview_of_economy_2014.pdf
17. Kelley, D., Singer, S., & Herrington, M. (2016). Global entrepreneurship monitor 2015/16. Global Report. www.gemconsortium.org
18. Cresco: About Us (2016). https://www.cresco.ee/
19. Ambient Sound Investments: Company (2016). http://www.asi.ee/company
20. Estonian Development Fund: Investment Success Stories (2016). http://www.arengufond.ee/ en/investments/investment-success-stories/
21. Labsoftlatvia: Baltic Startup Scene in Numbers (2015). http://arcticstartup.com/article/ baltic-startup-scene-in-numbers/
22. The GEDI (The Global Entrepreneurship and Development Institute): Profile of Estonian National System of Entrepreneurship (2013). *Intermediary analysis.*
23. Startup Estonia: Estonian startups (2016). http://www.startupestonia.ee/startups
24. Williamsgrut, O. (2015). *Transferwisefounderstelluswhyit'soktobeanunprofitableunicorn.* http:// www.businessinsider.com/interviewwithtransferwisestaavethinrikusandkristokaarmann201510
25. Lunden, I., & Lomas, N. (2015). Rakuten buys virtual fitting room startup Fits. Me in a fashion commerce play. https://techcrunch.com/2015/07/12/rakutenbuysvirtualfittingroomstart upfitsmeinafashioncommerceplay/
26. Raagmaa, G., Kalvet, T., & Kasesalu, R. (2014). Europeanization and de-Europeanization of Estonian regional policy. *European Planning Studies, 22*(4), 775–795.

Printed in the United States
By Bookmasters